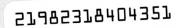

Shojo Beat

Yona of the Dawn

8

Story & Art by

Mizuho Kusanagi

Yona of the Dawn

Volume 8

CONTENTS

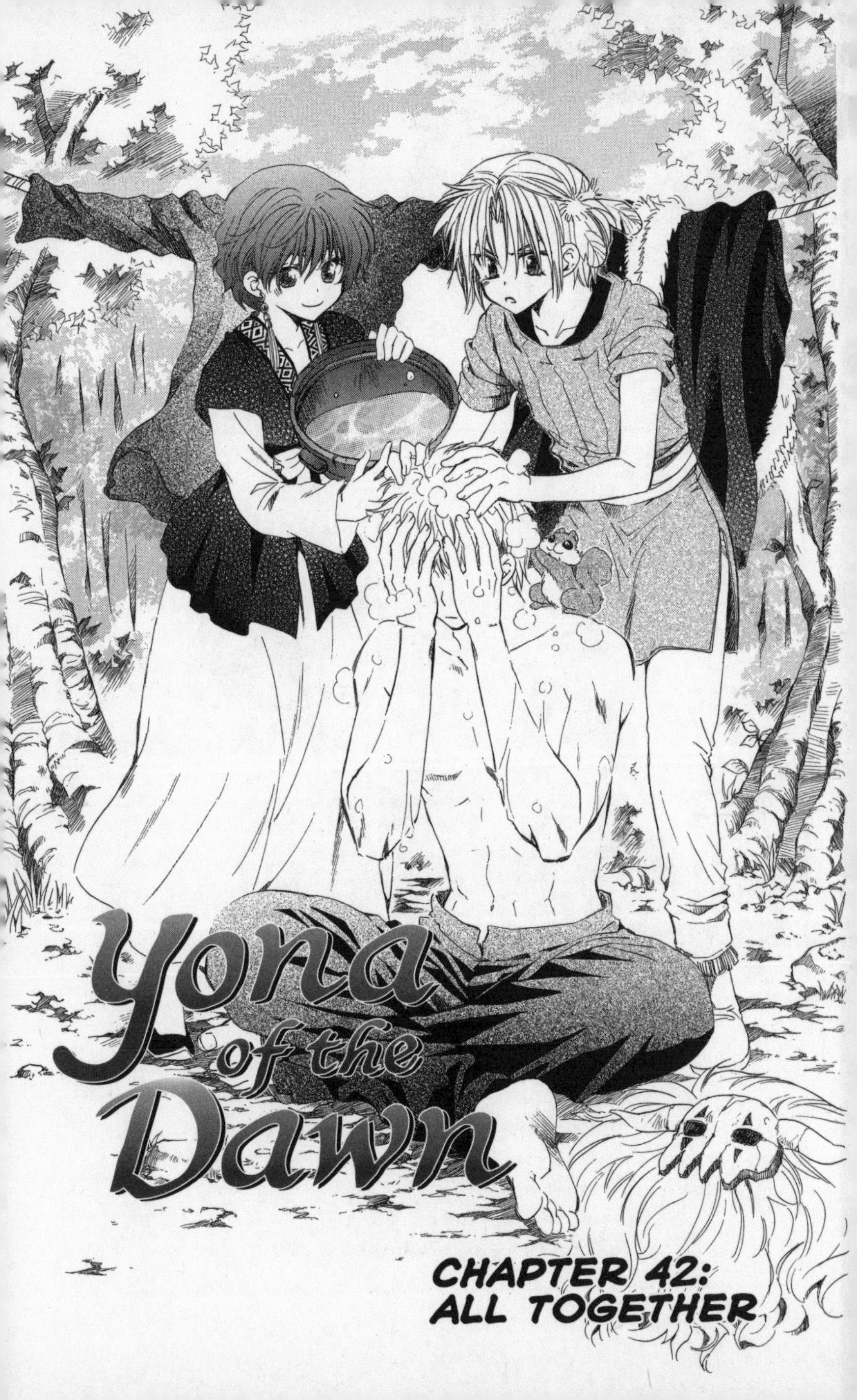
Yona of the Dawn
CHAPTER 42:
ALL TOGETHER

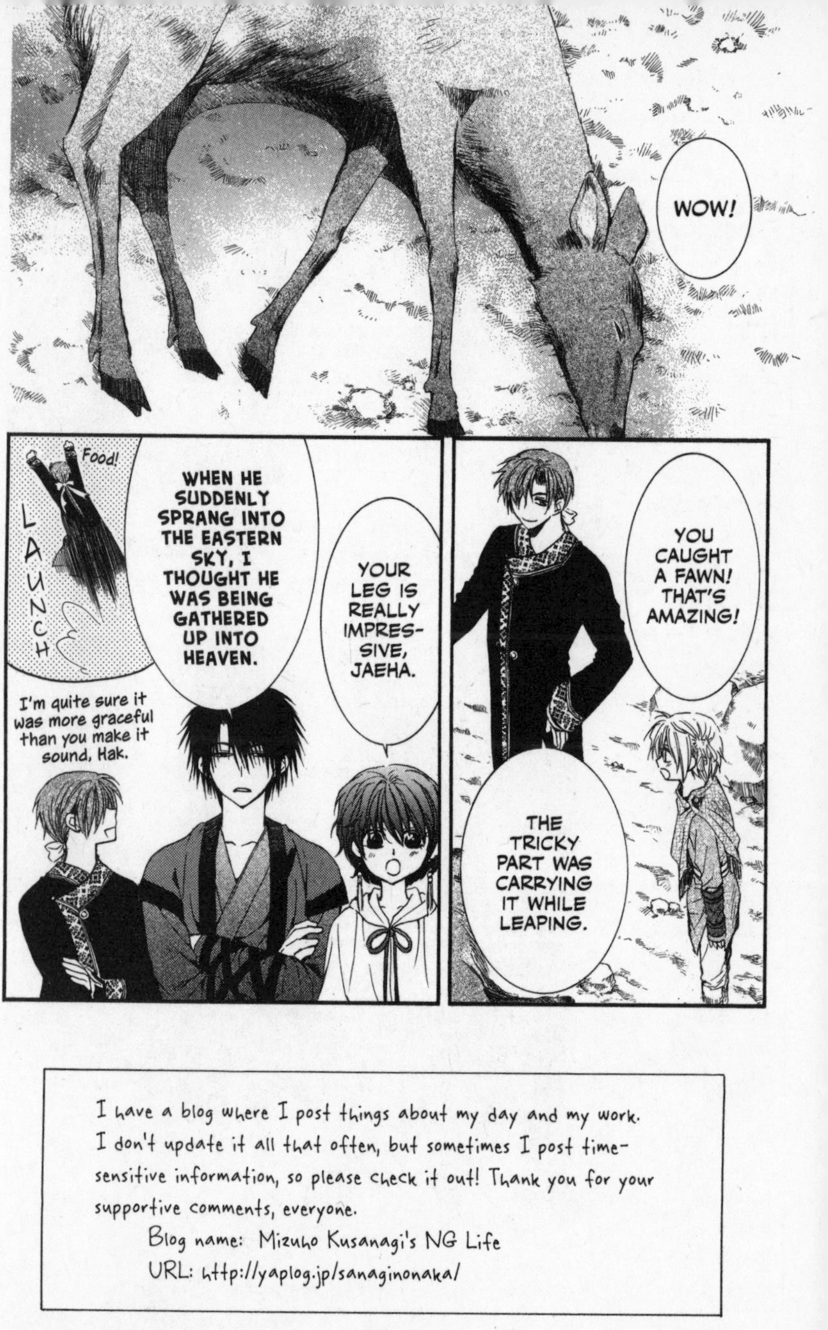
WOW!
YOU CAUGHT A FAWN! THAT'S AMAZING!
THE TRICKY PART WAS CARRYING IT WHILE LEAPING.
YOUR LEG IS REALLY IMPRESSIVE, JAEHA.
WHEN HE SUDDENLY SPRANG INTO THE EASTERN SKY, I THOUGHT HE WAS BEING GATHERED UP INTO HEAVEN.
Food!
LAUNCH
I'm quite sure it was more graceful than you make it sound, Hak.

I have a blog where I post things about my day and my work. I don't update it all that often, but sometimes I post time-sensitive information, so please check it out! Thank you for your supportive comments, everyone.

Blog name: Mizuho Kusanagi's NG Life

URL: http://yaplog.jp/sanaginonaka/

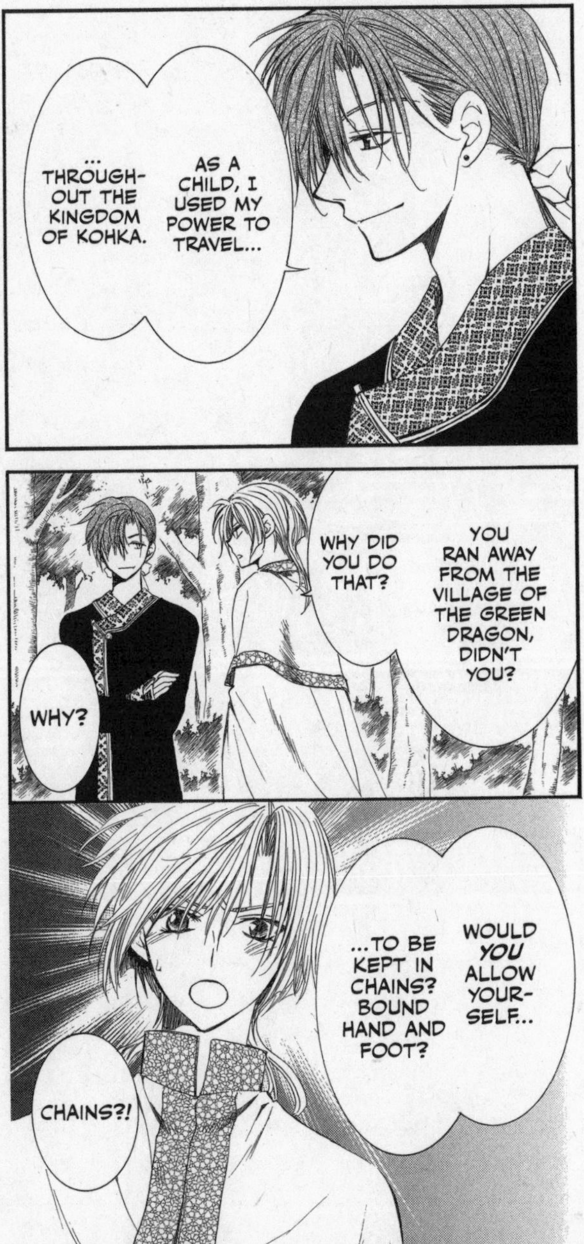
AS A CHILD, I USED MY POWER TO TRAVEL...
...THROUGH-OUT THE KINGDOM OF KOHKA.
YOU RAN AWAY FROM THE VILLAGE OF THE GREEN DRAGON, DIDN'T YOU?
WHY DID YOU DO THAT?
WHY?
WOULD *YOU* ALLOW YOUR-SELF...
...TO BE KEPT IN CHAINS? BOUND HAND AND FOOT?
CHAINS?!

Hello, this is Mizuho Kusanagi. Thank you for picking up volume 8 of Yona of the Dawn! Volume 8... My last series, *NG Life*, was already wrapping up when it got to this point, but Yona still has a long way to go. I hope you'll stay with her as she makes her journey.

Many people have said supportive things and made videos for me while I've been writing Yona. I have so much to be thankful for as a creator! When Kentaro Miura drew me a picture of Yona and Hak, I was so glad that I'd chosen to be a manga artist. I've received comments from other wonderful people too. I don't deserve such praise! To all of you who are thrilled about Yona, I'd like to thank you from the bottom of my heart. Now let's dig into volume 8!

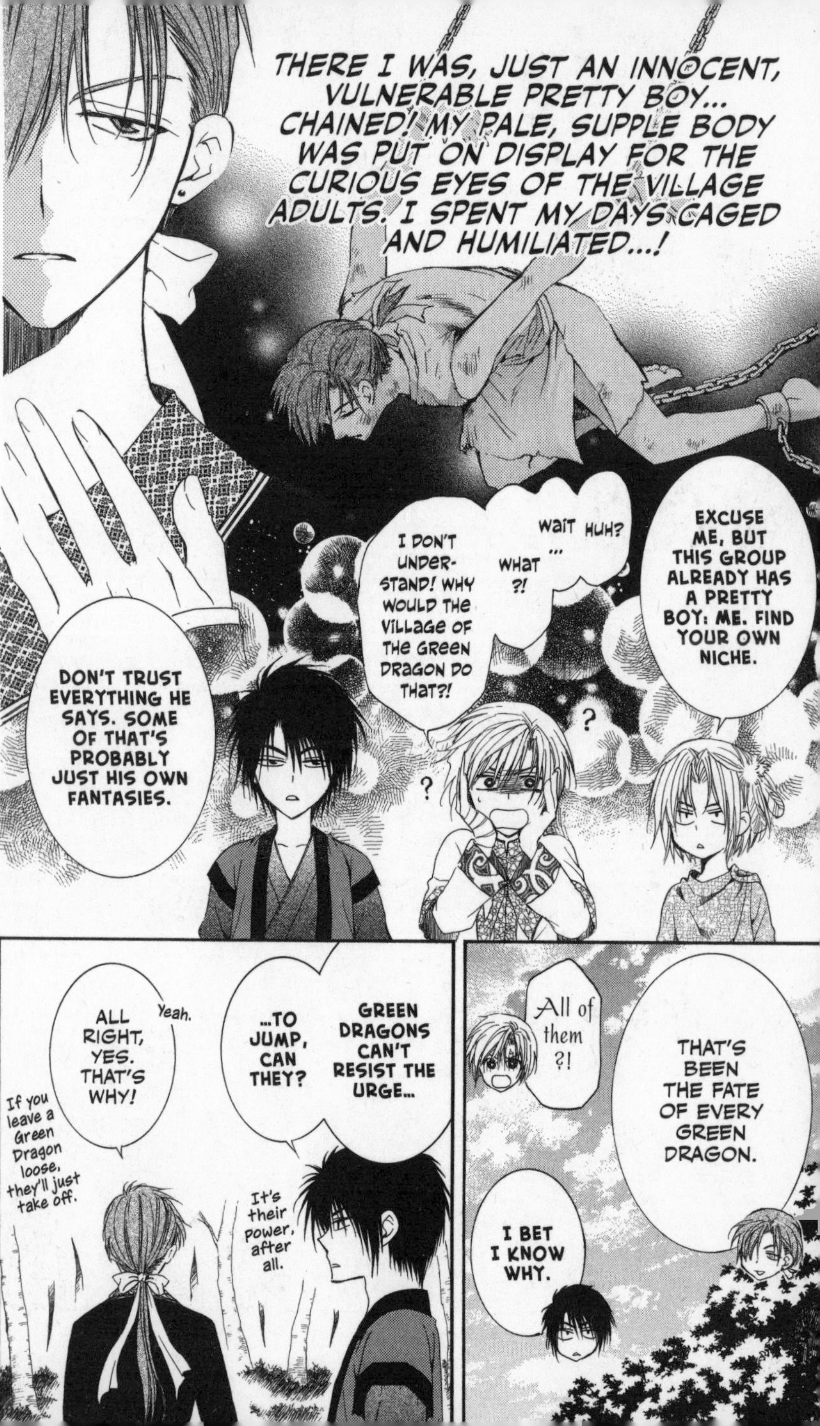
THERE I WAS, JUST AN INNOCENT, VULNERABLE PRETTY BOY... CHAINED! MY PALE, SUPPLE BODY WAS PUT ON DISPLAY FOR THE CURIOUS EYES OF THE VILLAGE ADULTS. I SPENT MY DAYS CAGED AND HUMILIATED...!
EXCUSE ME, BUT THIS GROUP ALREADY HAS A PRETTY BOY: ME. FIND YOUR OWN NICHE.
HUH?
Wait... WHAT?!
I DON'T UNDERSTAND! WHY WOULD THE VILLAGE OF THE GREEN DRAGON DO THAT?!
DON'T TRUST EVERYTHING HE SAYS. SOME OF THAT'S PROBABLY JUST HIS OWN FANTASIES.
THAT'S BEEN THE FATE OF EVERY GREEN DRAGON.
All of them?!
I BET I KNOW WHY.
GREEN DRAGONS CAN'T RESIST THE URGE...
...TO JUMP, CAN THEY?
It's their power, after all.
ALL RIGHT, YES. THAT'S WHY!
Yeah.
If you leave a Green Dragon loose, they'll just take off.

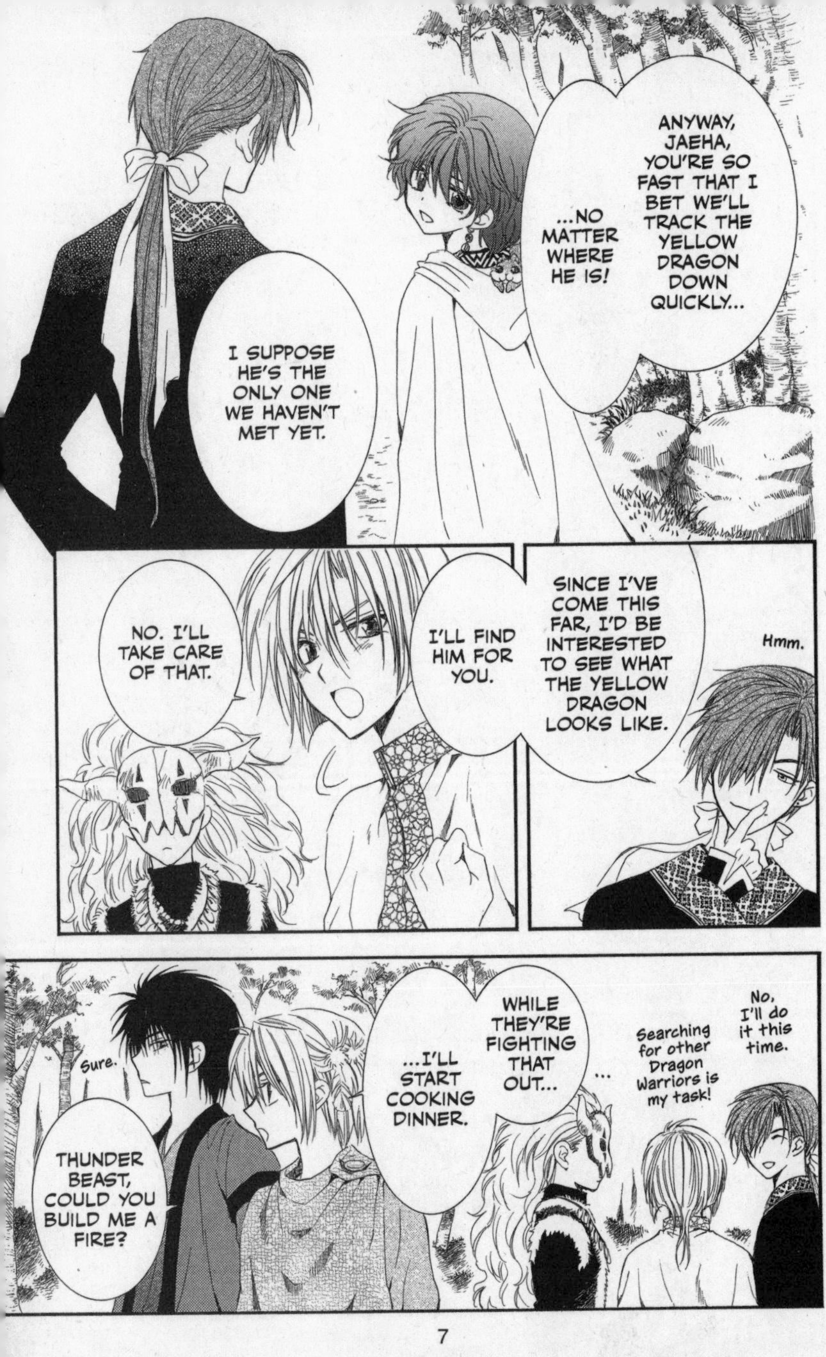
ANYWAY, JAEHA, YOU'RE SO FAST THAT I BET WE'LL TRACK THE YELLOW DRAGON DOWN QUICKLY...
...NO MATTER WHERE HE IS!
I SUPPOSE HE'S THE ONLY ONE WE HAVEN'T MET YET.
Hmm.
SINCE I'VE COME THIS FAR, I'D BE INTERESTED TO SEE WHAT THE YELLOW DRAGON LOOKS LIKE.
I'LL FIND HIM FOR YOU.
NO. I'LL TAKE CARE OF THAT.
No, I'll do it this time.
Searching for other Dragon Warriors is my task!
...
WHILE THEY'RE FIGHTING THAT OUT...
...I'LL START COOKING DINNER.
THUNDER BEAST, COULD YOU BUILD ME A FIRE?
Sure.

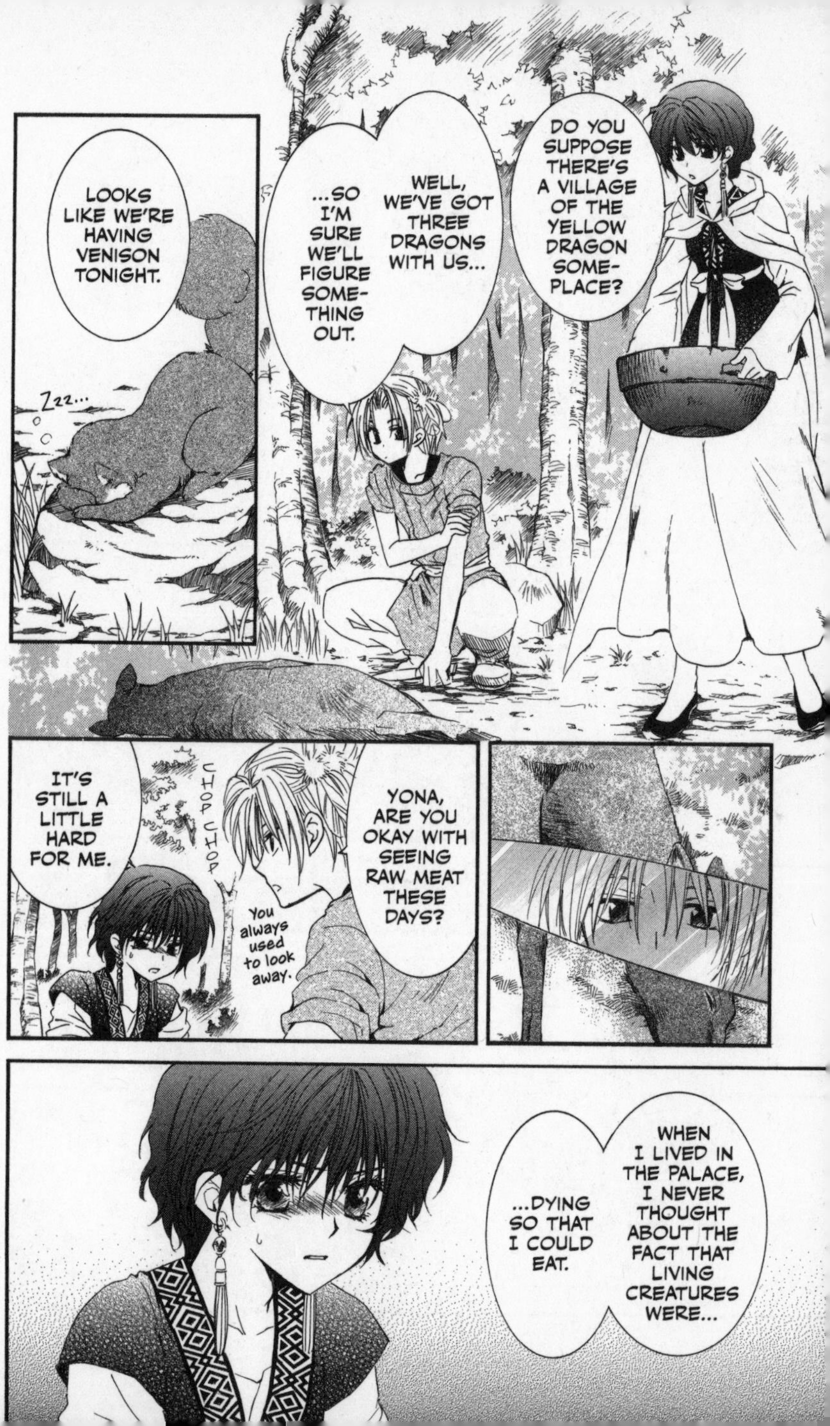
DO YOU SUPPOSE THERE'S A VILLAGE OF THE YELLOW DRAGON SOME-PLACE?
WELL, WE'VE GOT THREE DRAGONS WITH US...
...SO I'M SURE WE'LL FIGURE SOME-THING OUT.
LOOKS LIKE WE'RE HAVING VENISON TONIGHT.
Zzz...
YONA, ARE YOU OKAY WITH SEEING RAW MEAT THESE DAYS?
You always used to look away.
CHOP CHOP
IT'S STILL A LITTLE HARD FOR ME.
WHEN I LIVED IN THE PALACE, I NEVER THOUGHT ABOUT THE FACT THAT LIVING CREATURES WERE...
...DYING SO THAT I COULD EAT.

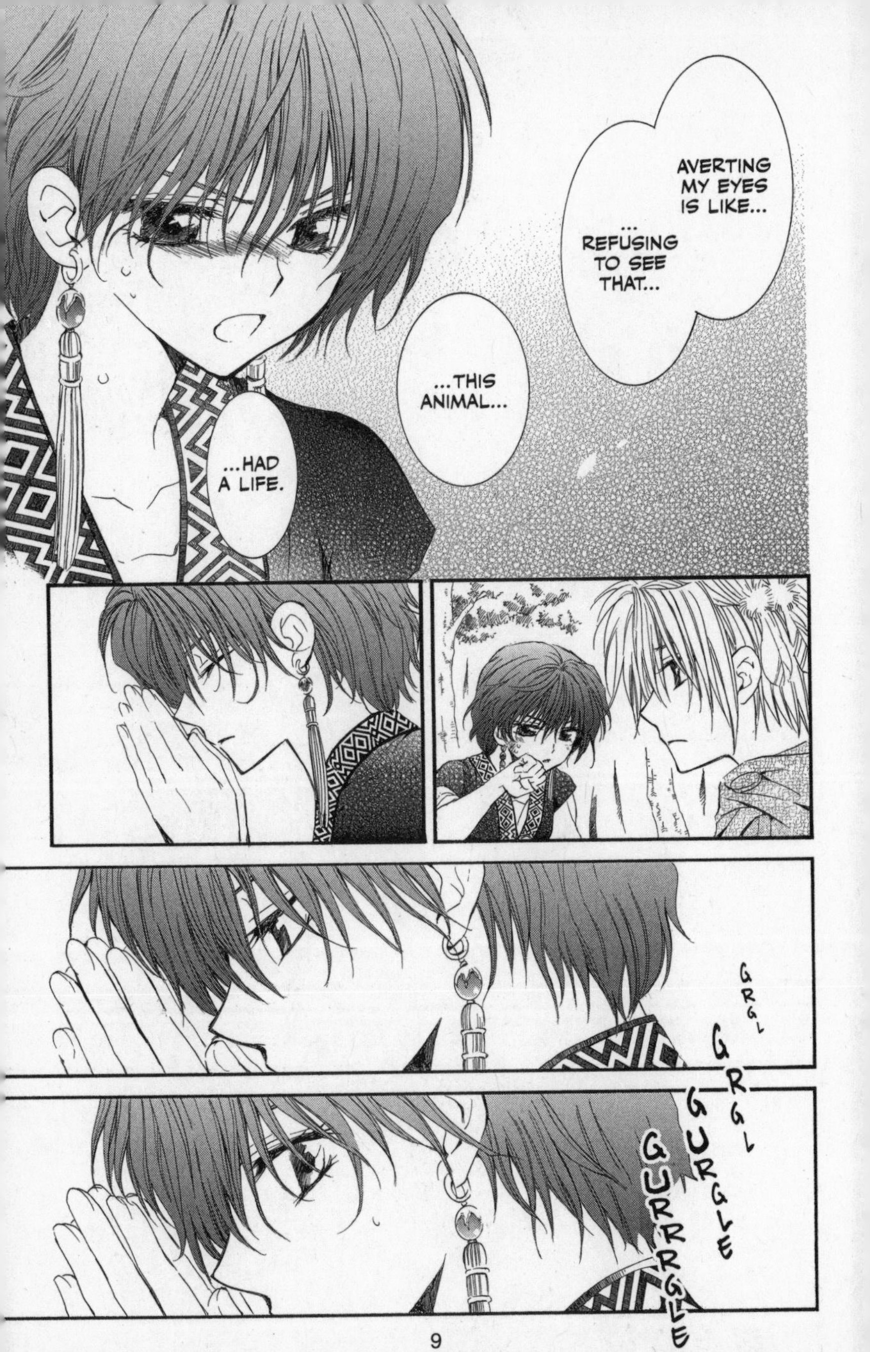
AVERTING MY EYES IS LIKE...
...REFUSING TO SEE THAT...
...THIS ANIMAL...
...HAD A LIFE.
GRGL
GRGL
GURGLE
GURRRGLE

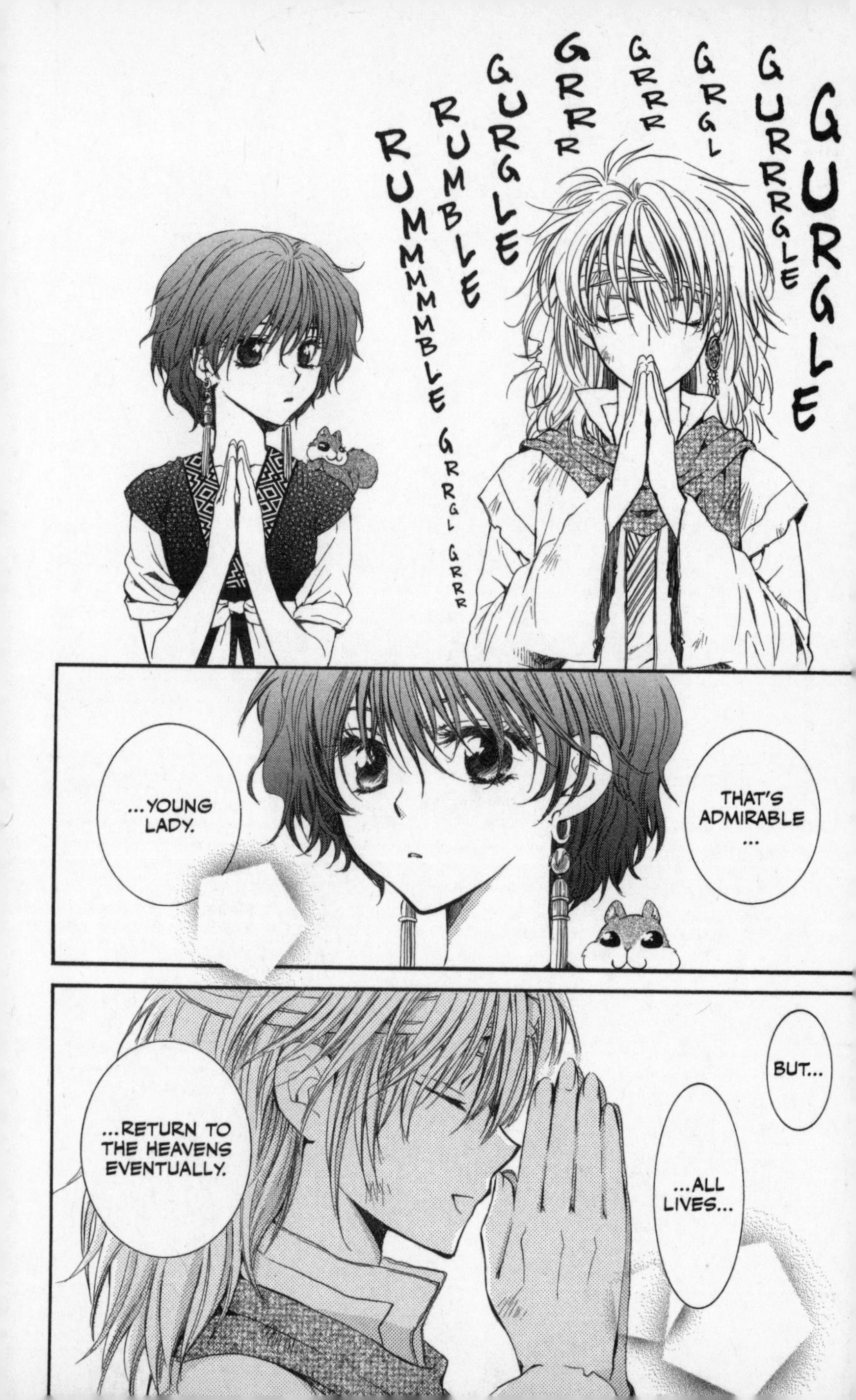
GURGLE
GURRRGLE
GRGL
GRRRR
GRRR
GURGLE
RUMBLE
RUMMMMMBLE
GRRGL GRRR
THAT'S ADMIRABLE ...
...YOUNG LADY.
BUT...
...ALL LIVES...
...RETURN TO THE HEAVENS EVENTUALLY.

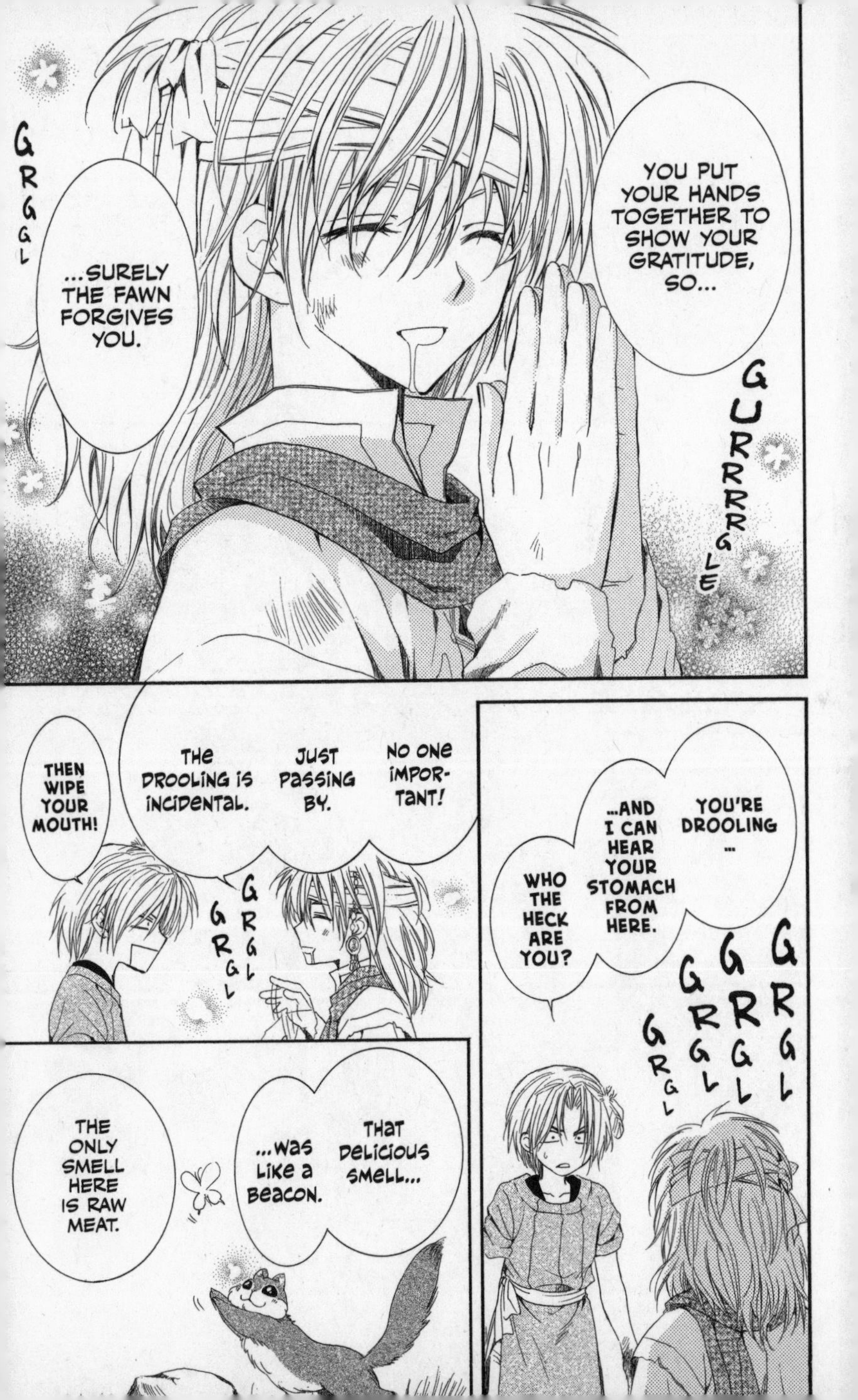
YOU PUT YOUR HANDS TOGETHER TO SHOW YOUR GRATITUDE, SO...
GURRRRGLE
...SURELY THE FAWN FORGIVES YOU.
GRGGL
YOU'RE DROOLING...
...AND I CAN HEAR YOUR STOMACH FROM HERE.
WHO THE HECK ARE YOU?
GRGL
GRGL
GRGL
GRGL
NO ONE IMPORTANT!
JUST PASSING BY.
THE DROOLING IS INCIDENTAL.
THEN WIPE YOUR MOUTH!
GRGL
GRGL
THAT DELICIOUS SMELL...
...WAS LIKE A BEACON.
THE ONLY SMELL HERE IS RAW MEAT.

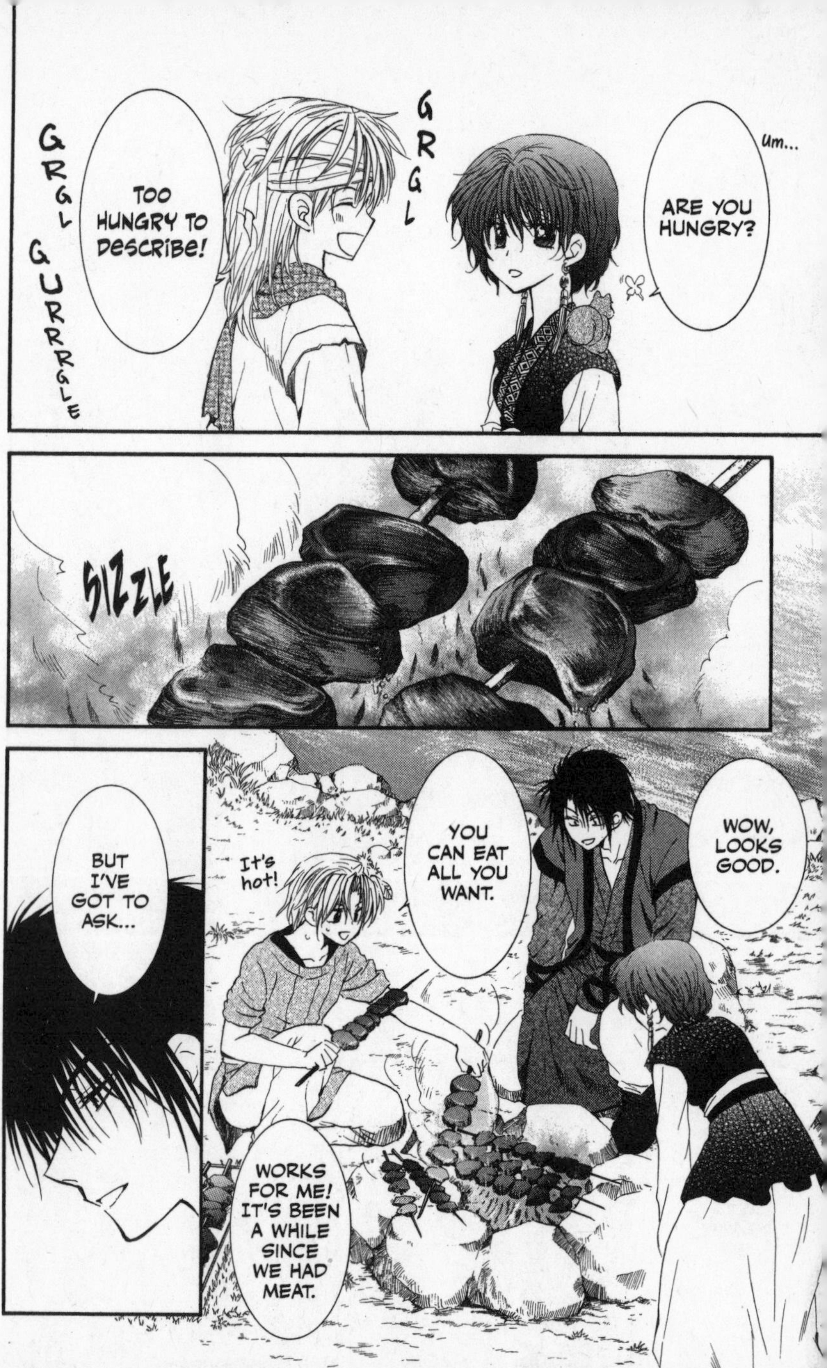
um...
ARE YOU HUNGRY?
GRGL
TOO HUNGRY TO DESCRIBE!
GRGL
GURRRGLE
SIZZLE
WOW, LOOKS GOOD.
YOU CAN EAT ALL YOU WANT.
It's hot!
WORKS FOR ME! IT'S BEEN A WHILE SINCE WE HAD MEAT.
BUT I'VE GOT TO ASK...

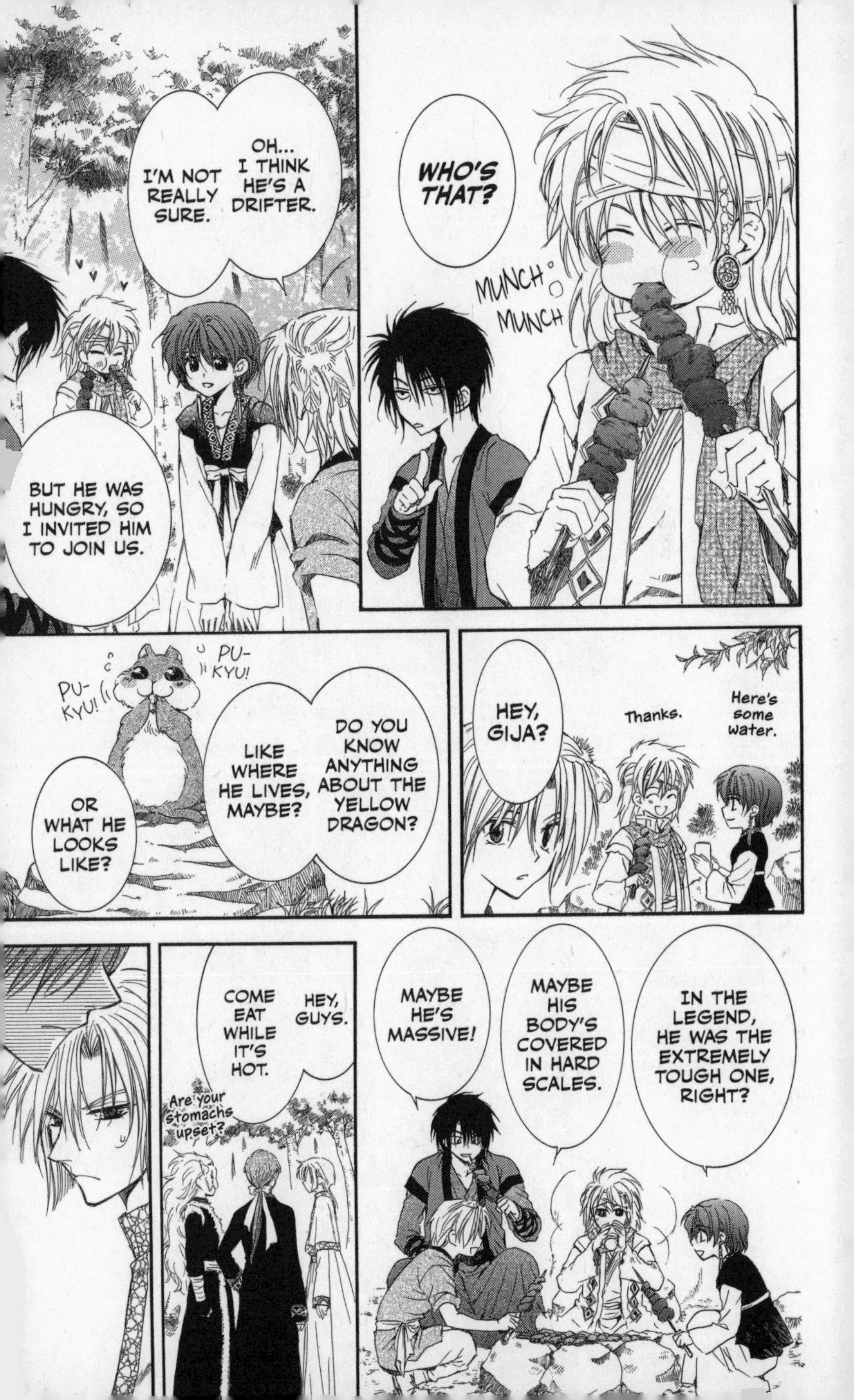
WHO'S THAT?
MUNCH MUNCH
OH... I THINK HE'S A DRIFTER.
I'M NOT REALLY SURE.
BUT HE WAS HUNGRY, SO I INVITED HIM TO JOIN US.
Here's some water.
Thanks.
HEY, GIJA?
DO YOU KNOW ANYTHING ABOUT THE YELLOW DRAGON?
LIKE WHERE HE LIVES, MAYBE?
PU-KYU!
PU-KYU!
OR WHAT HE LOOKS LIKE?
IN THE LEGEND, HE WAS THE EXTREMELY TOUGH ONE, RIGHT?
MAYBE HIS BODY'S COVERED IN HARD SCALES.
MAYBE HE'S MASSIVE!
HEY, GUYS.
COME EAT WHILE IT'S HOT.
Are your stomachs upset?

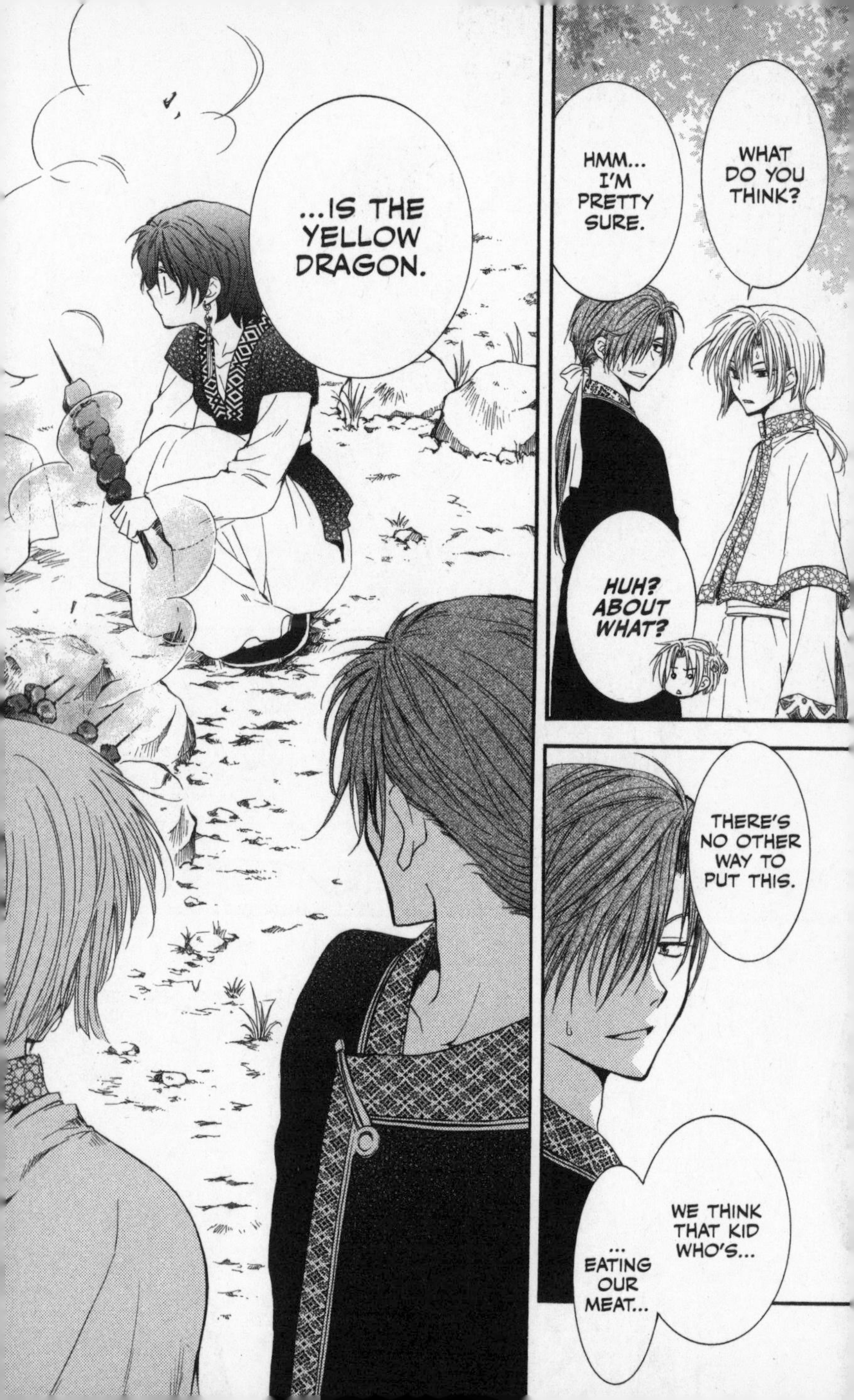
WHAT DO YOU THINK?
HMM... I'M PRETTY SURE.
HUH? ABOUT WHAT?
THERE'S NO OTHER WAY TO PUT THIS.
WE THINK THAT KID WHO'S...
... EATING OUR MEAT...
...IS THE YELLOW DRAGON.

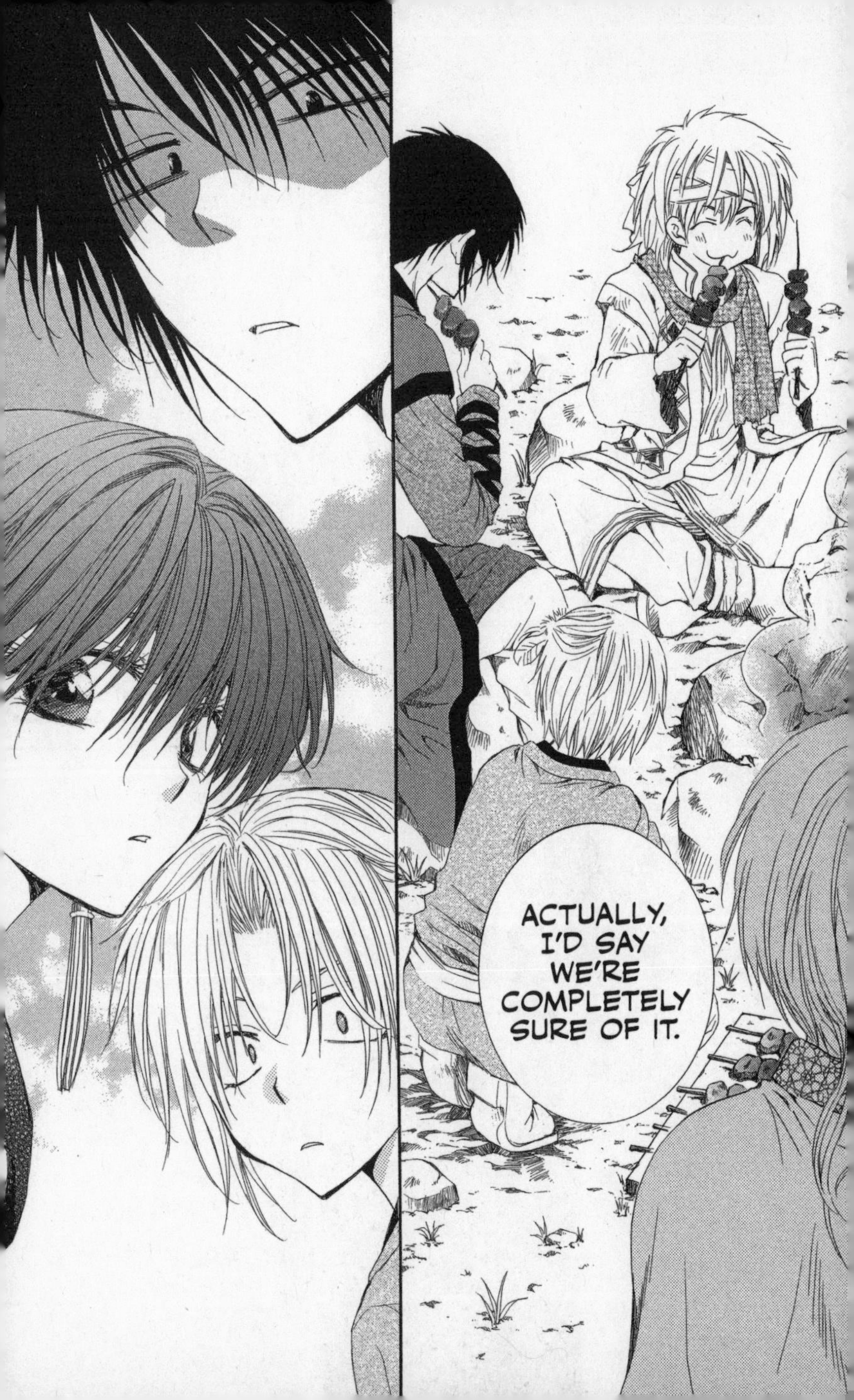
ACTUALLY, I'D SAY WE'RE COMPLETELY SURE OF IT.

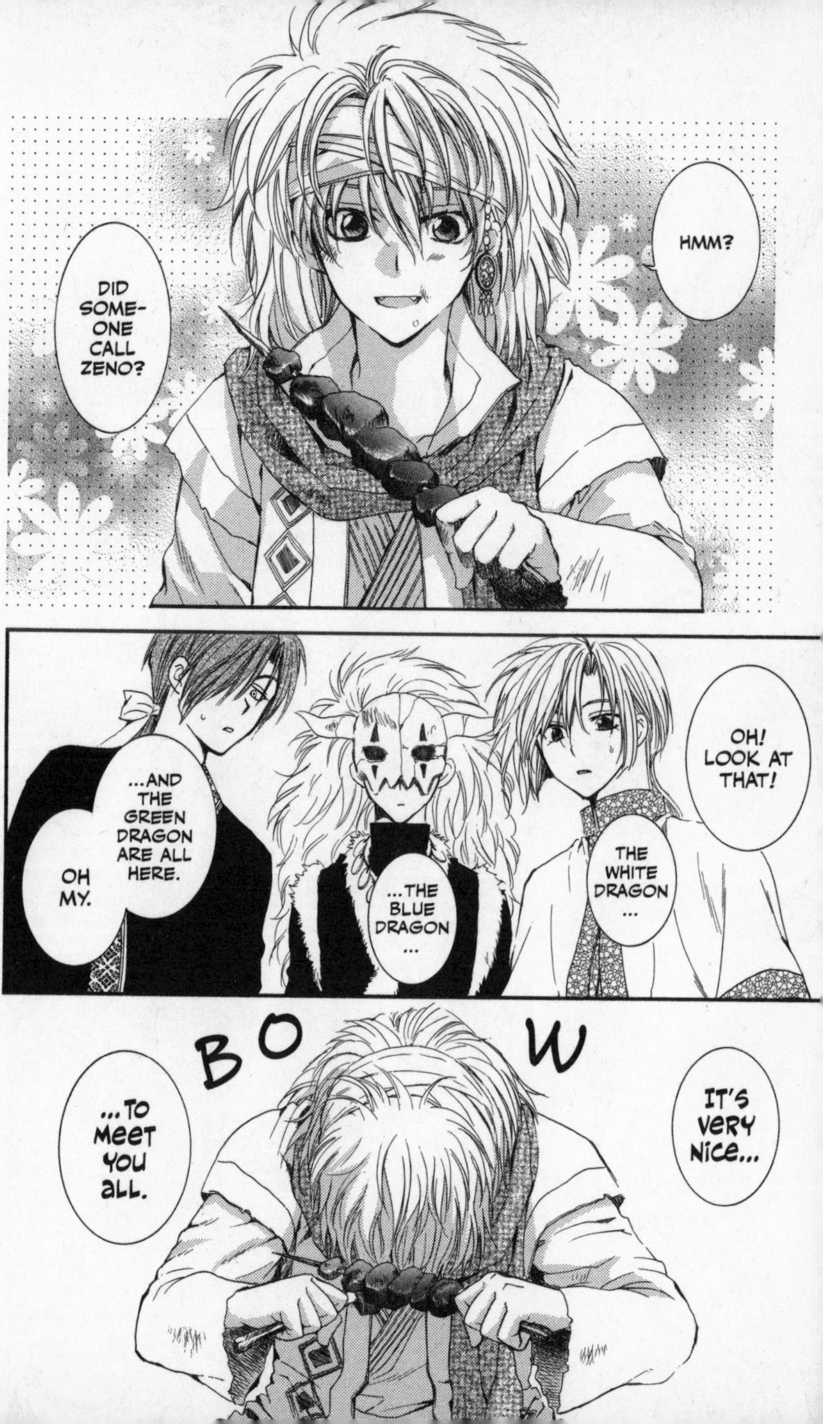
HMM?
DID SOME-ONE CALL ZENO?
OH! LOOK AT THAT!
THE WHITE DRAGON...
...THE BLUE DRAGON...
...AND THE GREEN DRAGON ARE ALL HERE.
OH MY.
BOW
IT'S VERY NICE...
...TO MEET YOU ALL.

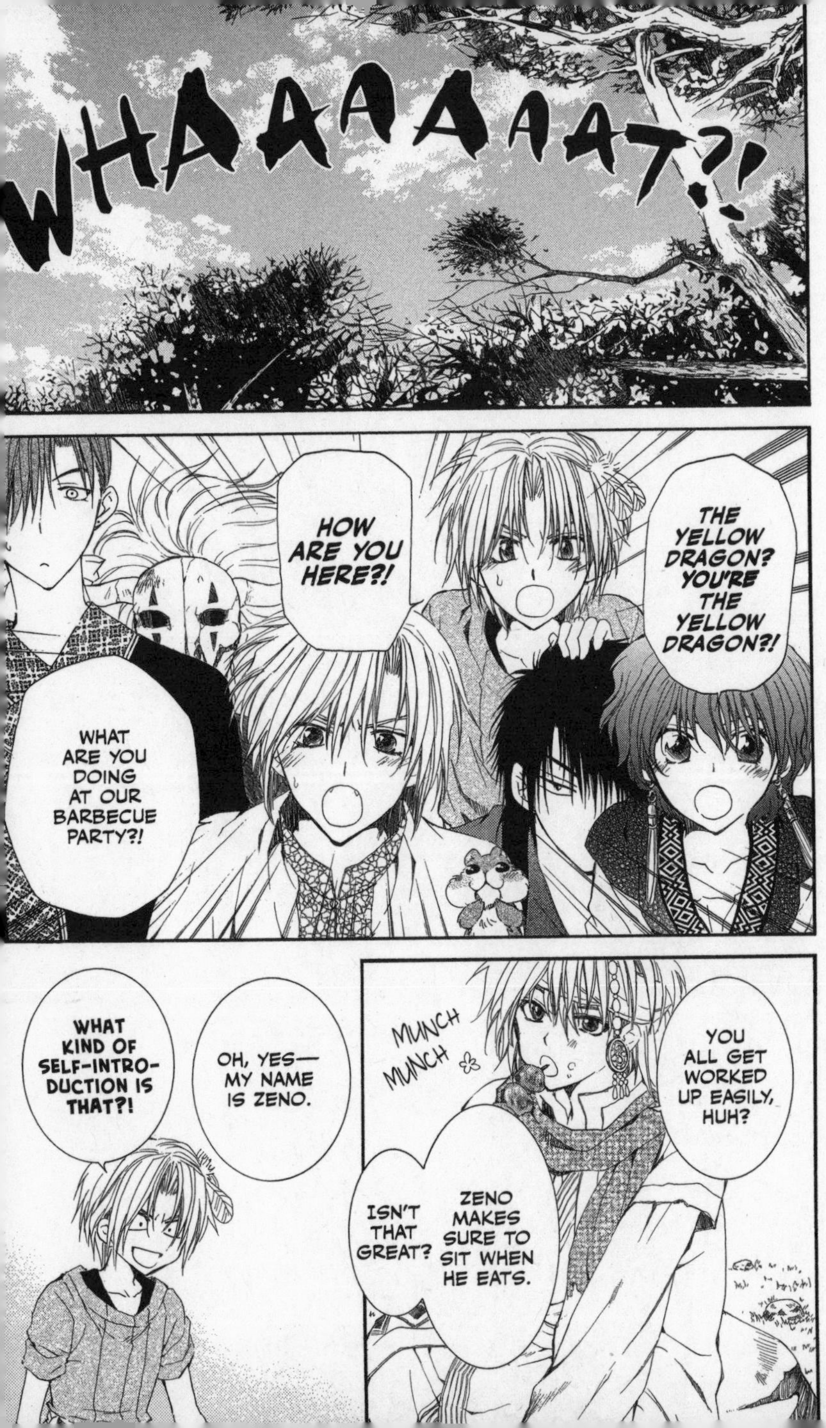
WHAAAAAAT?!
THE YELLOW DRAGON? YOU'RE THE YELLOW DRAGON?!
HOW ARE YOU HERE?!
WHAT ARE YOU DOING AT OUR BARBECUE PARTY?!
MUNCH MUNCH
YOU ALL GET WORKED UP EASILY, HUH?
ZENO MAKES SURE TO SIT WHEN HE EATS.
ISN'T THAT GREAT?
OH, YES— MY NAME IS ZENO.
WHAT KIND OF SELF-INTRO-DUCTION IS THAT?!

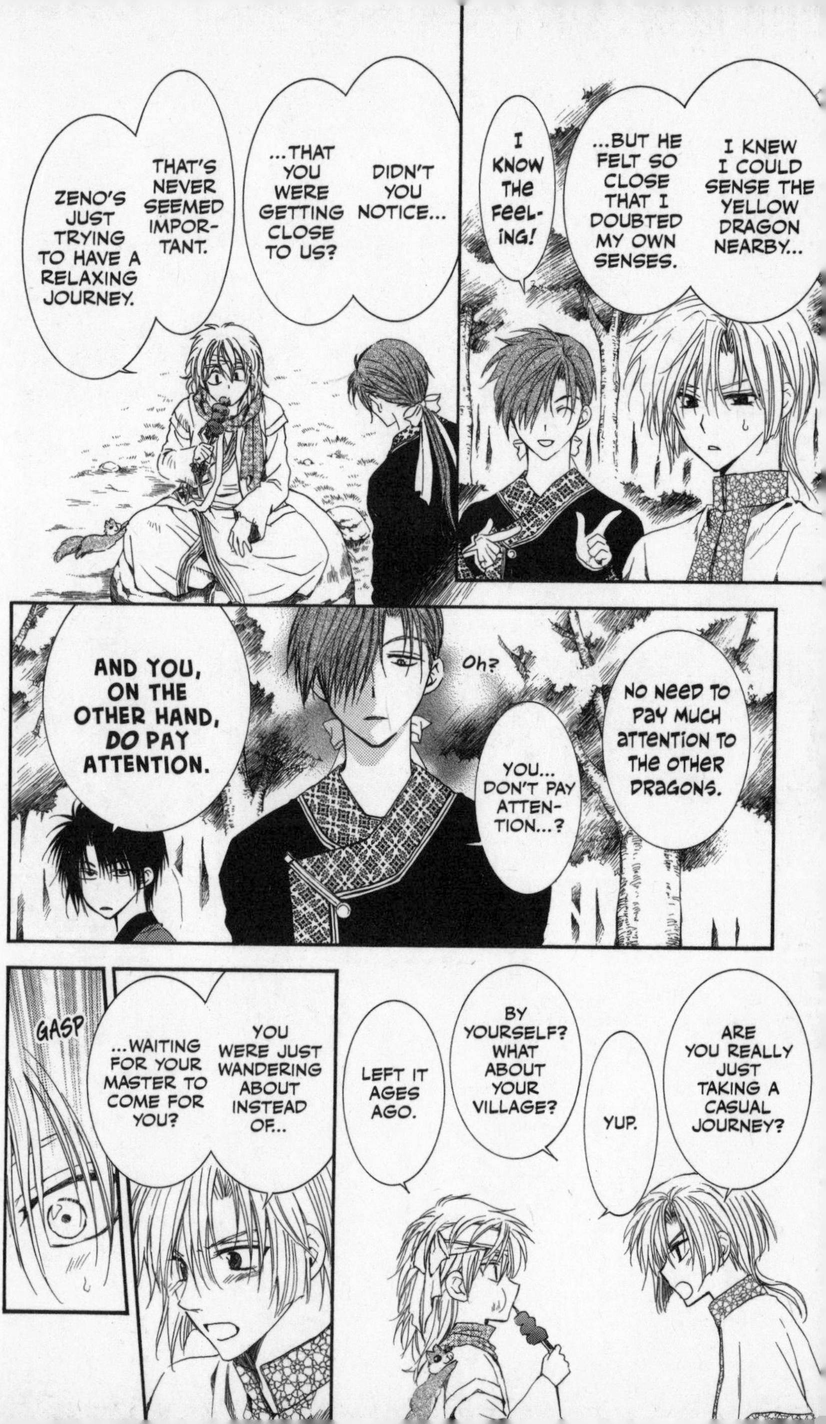
I KNEW I COULD SENSE THE YELLOW DRAGON NEARBY...
...BUT HE FELT SO CLOSE THAT I DOUBTED MY OWN SENSES.
I KNOW THE FEEL-ING!
DIDN'T YOU NOTICE...
...THAT YOU WERE GETTING CLOSE TO US?
THAT'S NEVER SEEMED IMPOR-TANT.
ZENO'S JUST TRYING TO HAVE A RELAXING JOURNEY.
NO NEED TO PAY MUCH ATTENTION TO THE OTHER DRAGONS.
Oh?
YOU... DON'T PAY ATTEN-TION...?
AND YOU, ON THE OTHER HAND, DO PAY ATTENTION.
ARE YOU REALLY JUST TAKING A CASUAL JOURNEY?
YUP.
BY YOURSELF? WHAT ABOUT YOUR VILLAGE?
LEFT IT AGES AGO.
YOU WERE JUST WANDERING ABOUT INSTEAD OF...
...WAITING FOR YOUR MASTER TO COME FOR YOU?
GASP

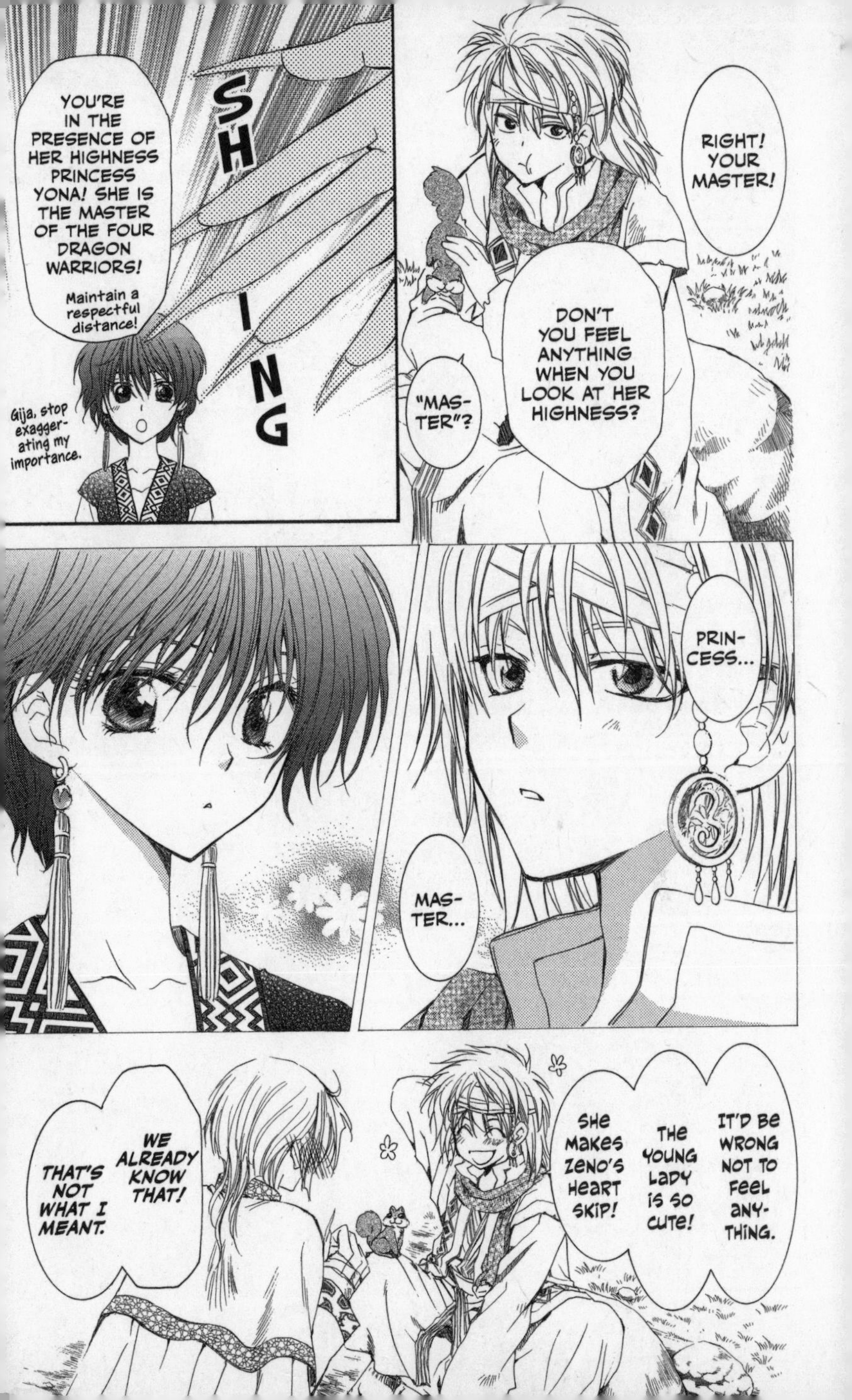
RIGHT! YOUR MASTER!
DON'T YOU FEEL ANYTHING WHEN YOU LOOK AT HER HIGHNESS?
"MAS-TER"?
SHING
YOU'RE IN THE PRESENCE OF HER HIGHNESS PRINCESS YONA! SHE IS THE MASTER OF THE FOUR DRAGON WARRIORS!
Maintain a respectful distance!
Gija, stop exagger-ating my importance.
PRIN-CESS...
MAS-TER...
IT'D BE WRONG NOT TO FEEL ANY-THING.
THE YOUNG LADY IS SO CUTE!
SHE MAKES ZENO'S HEART SKIP!
WE ALREADY KNOW THAT!
THAT'S NOT WHAT I MEANT.

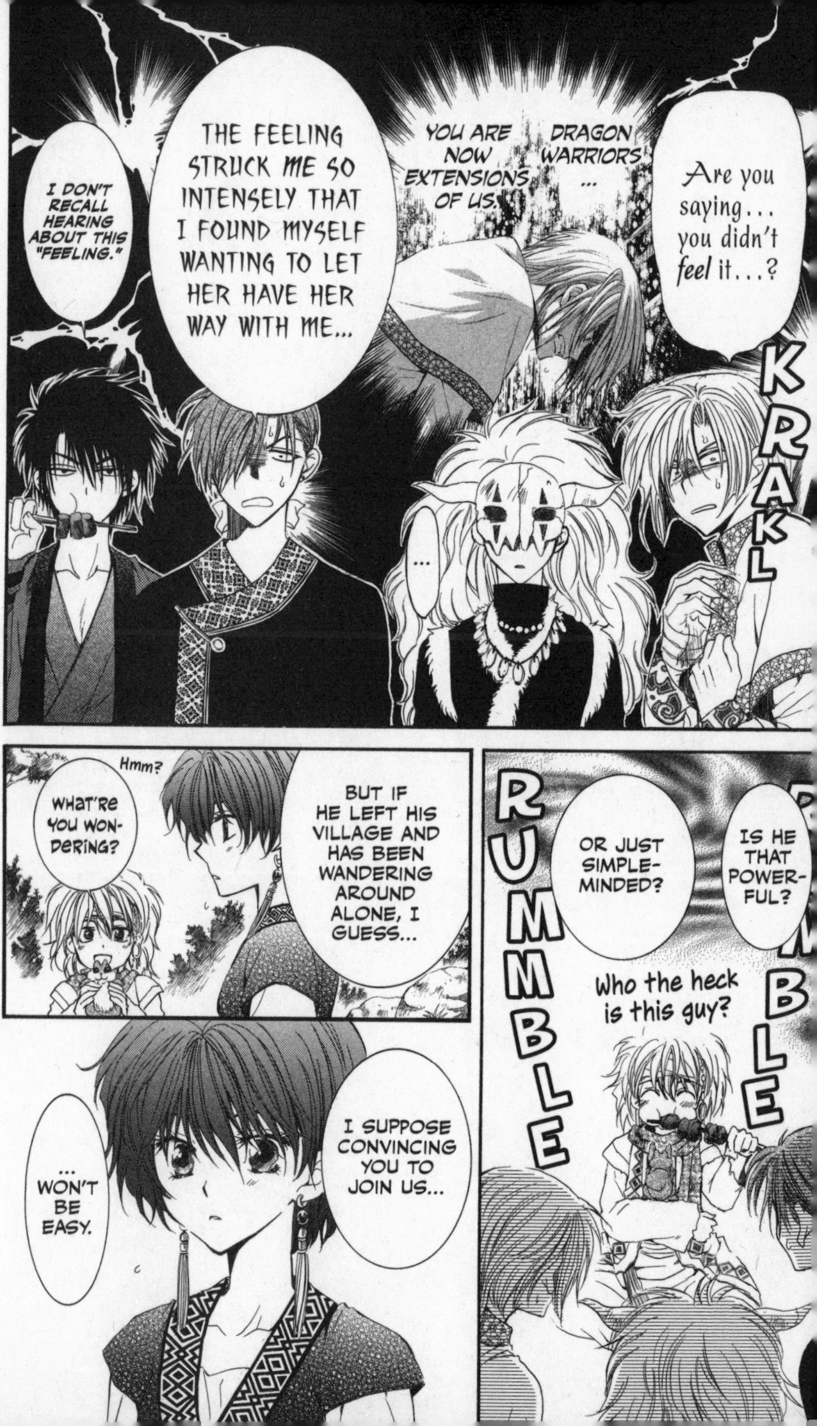

Are you saying... you didn't *feel* it...?
KRAKL
DRAGON WARRIORS...
YOU ARE NOW EXTENSIONS OF US.
THE FEELING STRUCK *ME* SO INTENSELY THAT I FOUND MYSELF WANTING TO LET HER HAVE HER WAY WITH ME...
I DON'T RECALL HEARING ABOUT THIS "FEELING."
...
MBLE
IS HE THAT POWERFUL?
OR JUST SIMPLE-MINDED?
RUMBLE
Who the heck is this guy?
BUT IF HE LEFT HIS VILLAGE AND HAS BEEN WANDERING AROUND ALONE, I GUESS...
Hmm?
WHAT'RE YOU WONDERING?
I SUPPOSE CONVINCING YOU TO JOIN US...
... WON'T BE EASY.

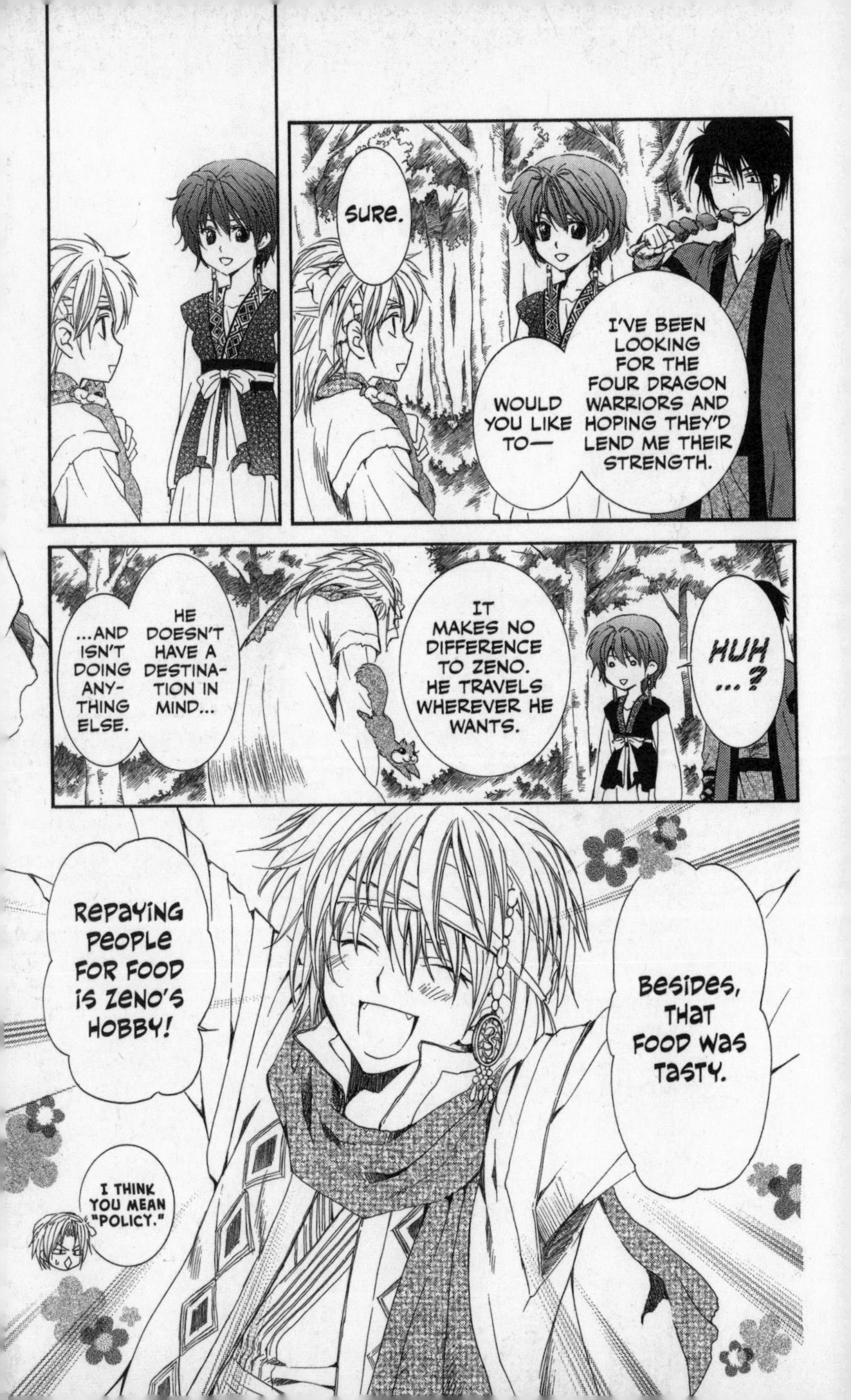
I'VE BEEN LOOKING FOR THE FOUR DRAGON WARRIORS AND HOPING THEY'D LEND ME THEIR STRENGTH.
WOULD YOU LIKE TO—
Sure.
HUH ...?
IT MAKES NO DIFFERENCE TO ZENO. HE TRAVELS WHEREVER HE WANTS.
HE DOESN'T HAVE A DESTINATION IN MIND...
...AND ISN'T DOING ANYTHING ELSE.
Besides, that food was tasty.
Repaying people for food is Zeno's hobby!
I THINK YOU MEAN "POLICY."

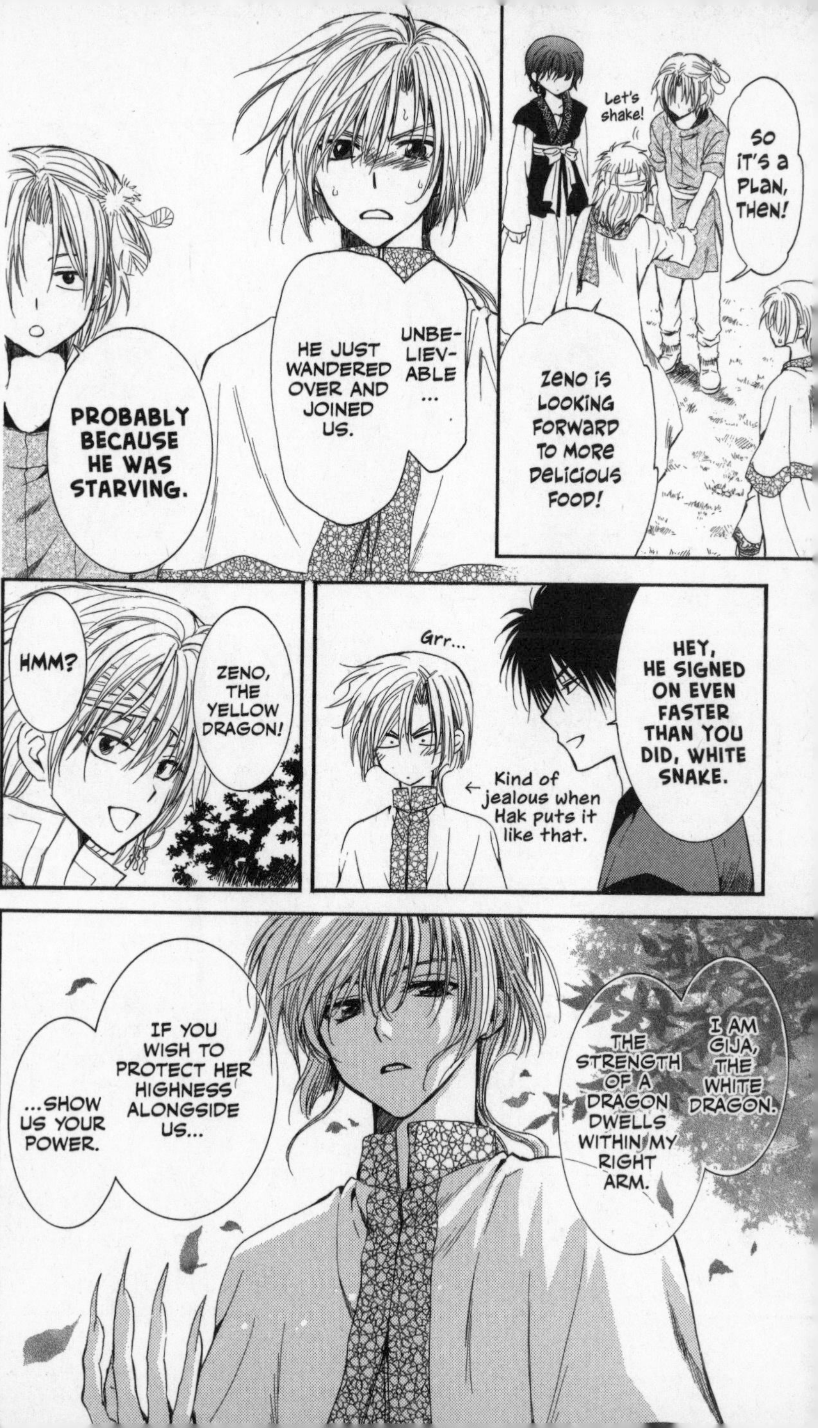
So it's a plan, then!
Let's shake!
Zeno is looking forward to more delicious food!
Unbe-liev-able...
He just wandered over and joined us.
Probably because he was starving.
Hey, he signed on even faster than you did, White Snake.
Grr...
← Kind of jealous when Hak puts it like that.
Zeno, the Yellow Dragon!
Hmm?
I am Gija, the White Dragon.
The strength of a dragon dwells within my right arm.
If you wish to protect her highness alongside us...
...show us your power.

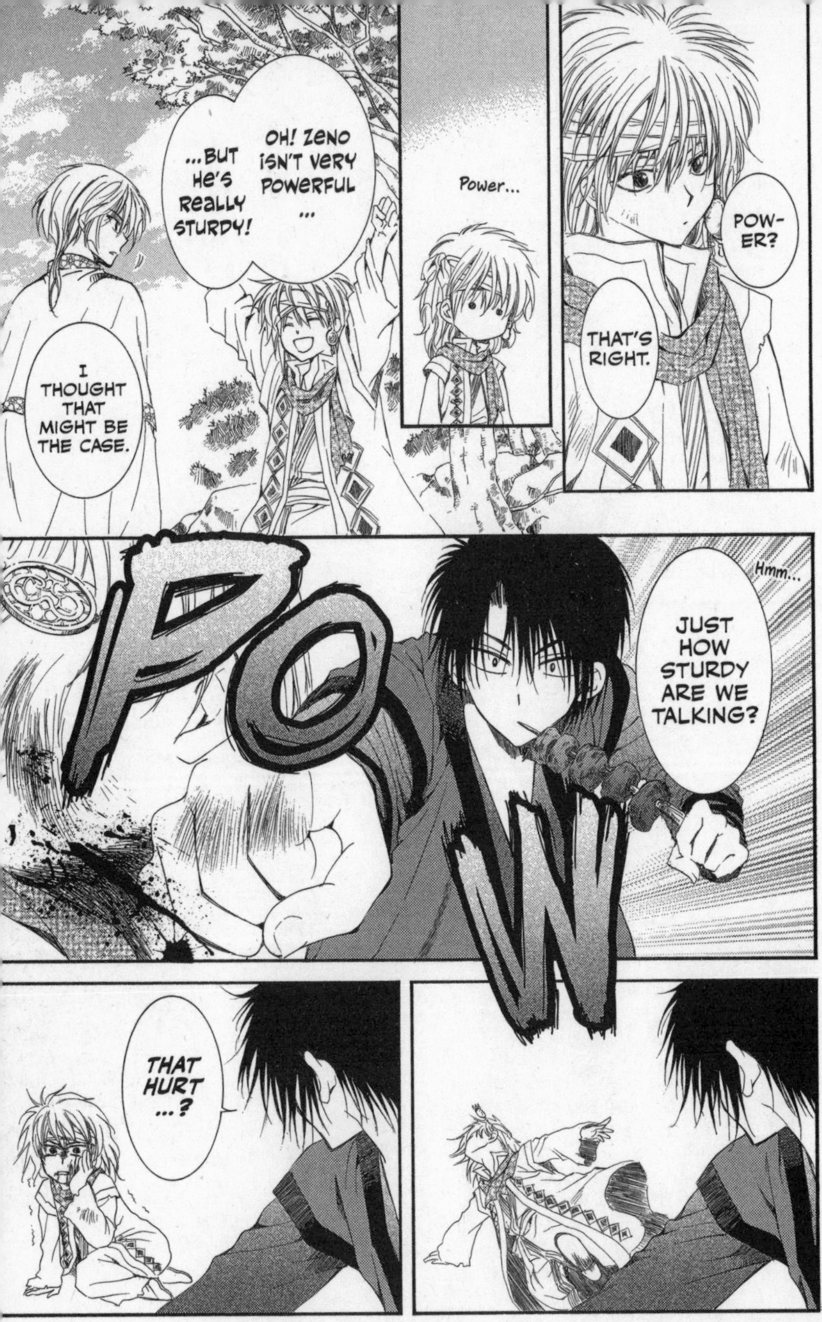
POW-ER?
THAT'S RIGHT.
Power...
OH! ZENO ISN'T VERY POWERFUL...
...BUT HE'S REALLY STURDY!
I THOUGHT THAT MIGHT BE THE CASE.
Hmm...
JUST HOW STURDY ARE WE TALKING?
POW
THAT HURT...?

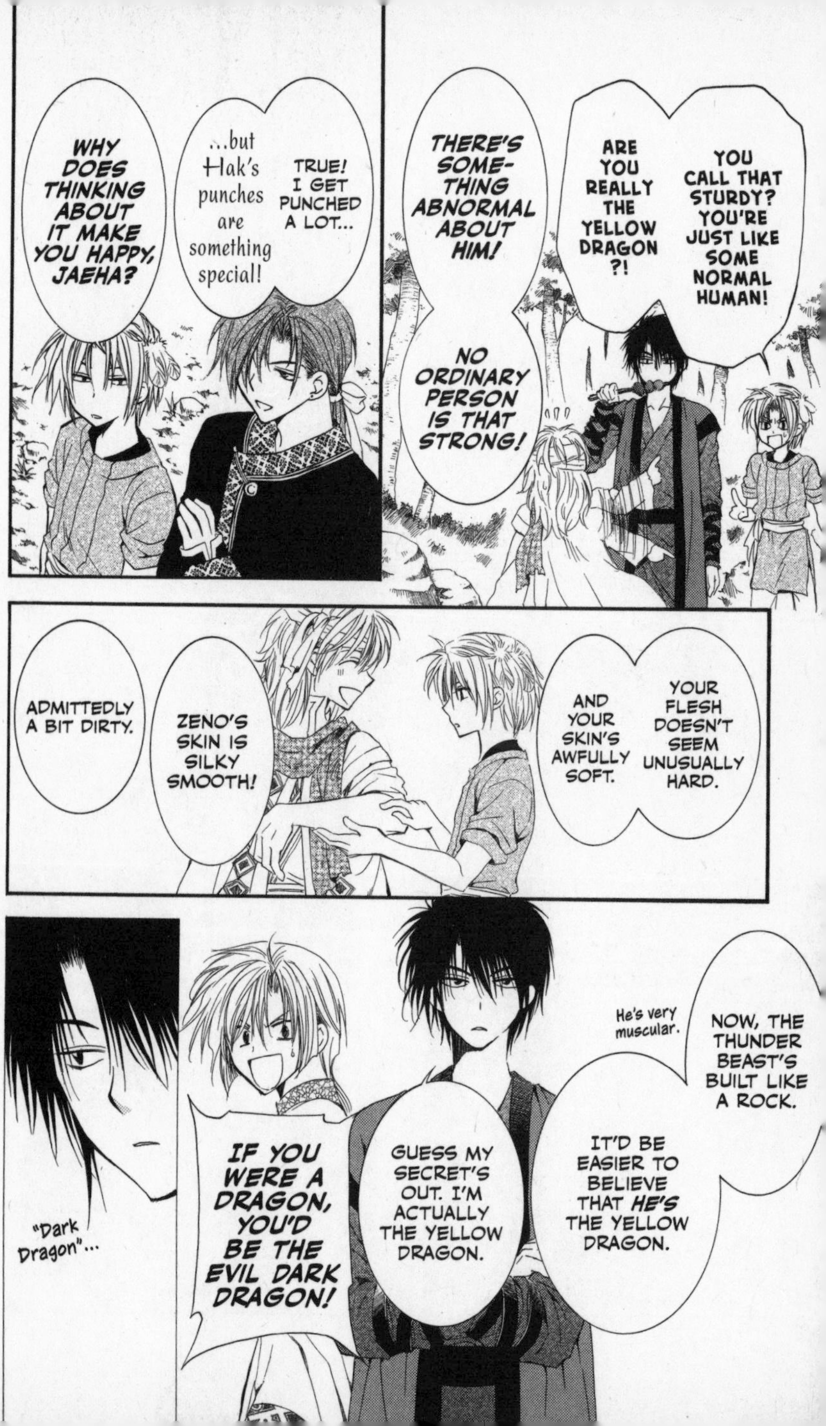
YOU CALL THAT STURDY? YOU'RE JUST LIKE SOME NORMAL HUMAN!
ARE YOU REALLY THE YELLOW DRAGON?!
THERE'S SOMETHING ABNORMAL ABOUT HIM!
NO ORDINARY PERSON IS THAT STRONG!
TRUE! I GET PUNCHED A LOT...
...but Hak's punches are something special!
WHY DOES THINKING ABOUT IT MAKE YOU HAPPY, JAEHA?
YOUR FLESH DOESN'T SEEM UNUSUALLY HARD.
AND YOUR SKIN'S AWFULLY SOFT.
ZENO'S SKIN IS SILKY SMOOTH!
ADMITTEDLY A BIT DIRTY.
NOW, THE THUNDER BEAST'S BUILT LIKE A ROCK.
He's very muscular.
IT'D BE EASIER TO BELIEVE THAT *HE'S* THE YELLOW DRAGON.
GUESS MY SECRET'S OUT. I'M ACTUALLY THE YELLOW DRAGON.
IF YOU WERE A DRAGON, YOU'D BE THE EVIL DARK DRAGON!
"Dark Dragon"...

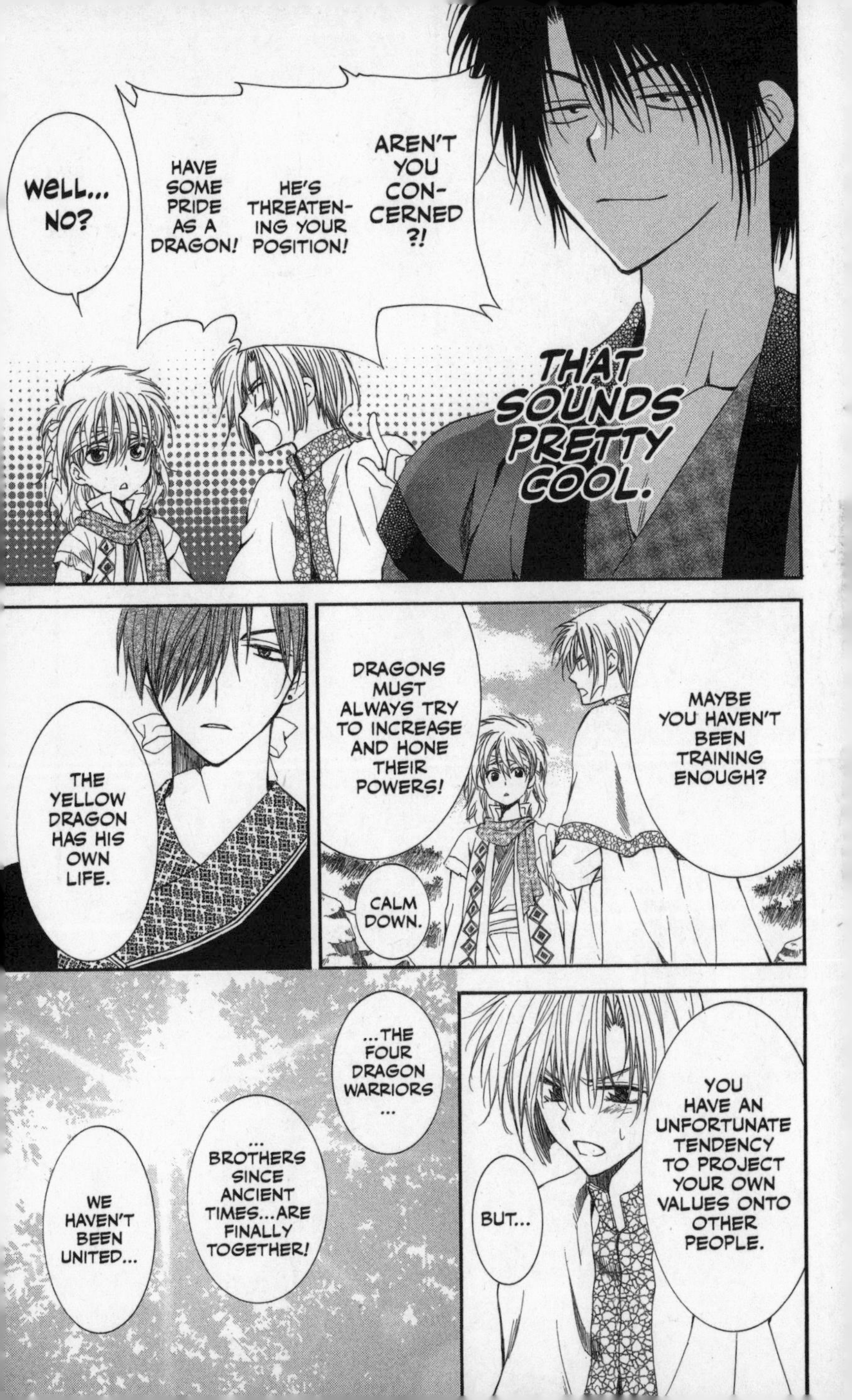
AREN'T YOU CONCERNED?!
HE'S THREATENING YOUR POSITION!
HAVE SOME PRIDE AS A DRAGON!
WELL... NO?
THAT SOUNDS PRETTY COOL.
MAYBE YOU HAVEN'T BEEN TRAINING ENOUGH?
DRAGONS MUST ALWAYS TRY TO INCREASE AND HONE THEIR POWERS!
CALM DOWN.
THE YELLOW DRAGON HAS HIS OWN LIFE.
YOU HAVE AN UNFORTUNATE TENDENCY TO PROJECT YOUR OWN VALUES ONTO OTHER PEOPLE.
BUT...
...THE FOUR DRAGON WARRIORS...
...BROTHERS SINCE ANCIENT TIMES...ARE FINALLY TOGETHER!
WE HAVEN'T BEEN UNITED...

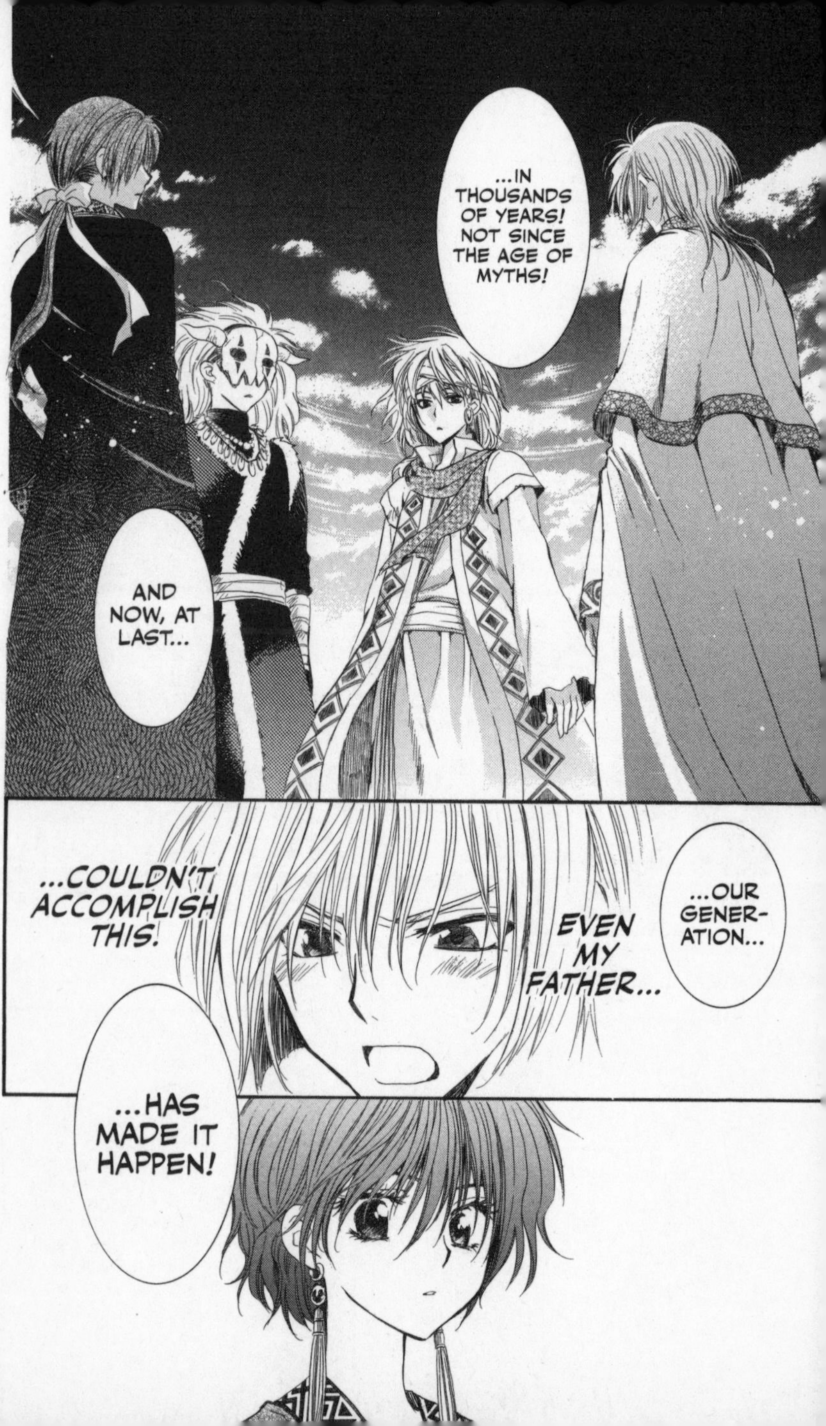
...IN THOUSANDS OF YEARS! NOT SINCE THE AGE OF MYTHS!
AND NOW, AT LAST...
...OUR GENERATION...
EVEN MY FATHER...
...COULDN'T ACCOMPLISH THIS.
...HAS MADE IT HAPPEN!

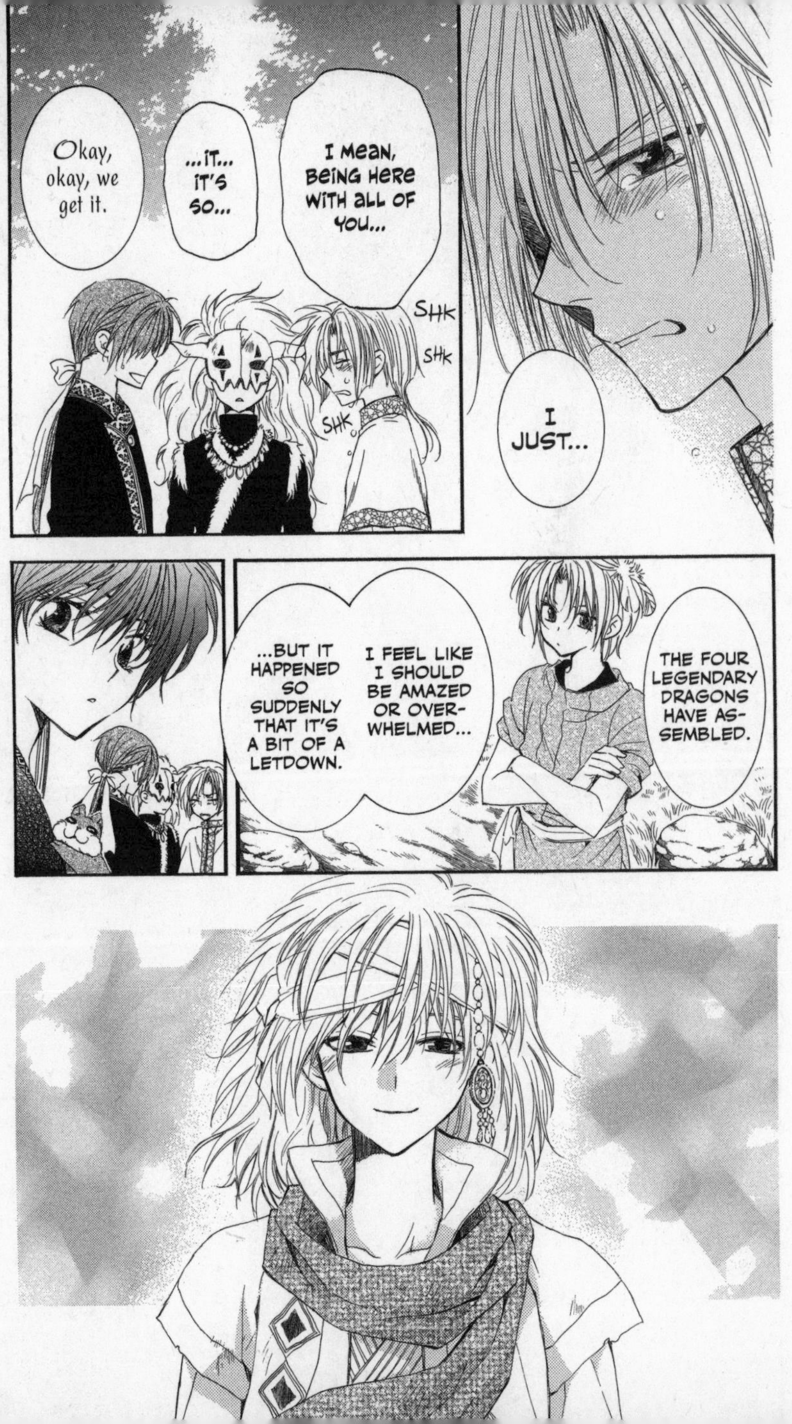
I JUST...
I MEAN, BEING HERE WITH ALL OF YOU...
SHK
SHK
SHK
...IT... IT'S SO...
Okay, okay, we get it.
THE FOUR LEGENDARY DRAGONS HAVE ASSEMBLED.
I FEEL LIKE I SHOULD BE AMAZED OR OVER-WHELMED...
...BUT IT HAPPENED SO SUDDENLY THAT IT'S A BIT OF A LETDOWN.

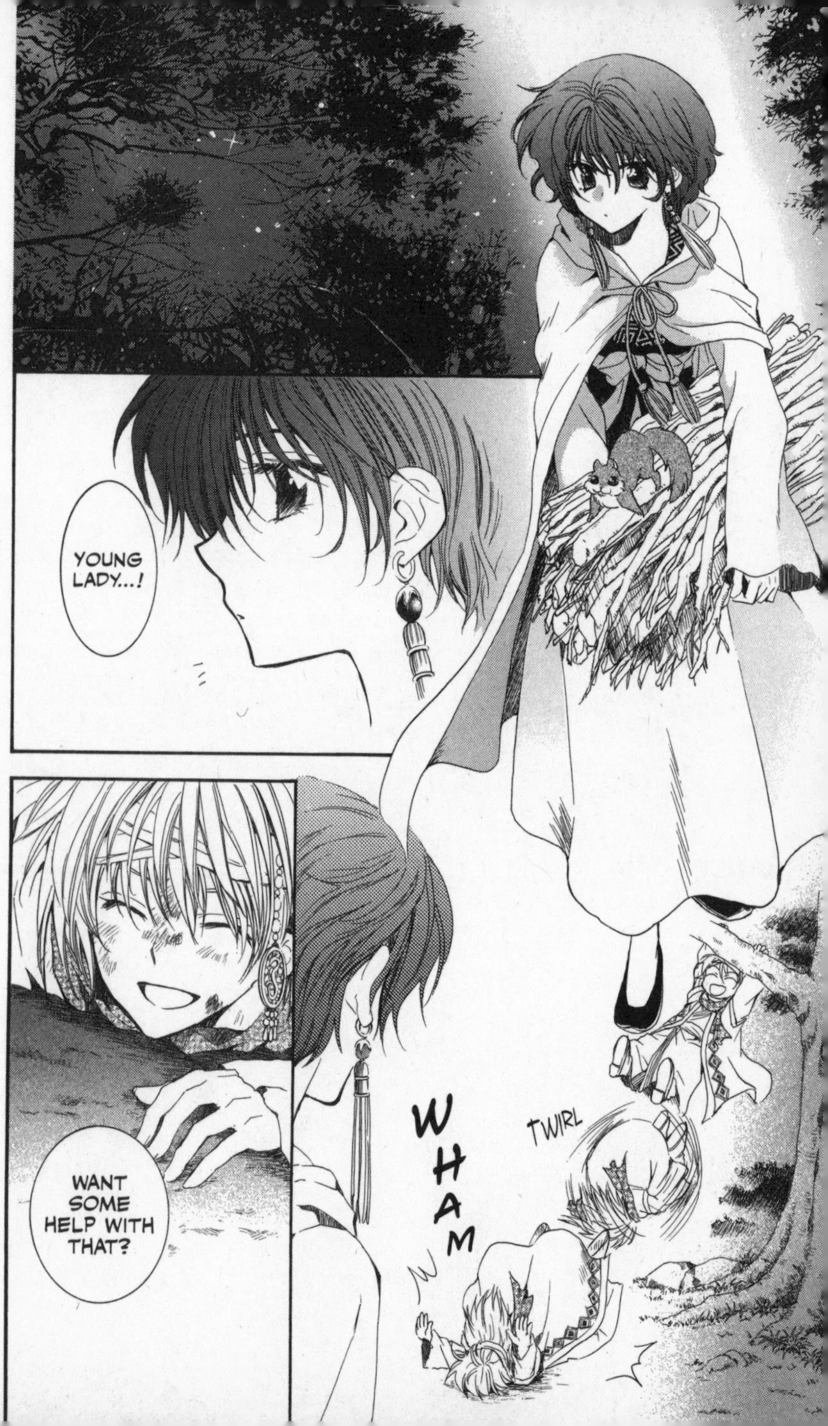
TWIRL
WHAM
YOUNG LADY...!
WANT SOME HELP WITH THAT?

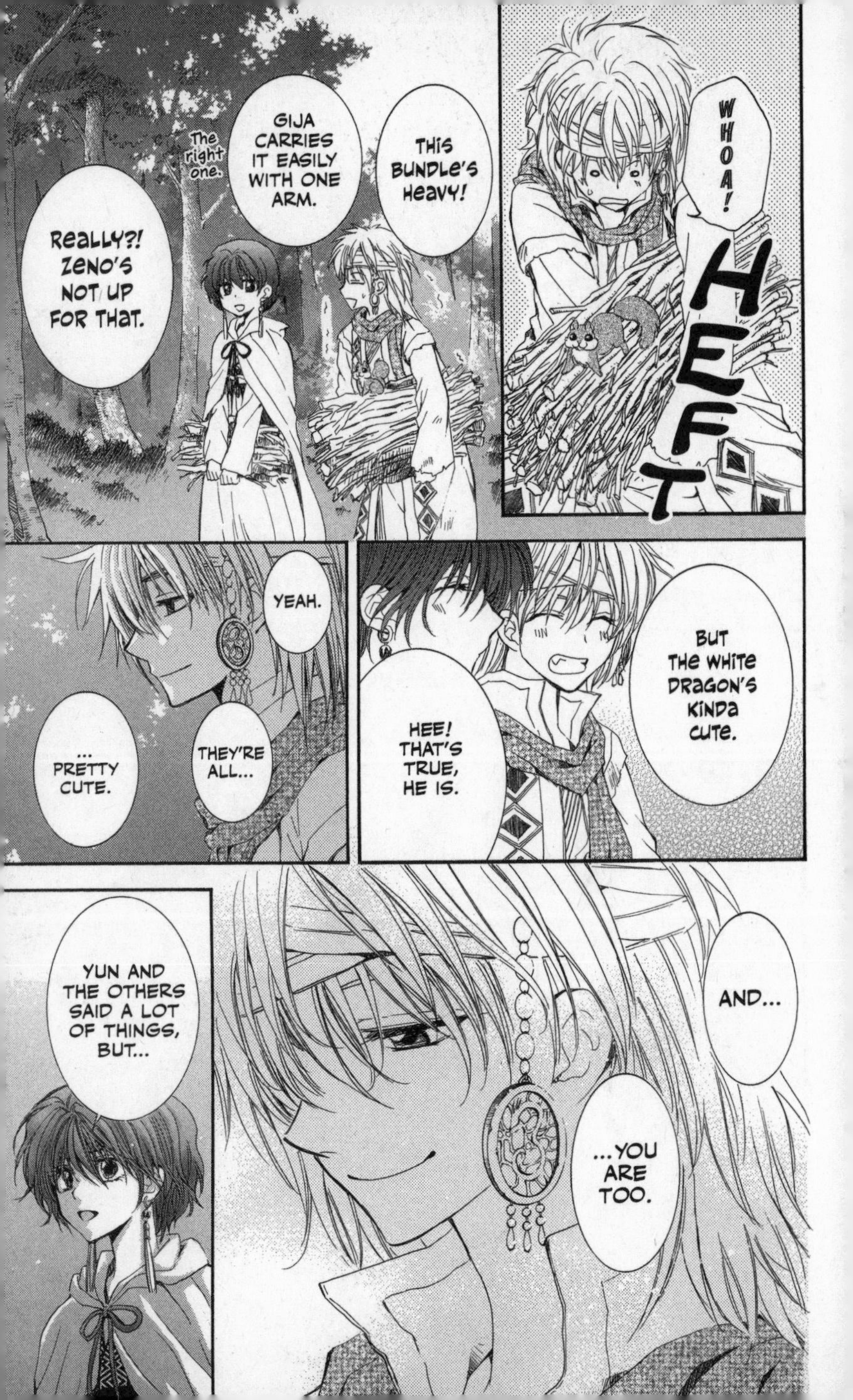
WHOA!
HEFT
THIS BUNDLE'S HEAVY!
GIJA CARRIES IT EASILY WITH ONE ARM.
The right one.
REALLY?! ZENO'S NOT UP FOR THAT.
BUT THE WHITE DRAGON'S KINDA CUTE.
HEE! THAT'S TRUE, HE IS.
YEAH.
THEY'RE ALL...
...PRETTY CUTE.
AND...
...YOU ARE TOO.
YUN AND THE OTHERS SAID A LOT OF THINGS, BUT...

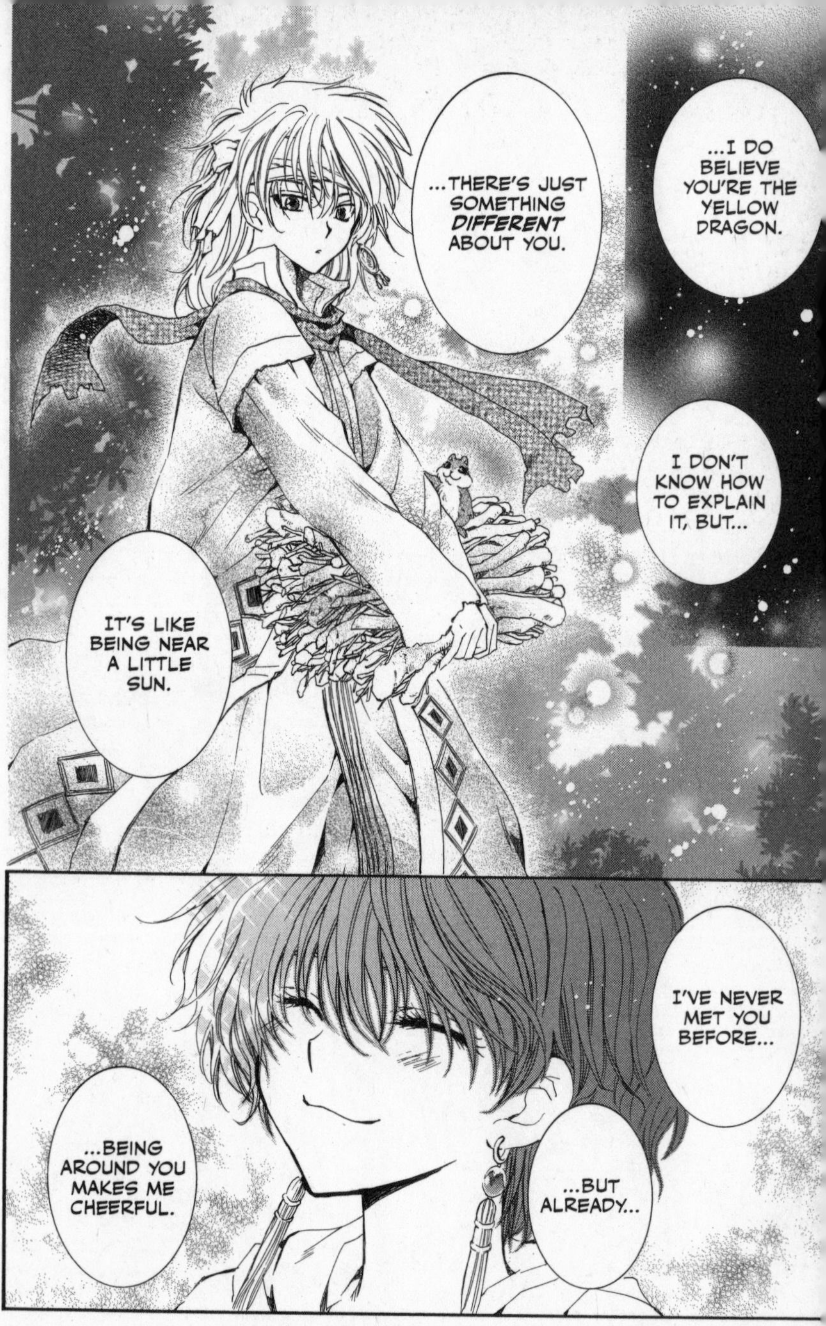
...I DO BELIEVE YOU'RE THE YELLOW DRAGON.
I DON'T KNOW HOW TO EXPLAIN IT, BUT...
...THERE'S JUST SOMETHING *DIFFERENT* ABOUT YOU.
IT'S LIKE BEING NEAR A LITTLE SUN.
I'VE NEVER MET YOU BEFORE...
...BUT ALREADY...
...BEING AROUND YOU MAKES ME CHEERFUL.

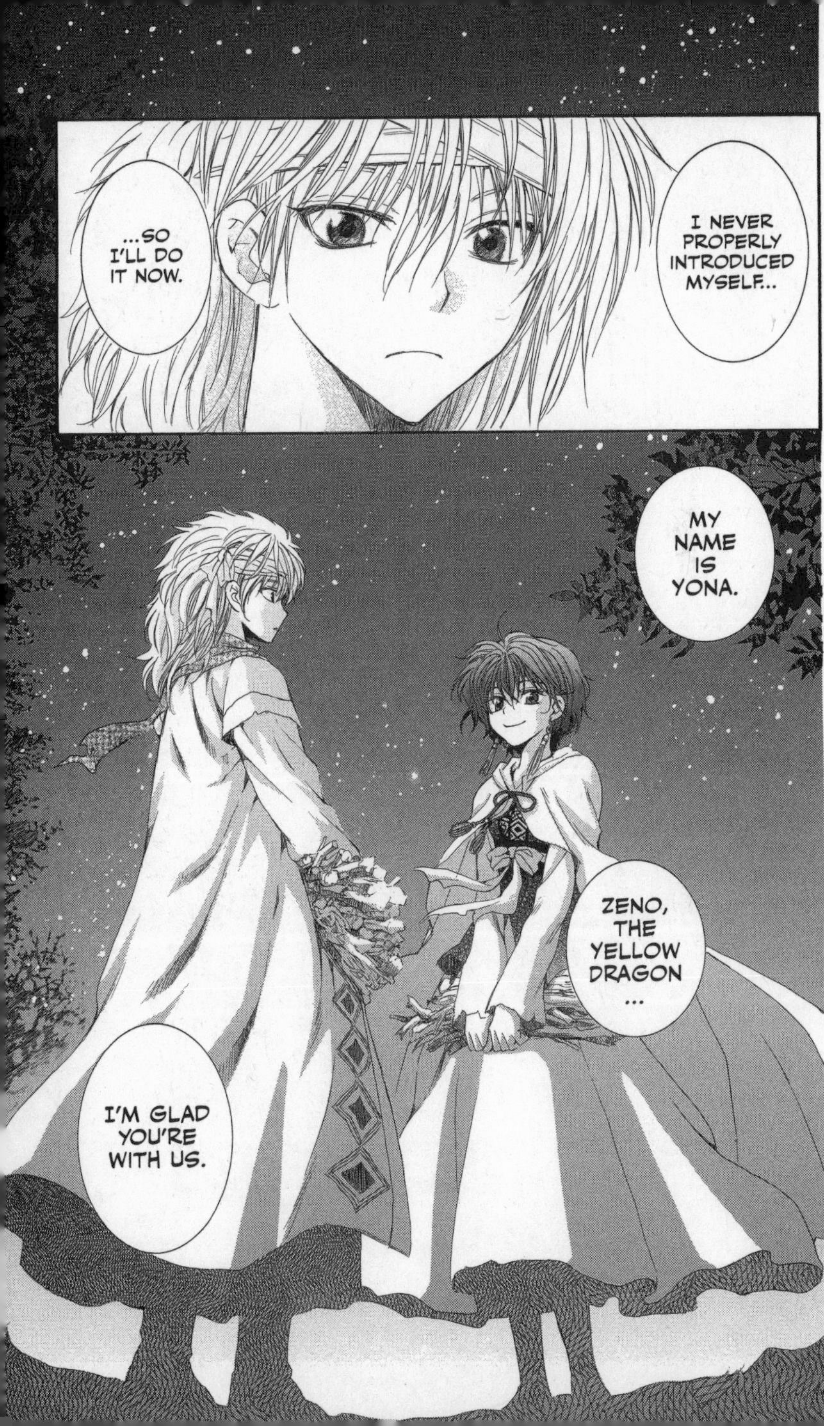
I NEVER PROPERLY INTRODUCED MYSELF...
...SO I'LL DO IT NOW.
MY NAME IS YONA.
ZENO, THE YELLOW DRAGON ...
I'M GLAD YOU'RE WITH US.

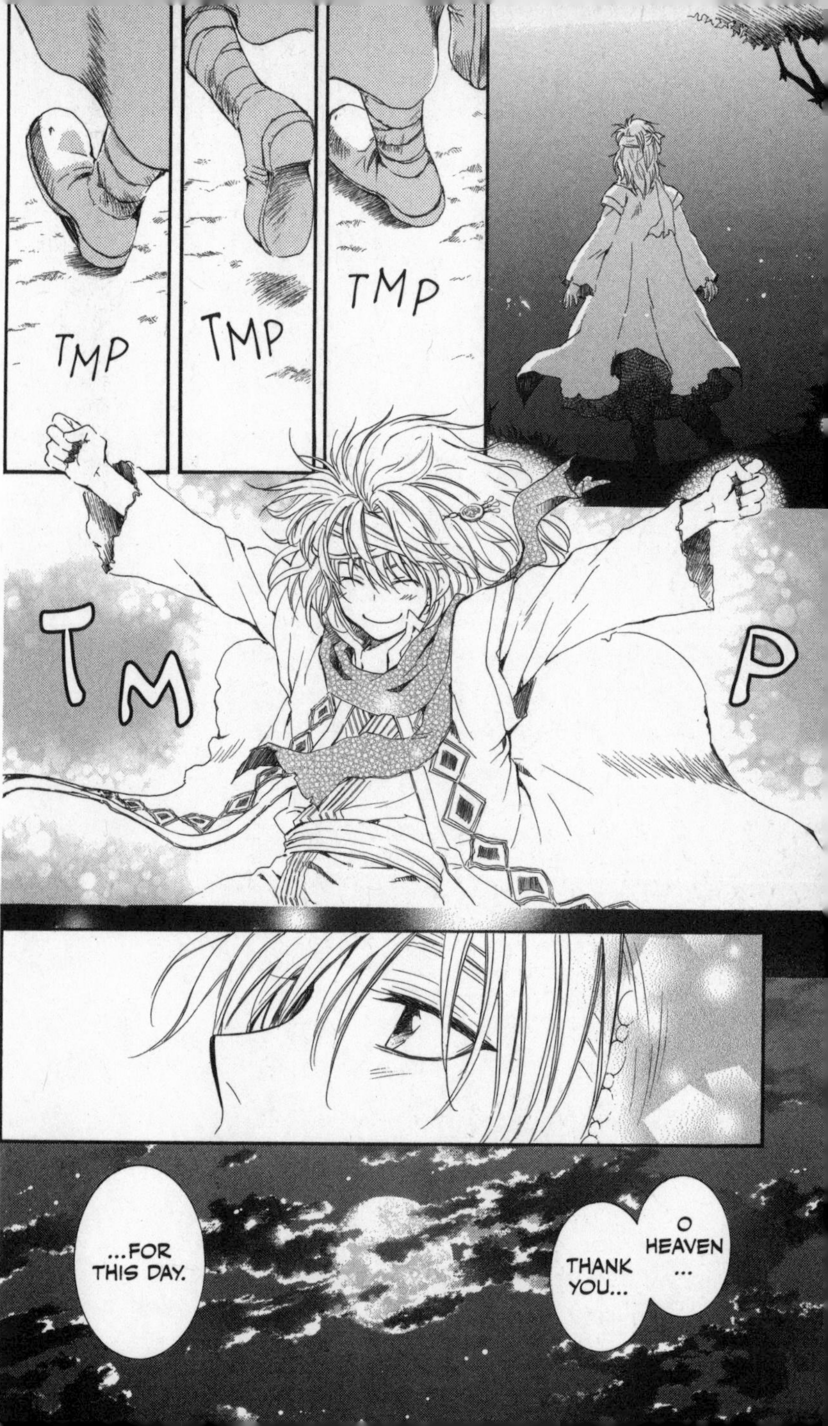
TMP
TMP
TMP
TMP
O HEAVEN ...
THANK YOU...
...FOR THIS DAY.

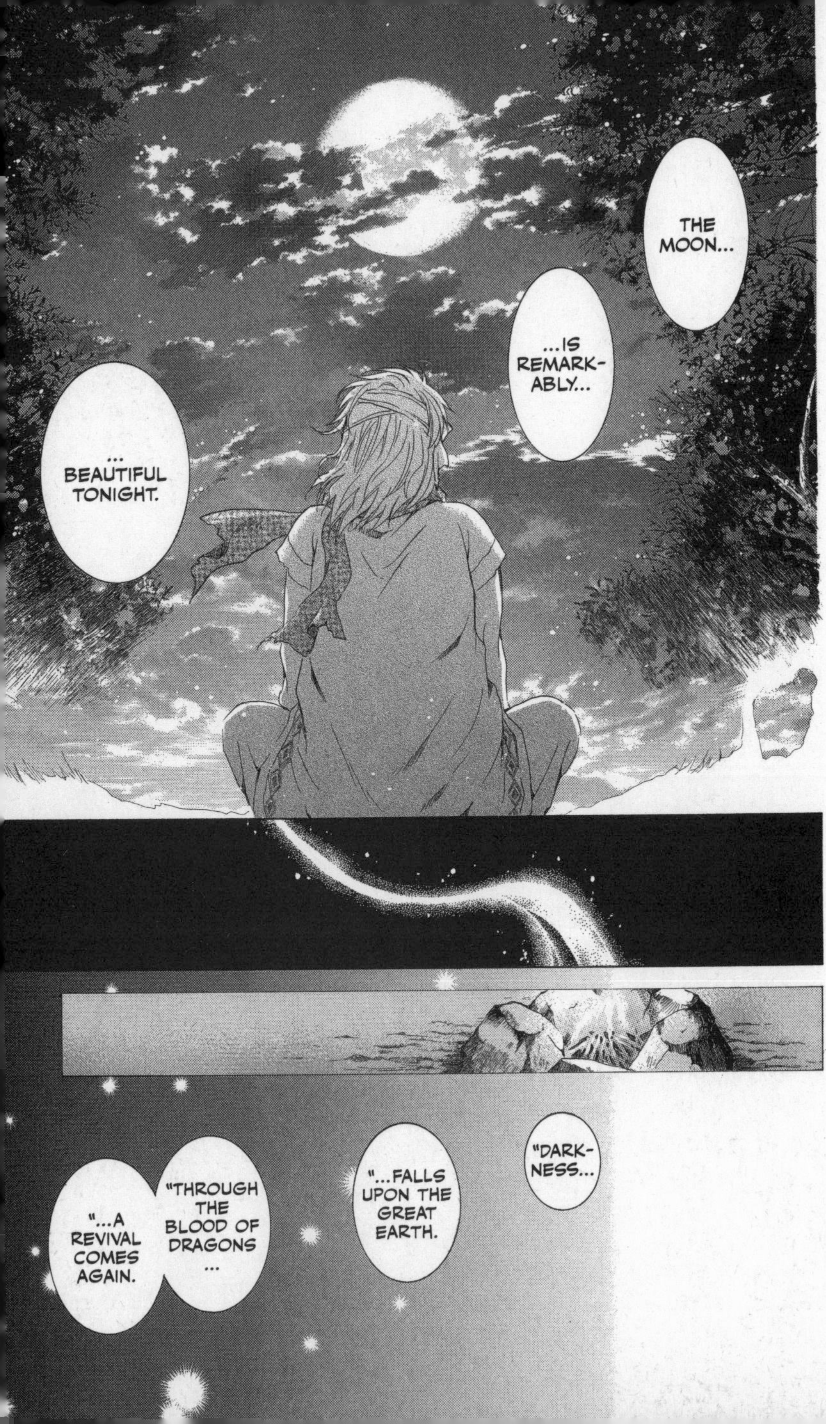
THE MOON...
...IS REMARK-ABLY...
...BEAUTIFUL TONIGHT.
"DARK-NESS...
"...FALLS UPON THE GREAT EARTH.
"THROUGH THE BLOOD OF DRAGONS...
"...A REVIVAL COMES AGAIN.

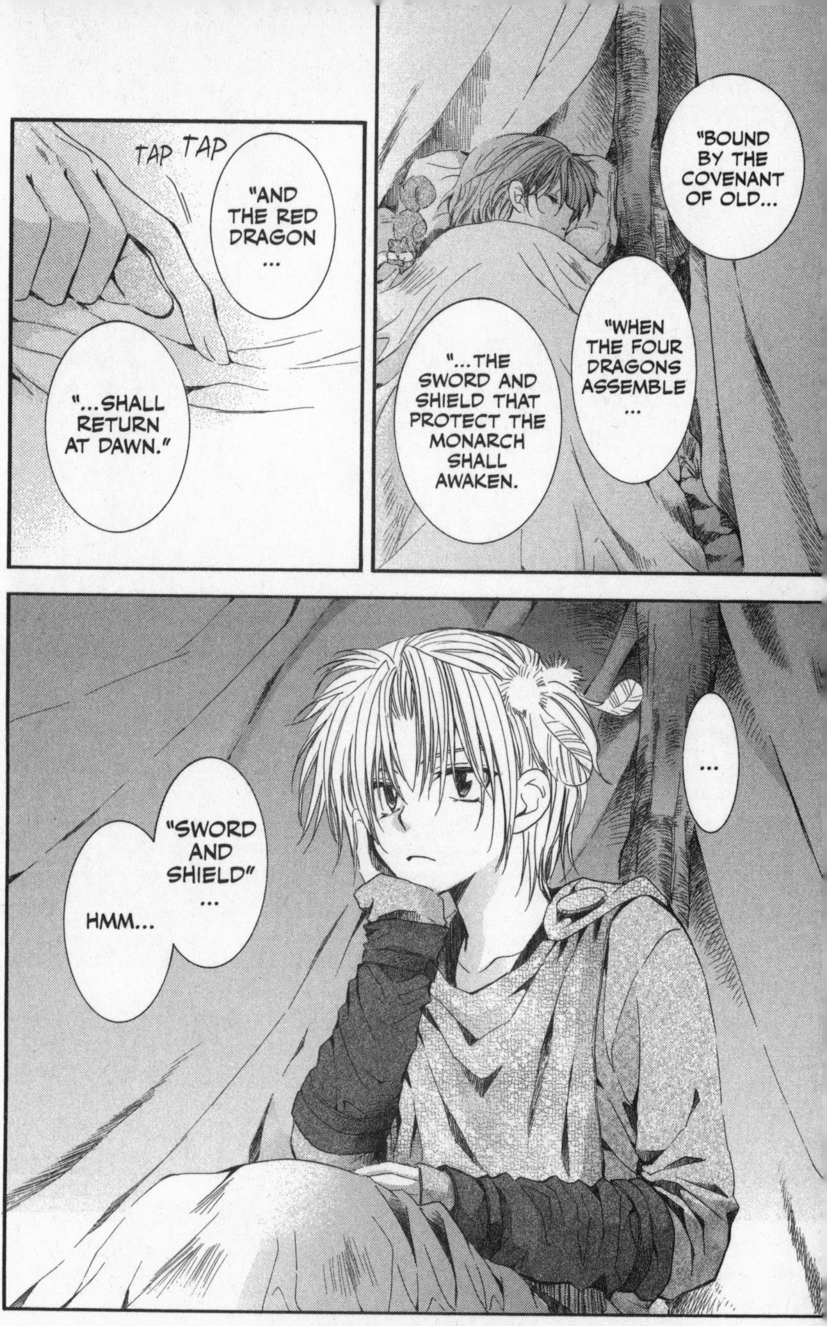
"BOUND BY THE COVENANT OF OLD...
"WHEN THE FOUR DRAGONS ASSEMBLE...
"...THE SWORD AND SHIELD THAT PROTECT THE MONARCH SHALL AWAKEN.
TAP TAP
"AND THE RED DRAGON...
"...SHALL RETURN AT DAWN."
...
"SWORD AND SHIELD"... HMM...

CHAPTER 42 / THE END

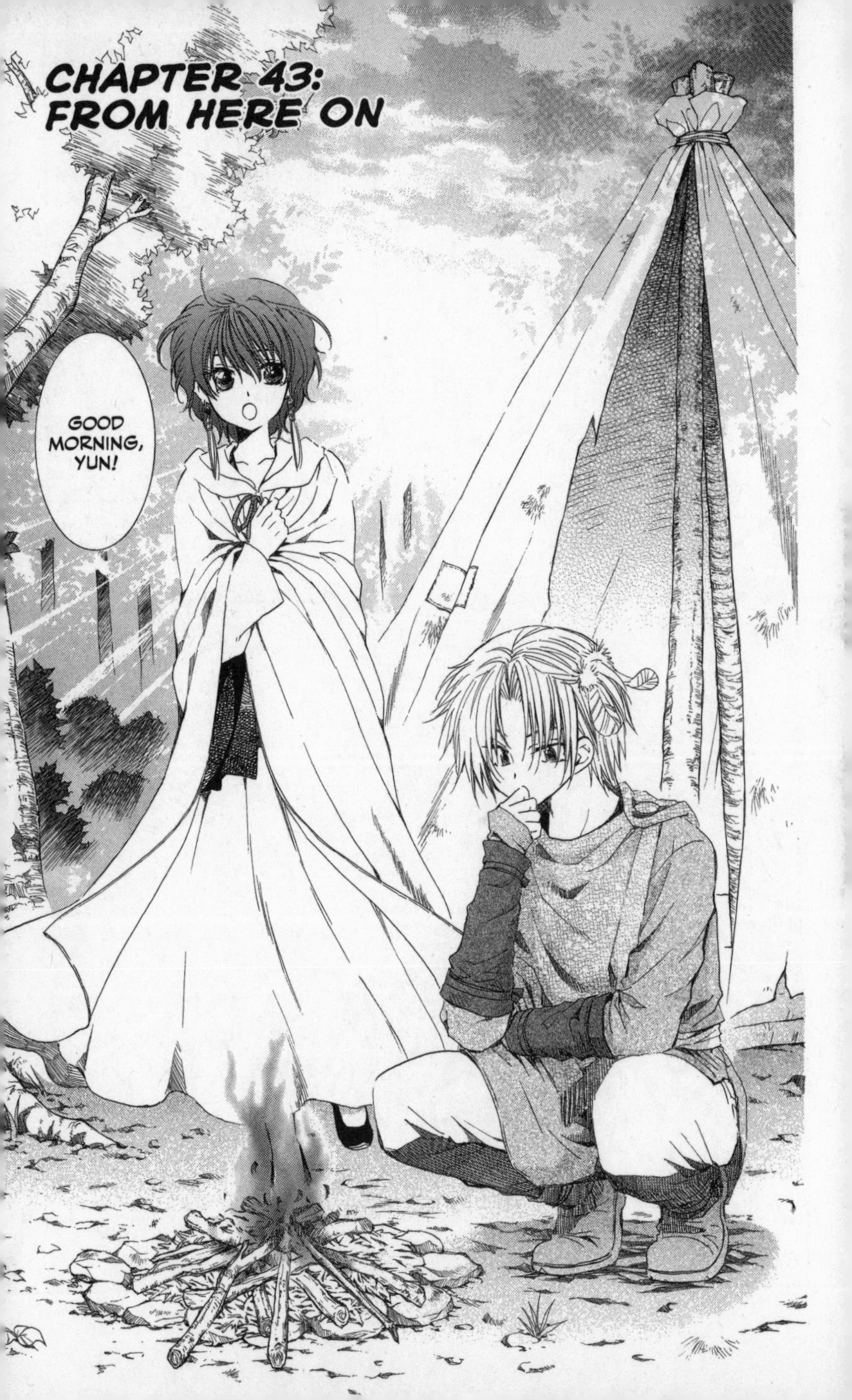
CHAPTER 43:
FROM HERE ON
GOOD MORNING, YUN!

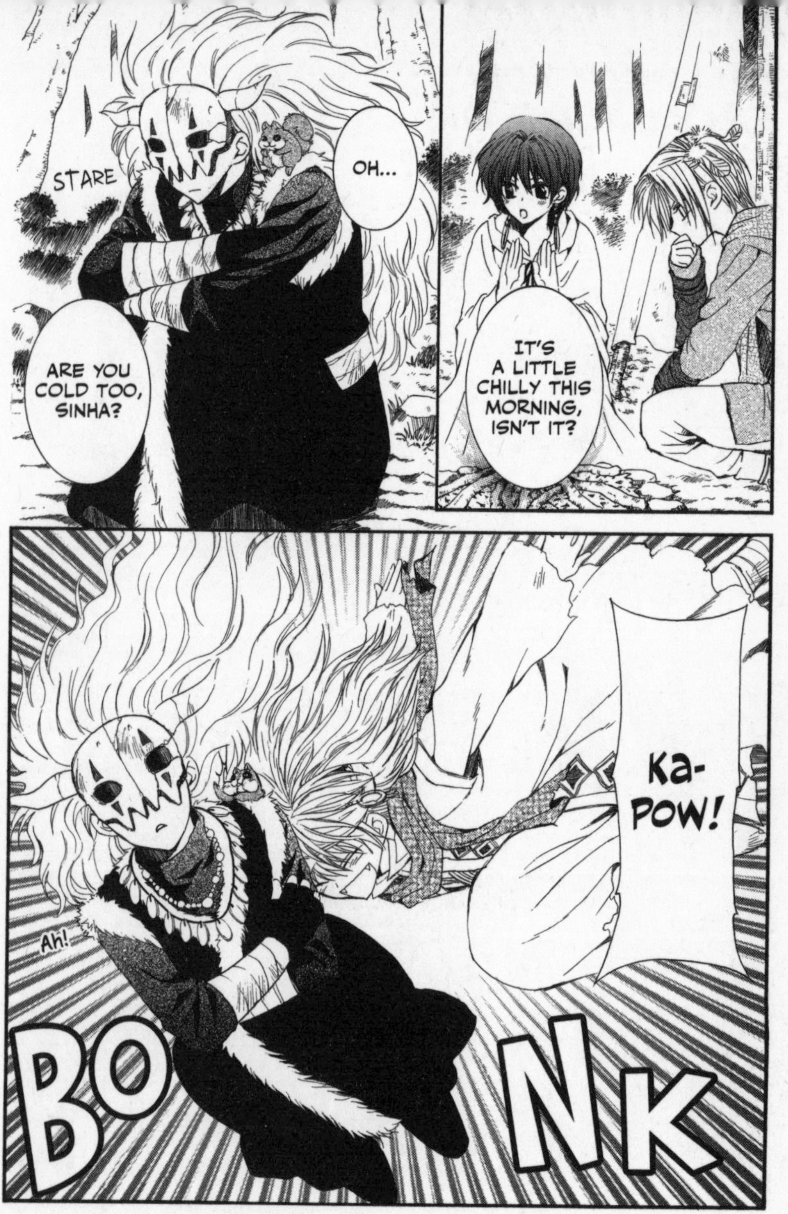
IT'S A LITTLE CHILLY THIS MORNING, ISN'T IT?
OH...
STARE
ARE YOU COLD TOO, SINHA?
KA-POW!
Ah!
BONK

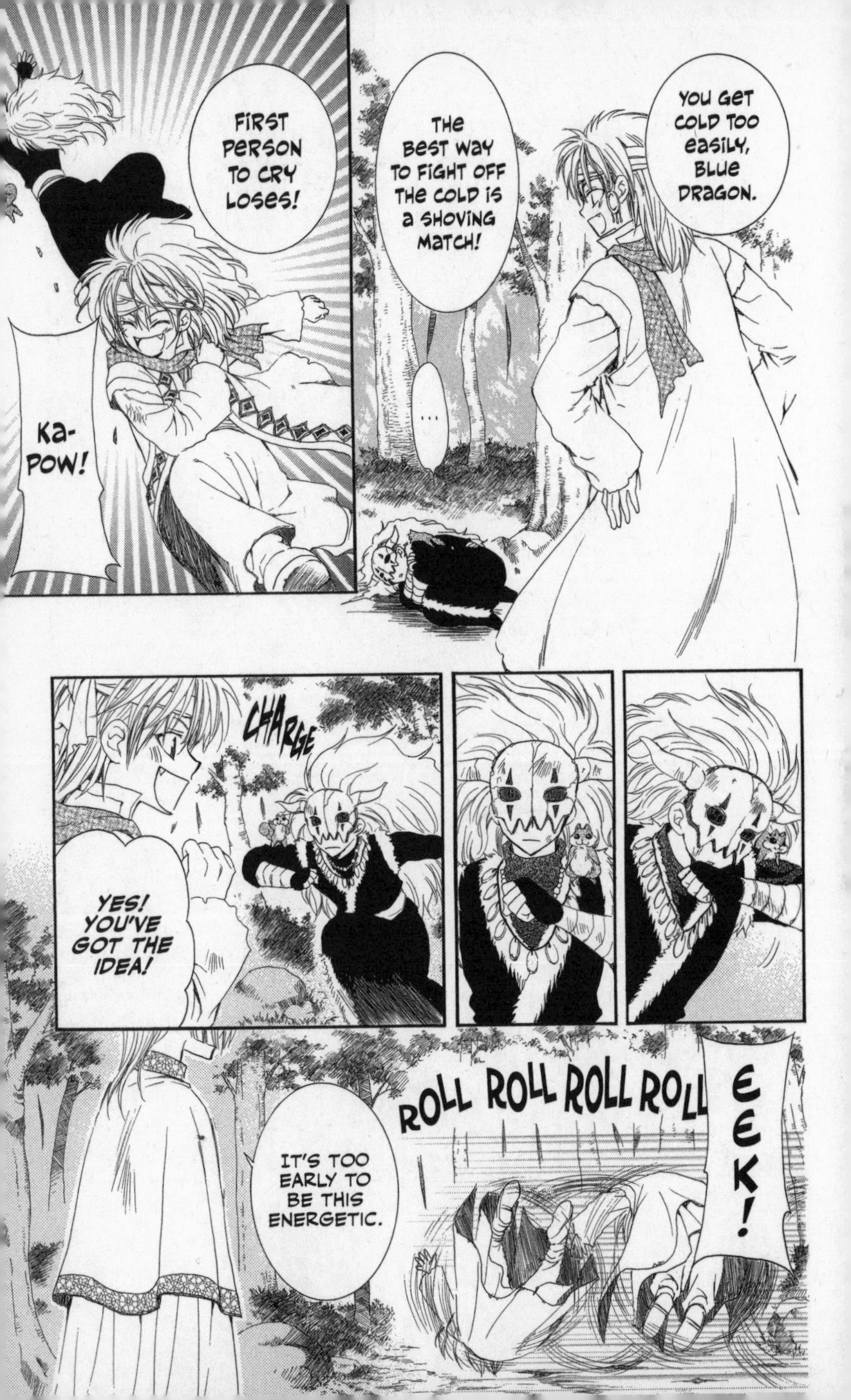
YOU GET COLD TOO EASILY, BLUE DRAGON.
THE BEST WAY TO FIGHT OFF THE COLD IS A SHOVING MATCH!
...
FIRST PERSON TO CRY LOSES!
KA-POW!
CHARGE
YES! YOU'VE GOT THE IDEA!
EEK!
ROLL ROLL ROLL ROLL
IT'S TOO EARLY TO BE THIS ENERGETIC.

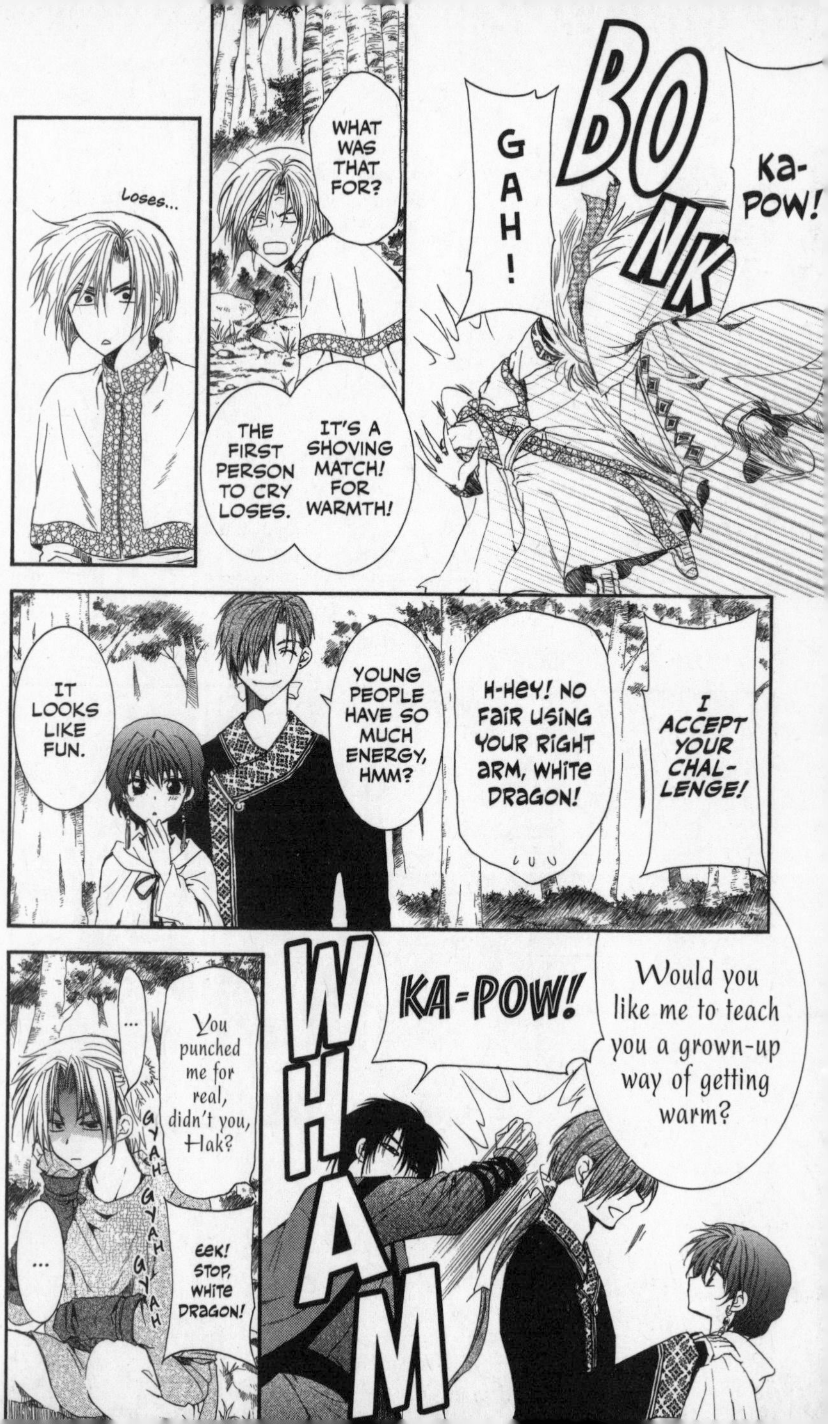

KA-POW!
BONK
GAH!
WHAT WAS THAT FOR?
IT'S A SHOVING MATCH! FOR WARMTH!
THE FIRST PERSON TO CRY LOSES.
Loses...
I ACCEPT YOUR CHALLENGE!
H-HEY! NO FAIR USING YOUR RIGHT ARM, WHITE DRAGON!
YOUNG PEOPLE HAVE SO MUCH ENERGY, HMM?
IT LOOKS LIKE FUN.
Would you like me to teach you a grown-up way of getting warm?
KA-POW!
WHAM
You punched me for real, didn't you, Hak?
...
GYAH GYAH GYAH
EEK! STOP, WHITE DRAGON!
...

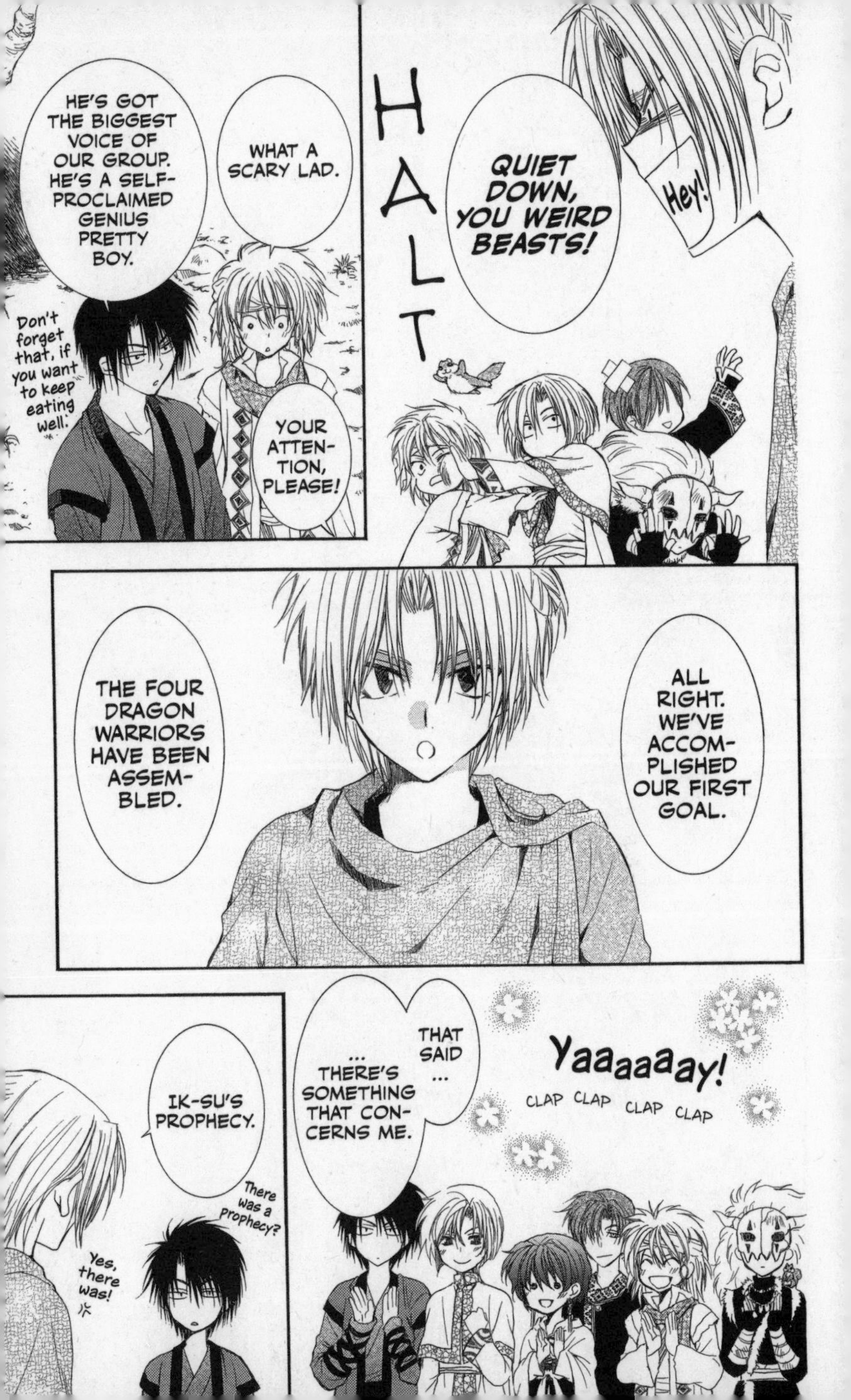
Hey!
QUIET DOWN, YOU WEIRD BEASTS!
HALT
WHAT A SCARY LAD.
HE'S GOT THE BIGGEST VOICE OF OUR GROUP. HE'S A SELF-PROCLAIMED GENIUS PRETTY BOY.
YOUR ATTENTION, PLEASE!
Don't forget that, if you want to keep eating well.
ALL RIGHT. WE'VE ACCOMPLISHED OUR FIRST GOAL.
THE FOUR DRAGON WARRIORS HAVE BEEN ASSEMBLED.
Yaaaaaay!
CLAP CLAP CLAP CLAP
THAT SAID ...
... THERE'S SOMETHING THAT CONCERNS ME.
IK-SU'S PROPHECY.
There was a prophecy?
Yes, there was!

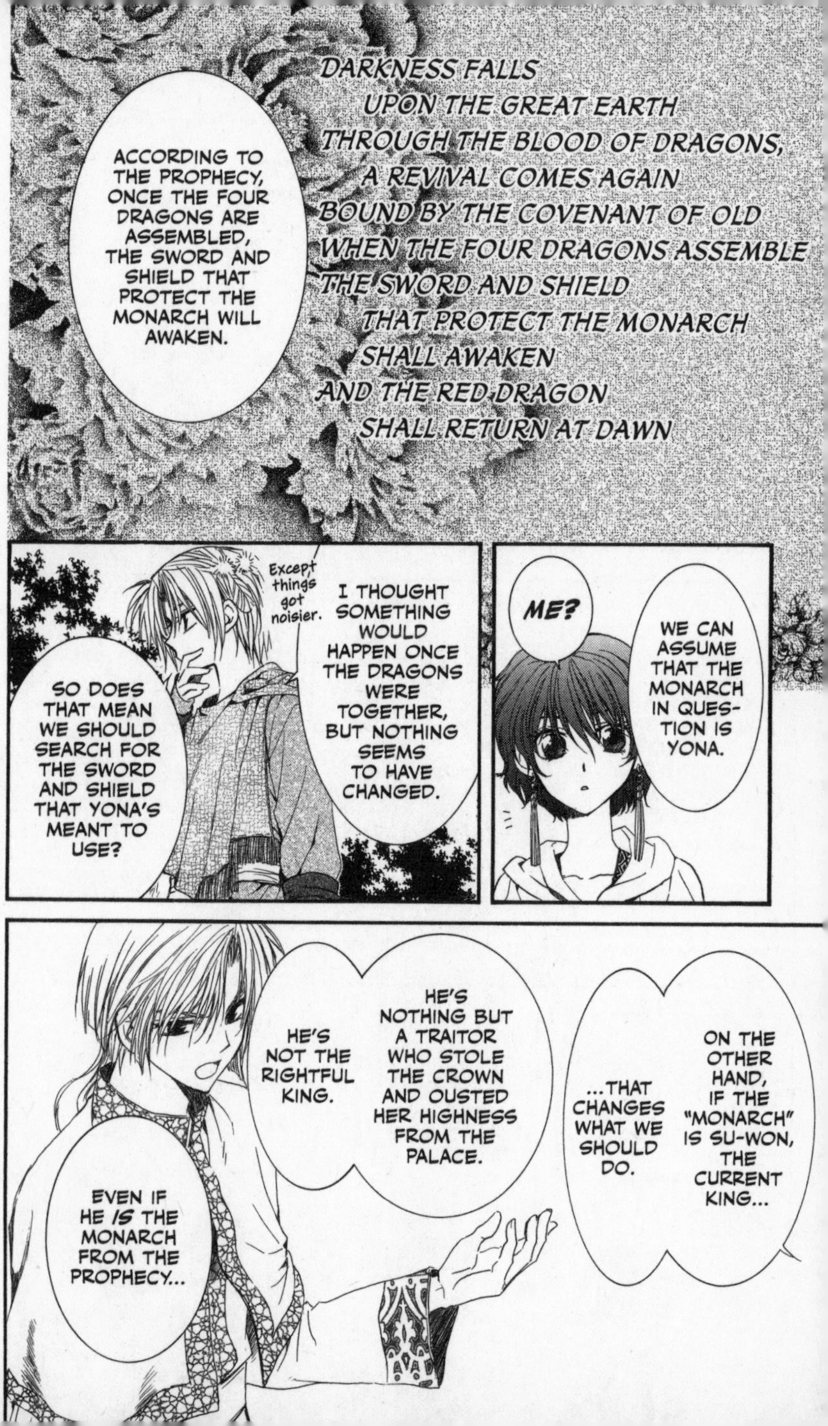

DARKNESS FALLS
UPON THE GREAT EARTH
THROUGH THE BLOOD OF DRAGONS,
A REVIVAL COMES AGAIN
BOUND BY THE COVENANT OF OLD
WHEN THE FOUR DRAGONS ASSEMBLE
THE SWORD AND SHIELD
THAT PROTECT THE MONARCH
SHALL AWAKEN
AND THE RED DRAGON
SHALL RETURN AT DAWN
ACCORDING TO THE PROPHECY, ONCE THE FOUR DRAGONS ARE ASSEMBLED, THE SWORD AND SHIELD THAT PROTECT THE MONARCH WILL AWAKEN.
WE CAN ASSUME THAT THE MONARCH IN QUESTION IS YONA.
ME?
I THOUGHT SOMETHING WOULD HAPPEN ONCE THE DRAGONS WERE TOGETHER, BUT NOTHING SEEMS TO HAVE CHANGED.
Except things got noisier.
SO DOES THAT MEAN WE SHOULD SEARCH FOR THE SWORD AND SHIELD THAT YONA'S MEANT TO USE?
ON THE OTHER HAND, IF THE "MONARCH" IS SU-WON, THE CURRENT KING...
...THAT CHANGES WHAT WE SHOULD DO.
HE'S NOTHING BUT A TRAITOR WHO STOLE THE CROWN AND OUSTED HER HIGHNESS FROM THE PALACE.
HE'S NOT THE RIGHTFUL KING.
EVEN IF HE *IS* THE MONARCH FROM THE PROPHECY...

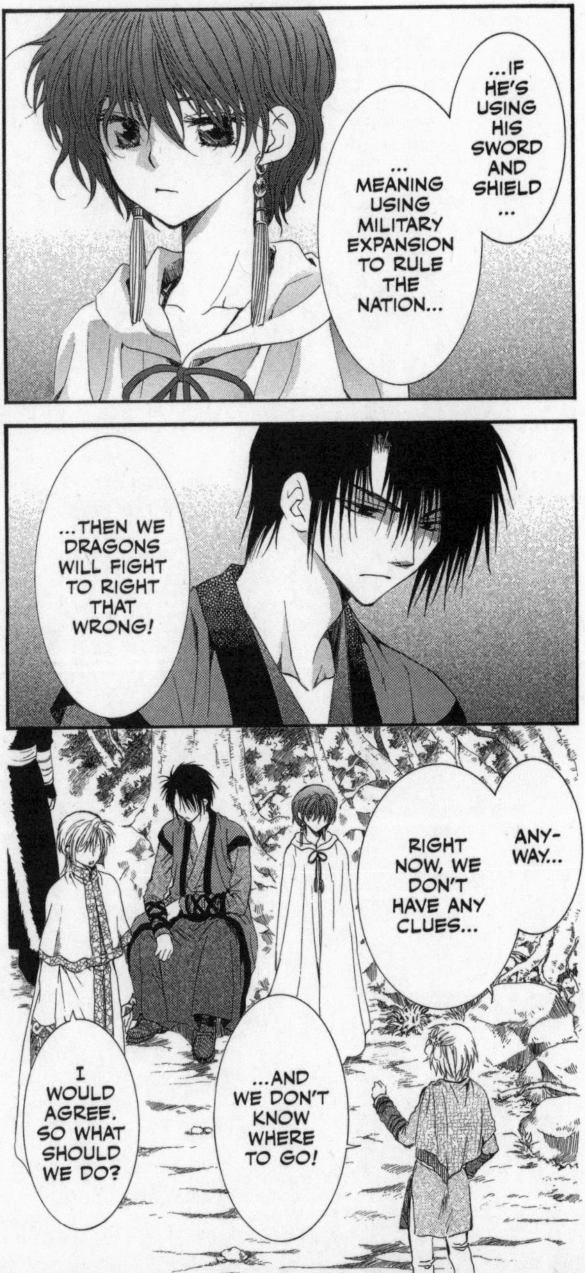
...IF HE'S USING HIS SWORD AND SHIELD...
...MEANING USING MILITARY EXPANSION TO RULE THE NATION...
...THEN WE DRAGONS WILL FIGHT TO RIGHT THAT WRONG!
ANYWAY...
RIGHT NOW, WE DON'T HAVE ANY CLUES...
...AND WE DON'T KNOW WHERE TO GO!
I WOULD AGREE. SO WHAT SHOULD WE DO?

As the cast of characters gets bigger, drawing them all takes longer. If we list them by height...

Hak → 188 cm (Roughly the same)
Jaeha → 188 cm
Sinha → 180 cm
Gija → 175 cm
Zeno → 166 cm
Yun → 162 cm
Yona → 157 cm
Plus
Su-won → 185 cm

I'm on the short side, so from my perspective, Hak and the others are giants.

If we sort them by age...

Jaeha → 25 years old
Gija → 20 years old
Hak → 18 years old
Sinha → 18 years old
Zeno → 17 years old
Yona → 16 years old
Yun → 15 years old
Pu-kyu → ?
(Su-won is 18 years old)

Hak...acts somewhat older, doesn't he?

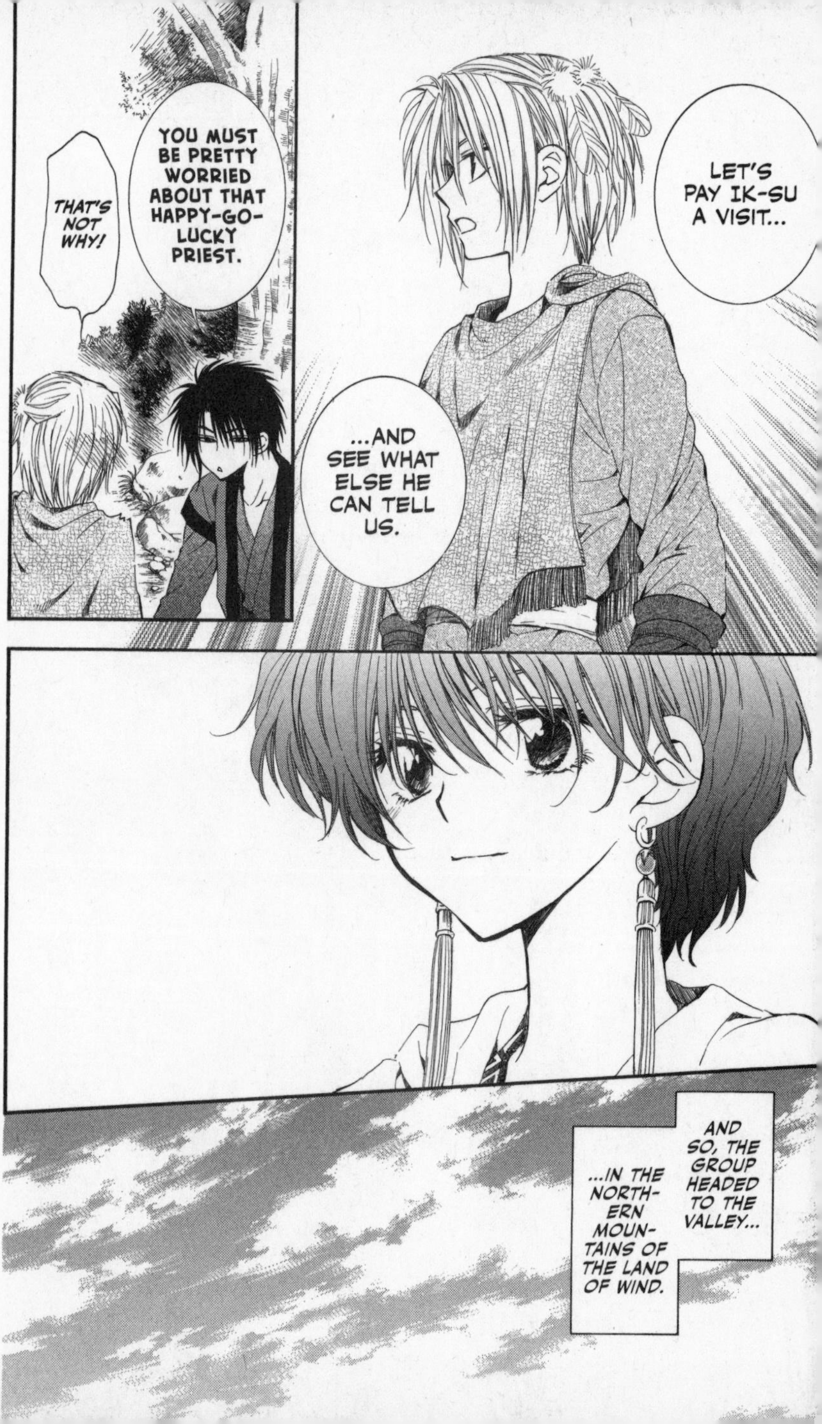
LET'S PAY IK-SU A VISIT...
...AND SEE WHAT ELSE HE CAN TELL US.
YOU MUST BE PRETTY WORRIED ABOUT THAT HAPPY-GO-LUCKY PRIEST.
THAT'S NOT WHY!
AND SO, THE GROUP HEADED TO THE VALLEY...
...IN THE NORTHERN MOUNTAINS OF THE LAND OF WIND.

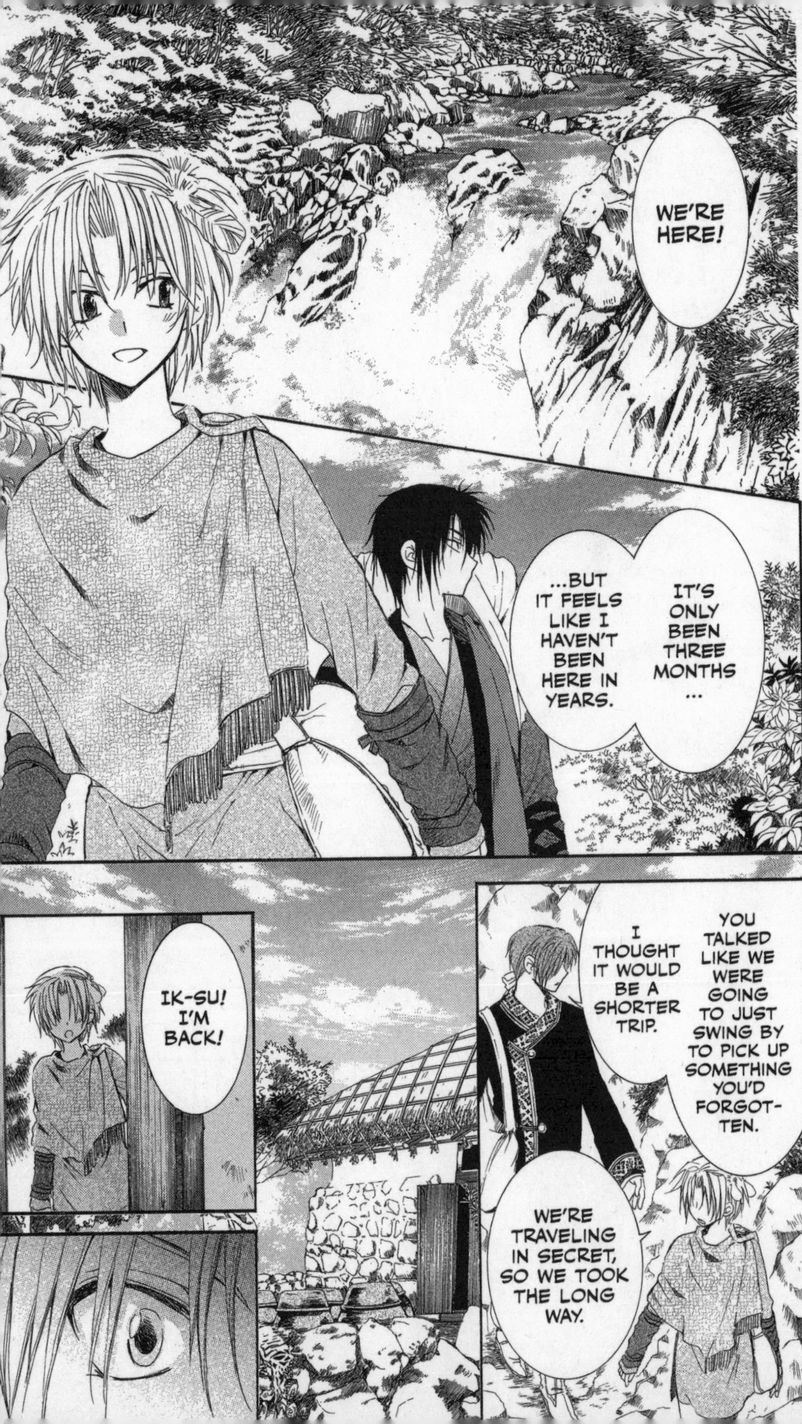
WE'RE HERE!
IT'S ONLY BEEN THREE MONTHS...
...BUT IT FEELS LIKE I HAVEN'T BEEN HERE IN YEARS.
YOU TALKED LIKE WE WERE GOING TO JUST SWING BY TO PICK UP SOMETHING YOU'D FORGOT-TEN.
I THOUGHT IT WOULD BE A SHORTER TRIP.
WE'RE TRAVELING IN SECRET, SO WE TOOK THE LONG WAY.
IK-SU! I'M BACK!

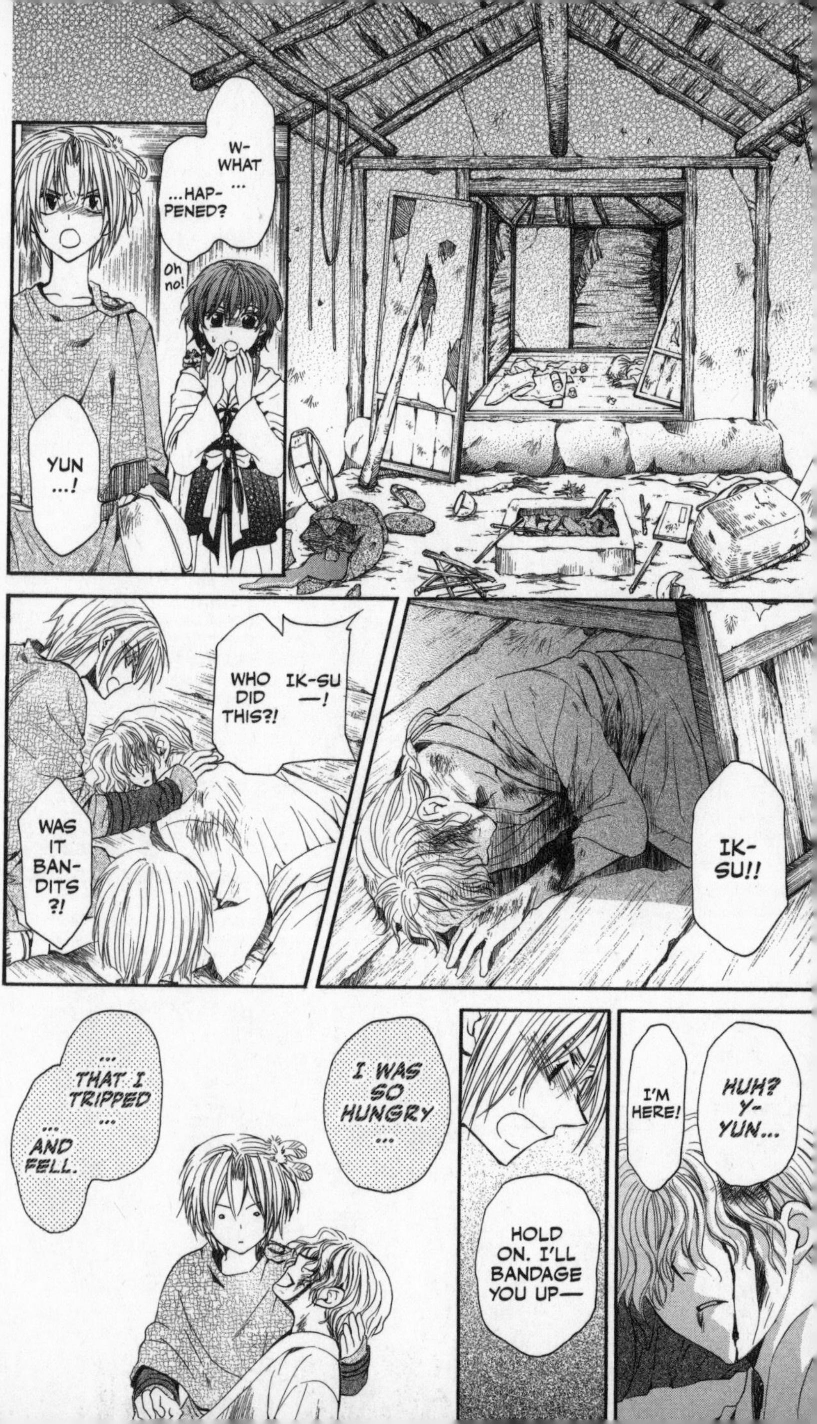
W-WHAT ... ...HAPPENED?
Oh no!
YUN ...!
IK-SU!!
IK-SU —!
WHO DID THIS?!
WAS IT BANDITS ?!
HUH? Y-YUN...
I'M HERE!
HOLD ON. I'LL BANDAGE YOU UP—
I WAS SO HUNGRY ...
... THAT I TRIPPED ... ... AND FELL.

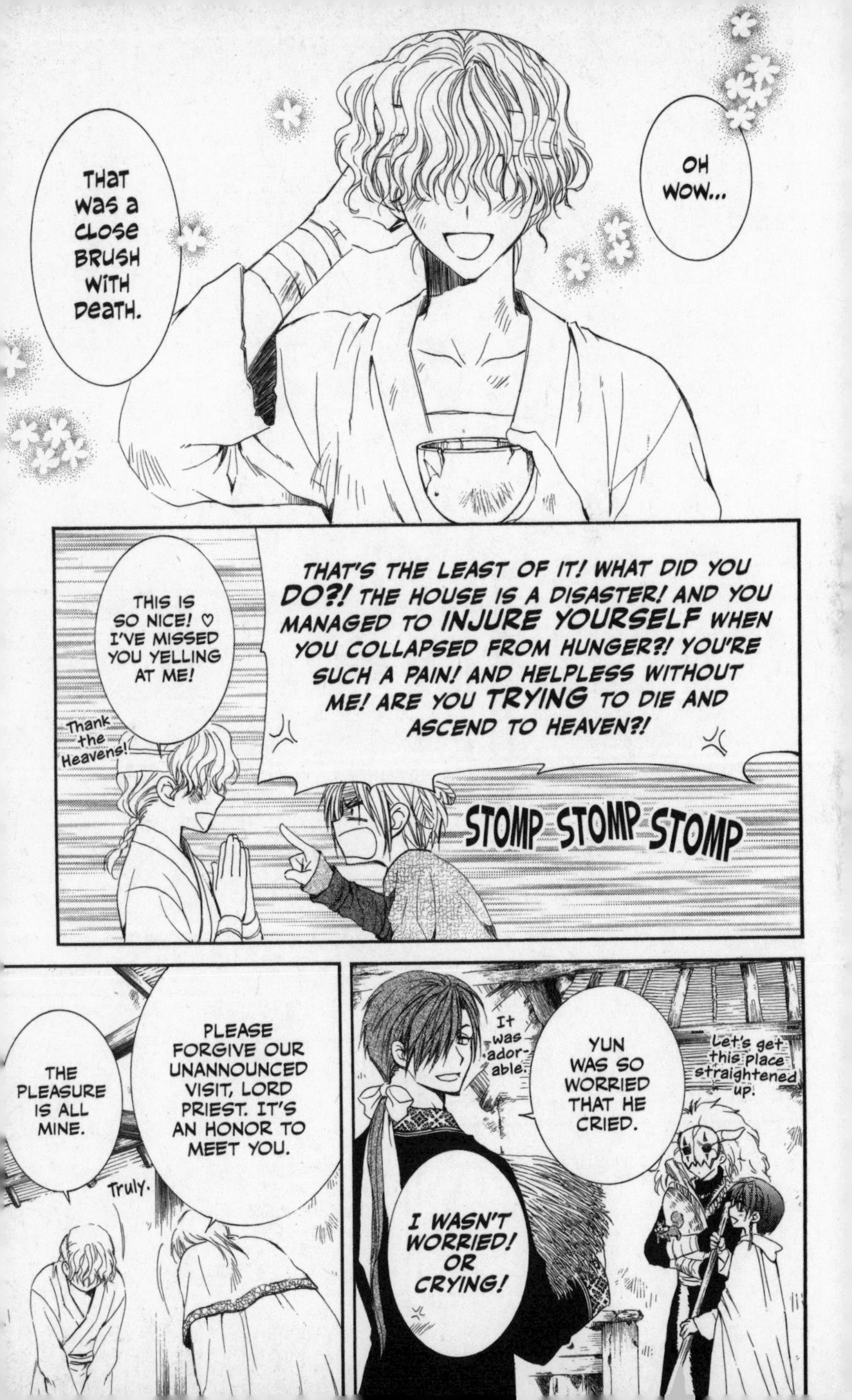
OH WOW...
THAT WAS A CLOSE BRUSH WITH DEATH.
THAT'S THE LEAST OF IT! WHAT DID YOU DO?! THE HOUSE IS A DISASTER! AND YOU MANAGED TO INJURE YOURSELF WHEN YOU COLLAPSED FROM HUNGER?! YOU'RE SUCH A PAIN! AND HELPLESS WITHOUT ME! ARE YOU TRYING TO DIE AND ASCEND TO HEAVEN?!
THIS IS SO NICE! ♡ I'VE MISSED YOU YELLING AT ME!
Thank the Heavens!
STOMP STOMP STOMP
Let's get this place straightened up.
YUN WAS SO WORRIED THAT HE CRIED.
It was adorable.
I WASN'T WORRIED! OR CRYING!
PLEASE FORGIVE OUR UNANNOUNCED VISIT, LORD PRIEST. IT'S AN HONOR TO MEET YOU.
THE PLEASURE IS ALL MINE.
Truly.

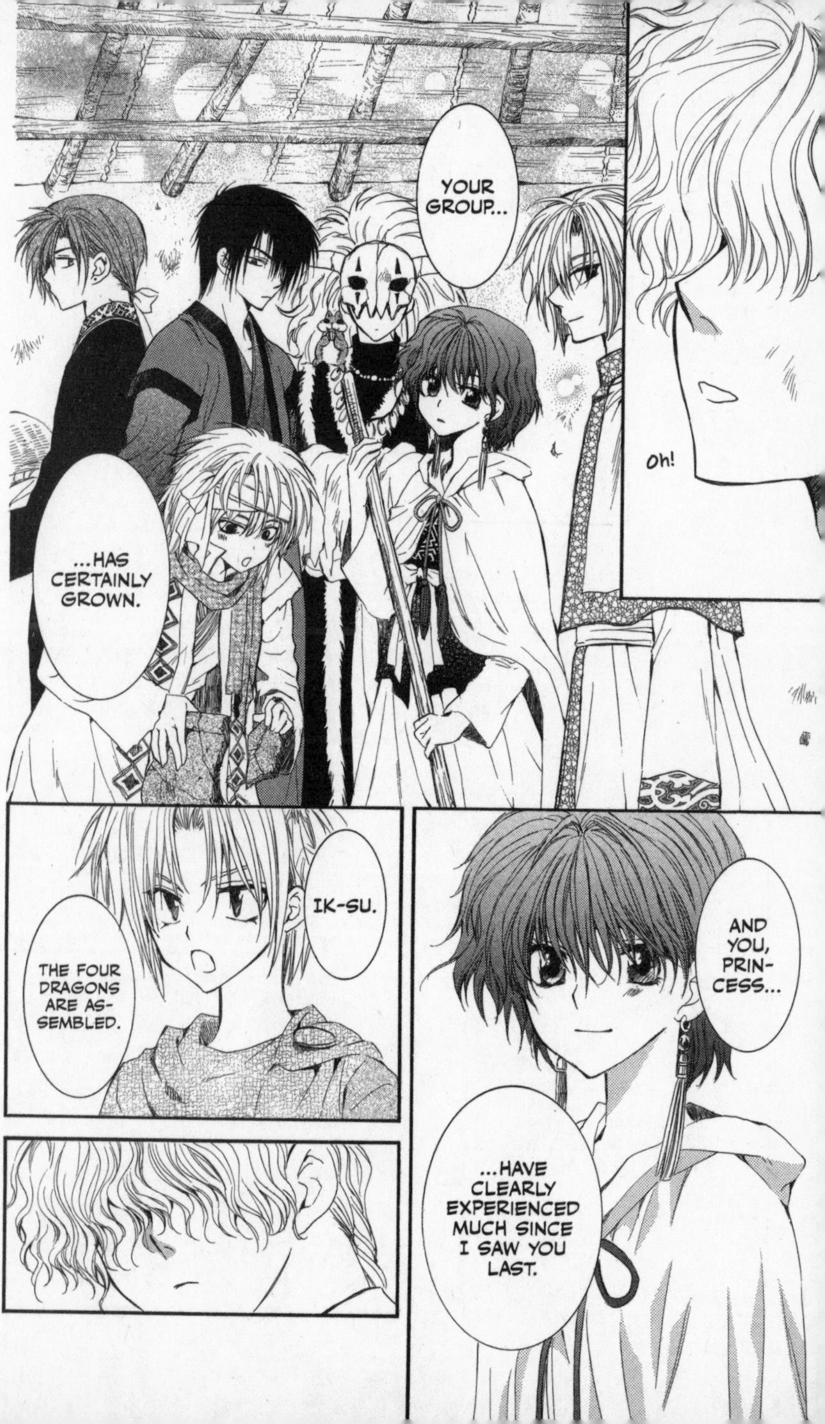
Oh!
YOUR GROUP...
...HAS CERTAINLY GROWN.
AND YOU, PRIN-CESS...
...HAVE CLEARLY EXPERIENCED MUCH SINCE I SAW YOU LAST.
IK-SU.
THE FOUR DRAGONS ARE AS-SEMBLED.

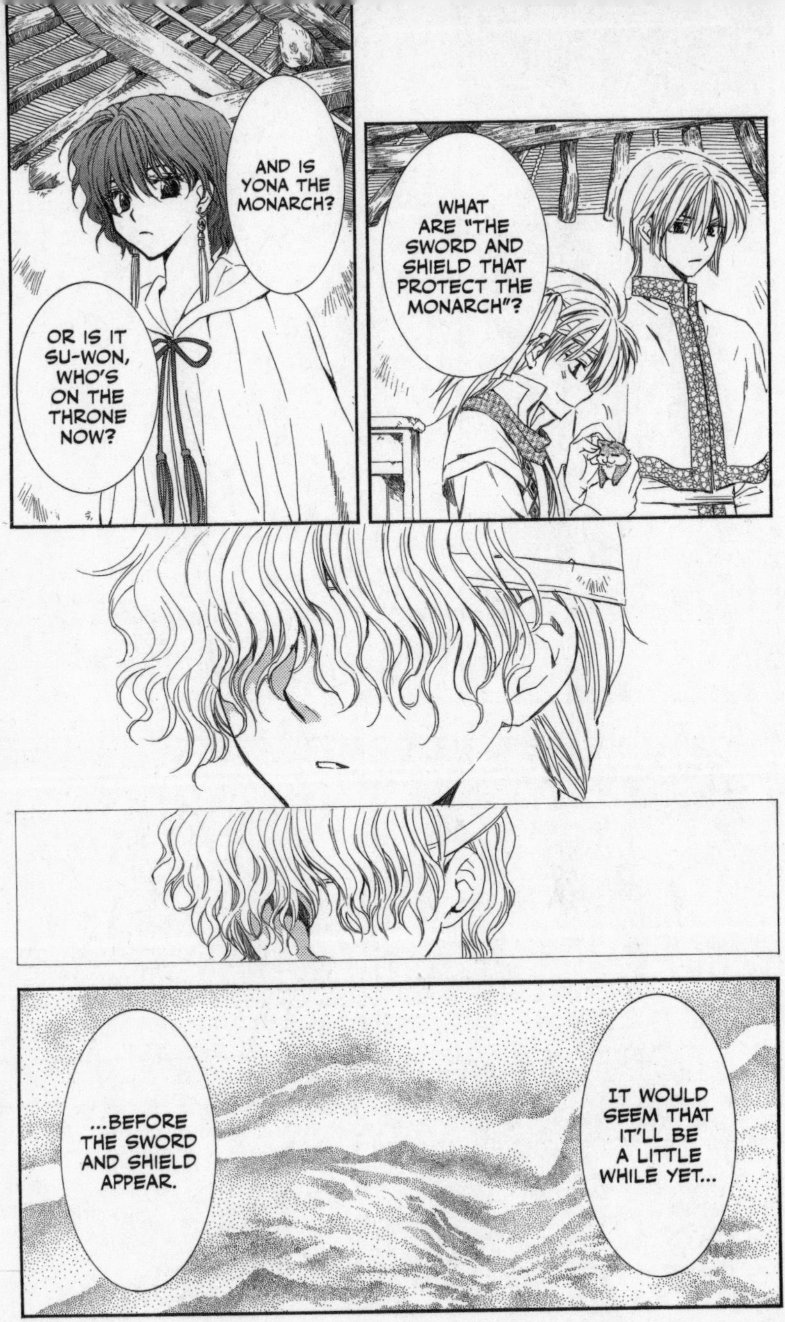
WHAT ARE "THE SWORD AND SHIELD THAT PROTECT THE MONARCH"?
AND IS YONA THE MONARCH?
OR IS IT SU-WON, WHO'S ON THE THRONE NOW?
IT WOULD SEEM THAT IT'LL BE A LITTLE WHILE YET...
...BEFORE THE SWORD AND SHIELD APPEAR.

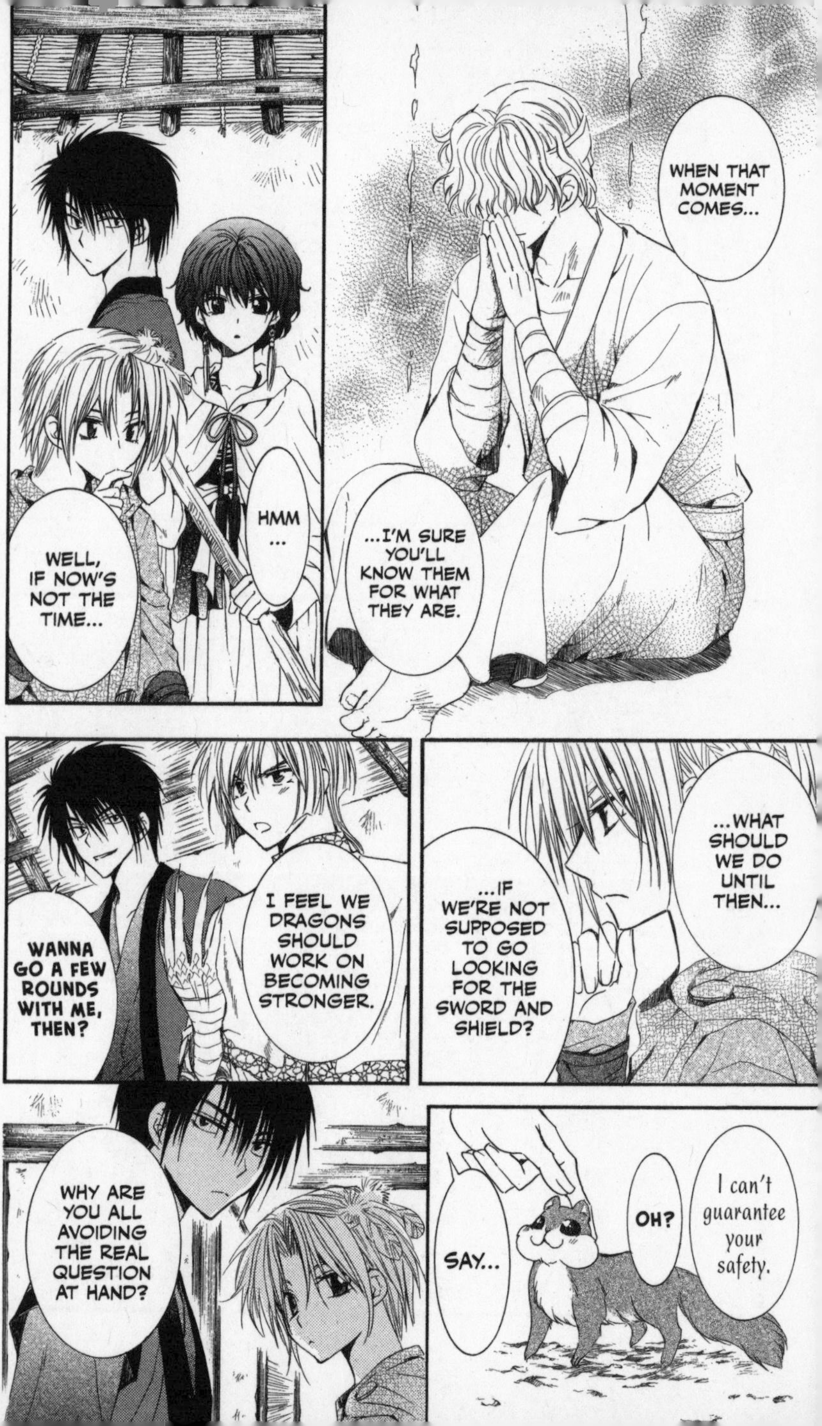
WHEN THAT MOMENT COMES...
...I'M SURE YOU'LL KNOW THEM FOR WHAT THEY ARE.
HMM ...
WELL, IF NOW'S NOT THE TIME...
...WHAT SHOULD WE DO UNTIL THEN...
...IF WE'RE NOT SUPPOSED TO GO LOOKING FOR THE SWORD AND SHIELD?
I FEEL WE DRAGONS SHOULD WORK ON BECOMING STRONGER.
WANNA GO A FEW ROUNDS WITH ME, THEN?
I can't guarantee your safety.
OH?
SAY...
WHY ARE YOU ALL AVOIDING THE REAL QUESTION AT HAND?

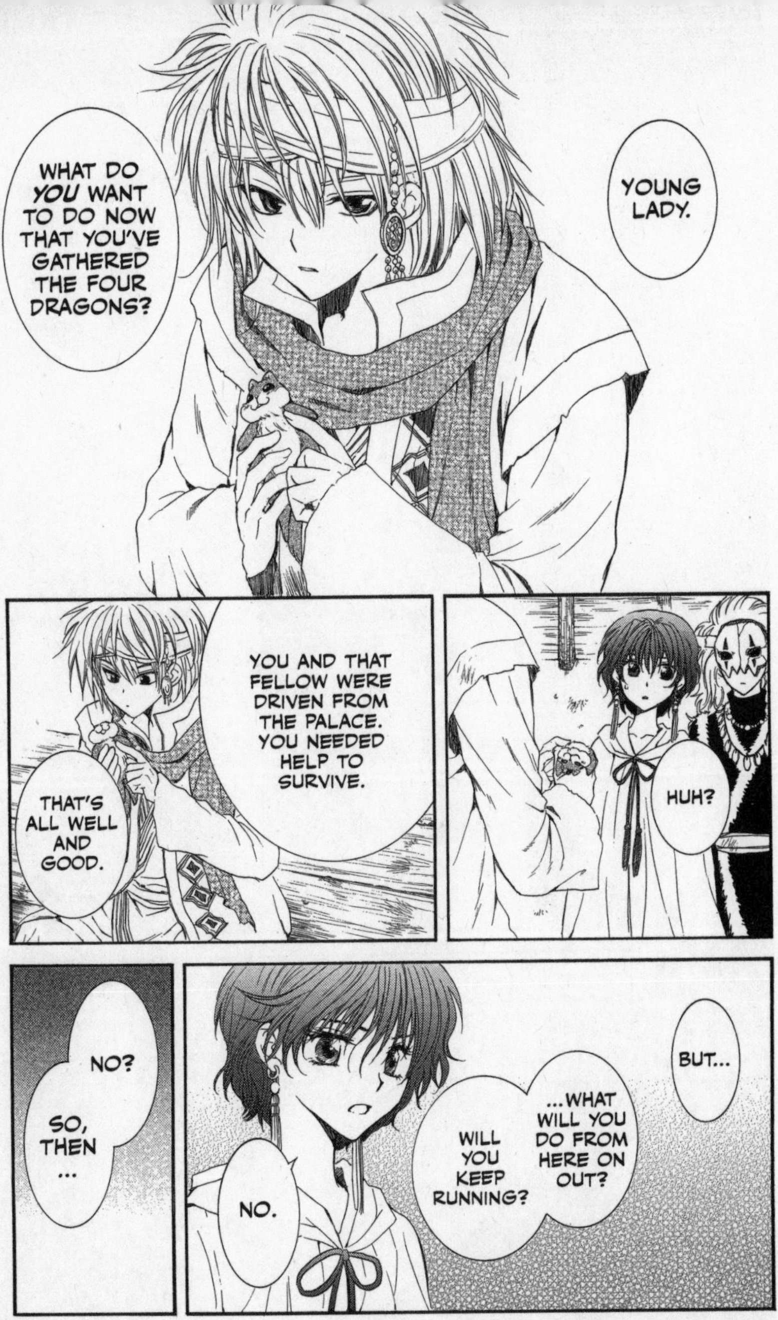
YOUNG LADY.
WHAT DO *YOU* WANT TO DO NOW THAT YOU'VE GATHERED THE FOUR DRAGONS?
HUH?
YOU AND THAT FELLOW WERE DRIVEN FROM THE PALACE. YOU NEEDED HELP TO SURVIVE.
THAT'S ALL WELL AND GOOD.
BUT...
...WHAT WILL YOU DO FROM HERE ON OUT?
WILL YOU KEEP RUNNING?
NO.
NO?
SO, THEN ...

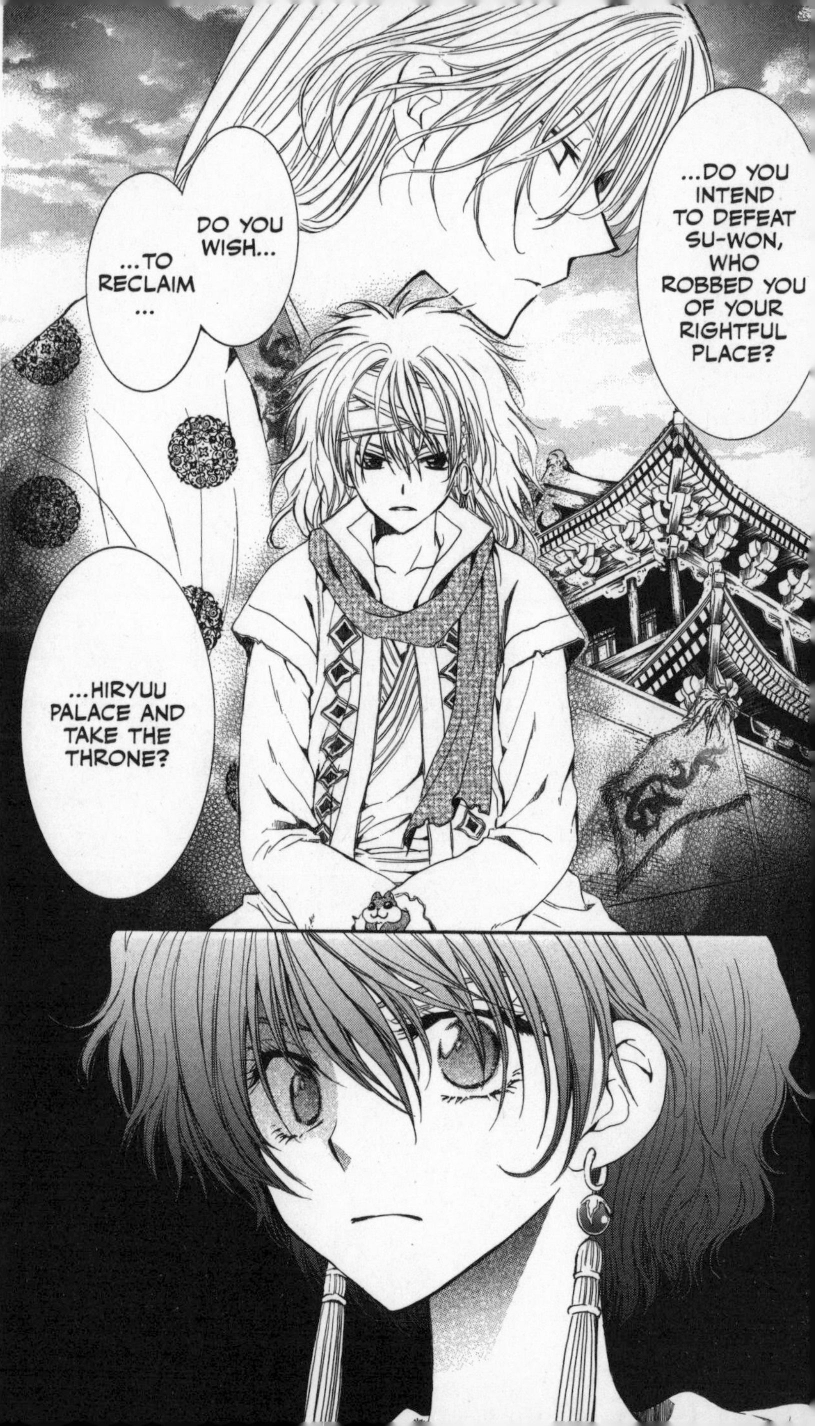
...DO YOU INTEND TO DEFEAT SU-WON, WHO ROBBED YOU OF YOUR RIGHTFUL PLACE?
DO YOU WISH...
...TO RECLAIM ...
...HIRYUU PALACE AND TAKE THE THRONE?

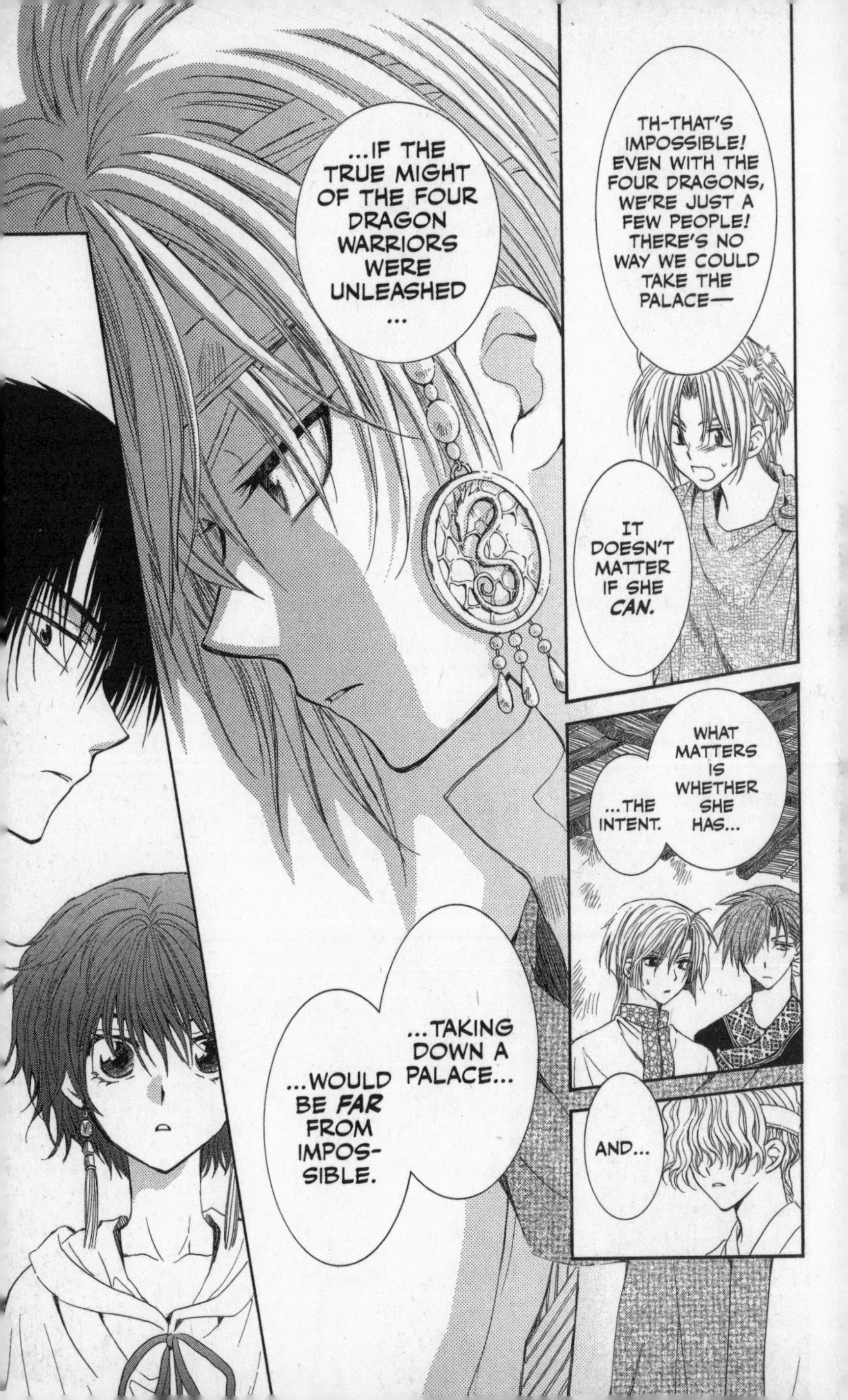
TH-THAT'S IMPOSSIBLE! EVEN WITH THE FOUR DRAGONS, WE'RE JUST A FEW PEOPLE! THERE'S NO WAY WE COULD TAKE THE PALACE—
IT DOESN'T MATTER IF SHE *CAN.*
WHAT MATTERS IS WHETHER SHE HAS...
...THE INTENT.
AND...
...IF THE TRUE MIGHT OF THE FOUR DRAGON WARRIORS WERE UNLEASHED...
...TAKING DOWN A PALACE...
...WOULD BE *FAR* FROM IMPOSSIBLE.

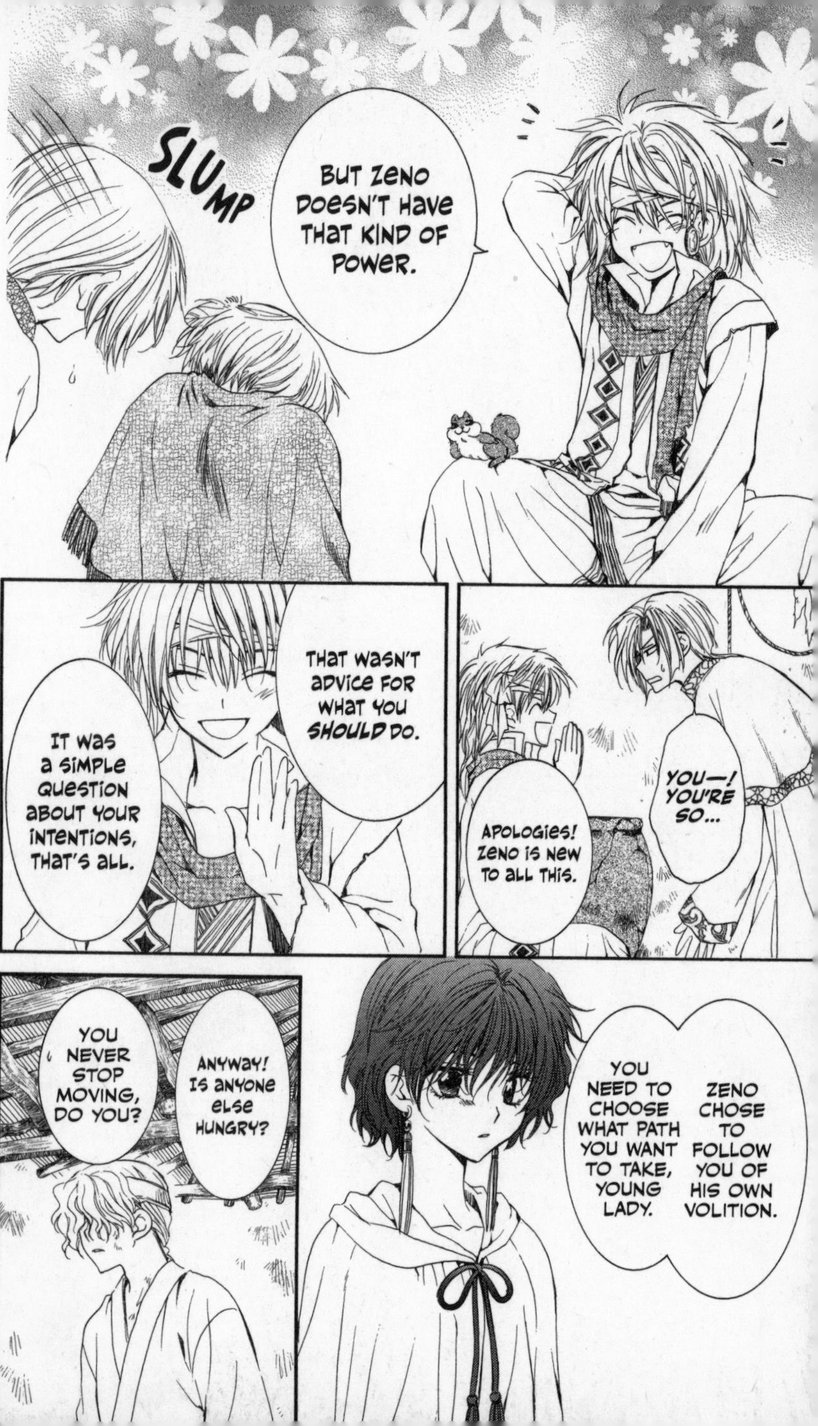
BUT ZENO DOESN'T HAVE THAT KIND OF POWER.
SLUMP
YOU—! YOU'RE SO...
APOLOGIES! ZENO IS NEW TO ALL THIS.
THAT WASN'T ADVICE FOR WHAT YOU SHOULD DO.
IT WAS A SIMPLE QUESTION ABOUT YOUR INTENTIONS, THAT'S ALL.
ZENO CHOSE TO FOLLOW YOU OF HIS OWN VOLITION.
YOU NEED TO CHOOSE WHAT PATH YOU WANT TO TAKE, YOUNG LADY.
ANYWAY! IS ANYONE ELSE HUNGRY?
YOU NEVER STOP MOVING, DO YOU?

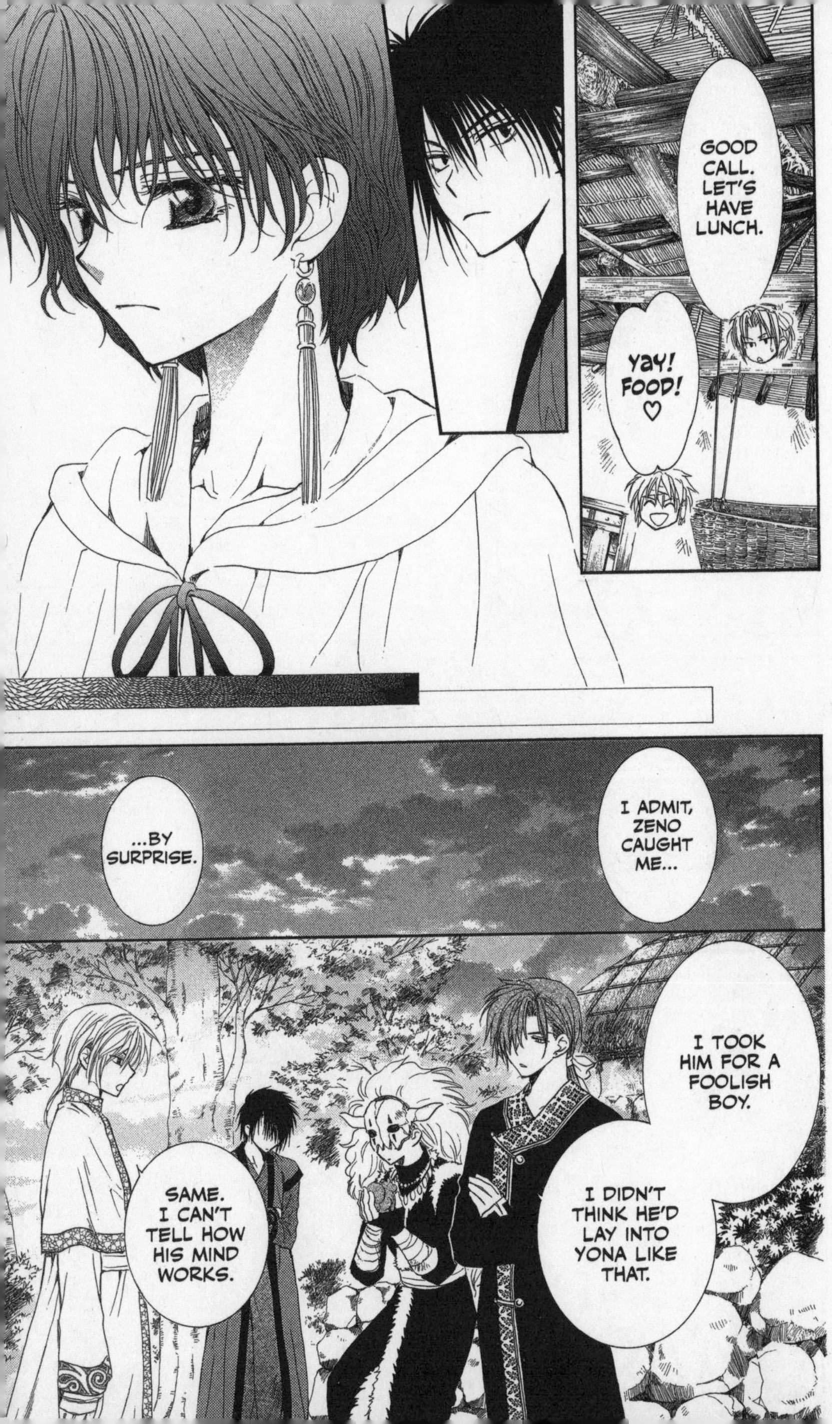
GOOD CALL. LET'S HAVE LUNCH.
yay! FOOD! ♡
I ADMIT, ZENO CAUGHT ME...
...BY SURPRISE.
I TOOK HIM FOR A FOOLISH BOY.
I DIDN'T THINK HE'D LAY INTO YONA LIKE THAT.
SAME. I CAN'T TELL HOW HIS MIND WORKS.

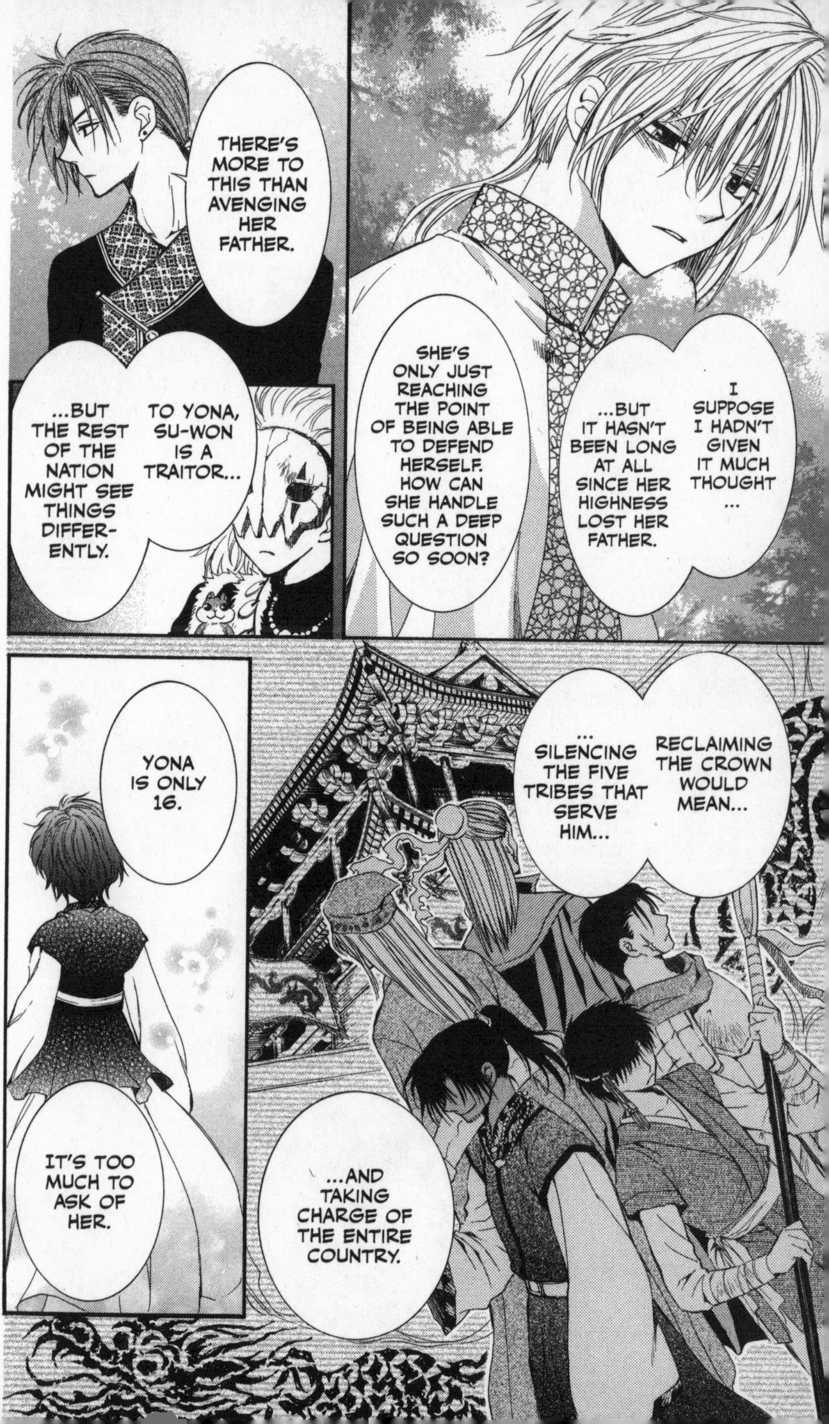
I SUPPOSE I HADN'T GIVEN IT MUCH THOUGHT...
...BUT IT HASN'T BEEN LONG AT ALL SINCE HER HIGHNESS LOST HER FATHER.
SHE'S ONLY JUST REACHING THE POINT OF BEING ABLE TO DEFEND HERSELF. HOW CAN SHE HANDLE SUCH A DEEP QUESTION SO SOON?
THERE'S MORE TO THIS THAN AVENGING HER FATHER.
TO YONA, SU-WON IS A TRAITOR...
...BUT THE REST OF THE NATION MIGHT SEE THINGS DIFFER-ENTLY.
RECLAIMING THE CROWN WOULD MEAN...
...SILENCING THE FIVE TRIBES THAT SERVE HIM...
...AND TAKING CHARGE OF THE ENTIRE COUNTRY.
YONA IS ONLY 16.
IT'S TOO MUCH TO ASK OF HER.

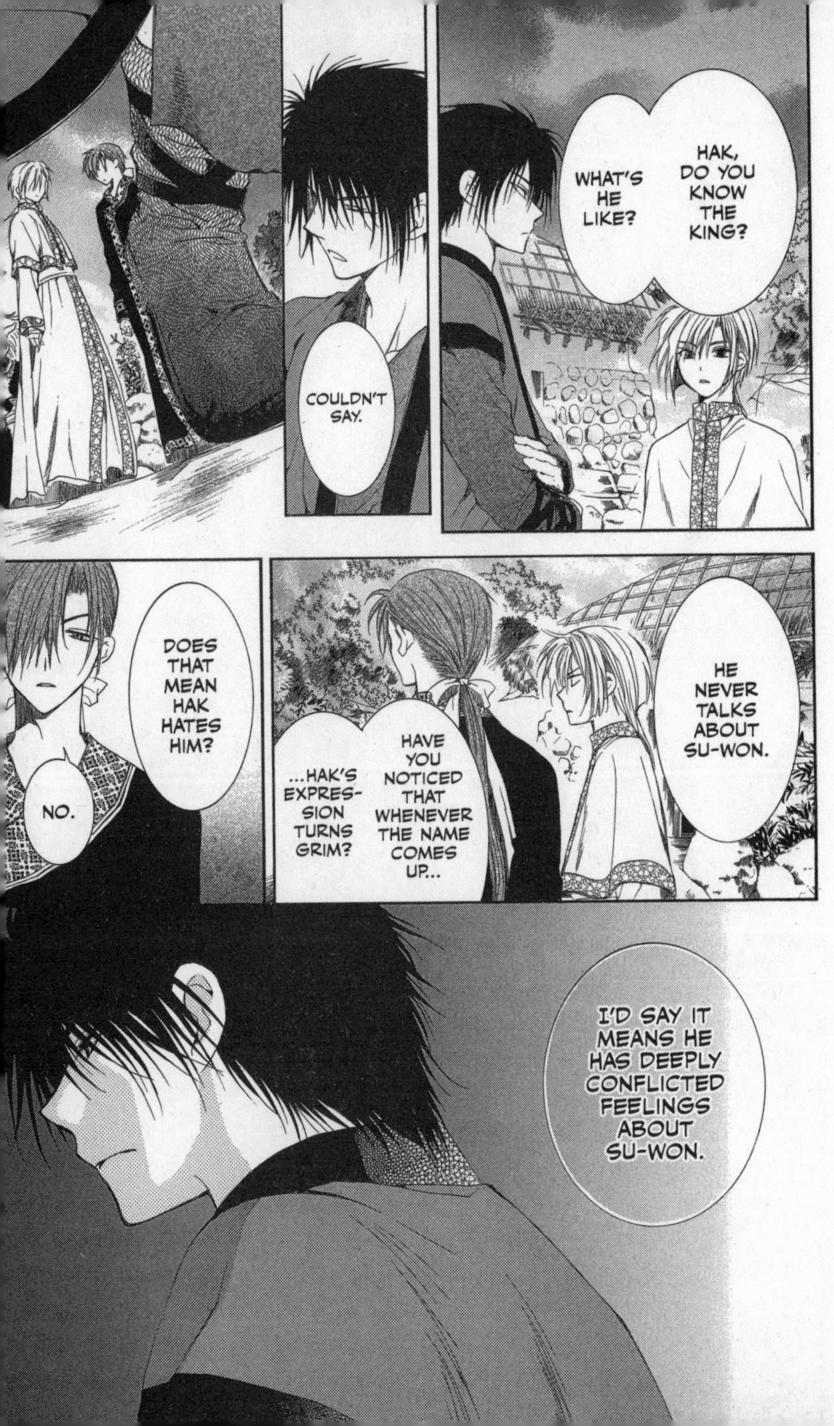
HAK, DO YOU KNOW THE KING?
WHAT'S HE LIKE?
COULDN'T SAY.
HE NEVER TALKS ABOUT SU-WON.
HAVE YOU NOTICED THAT WHENEVER THE NAME COMES UP...
...HAK'S EXPRES-SION TURNS GRIM?
DOES THAT MEAN HAK HATES HIM?
NO.
I'D SAY IT MEANS HE HAS DEEPLY CONFLICTED FEELINGS ABOUT SU-WON.

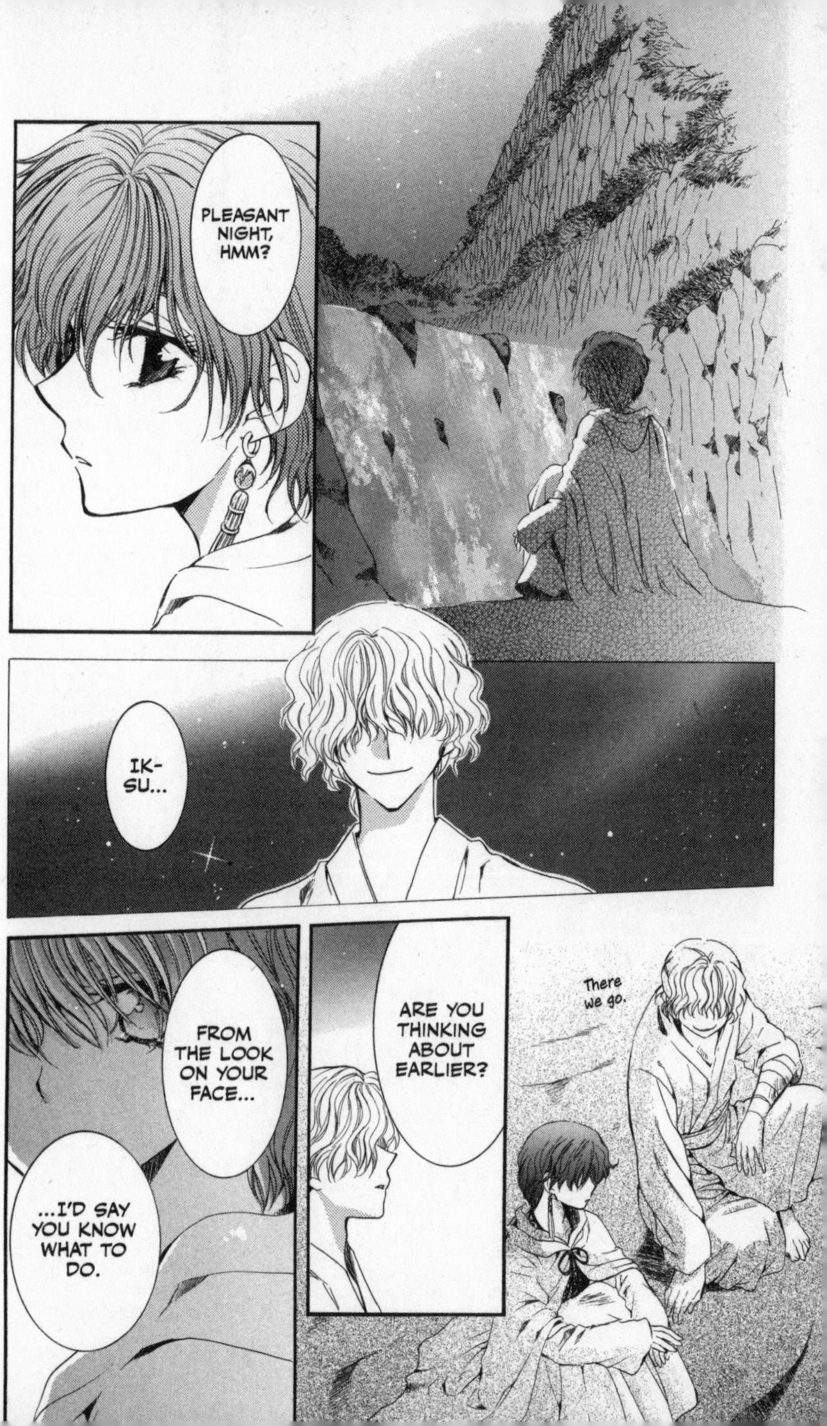
PLEASANT NIGHT, HMM?
IK-SU...
There we go.
ARE YOU THINKING ABOUT EARLIER?
FROM THE LOOK ON YOUR FACE...
...I'D SAY YOU KNOW WHAT TO DO.

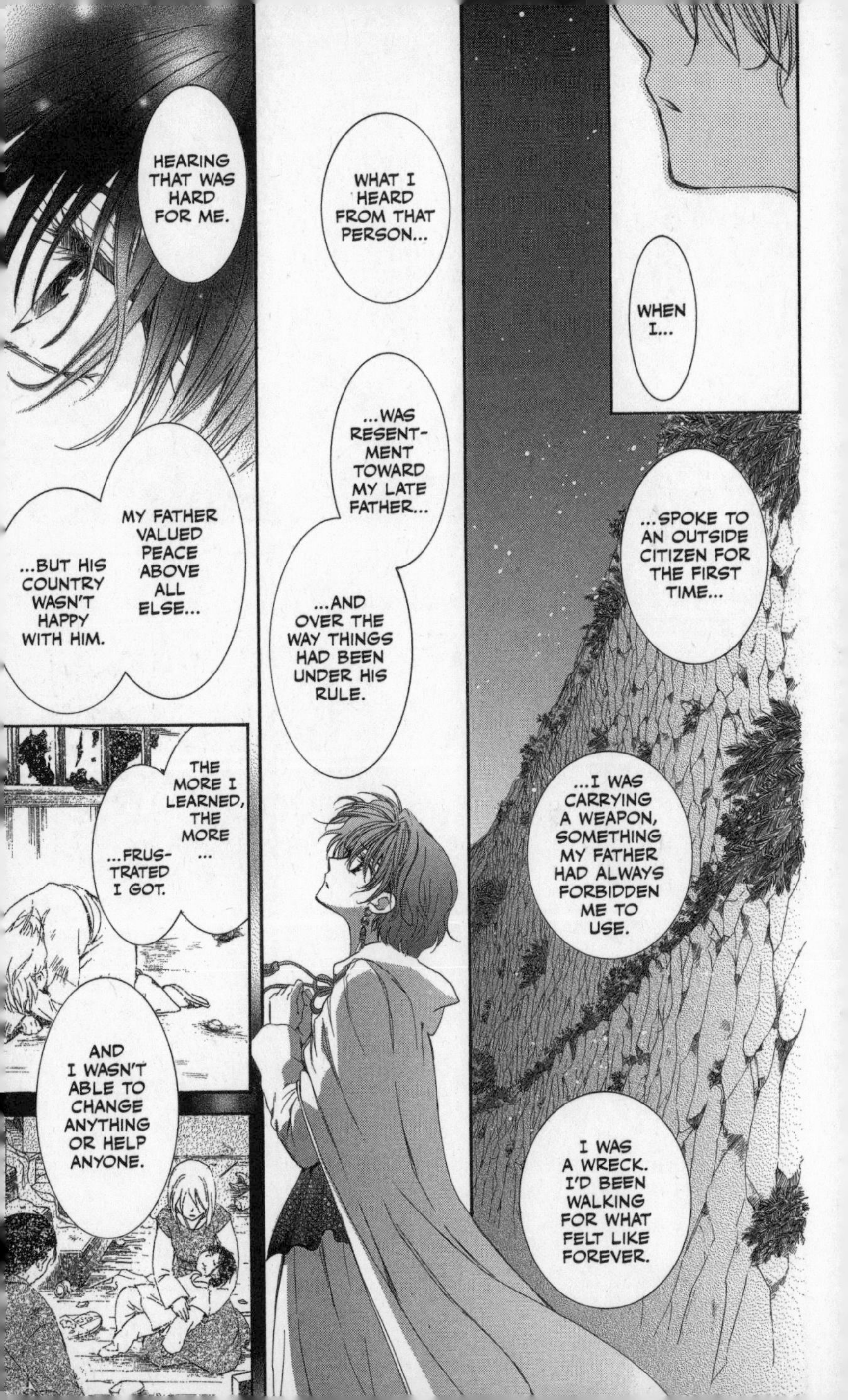
WHEN I...
...SPOKE TO AN OUTSIDE CITIZEN FOR THE FIRST TIME...
...I WAS CARRYING A WEAPON, SOMETHING MY FATHER HAD ALWAYS FORBIDDEN ME TO USE.
I WAS A WRECK. I'D BEEN WALKING FOR WHAT FELT LIKE FOREVER.
WHAT I HEARD FROM THAT PERSON...
...WAS RESENT-MENT TOWARD MY LATE FATHER...
...AND OVER THE WAY THINGS HAD BEEN UNDER HIS RULE.
HEARING THAT WAS HARD FOR ME.
MY FATHER VALUED PEACE ABOVE ALL ELSE...
...BUT HIS COUNTRY WASN'T HAPPY WITH HIM.
THE MORE I LEARNED, THE MORE ...
...FRUS-TRATED I GOT.
AND I WASN'T ABLE TO CHANGE ANYTHING OR HELP ANYONE.

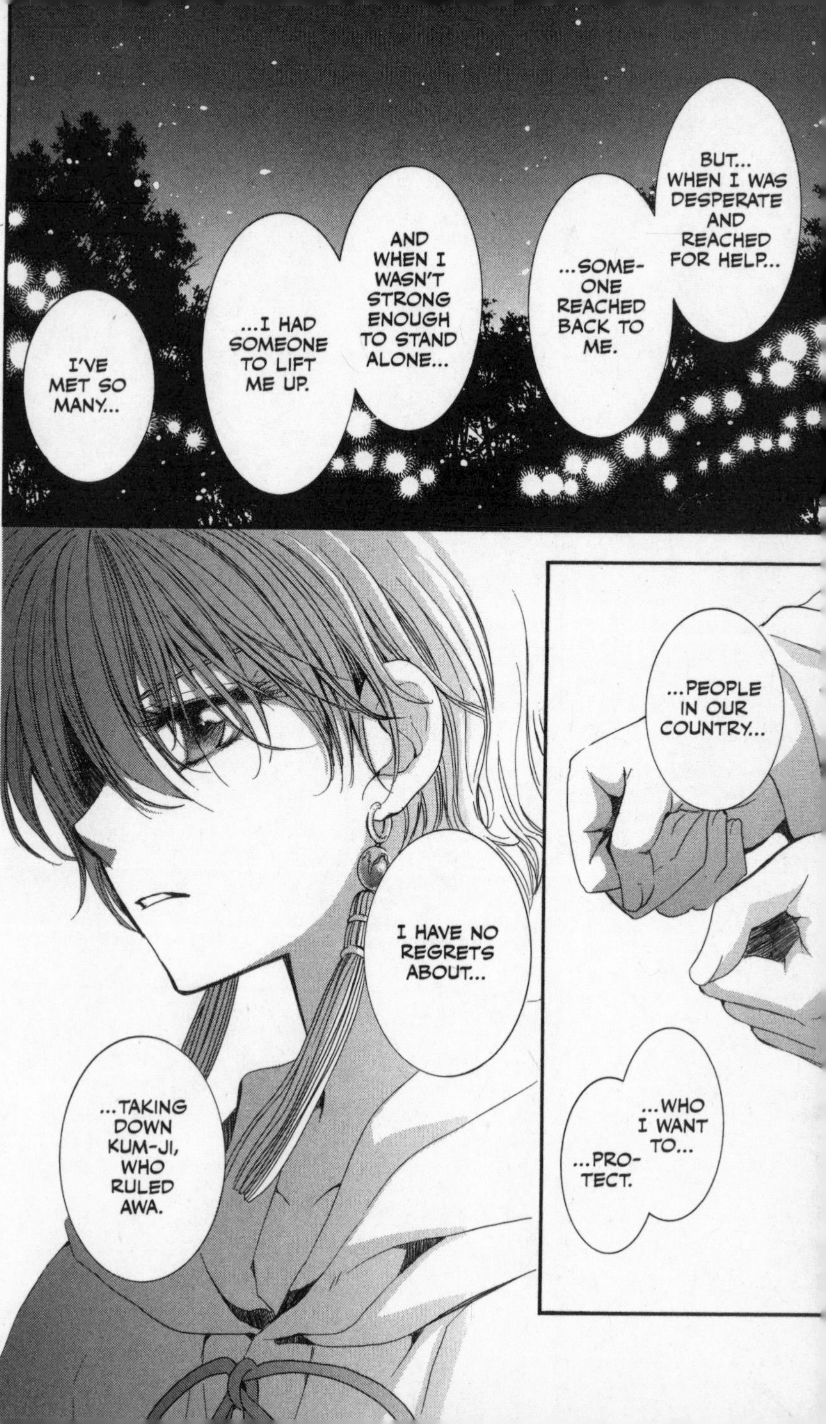
BUT... WHEN I WAS DESPERATE AND REACHED FOR HELP...
...SOME-ONE REACHED BACK TO ME.
AND WHEN I WASN'T STRONG ENOUGH TO STAND ALONE...
...I HAD SOMEONE TO LIFT ME UP.
I'VE MET SO MANY...
...PEOPLE IN OUR COUNTRY...
...WHO I WANT TO...
...PRO-TECT.
I HAVE NO REGRETS ABOUT...
...TAKING DOWN KUM-JI, WHO RULED AWA.

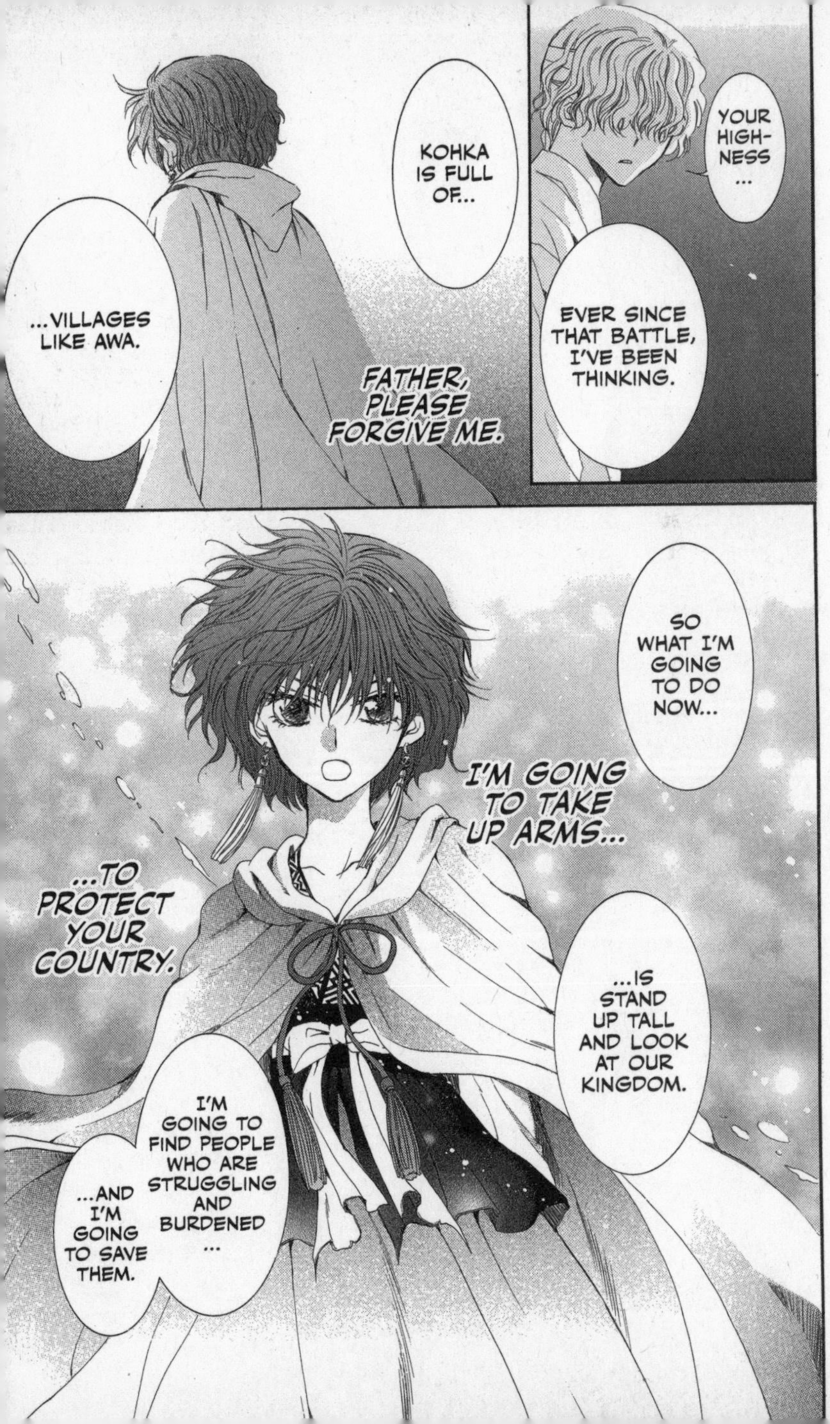
YOUR HIGH-NESS ...
EVER SINCE THAT BATTLE, I'VE BEEN THINKING.
KOHKA IS FULL OF...
...VILLAGES LIKE AWA.
FATHER, PLEASE FORGIVE ME.
SO WHAT I'M GOING TO DO NOW...
I'M GOING TO TAKE UP ARMS...
...TO PROTECT YOUR COUNTRY.
...IS STAND UP TALL AND LOOK AT OUR KINGDOM.
I'M GOING TO FIND PEOPLE WHO ARE STRUGGLING AND BURDENED ...
...AND I'M GOING TO SAVE THEM.

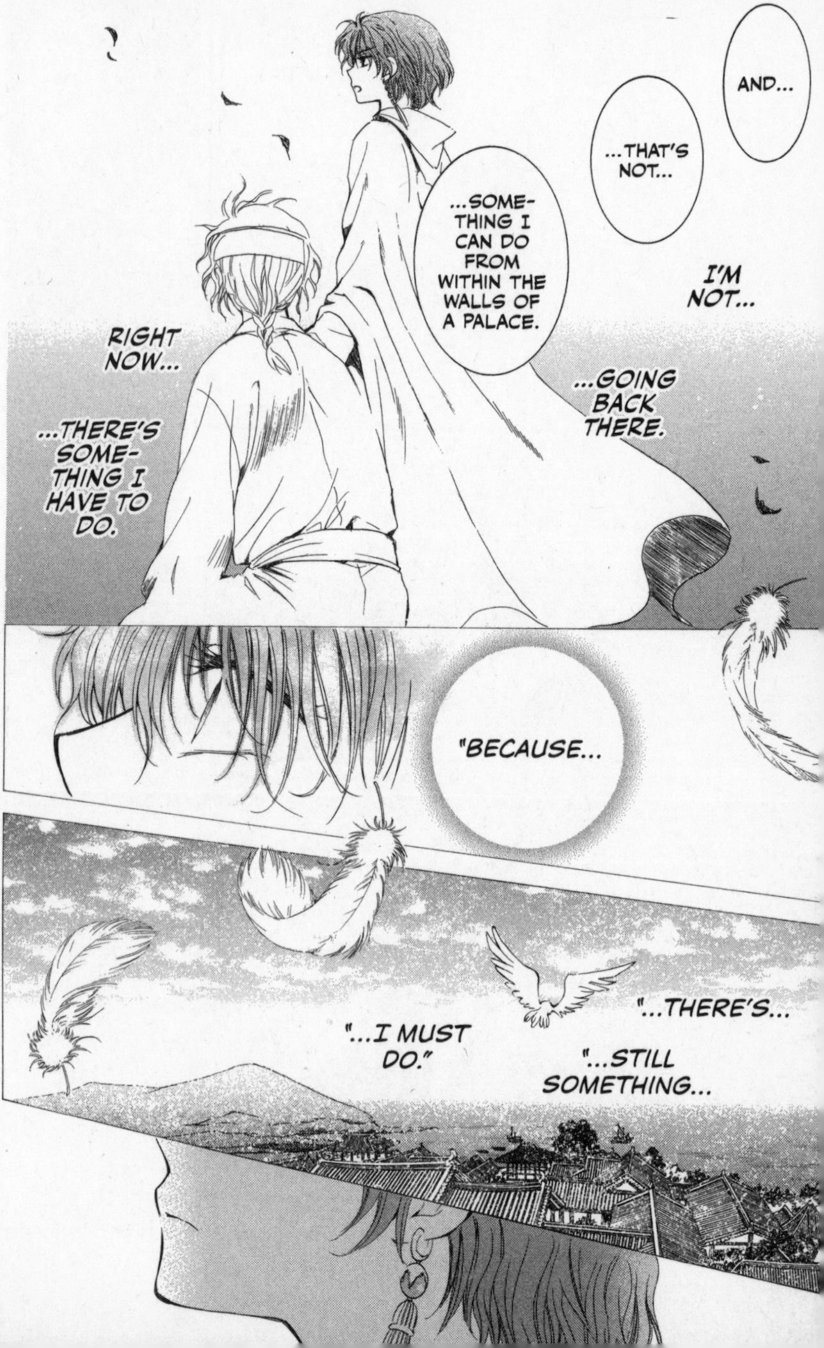
AND...
...THAT'S NOT...
...SOMETHING I CAN DO FROM WITHIN THE WALLS OF A PALACE.
I'M NOT...
...GOING BACK THERE.
RIGHT NOW...
...THERE'S SOMETHING I HAVE TO DO.
"BECAUSE...
"...THERE'S...
"...STILL SOMETHING...
"...I MUST DO."

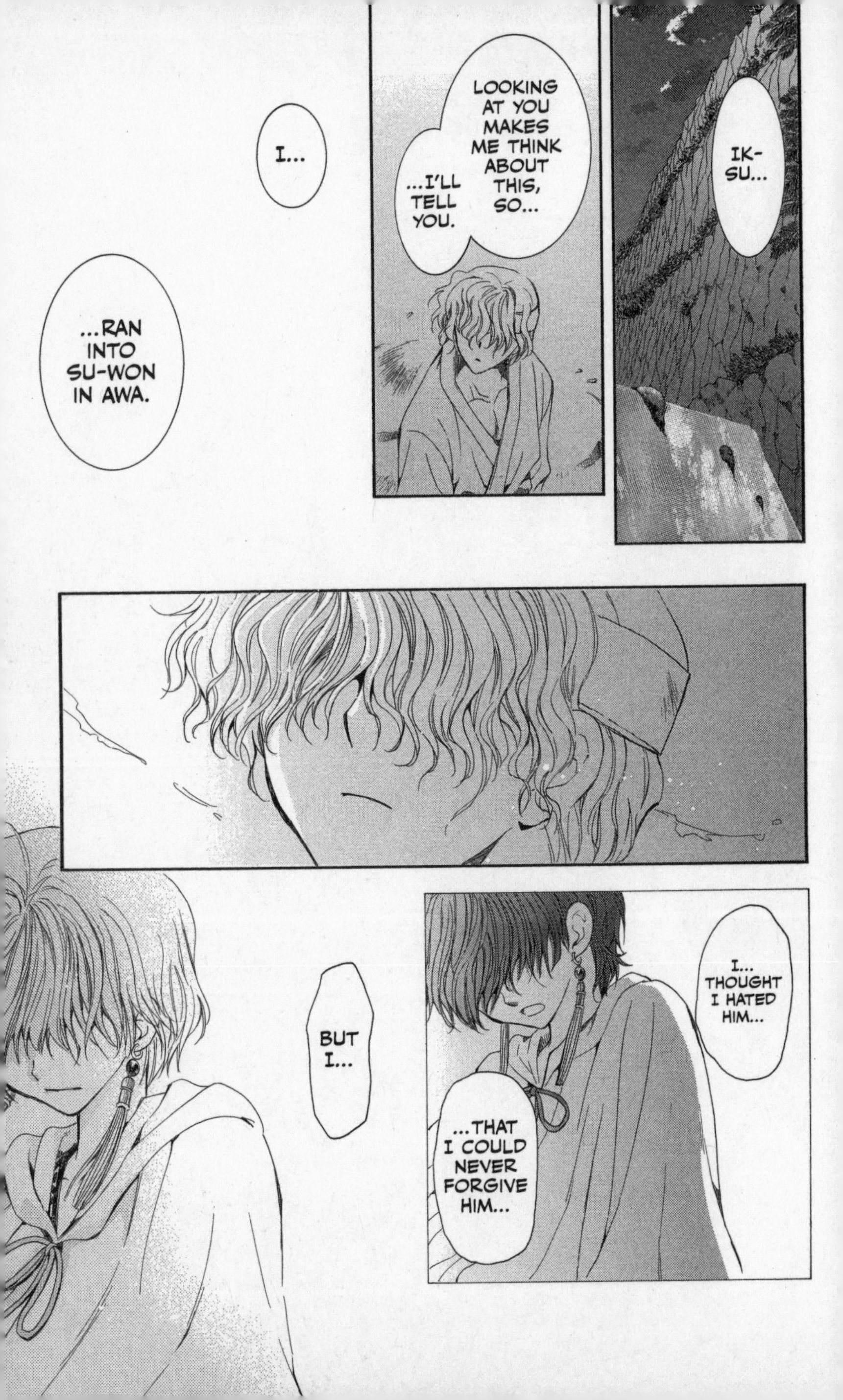
IK-SU...
LOOKING AT YOU MAKES ME THINK ABOUT THIS, SO...
...I'LL TELL YOU.
I...
...RAN INTO SU-WON IN AWA.
I... THOUGHT I HATED HIM...
...THAT I COULD NEVER FORGIVE HIM...
BUT I...

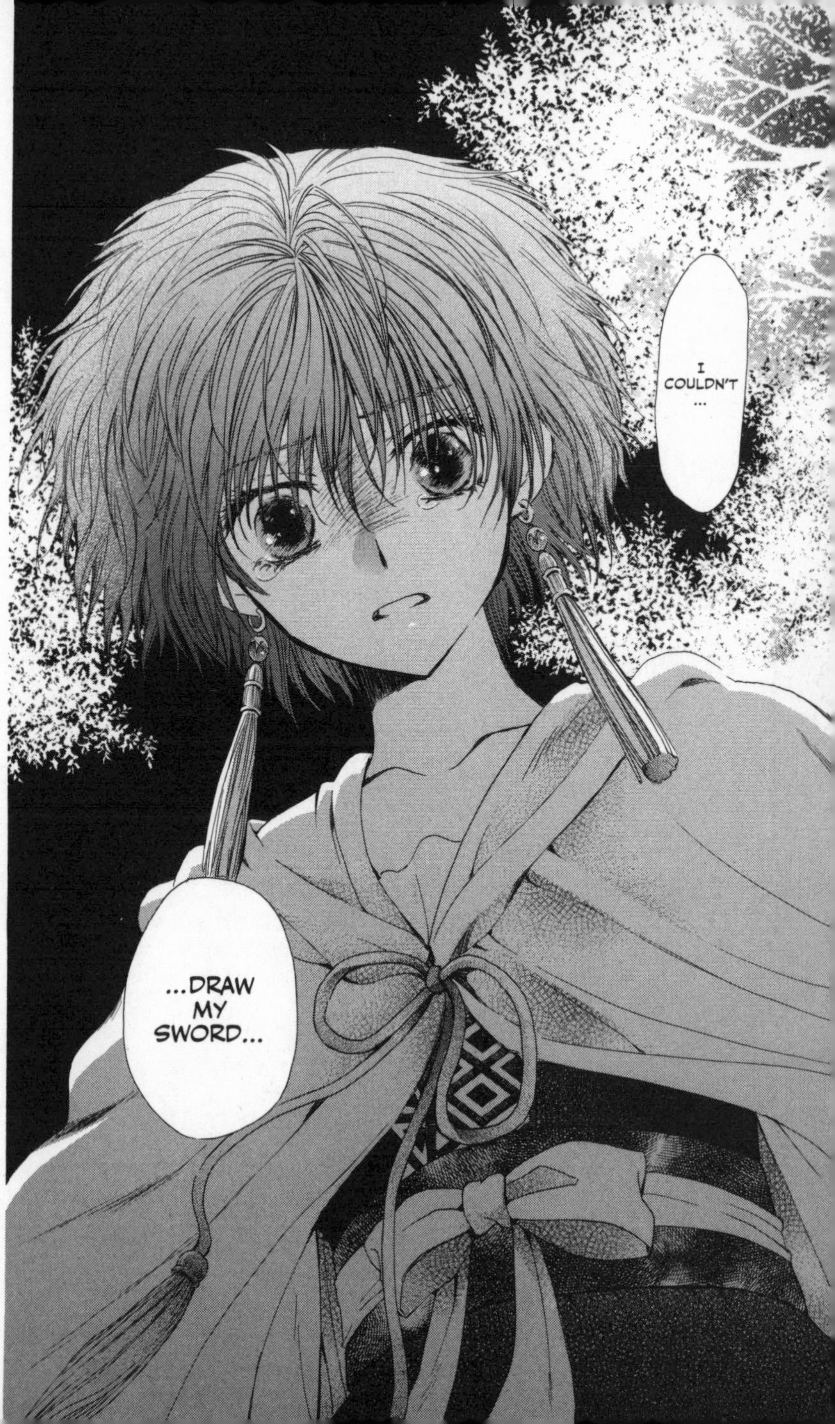
I COULDN'T ...
...DRAW MY SWORD...

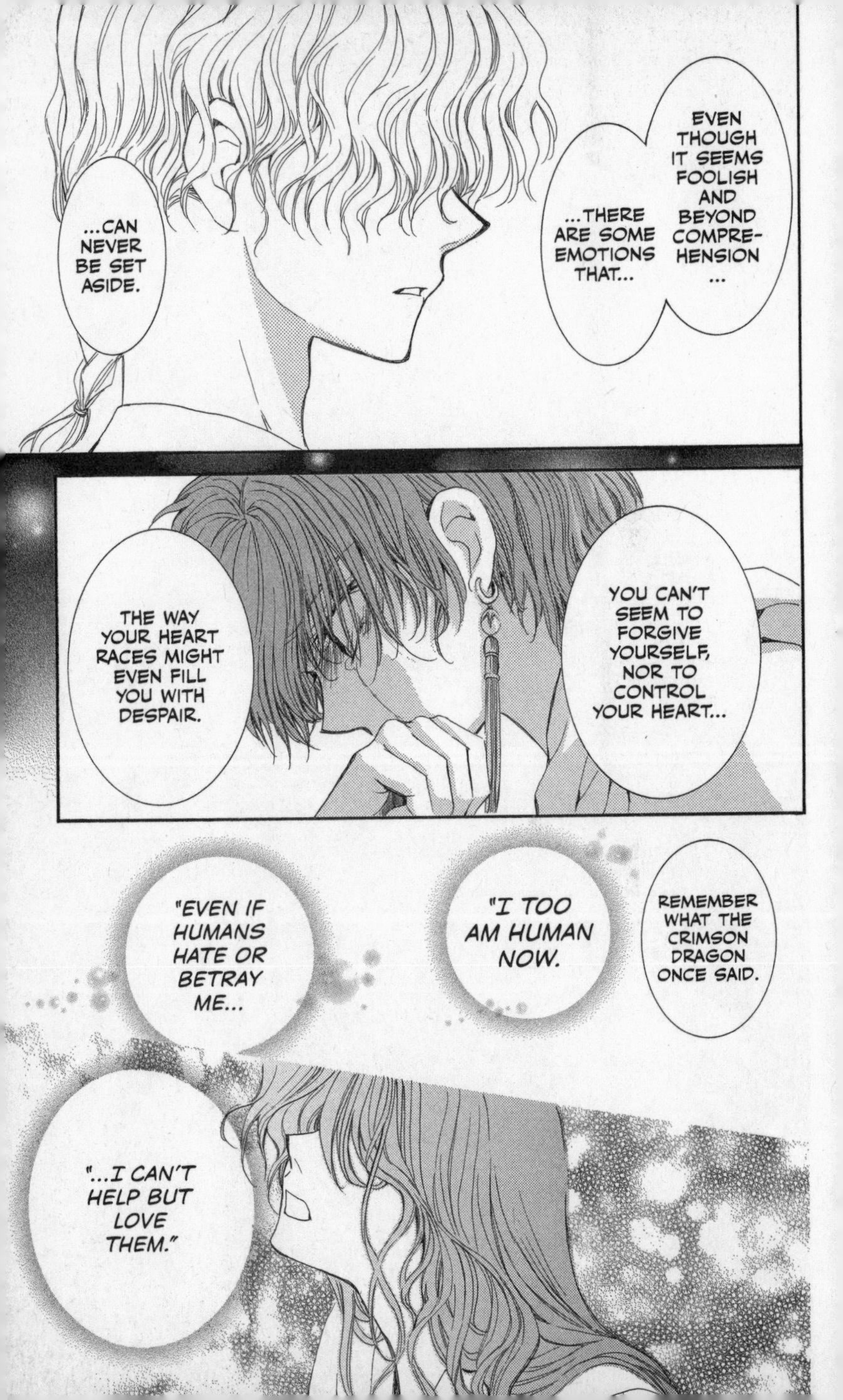
EVEN THOUGH IT SEEMS FOOLISH AND BEYOND COMPREHENSION...
...THERE ARE SOME EMOTIONS THAT...
...CAN NEVER BE SET ASIDE.
YOU CAN'T SEEM TO FORGIVE YOURSELF, NOR TO CONTROL YOUR HEART...
THE WAY YOUR HEART RACES MIGHT EVEN FILL YOU WITH DESPAIR.
REMEMBER WHAT THE CRIMSON DRAGON ONCE SAID.
"I TOO AM HUMAN NOW.
"EVEN IF HUMANS HATE OR BETRAY ME...
"...I CAN'T HELP BUT LOVE THEM."

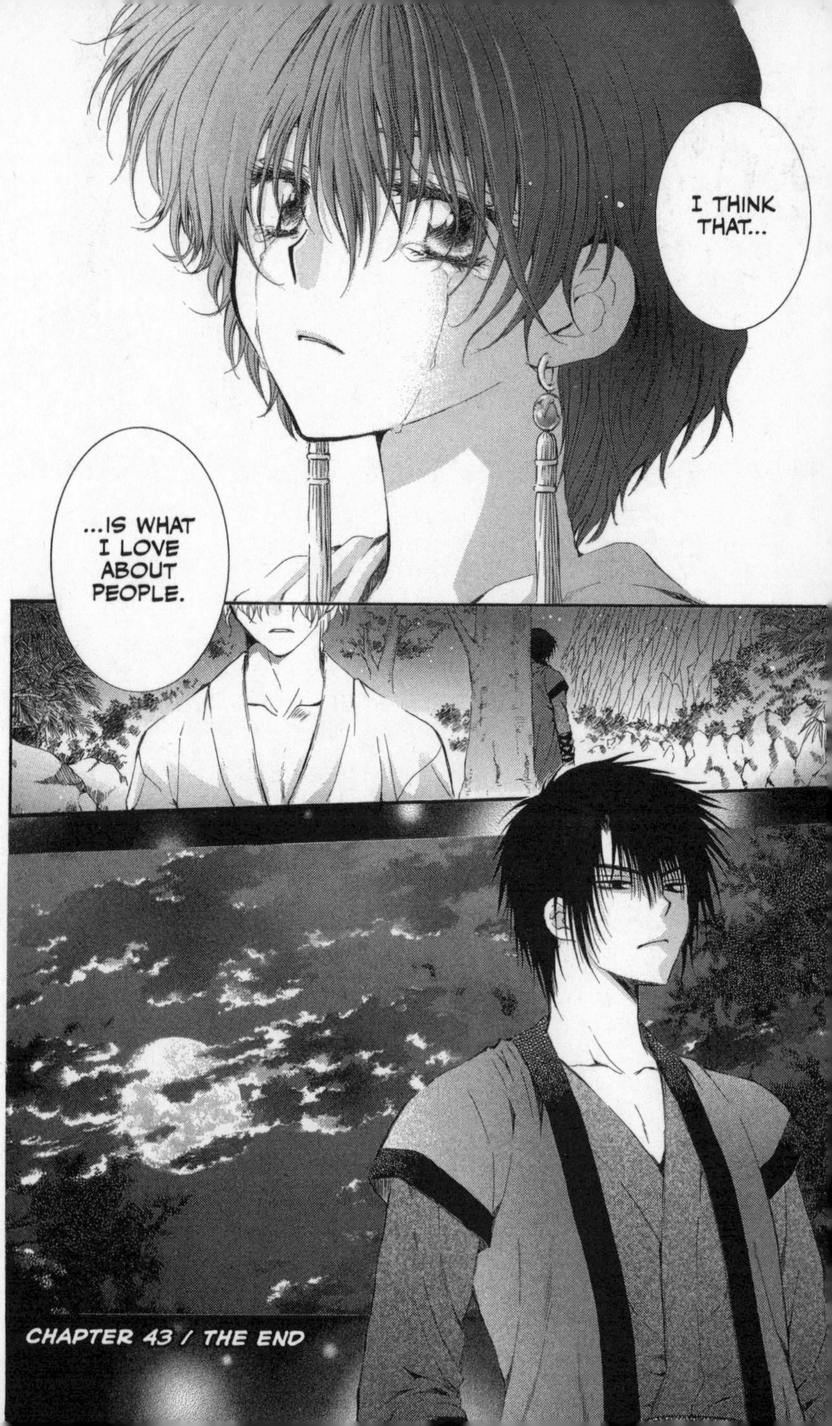
I THINK THAT...
...IS WHAT I LOVE ABOUT PEOPLE.
CHAPTER 43 / THE END

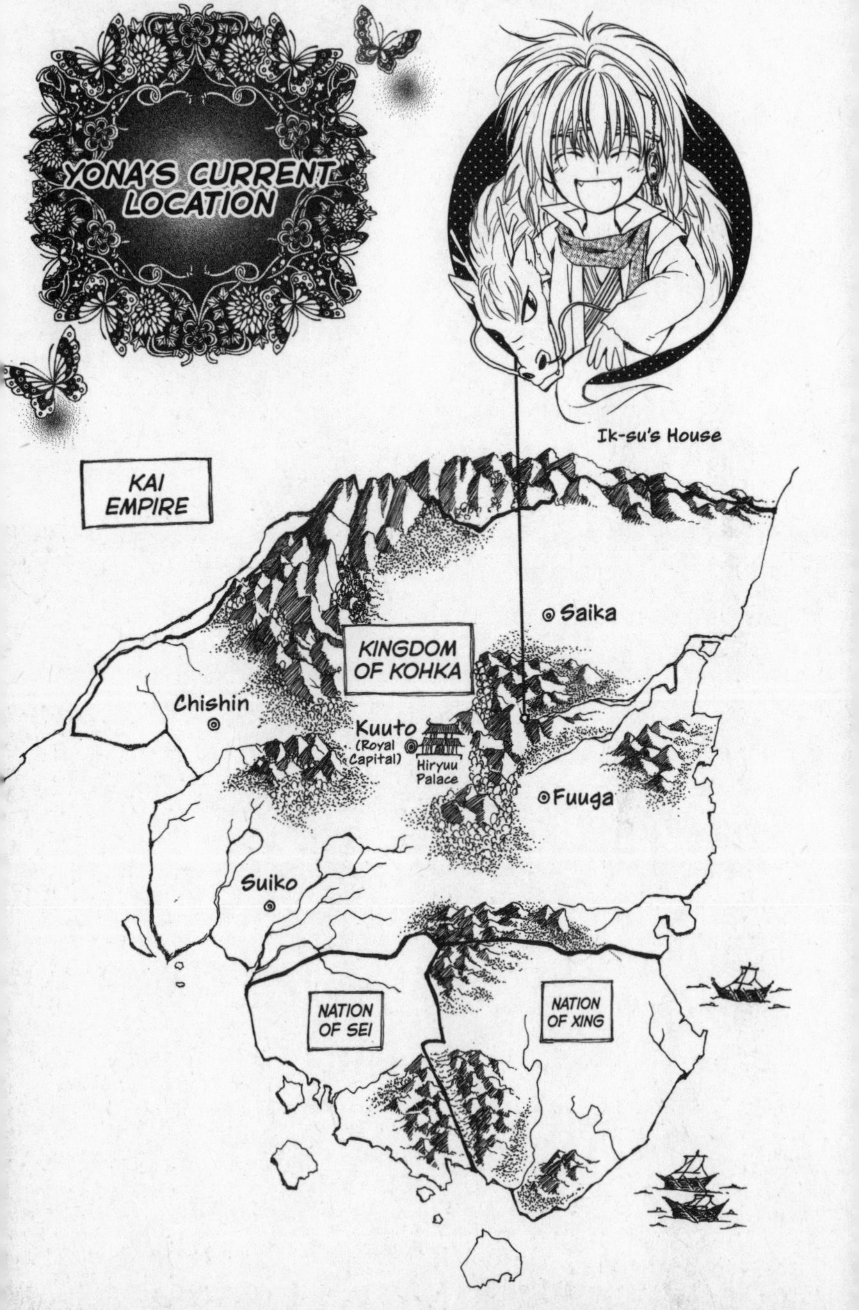
YONA'S CURRENT LOCATION
Ik-su's House
KAI EMPIRE
Saika
KINGDOM OF KOHKA
Chishin
Kuuto (Royal Capital)
Hiryuu Palace
Fuuga
Suiko
NATION OF SEI
NATION OF XING

CHAPTER 44: PEOPLE'S EXPECTATIONS

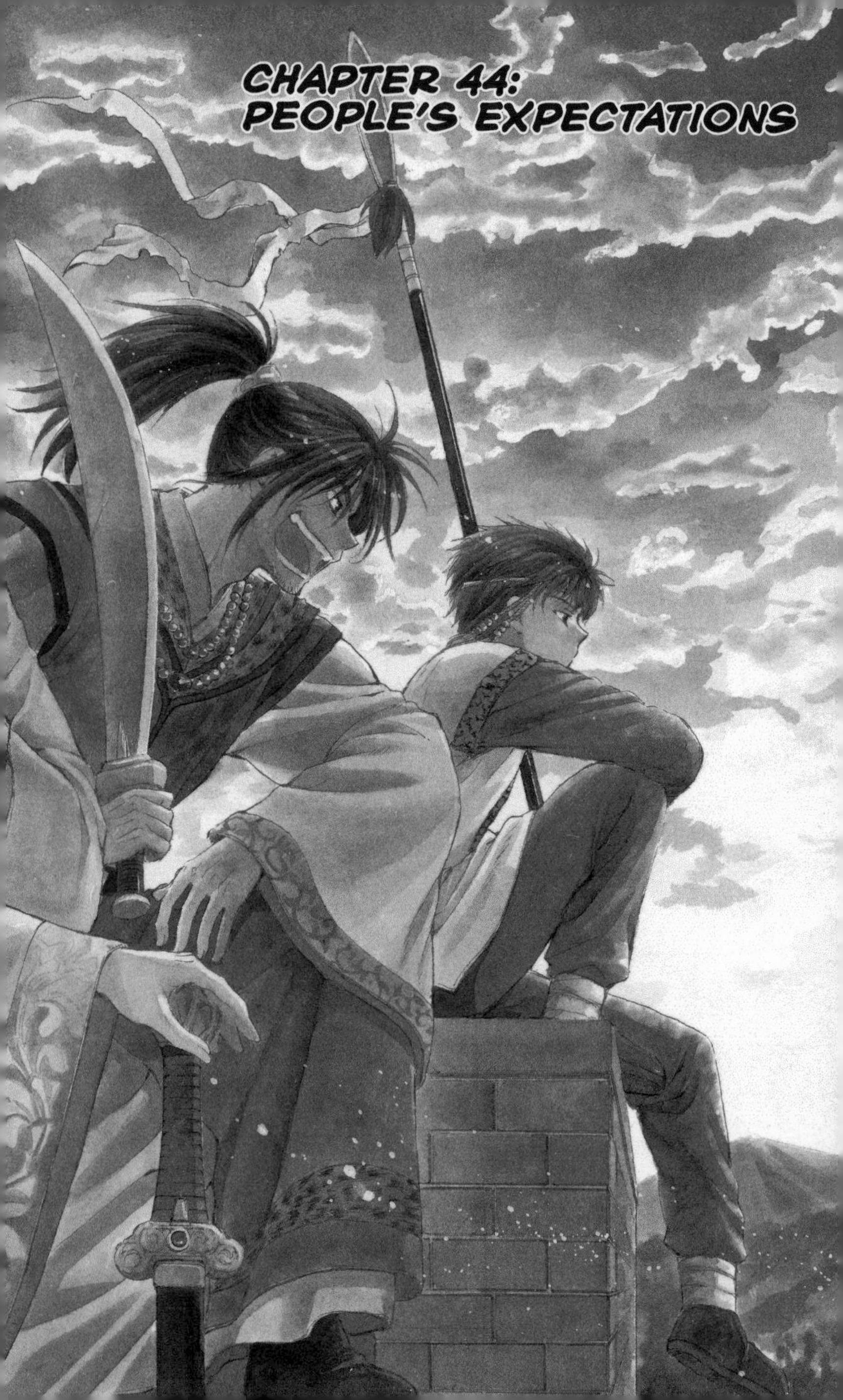

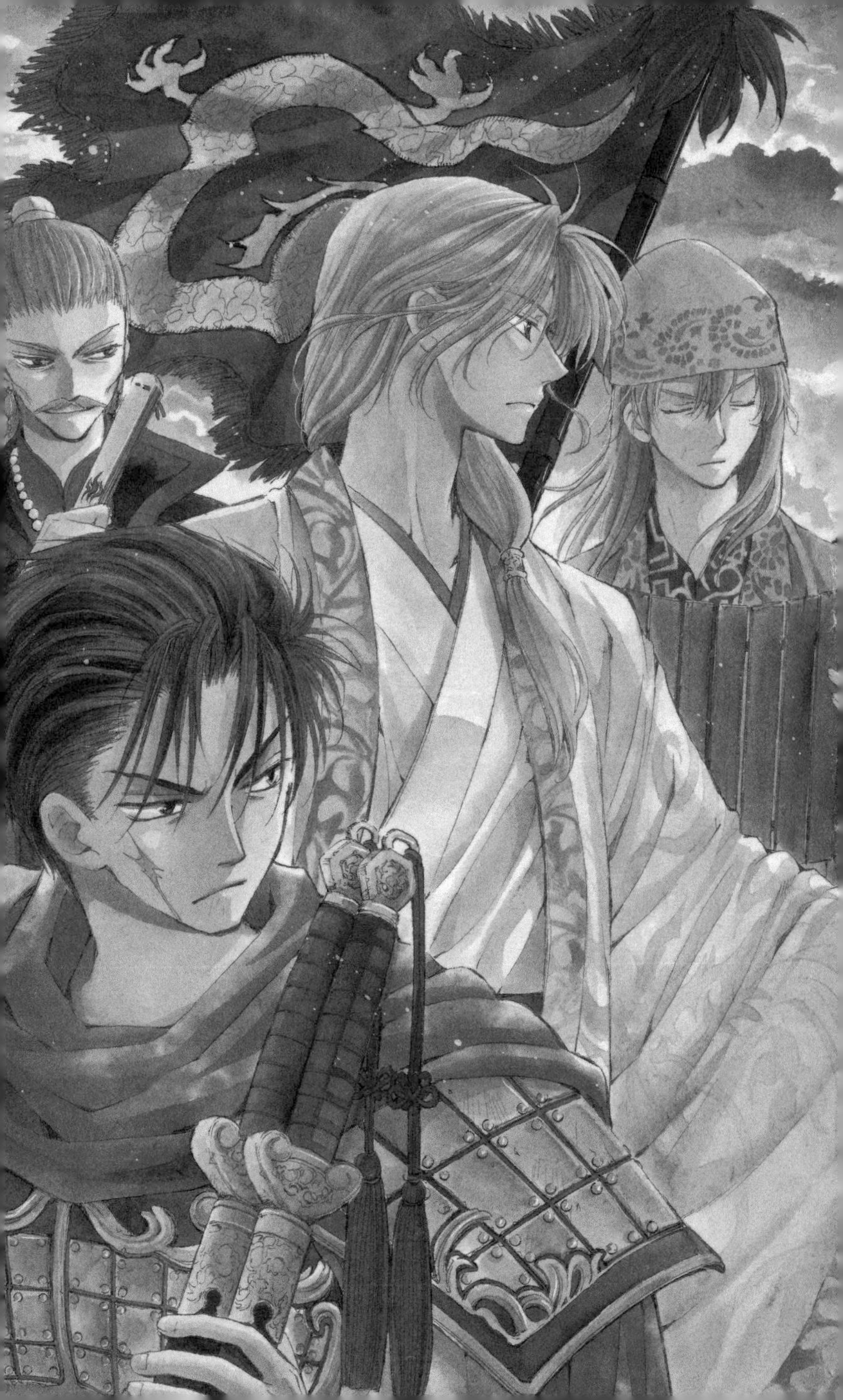

Wind Tribe Chief Tae-u
Today's task: Babysitting

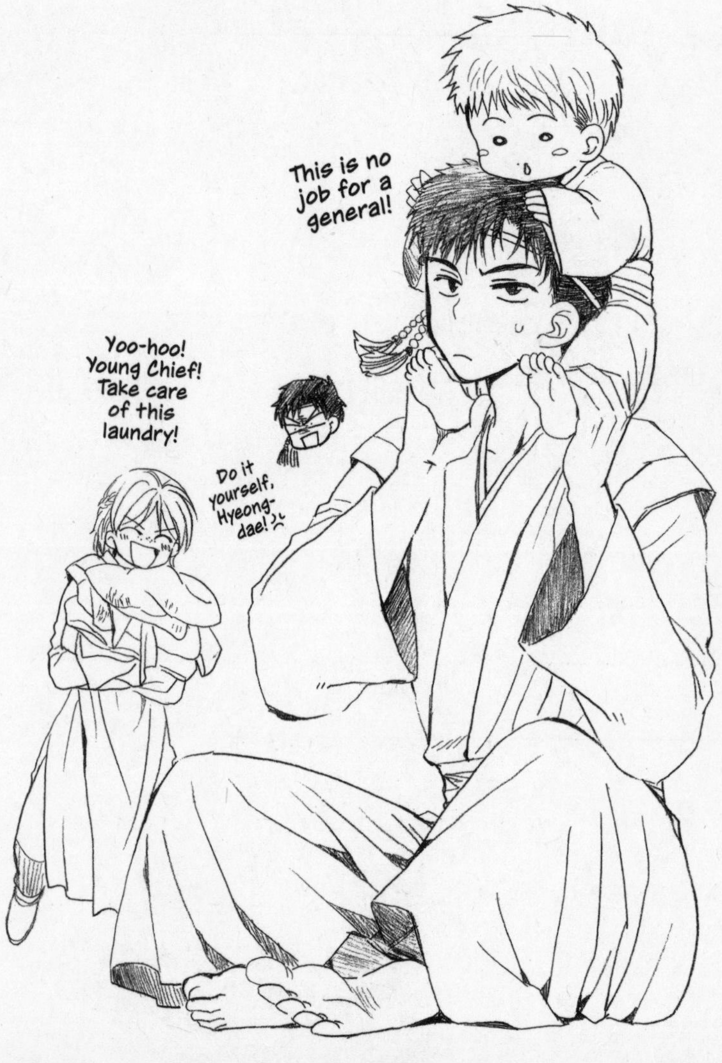
This is no job for a general!
Yoo-hoo! Young Chief! Take care of this laundry!
Do it yourself, Hyeong-dae!

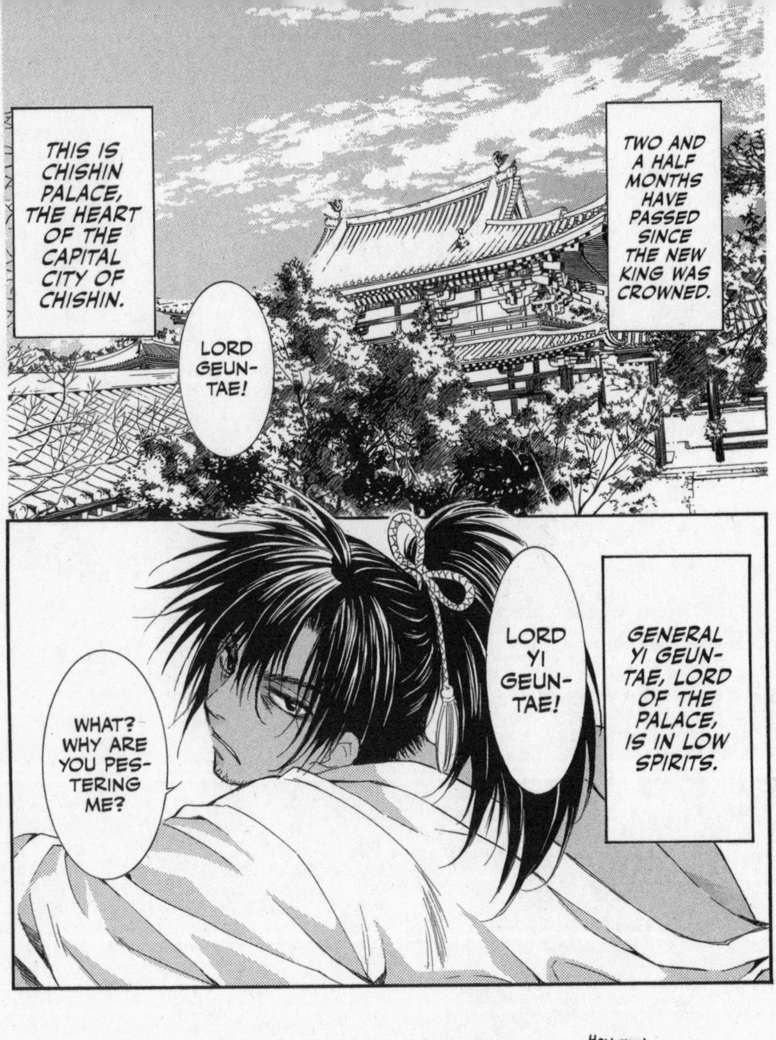
TWO AND A HALF MONTHS HAVE PASSED SINCE THE NEW KING WAS CROWNED.
THIS IS CHISHIN PALACE, THE HEART OF THE CAPITAL CITY OF CHISHIN.
LORD GEUN-TAE!
GENERAL YI GEUN-TAE, LORD OF THE PALACE, IS IN LOW SPIRITS.
LORD YI GEUN-TAE!
WHAT? WHY ARE YOU PES-TERING ME?

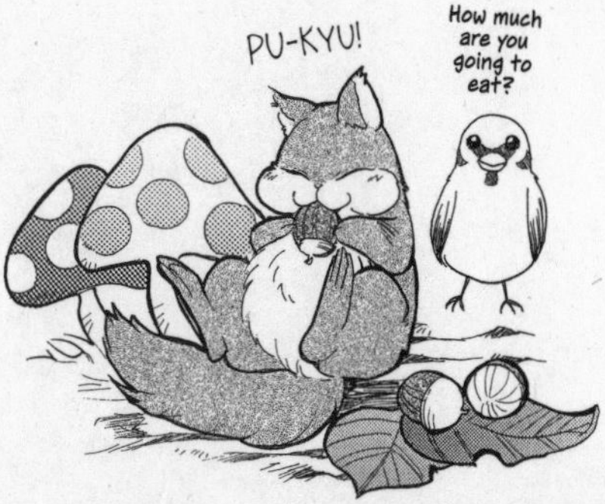
How much are you going to eat?
PU-KYU!

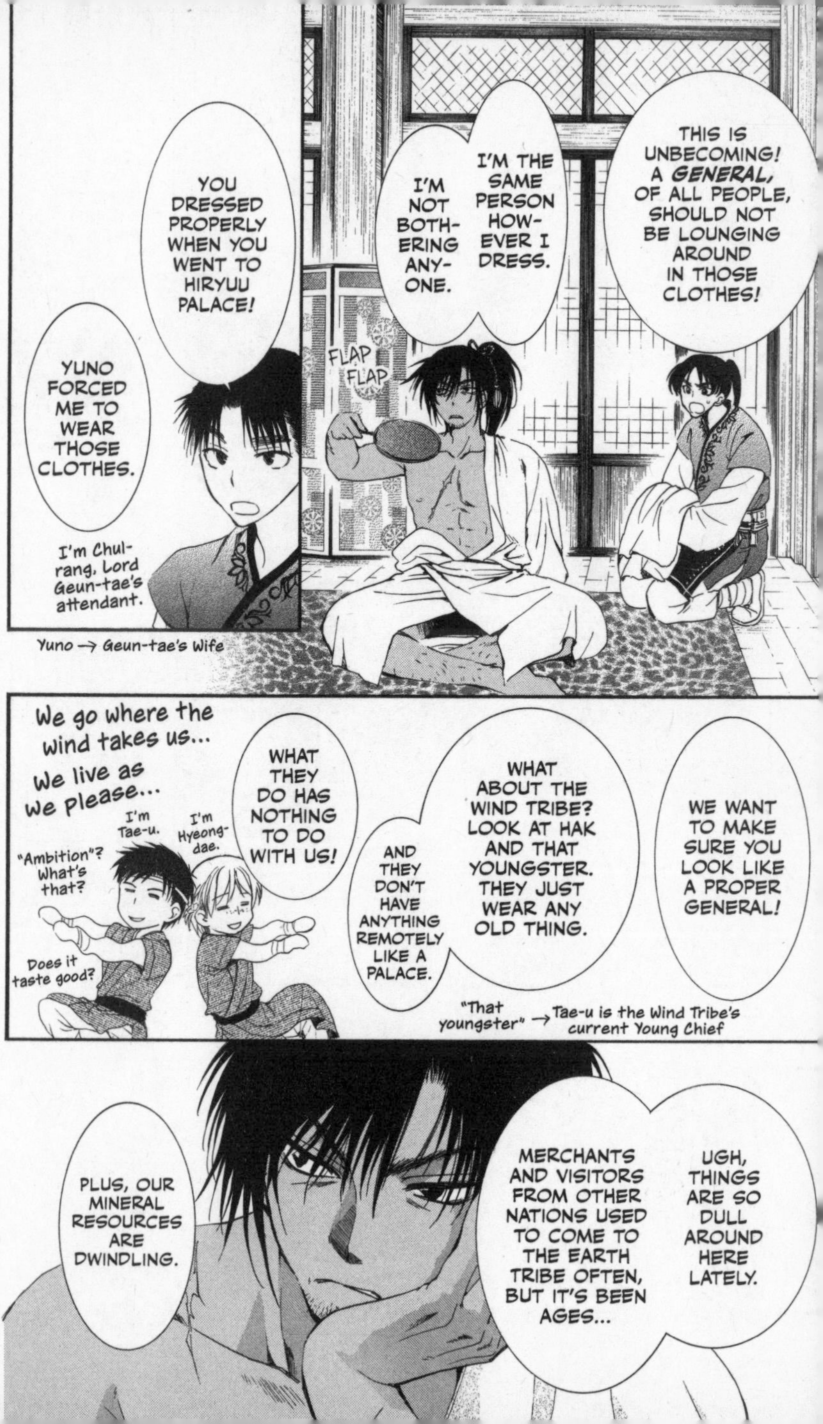
THIS IS UNBECOMING! A GENERAL, OF ALL PEOPLE, SHOULD NOT BE LOUNGING AROUND IN THOSE CLOTHES!
I'M THE SAME PERSON HOWEVER I DRESS.
I'M NOT BOTHERING ANYONE.
FLAP FLAP
YOU DRESSED PROPERLY WHEN YOU WENT TO HIRYUU PALACE!
YUNO FORCED ME TO WEAR THOSE CLOTHES.
I'm Chul-rang, Lord Geun-tae's attendant.
Yuno → Geun-tae's Wife
WE WANT TO MAKE SURE YOU LOOK LIKE A PROPER GENERAL!
WHAT ABOUT THE WIND TRIBE? LOOK AT HAK AND THAT YOUNGSTER. THEY JUST WEAR ANY OLD THING.
AND THEY DON'T HAVE ANYTHING REMOTELY LIKE A PALACE.
WHAT THEY DO HAS NOTHING TO DO WITH US!
We go where the wind takes us...
We live as we please...
I'm Hyeong-dae.
I'm Tae-u.
"Ambition"? What's that?
Does it taste good?
"That youngster" → Tae-u is the Wind Tribe's current Young Chief
UGH, THINGS ARE SO DULL AROUND HERE LATELY.
MERCHANTS AND VISITORS FROM OTHER NATIONS USED TO COME TO THE EARTH TRIBE OFTEN, BUT IT'S BEEN AGES...
PLUS, OUR MINERAL RESOURCES ARE DWINDLING.

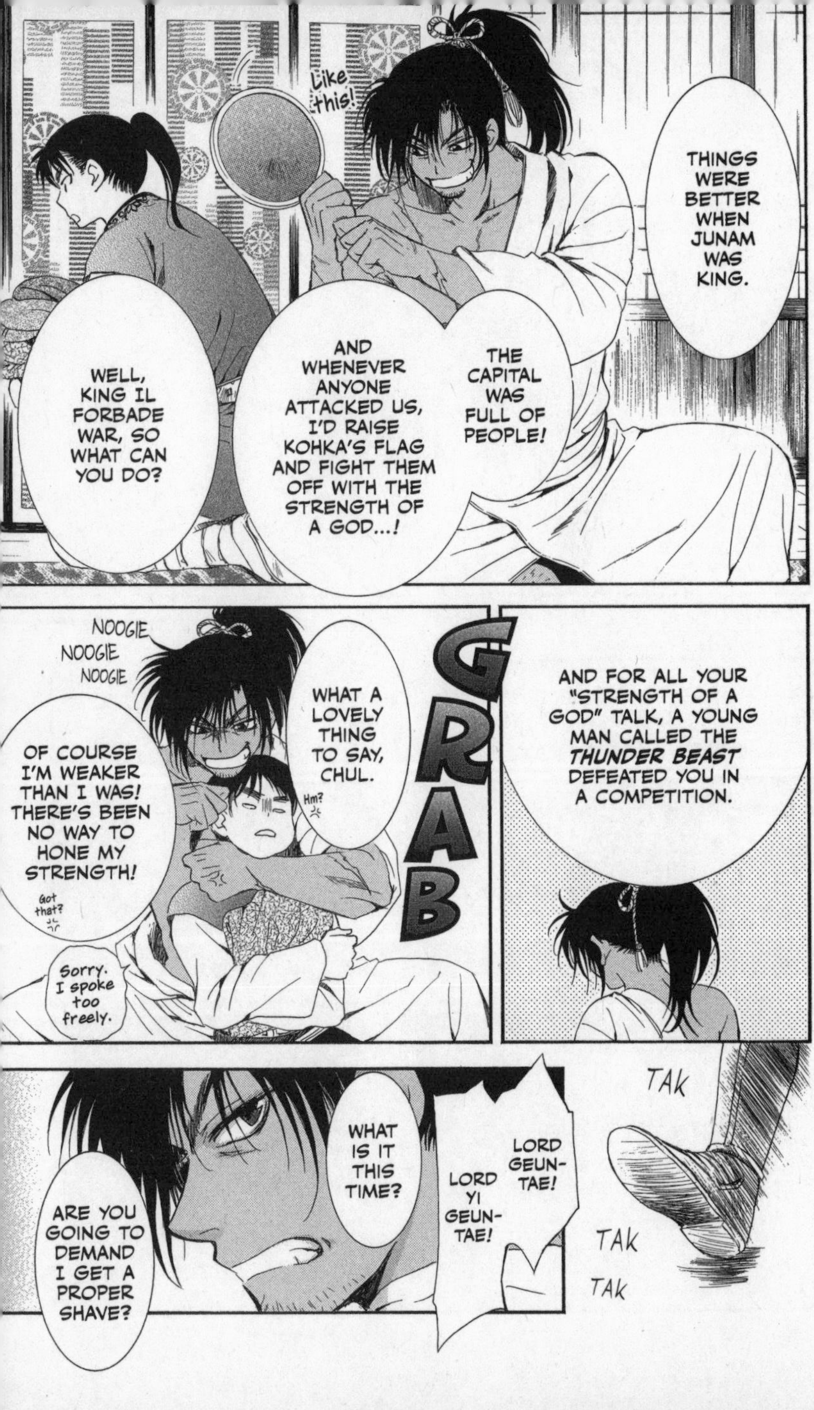

THINGS WERE BETTER WHEN JUNAM WAS KING.
THE CAPITAL WAS FULL OF PEOPLE!
AND WHENEVER ANYONE ATTACKED US, I'D RAISE KOHKA'S FLAG AND FIGHT THEM OFF WITH THE STRENGTH OF A GOD...!
Like this!
WELL, KING IL FORBADE WAR, SO WHAT CAN YOU DO?
AND FOR ALL YOUR "STRENGTH OF A GOD" TALK, A YOUNG MAN CALLED THE ***THUNDER BEAST*** DEFEATED YOU IN A COMPETITION.
GRAB
WHAT A LOVELY THING TO SAY, CHUL.
Hm?
NOOGIE
NOOGIE
NOOGIE
OF COURSE I'M WEAKER THAN I WAS! THERE'S BEEN NO WAY TO HONE MY STRENGTH!
Got that?
Sorry. I spoke too freely.
TAK
TAK
TAK
LORD GEUN-TAE!
LORD YI GEUN-TAE!
WHAT IS IT THIS TIME?
ARE YOU GOING TO DEMAND I GET A PROPER SHAVE?

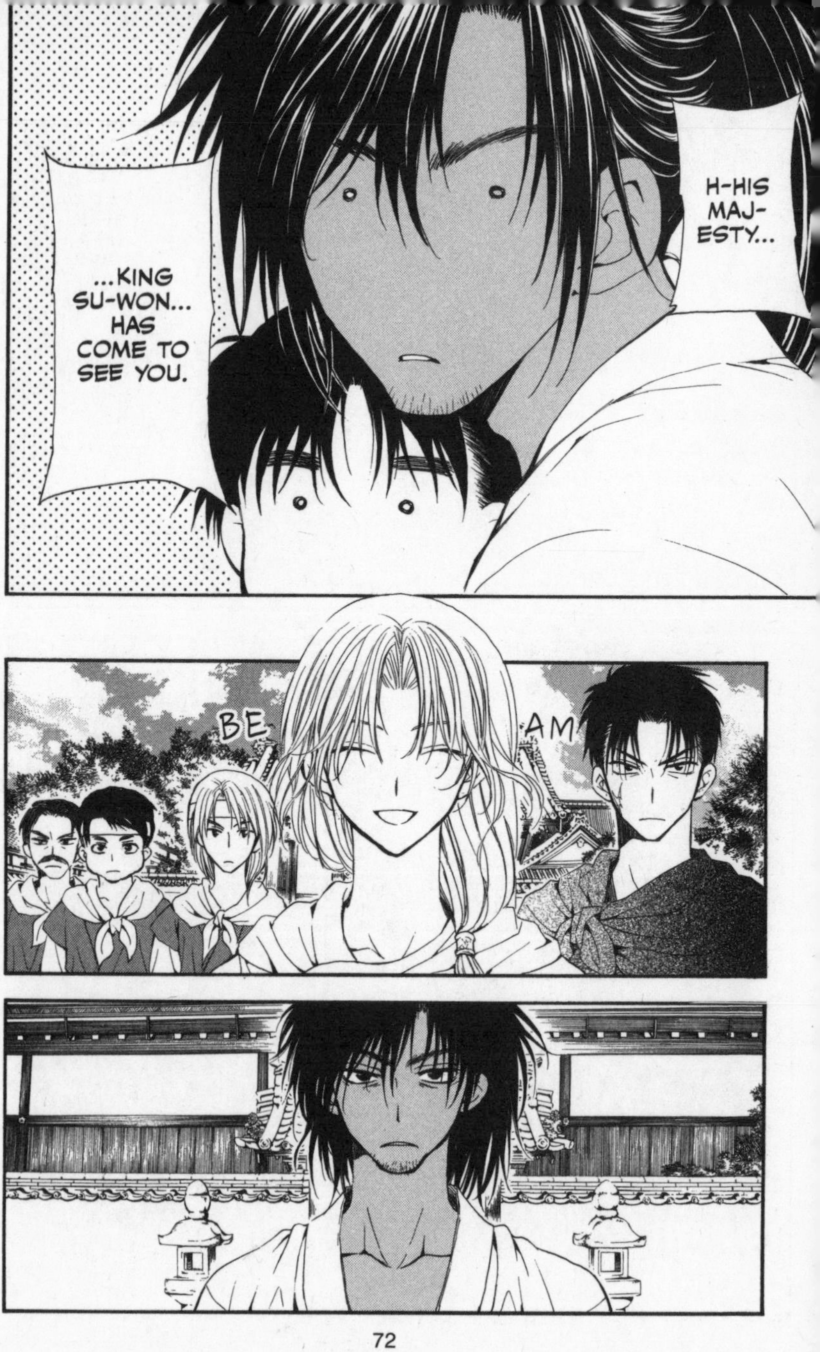
H-HIS MAJ-ESTY...
...KING SU-WON... HAS COME TO SEE YOU.
BE
AM

Starting with this chapter, we're having a Su-won storyline. It's been a while since I drew Su-won so much!

Some readers didn't know who the characters on the chapter's title page were. That's Su-won and the generals of the five tribes.
Sky→General Han Ju-do
Fire→General Kang Su-jin
Earth→General Yi Geun-tae
Water→General Ahn Jung-gi
Wind→General Tae-u
(Because Hak stepped down, Tae-u is now the Wind Tribe's chief.)

They all appeared briefly in volume 2, chapter 6. I figured none of them were very well known, so I colored them the way I felt like doing it. I'm satisfied with how I drew them. ✧

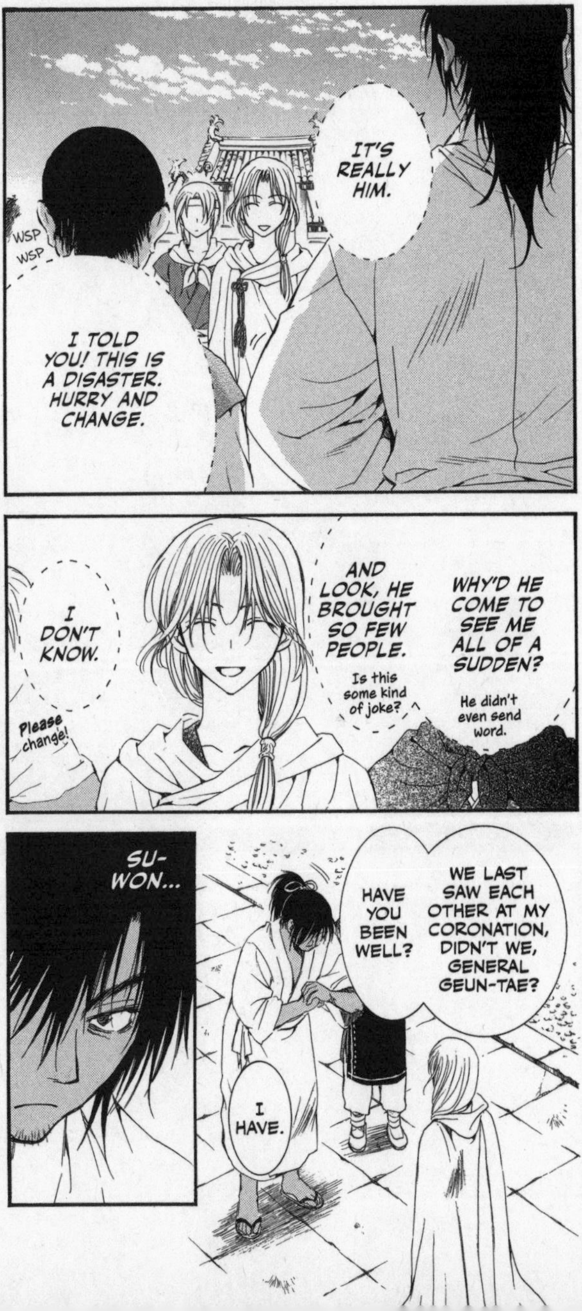
IT'S REALLY HIM.
WSP WSP
I TOLD YOU! THIS IS A DISASTER. HURRY AND CHANGE.
WHY'D HE COME TO SEE ME ALL OF A SUDDEN?
He didn't even send word.
AND LOOK, HE BROUGHT SO FEW PEOPLE.
Is this some kind of joke?
I DON'T KNOW.
Please change!
WE LAST SAW EACH OTHER AT MY CORONATION, DIDN'T WE, GENERAL GEUN-TAE?
HAVE YOU BEEN WELL?
I HAVE.
SU-WON...

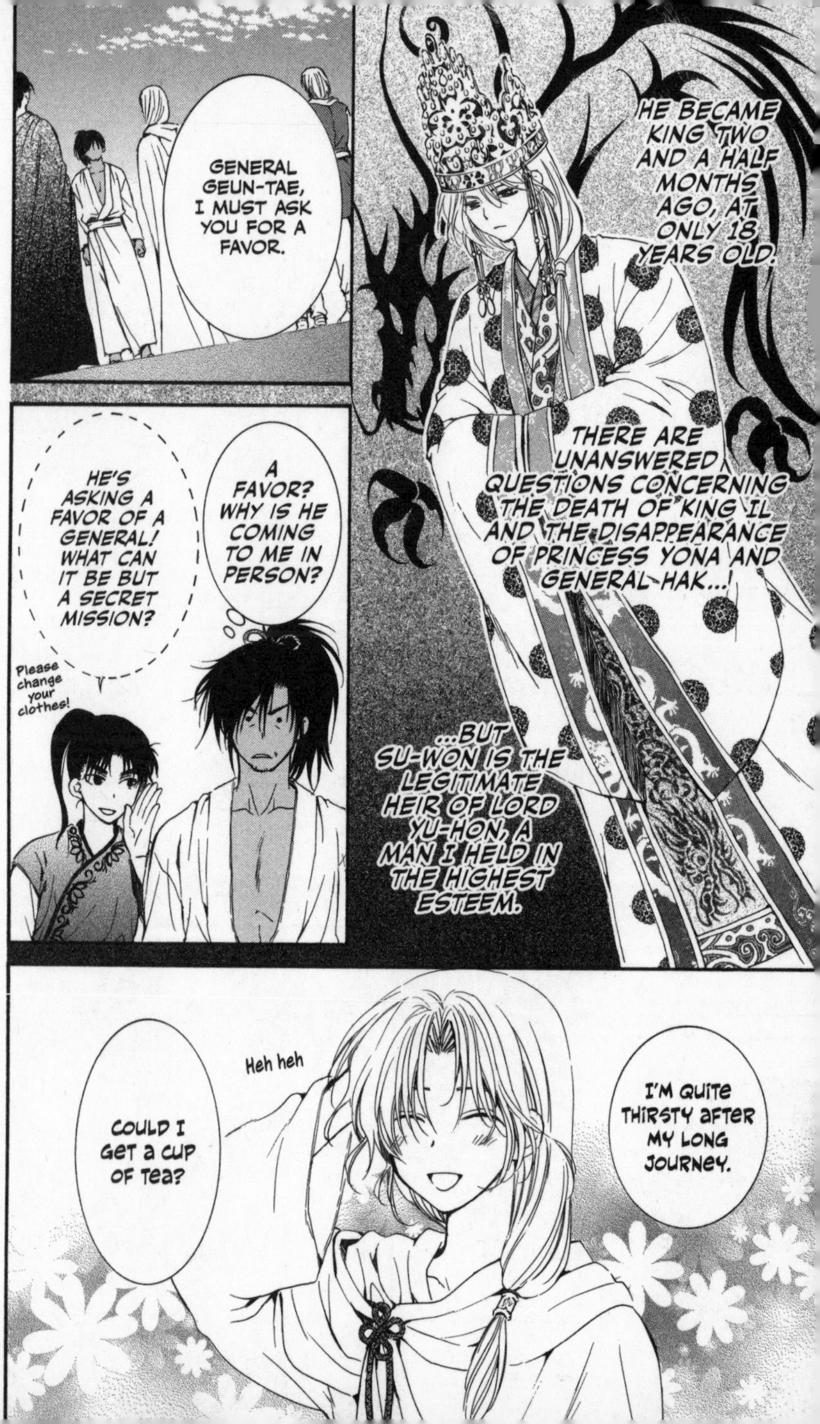
HE BECAME KING TWO AND A HALF MONTHS AGO, AT ONLY 18 YEARS OLD.
THERE ARE UNANSWERED QUESTIONS CONCERNING THE DEATH OF KING IL AND THE DISAPPEARANCE OF PRINCESS YONA AND GENERAL HAK...!
...BUT SU-WON IS THE LEGITIMATE HEIR OF LORD YU-HON, A MAN I HELD IN THE HIGHEST ESTEEM.
GENERAL GEUN-TAE, I MUST ASK YOU FOR A FAVOR.
A FAVOR? WHY IS HE COMING TO ME IN PERSON?
HE'S ASKING A FAVOR OF A GENERAL! WHAT CAN IT BE BUT A SECRET MISSION?
Please change your clothes!
I'M QUITE THIRSTY AFTER MY LONG JOURNEY.
Heh heh
COULD I GET A CUP OF TEA?

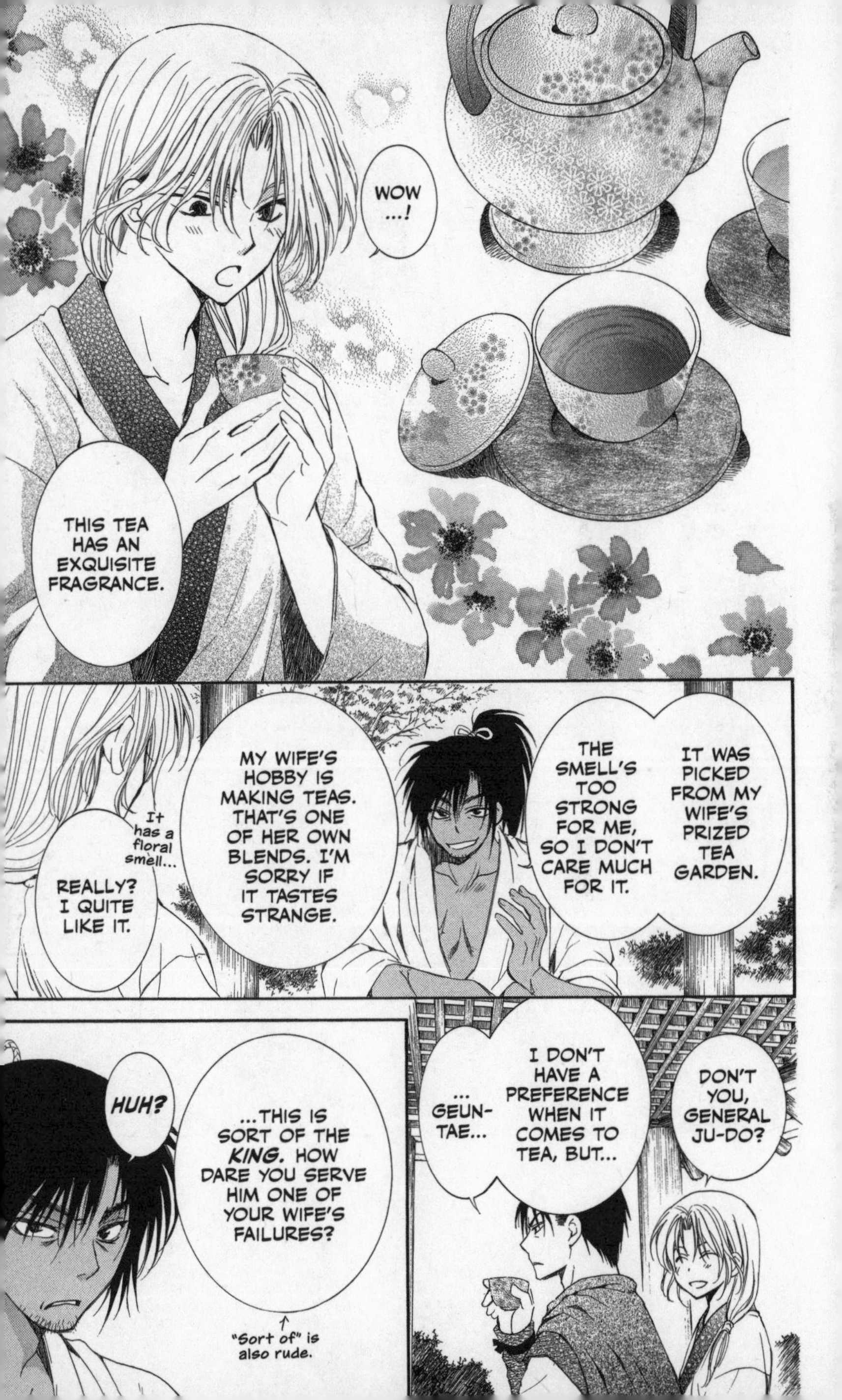
WOW ...!
THIS TEA HAS AN EXQUISITE FRAGRANCE.
IT WAS PICKED FROM MY WIFE'S PRIZED TEA GARDEN.
THE SMELL'S TOO STRONG FOR ME, SO I DON'T CARE MUCH FOR IT.
MY WIFE'S HOBBY IS MAKING TEAS. THAT'S ONE OF HER OWN BLENDS. I'M SORRY IF IT TASTES STRANGE.
It has a floral smell...
REALLY? I QUITE LIKE IT.
DON'T YOU, GENERAL JU-DO?
I DON'T HAVE A PREFERENCE WHEN IT COMES TO TEA, BUT...
... GEUN-TAE...
HUH?
...THIS IS SORT OF THE *KING*. HOW DARE YOU SERVE HIM ONE OF YOUR WIFE'S FAILURES?
"Sort of" is also rude.

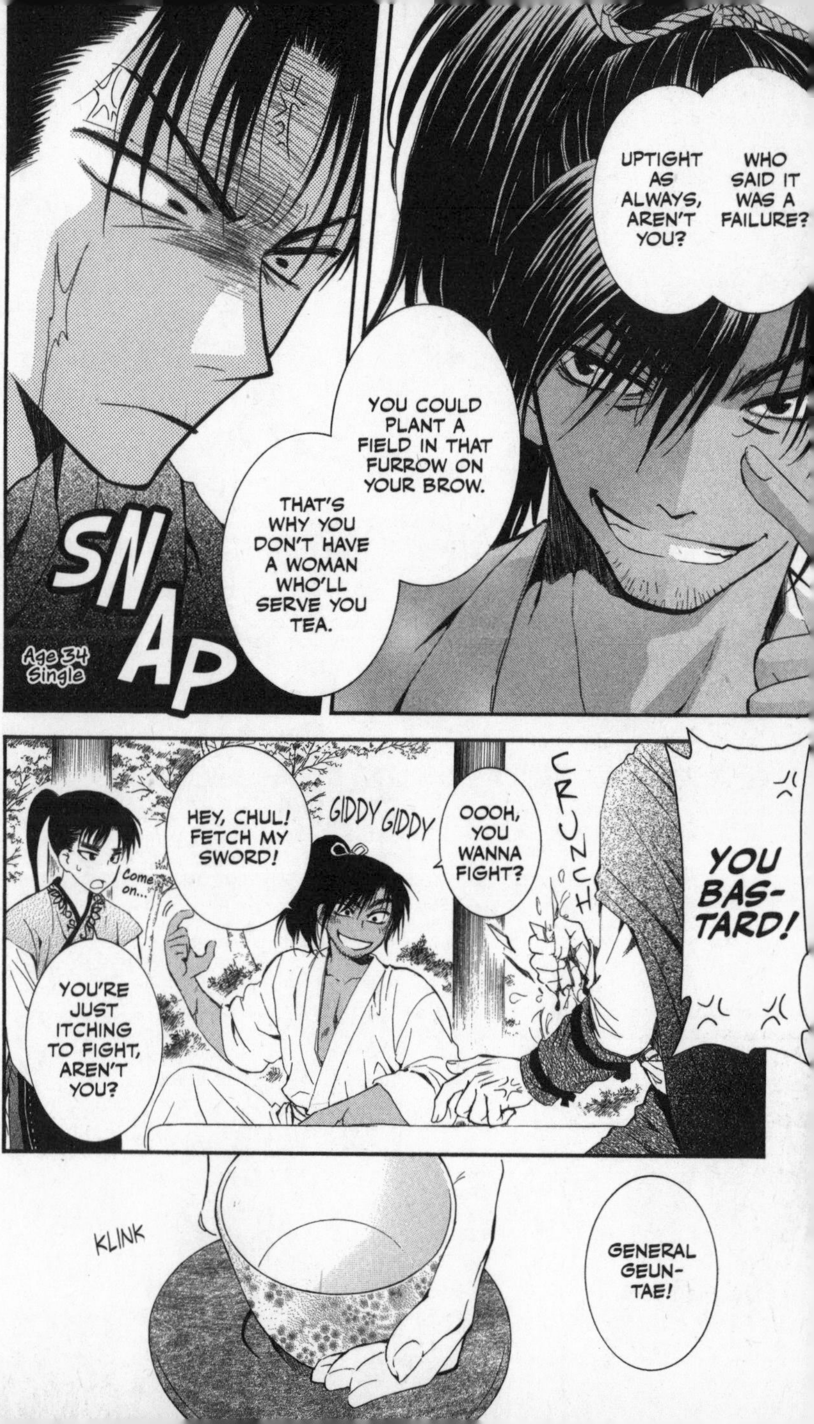
WHO SAID IT WAS A FAILURE?
UPTIGHT AS ALWAYS, AREN'T YOU?
YOU COULD PLANT A FIELD IN THAT FURROW ON YOUR BROW.
THAT'S WHY YOU DON'T HAVE A WOMAN WHO'LL SERVE YOU TEA.
SNAP
Age 34 Single
YOU BAS-TARD!
CRUNCH
OOOH, YOU WANNA FIGHT?
GIDDY GIDDY
HEY, CHUL! FETCH MY SWORD!
Come on...
YOU'RE JUST ITCHING TO FIGHT, AREN'T YOU?
GENERAL GEUN-TAE!
KLINK

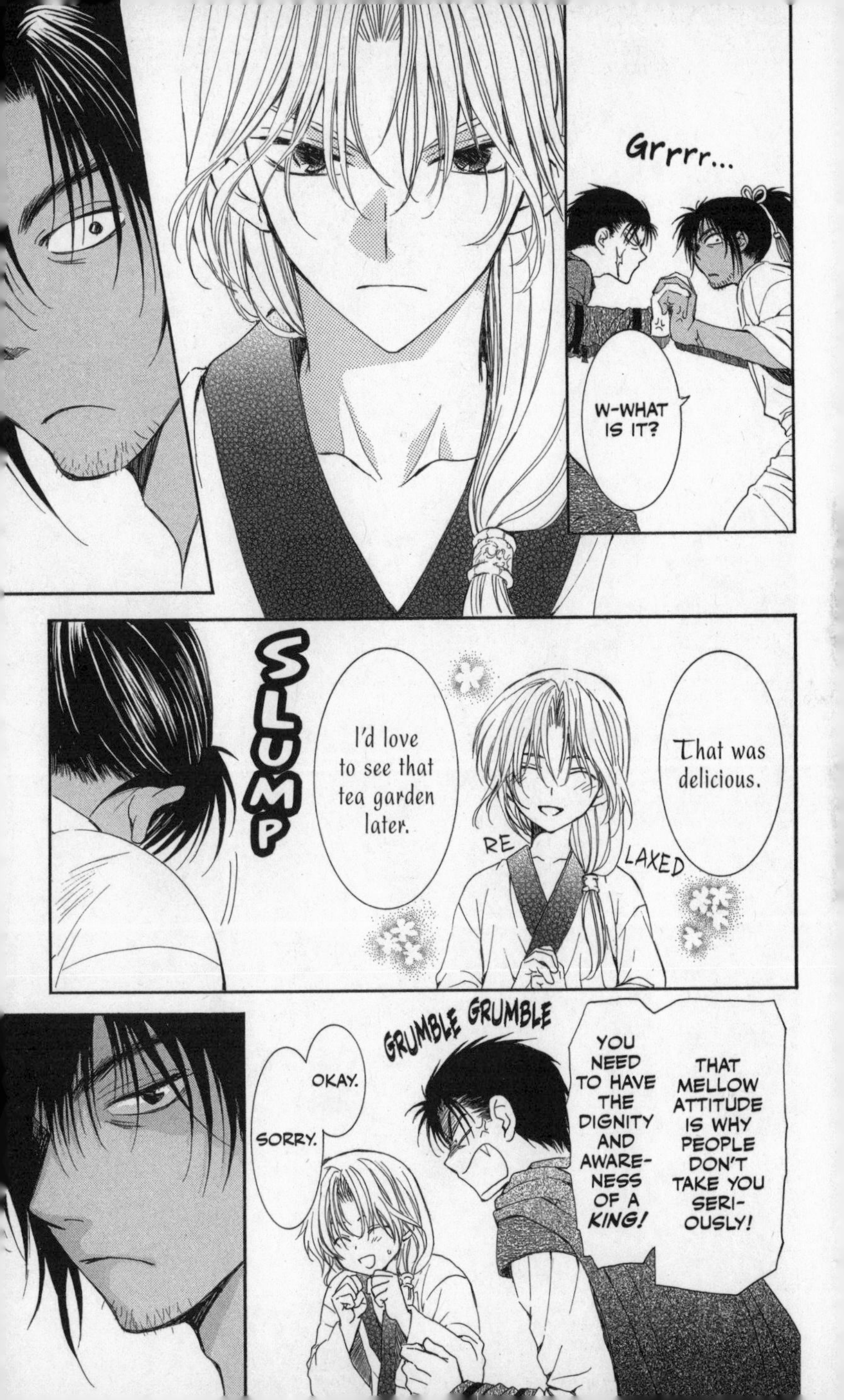
Grrrr...
W-WHAT IS IT?
That was delicious.
RE LAXED
I'd love to see that tea garden later.
SLUMP
THAT MELLOW ATTITUDE IS WHY PEOPLE DON'T TAKE YOU SERI-OUSLY!
YOU NEED TO HAVE THE DIGNITY AND AWARE-NESS OF A KING!
GRUMBLE GRUMBLE
OKAY.
SORRY.

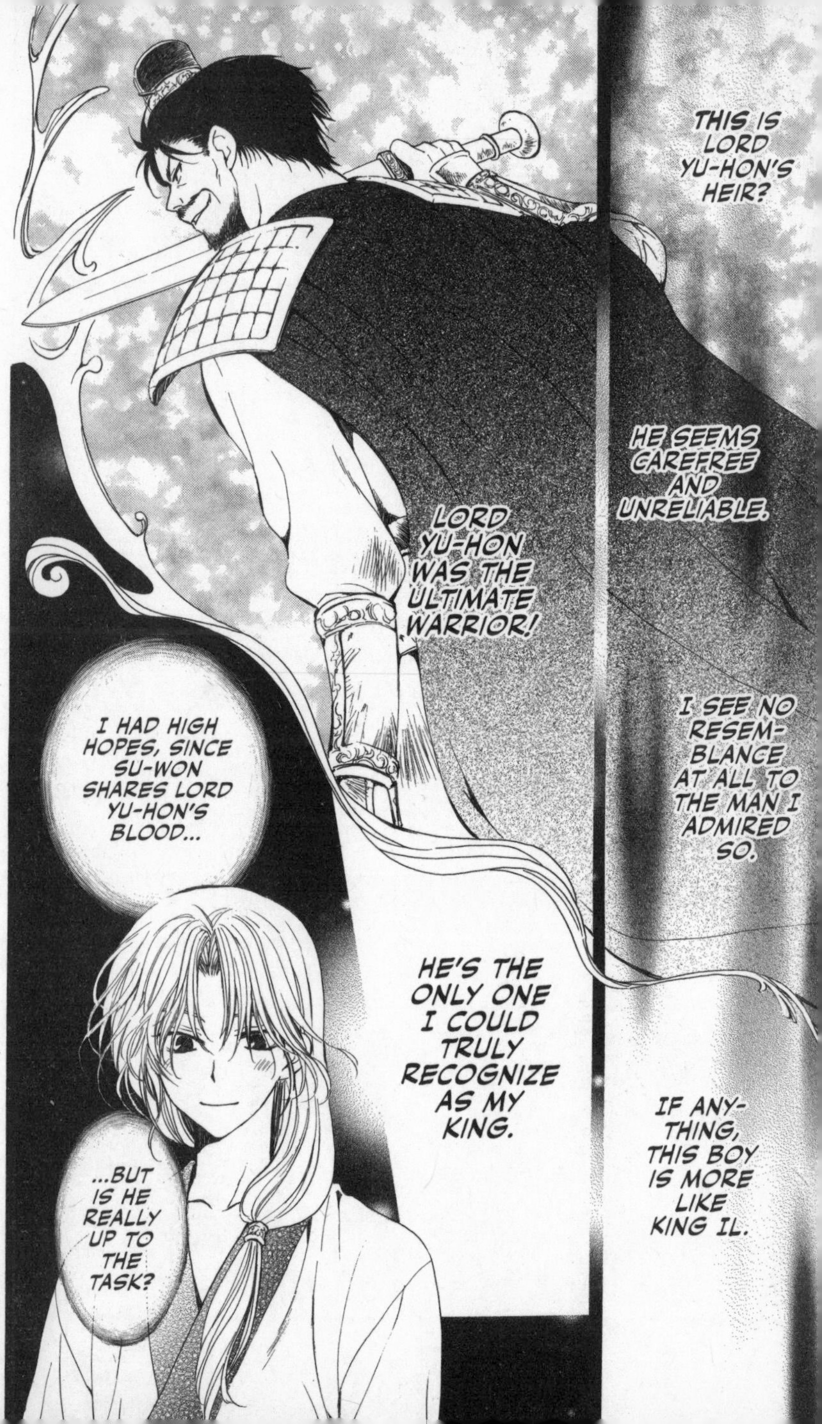
THIS IS LORD YU-HON'S HEIR?
HE SEEMS CAREFREE AND UNRELIABLE.
I SEE NO RESEM-BLANCE AT ALL TO THE MAN I ADMIRED SO.
IF ANY-THING, THIS BOY IS MORE LIKE KING IL.
LORD YU-HON WAS THE ULTIMATE WARRIOR!
HE'S THE ONLY ONE I COULD TRULY RECOGNIZE AS MY KING.
I HAD HIGH HOPES, SINCE SU-WON SHARES LORD YU-HON'S BLOOD...
...BUT IS HE REALLY UP TO THE TASK?

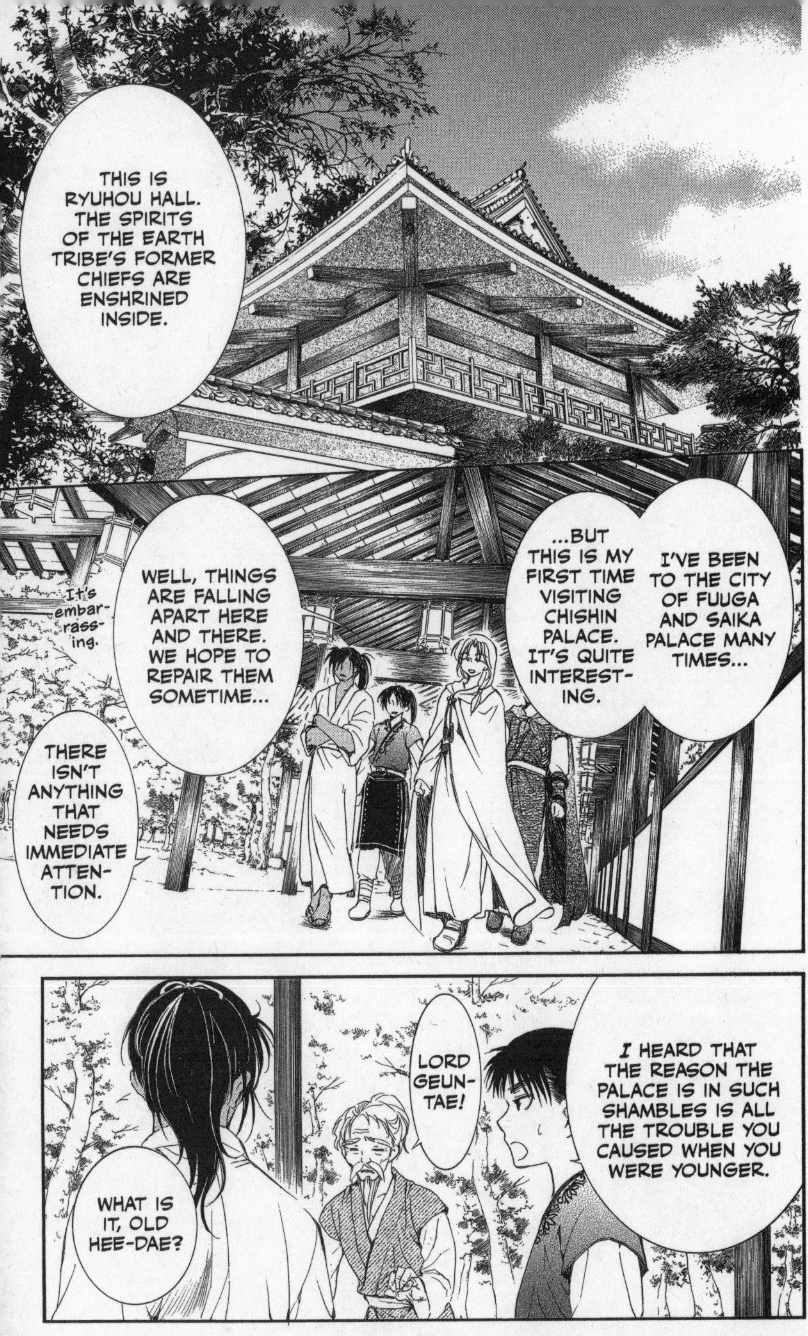
THIS IS RYUHOU HALL. THE SPIRITS OF THE EARTH TRIBE'S FORMER CHIEFS ARE ENSHRINED INSIDE.
I'VE BEEN TO THE CITY OF FUUGA AND SAIKA PALACE MANY TIMES...
...BUT THIS IS MY FIRST TIME VISITING CHISHIN PALACE. IT'S QUITE INTEREST-ING.
WELL, THINGS ARE FALLING APART HERE AND THERE. WE HOPE TO REPAIR THEM SOMETIME...
It's embar-rass-ing.
THERE ISN'T ANYTHING THAT NEEDS IMMEDIATE ATTEN-TION.
I HEARD THAT THE REASON THE PALACE IS IN SUCH SHAMBLES IS ALL THE TROUBLE YOU CAUSED WHEN YOU WERE YOUNGER.
LORD GEUN-TAE!
WHAT IS IT, OLD HEE-DAE?

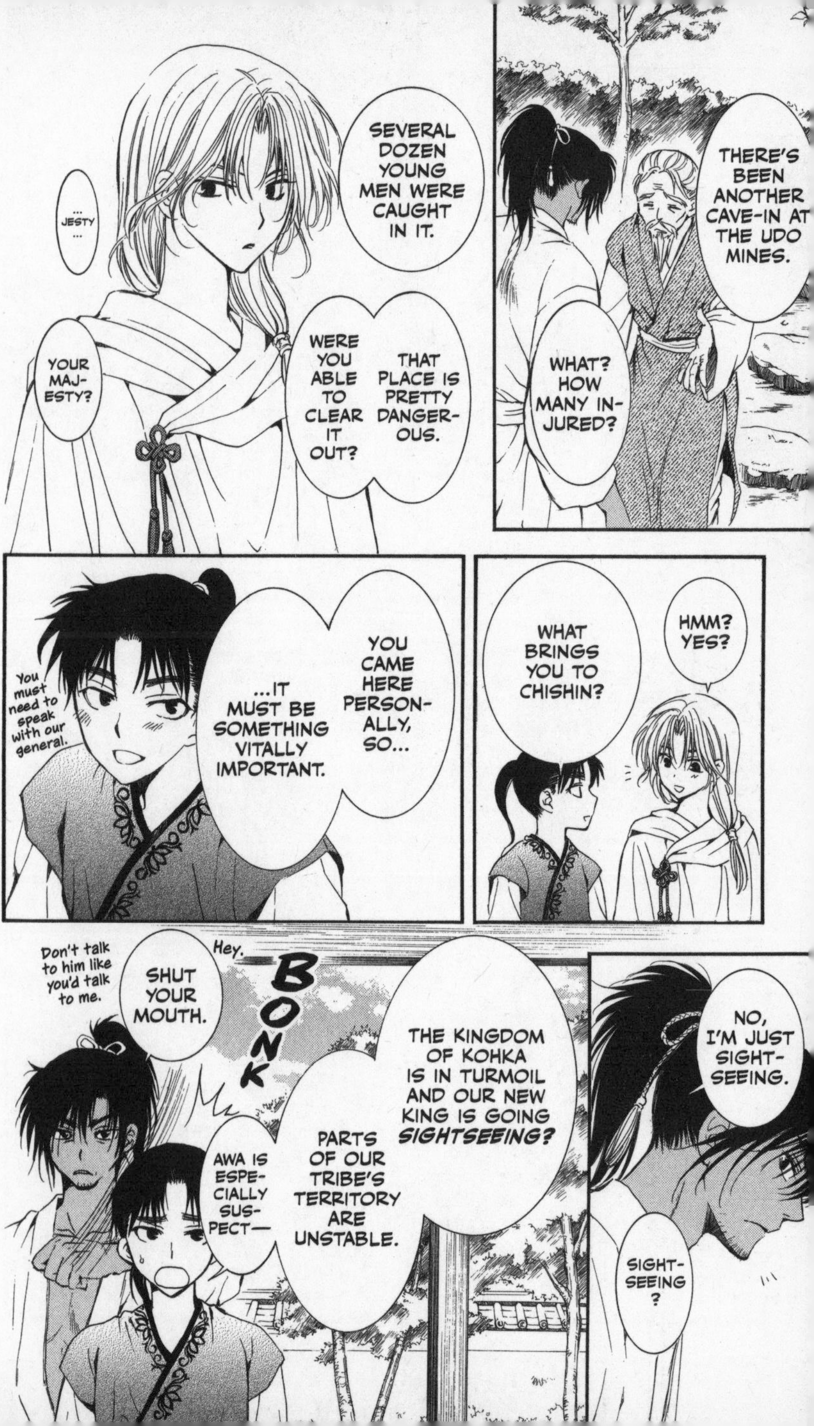
THERE'S BEEN ANOTHER CAVE-IN AT THE UDO MINES.
WHAT? HOW MANY INJURED?
SEVERAL DOZEN YOUNG MEN WERE CAUGHT IN IT.
...JESTY...
THAT PLACE IS PRETTY DANGEROUS.
WERE YOU ABLE TO CLEAR IT OUT?
YOUR MAJESTY?
HMM? YES?
WHAT BRINGS YOU TO CHISHIN?
YOU CAME HERE PERSONALLY, SO...
...IT MUST BE SOMETHING VITALLY IMPORTANT.
You must need to speak with our general.
NO, I'M JUST SIGHTSEEING.
SIGHTSEEING?
THE KINGDOM OF KOHKA IS IN TURMOIL AND OUR NEW KING IS GOING *SIGHTSEEING?*
BONK
Hey.
SHUT YOUR MOUTH.
Don't talk to him like you'd talk to me.
PARTS OF OUR TRIBE'S TERRITORY ARE UNSTABLE.
AWA IS ESPECIALLY SUSPECT—

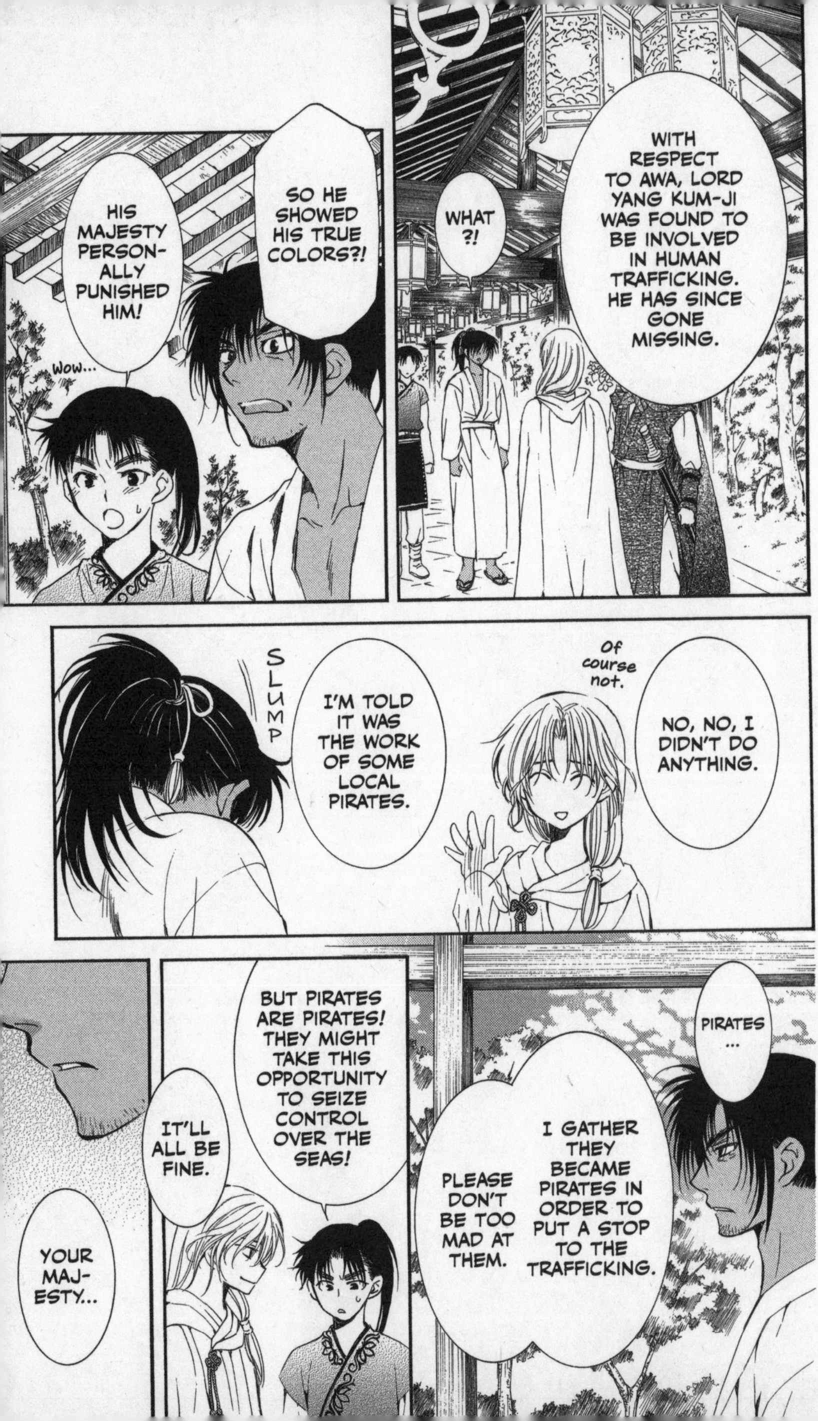
WITH RESPECT TO AWA, LORD YANG KUM-JI WAS FOUND TO BE INVOLVED IN HUMAN TRAFFICKING. HE HAS SINCE GONE MISSING.
WHAT?!
SO HE SHOWED HIS TRUE COLORS?!
HIS MAJESTY PERSON-ALLY PUNISHED HIM!
Wow...
NO, NO, I DIDN'T DO ANYTHING.
Of course not.
I'M TOLD IT WAS THE WORK OF SOME LOCAL PIRATES.
SLUMP
PIRATES...
I GATHER THEY BECAME PIRATES IN ORDER TO PUT A STOP TO THE TRAFFICKING.
PLEASE DON'T BE TOO MAD AT THEM.
BUT PIRATES ARE PIRATES! THEY MIGHT TAKE THIS OPPORTUNITY TO SEIZE CONTROL OVER THE SEAS!
IT'LL ALL BE FINE.
YOUR MAJ-ESTY...

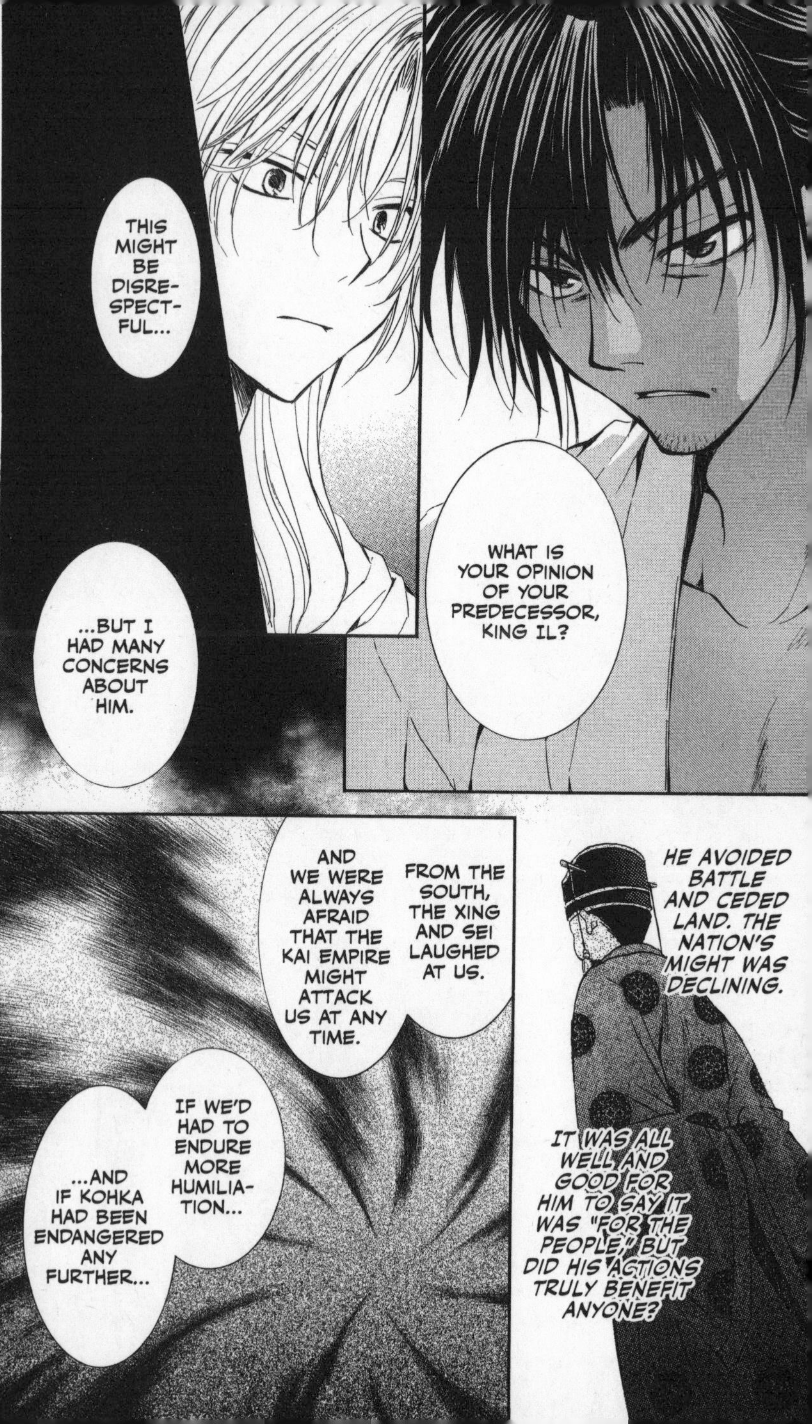
WHAT IS YOUR OPINION OF YOUR PREDECESSOR, KING IL?
THIS MIGHT BE DISRESPECTFUL...
...BUT I HAD MANY CONCERNS ABOUT HIM.
HE AVOIDED BATTLE AND CEDED LAND. THE NATION'S MIGHT WAS DECLINING.
IT WAS ALL WELL AND GOOD FOR HIM TO SAY IT WAS "FOR THE PEOPLE," BUT DID HIS ACTIONS TRULY BENEFIT ANYONE?
FROM THE SOUTH, THE XING AND SEI LAUGHED AT US.
AND WE WERE ALWAYS AFRAID THAT THE KAI EMPIRE MIGHT ATTACK US AT ANY TIME.
IF WE'D HAD TO ENDURE MORE HUMILIATION...
...AND IF KOHKA HAD BEEN ENDANGERED ANY FURTHER...

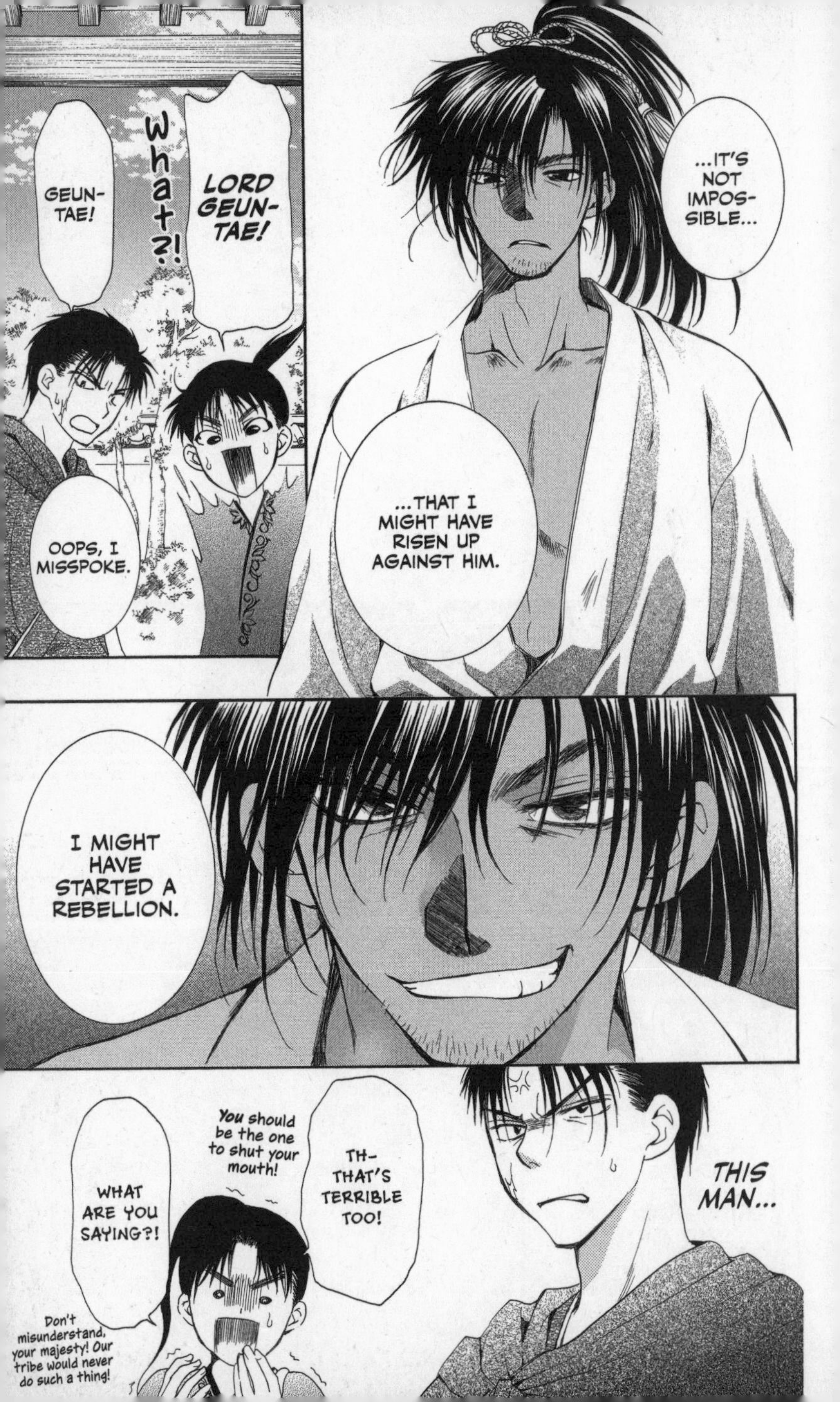
...IT'S NOT IMPOSSIBLE...
...THAT I MIGHT HAVE RISEN UP AGAINST HIM.
LORD GEUN-TAE!
What?!
GEUN-TAE!
OOPS, I MISSPOKE.
I MIGHT HAVE STARTED A REBELLION.
THIS MAN...
TH-THAT'S TERRIBLE TOO!
You should be the one to shut your mouth!
WHAT ARE YOU SAYING?!
Don't misunderstand, your majesty! Our tribe would never do such a thing!

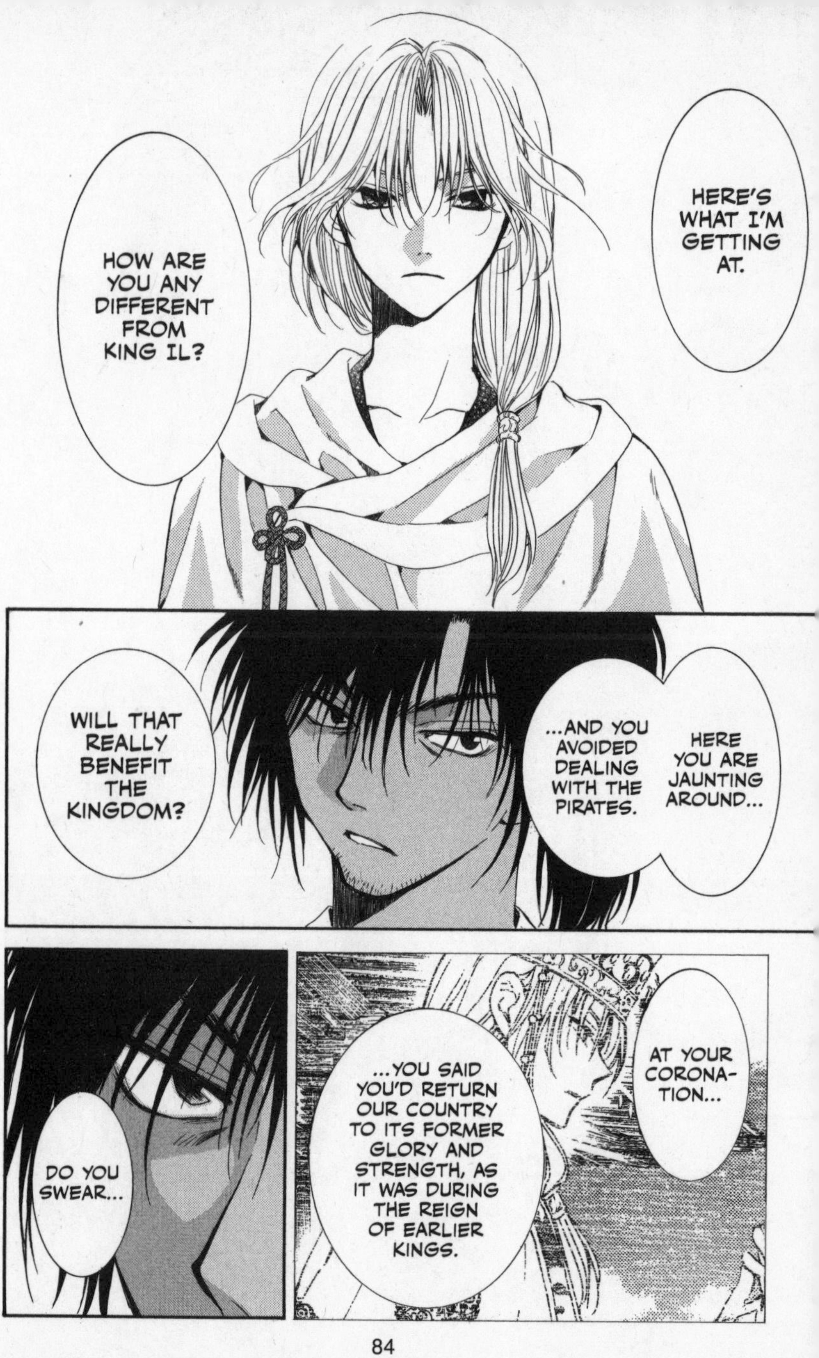
HERE'S WHAT I'M GETTING AT.
HOW ARE YOU ANY DIFFERENT FROM KING IL?
HERE YOU ARE JAUNTING AROUND...
...AND YOU AVOIDED DEALING WITH THE PIRATES.
WILL THAT REALLY BENEFIT THE KINGDOM?
AT YOUR CORONATION...
...YOU SAID YOU'D RETURN OUR COUNTRY TO ITS FORMER GLORY AND STRENGTH, AS IT WAS DURING THE REIGN OF EARLIER KINGS.
DO YOU SWEAR...

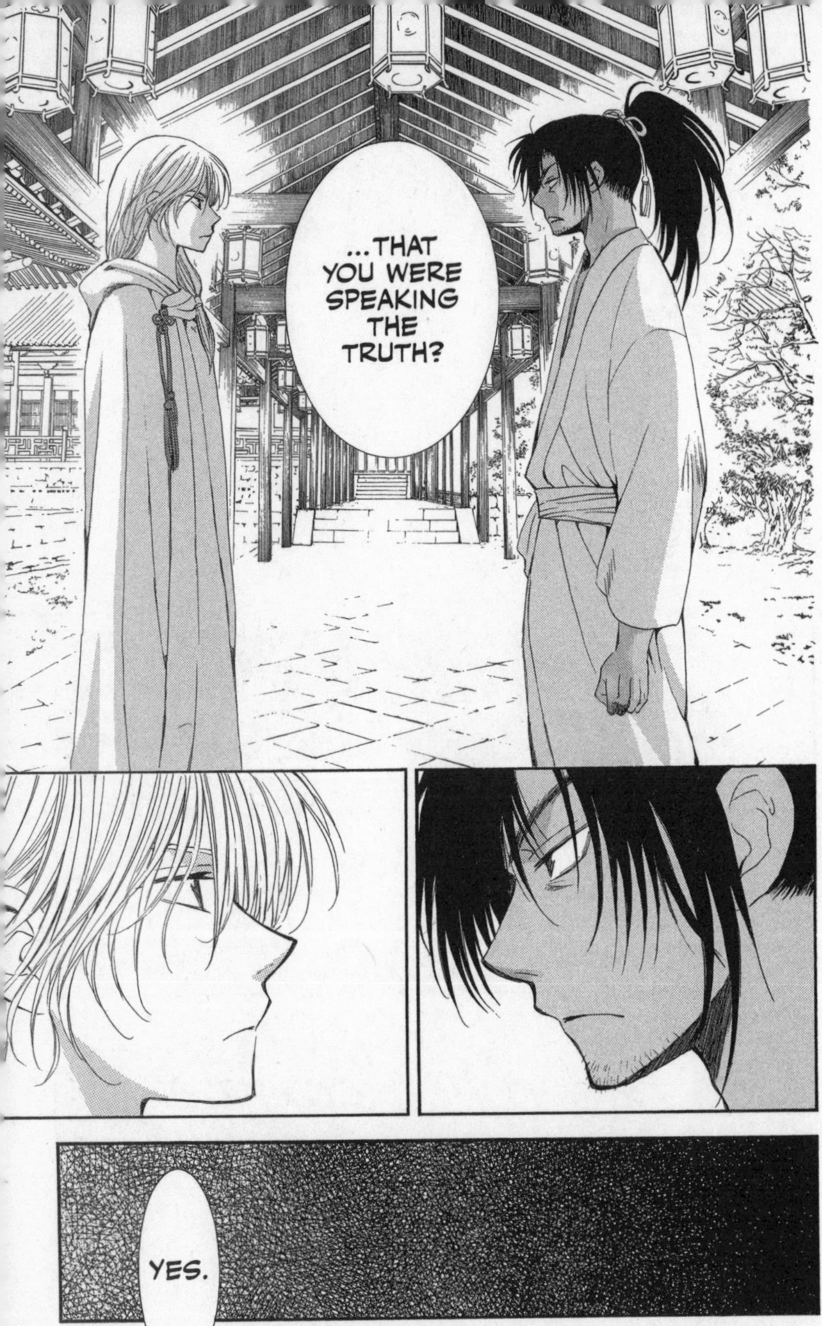
...THAT YOU WERE SPEAKING THE TRUTH?
YES.

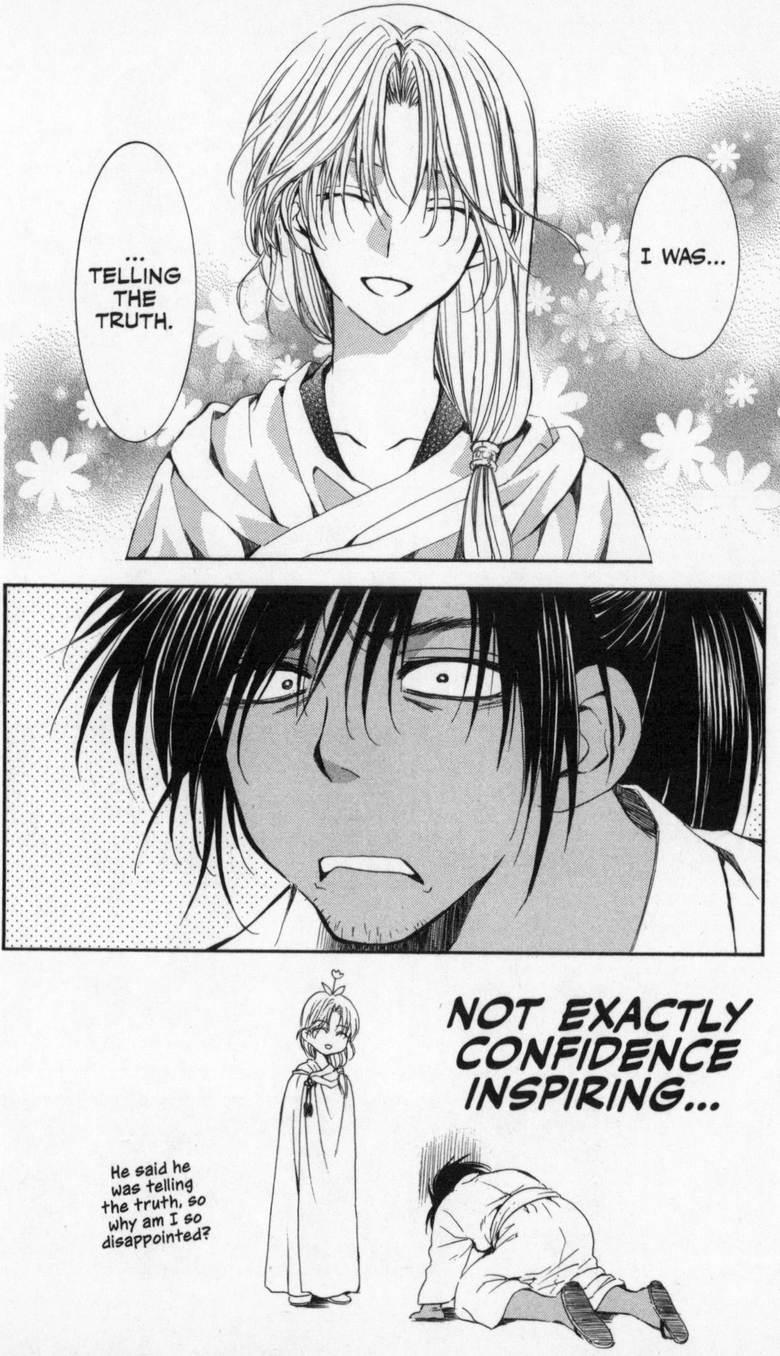
I WAS...
... TELLING THE TRUTH.
NOT EXACTLY CONFIDENCE INSPIRING...
He said he was telling the truth, so why am I so disappointed?

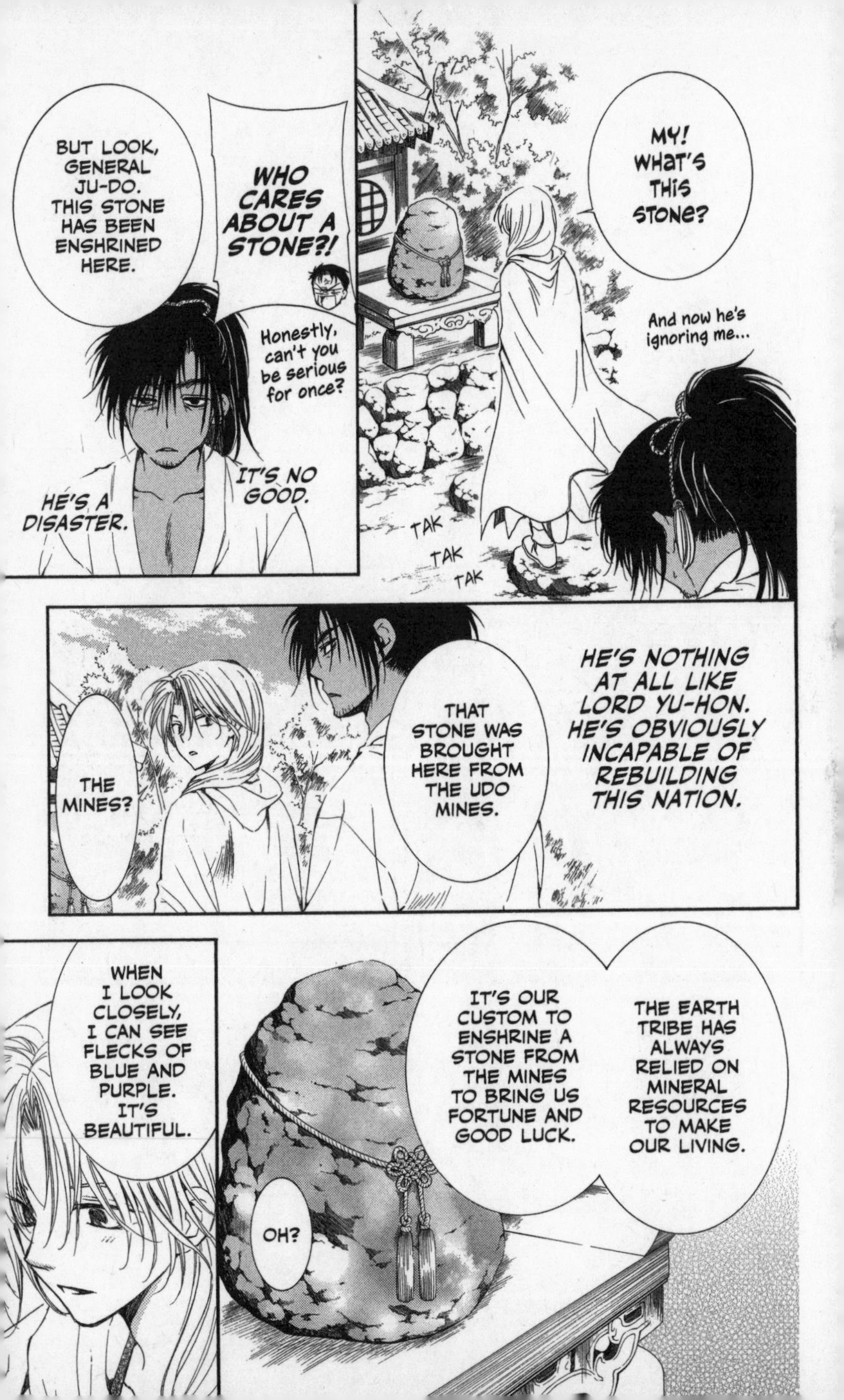
MY! WHAT'S THIS STONE?
And now he's ignoring me...
TAK
TAK
TAK
WHO CARES ABOUT A STONE?!
BUT LOOK, GENERAL JU-DO. THIS STONE HAS BEEN ENSHRINED HERE.
Honestly, can't you be serious for once?
IT'S NO GOOD.
HE'S A DISASTER.
HE'S NOTHING AT ALL LIKE LORD YU-HON. HE'S OBVIOUSLY INCAPABLE OF REBUILDING THIS NATION.
THAT STONE WAS BROUGHT HERE FROM THE UDO MINES.
THE MINES?
THE EARTH TRIBE HAS ALWAYS RELIED ON MINERAL RESOURCES TO MAKE OUR LIVING.
IT'S OUR CUSTOM TO ENSHRINE A STONE FROM THE MINES TO BRING US FORTUNE AND GOOD LUCK.
OH?
WHEN I LOOK CLOSELY, I CAN SEE FLECKS OF BLUE AND PURPLE. IT'S BEAUTIFUL.

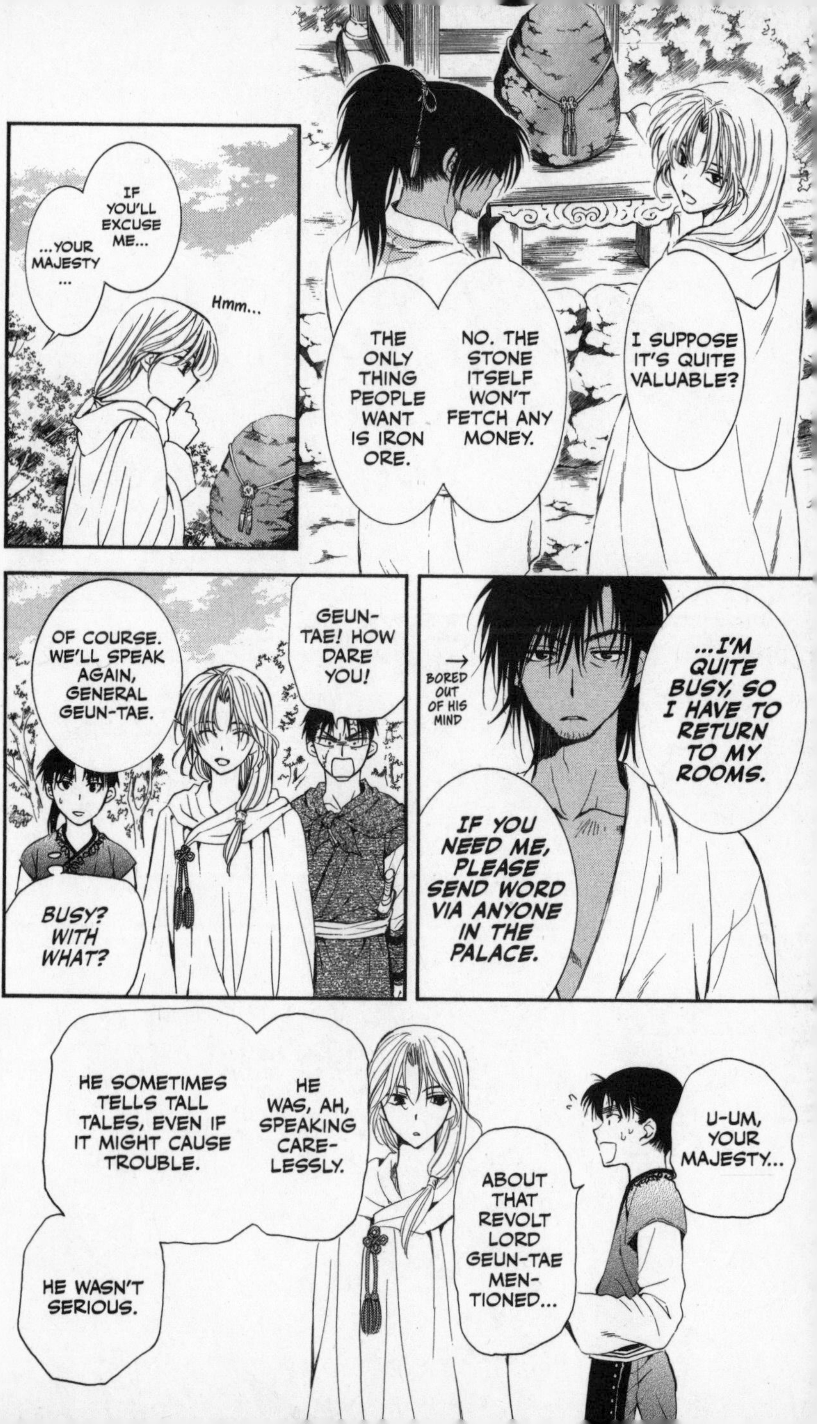

I SUPPOSE IT'S QUITE VALUABLE?
NO. THE STONE ITSELF WON'T FETCH ANY MONEY.
THE ONLY THING PEOPLE WANT IS IRON ORE.
Hmm...
IF YOU'LL EXCUSE ME... ...YOUR MAJESTY ...
...I'M QUITE BUSY, SO I HAVE TO RETURN TO MY ROOMS.
→ BORED OUT OF HIS MIND
IF YOU NEED ME, PLEASE SEND WORD VIA ANYONE IN THE PALACE.
GEUN-TAE! HOW DARE YOU!
OF COURSE. WE'LL SPEAK AGAIN, GENERAL GEUN-TAE.
BUSY? WITH WHAT?
U-UM, YOUR MAJESTY...
ABOUT THAT REVOLT LORD GEUN-TAE MEN-TIONED...
HE WAS, AH, SPEAKING CARE-LESSLY.
HE SOMETIMES TELLS TALL TALES, EVEN IF IT MIGHT CAUSE TROUBLE.
HE WASN'T SERIOUS.

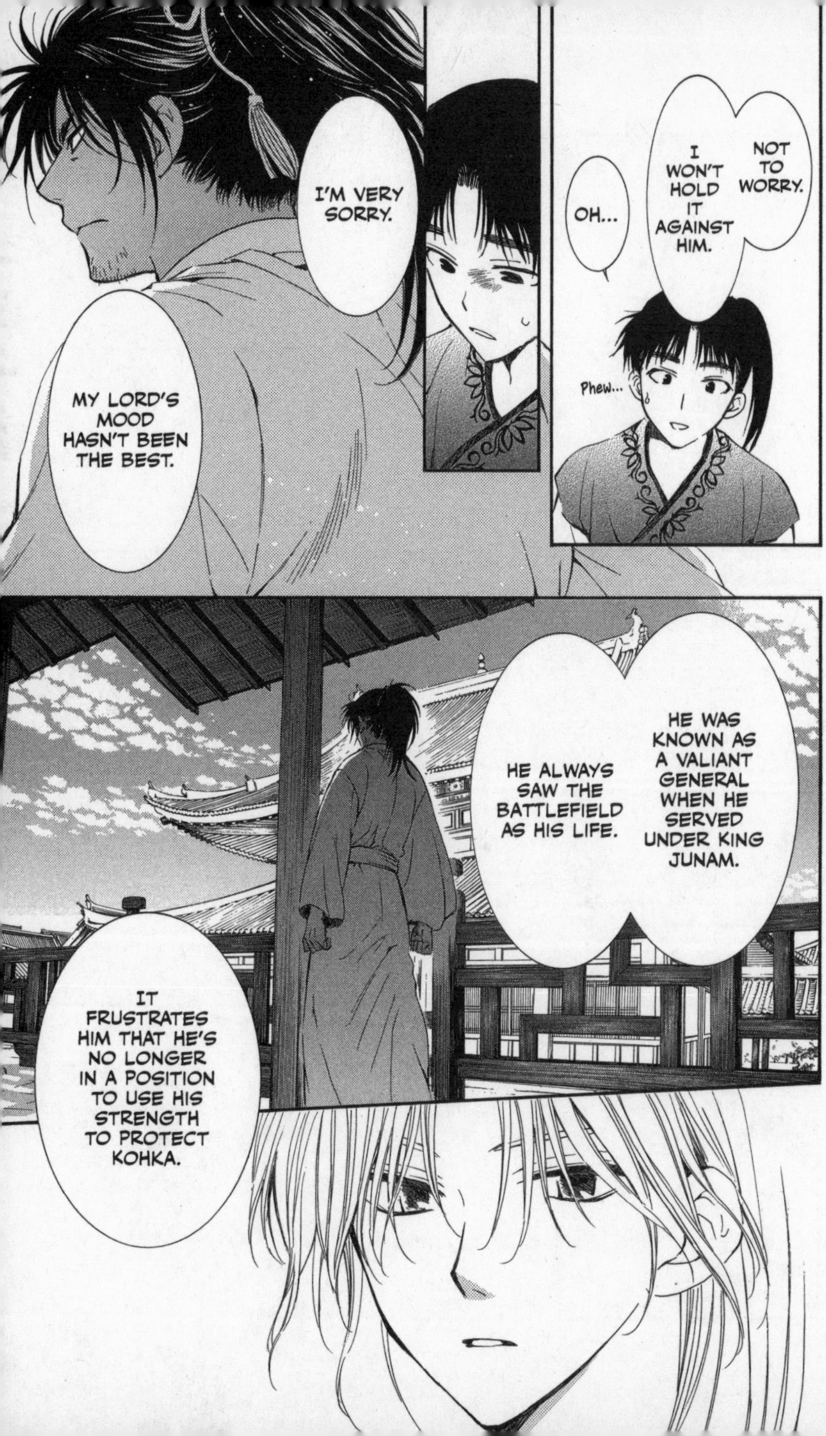
NOT TO WORRY.
I WON'T HOLD IT AGAINST HIM.
OH...
Phew...
I'M VERY SORRY.
MY LORD'S MOOD HASN'T BEEN THE BEST.
HE WAS KNOWN AS A VALIANT GENERAL WHEN HE SERVED UNDER KING JUNAM.
HE ALWAYS SAW THE BATTLEFIELD AS HIS LIFE.
IT FRUSTRATES HIM THAT HE'S NO LONGER IN A POSITION TO USE HIS STRENGTH TO PROTECT KOHKA.

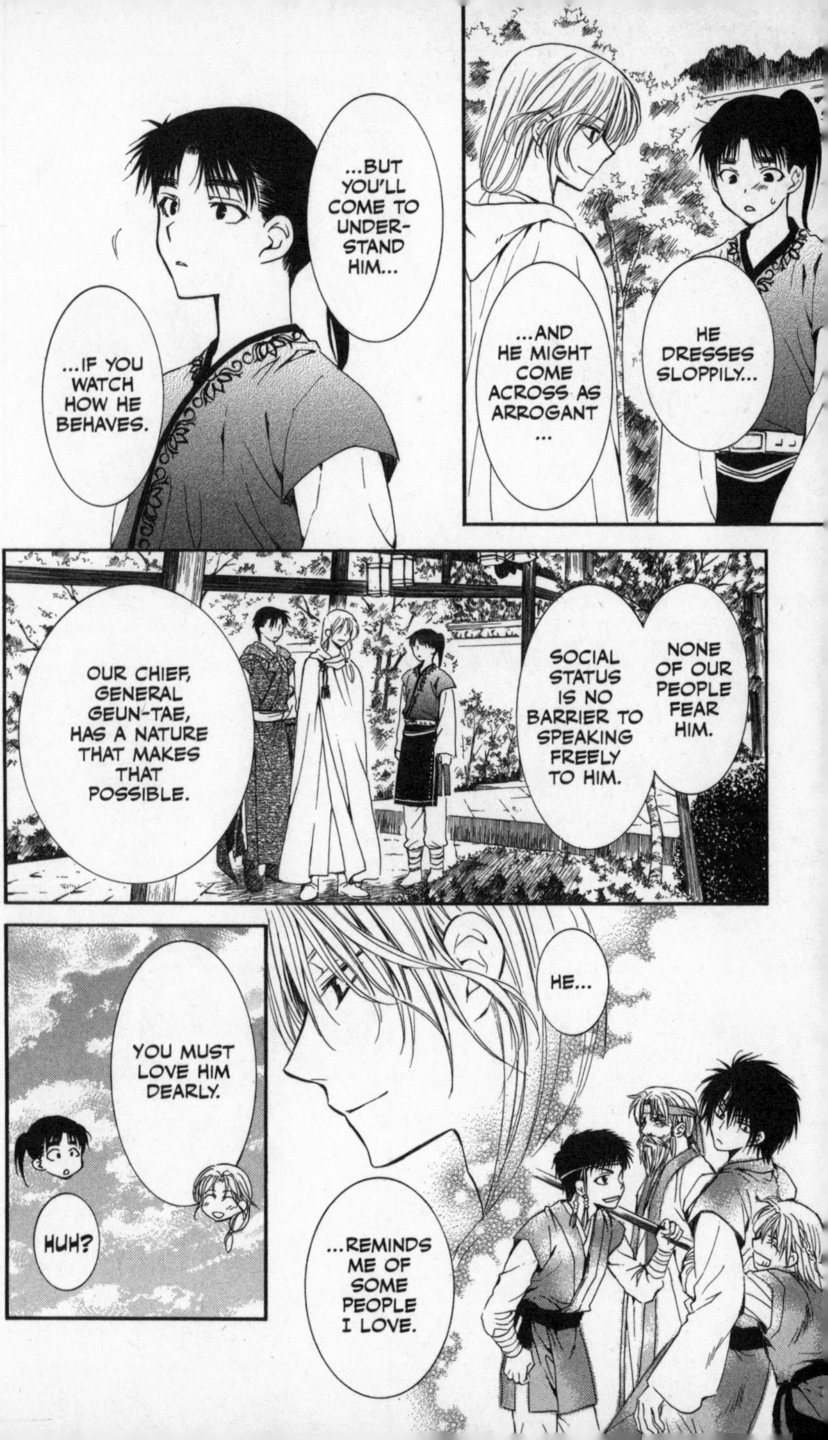
HE DRESSES SLOPPILY...
...AND HE MIGHT COME ACROSS AS ARROGANT...
...BUT YOU'LL COME TO UNDER-STAND HIM...
...IF YOU WATCH HOW HE BEHAVES.
NONE OF OUR PEOPLE FEAR HIM.
SOCIAL STATUS IS NO BARRIER TO SPEAKING FREELY TO HIM.
OUR CHIEF, GENERAL GEUN-TAE, HAS A NATURE THAT MAKES THAT POSSIBLE.
HE...
...REMINDS ME OF SOME PEOPLE I LOVE.
YOU MUST LOVE HIM DEARLY.
HUH?

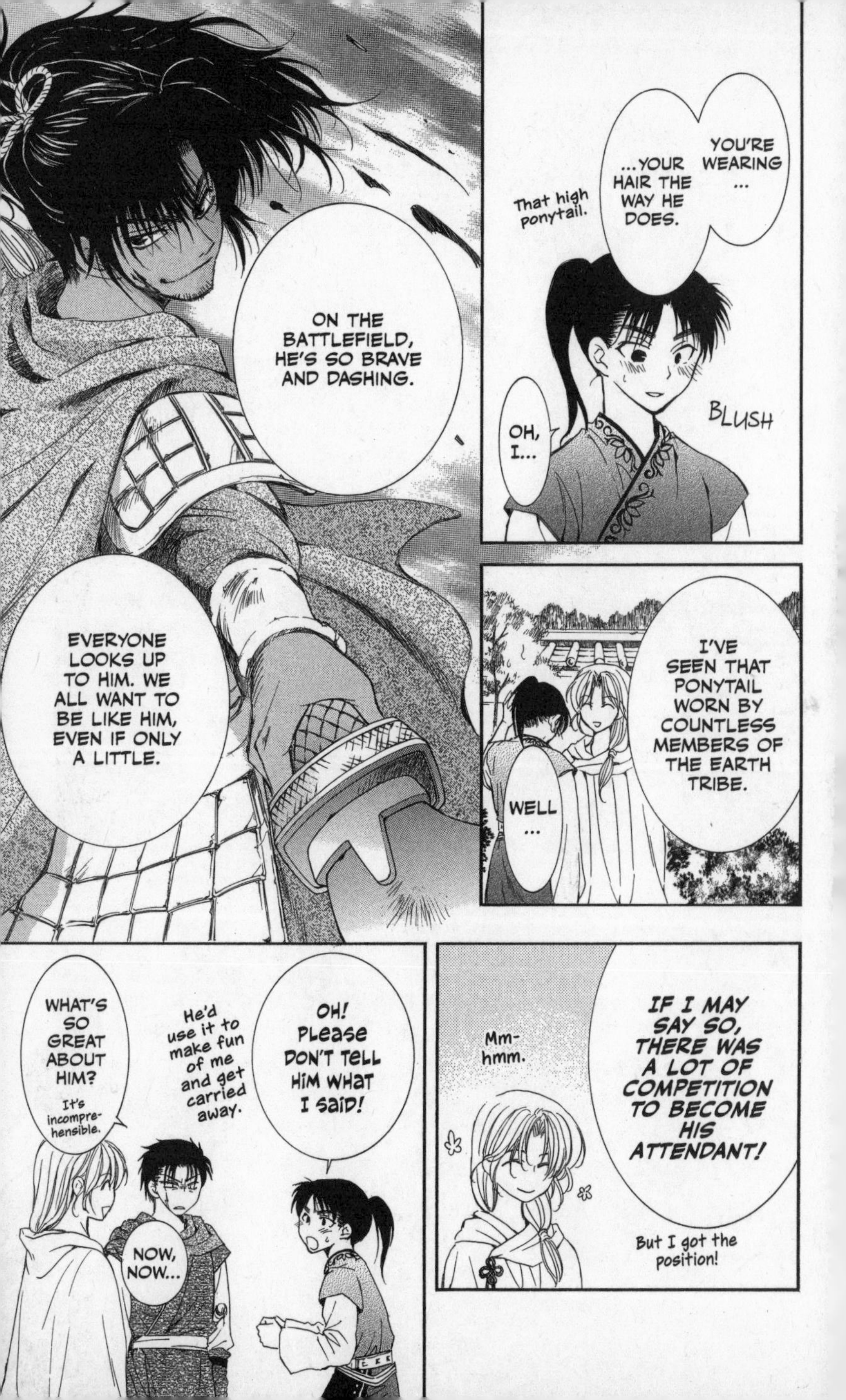
YOU'RE WEARING ...
...YOUR HAIR THE WAY HE DOES.
That high ponytail.
OH, I...
BLUSH
I'VE SEEN THAT PONYTAIL WORN BY COUNTLESS MEMBERS OF THE EARTH TRIBE.
WELL ...
ON THE BATTLEFIELD, HE'S SO BRAVE AND DASHING.
EVERYONE LOOKS UP TO HIM. WE ALL WANT TO BE LIKE HIM, EVEN IF ONLY A LITTLE.
IF I MAY SAY SO, THERE WAS A LOT OF COMPETITION TO BECOME HIS ATTENDANT!
Mm-hmm.
But I got the position!
OH! PLEASE DON'T TELL HIM WHAT I SAID!
He'd use it to make fun of me and get carried away.
WHAT'S SO GREAT ABOUT HIM?
It's incomprehensible.
NOW, NOW...

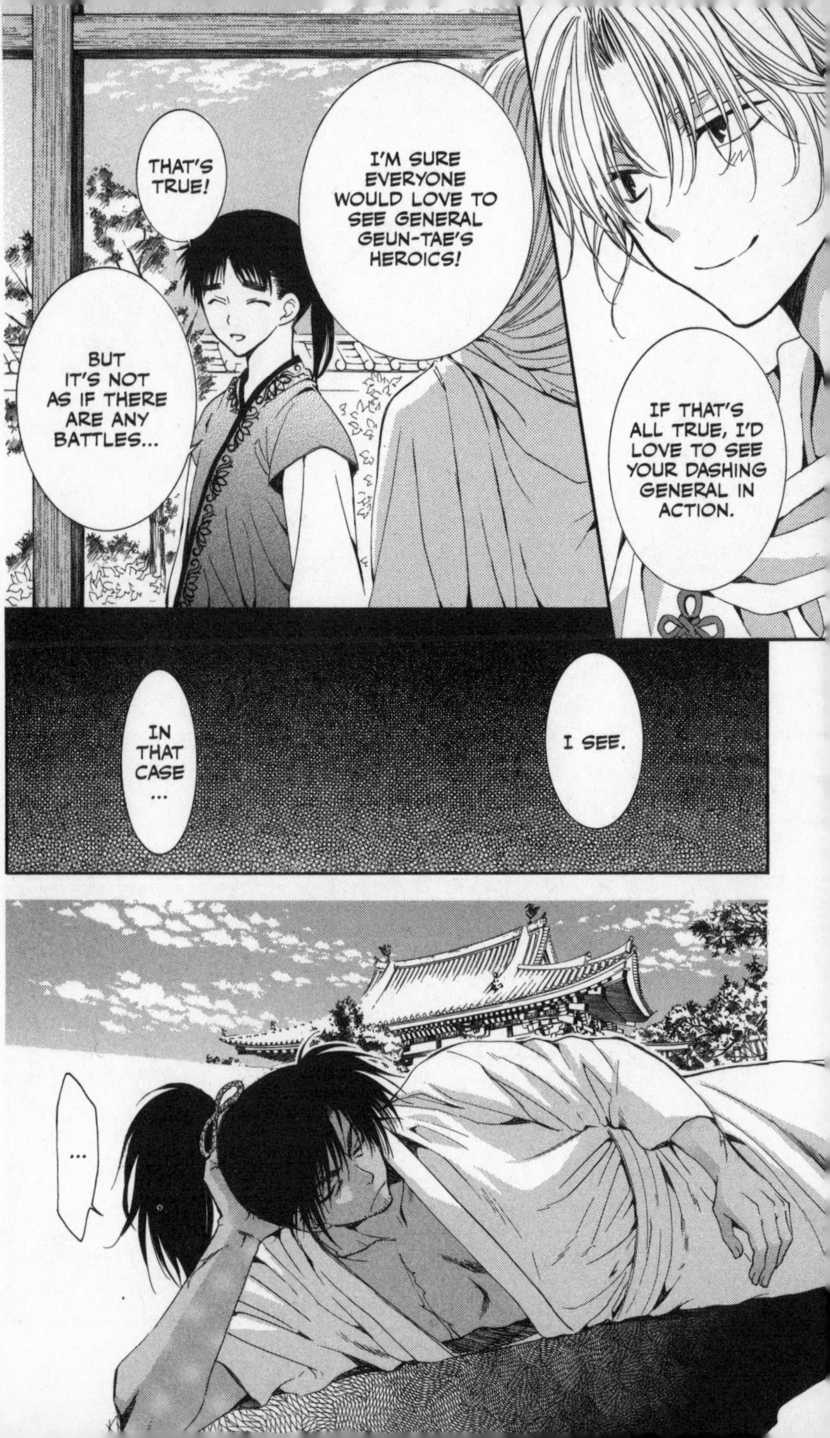
I'M SURE EVERYONE WOULD LOVE TO SEE GENERAL GEUN-TAE'S HEROICS!
THAT'S TRUE!
BUT IT'S NOT AS IF THERE ARE ANY BATTLES...
IF THAT'S ALL TRUE, I'D LOVE TO SEE YOUR DASHING GENERAL IN ACTION.
I SEE.
IN THAT CASE...
...

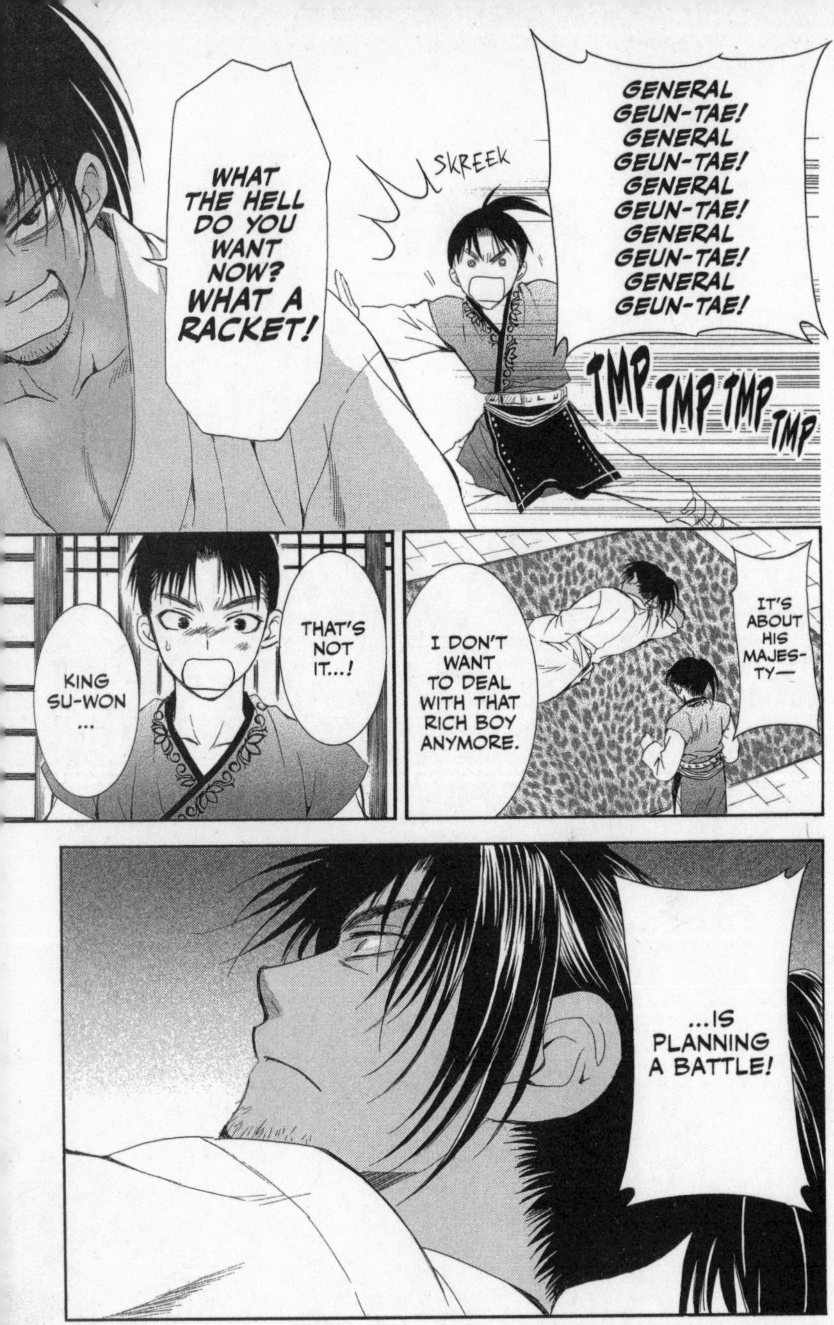
GENERAL GEUN-TAE! GENERAL GEUN-TAE! GENERAL GEUN-TAE! GENERAL GEUN-TAE! GENERAL GEUN-TAE!
SKREEK
TMP TMP TMP TMP
WHAT THE HELL DO YOU WANT NOW? WHAT A RACKET!
IT'S ABOUT HIS MAJES-TY—
I DON'T WANT TO DEAL WITH THAT RICH BOY ANYMORE.
THAT'S NOT IT...!
KING SU-WON ...
...IS PLANNING A BATTLE!

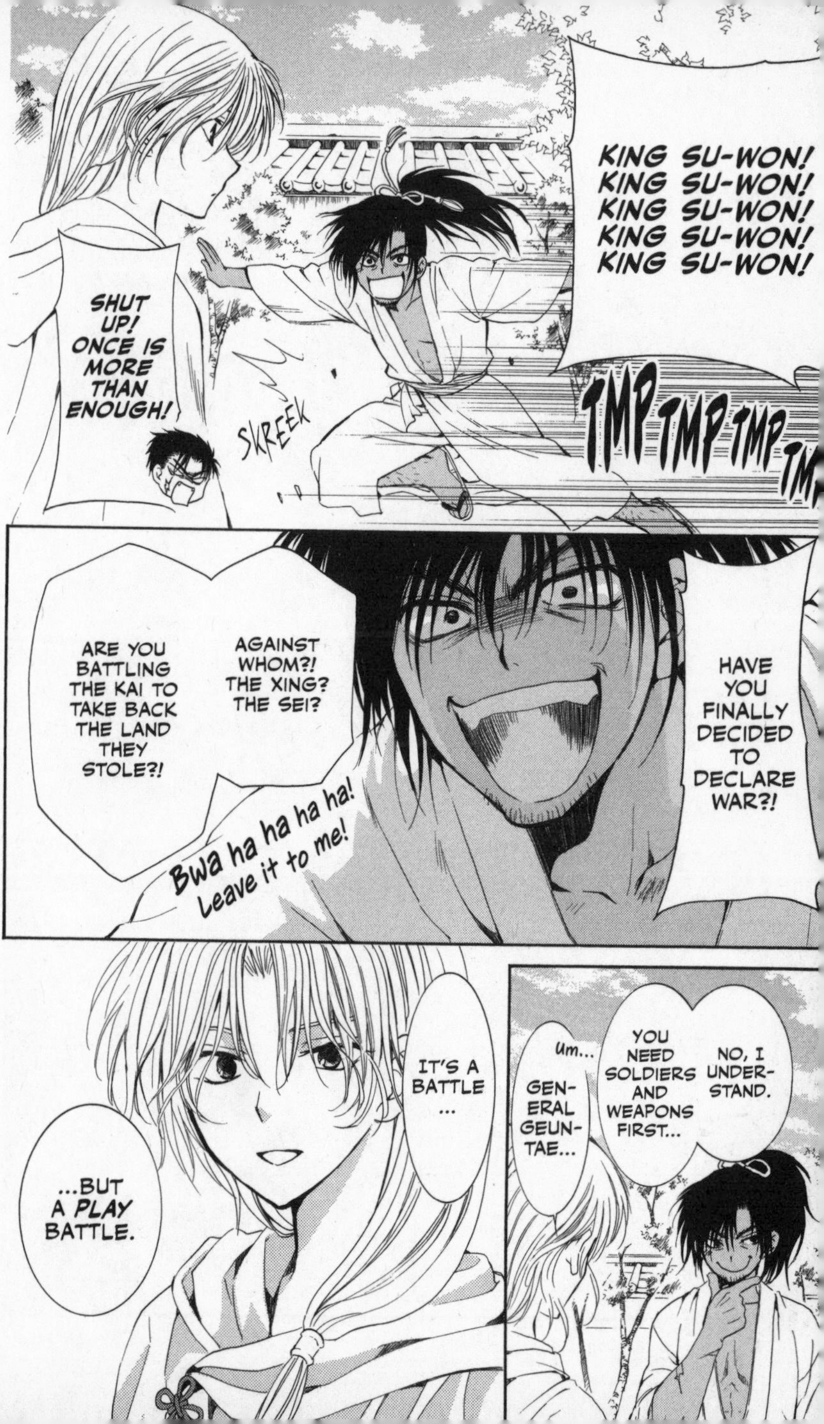
KING SU-WON! KING SU-WON! KING SU-WON! KING SU-WON! KING SU-WON!
TMP TMP TMP TMP
SKREEK
SHUT UP! ONCE IS MORE THAN ENOUGH!
HAVE YOU FINALLY DECIDED TO DECLARE WAR?!
AGAINST WHOM?! THE XING? THE SEI?
ARE YOU BATTLING THE KAI TO TAKE BACK THE LAND THEY STOLE?!
Bwa ha ha ha ha! Leave it to me!
NO, I UNDER-STAND.
YOU NEED SOLDIERS AND WEAPONS FIRST...
Um...
GEN-ERAL GEUN-TAE...
IT'S A BATTLE...
...BUT A PLAY BATTLE.

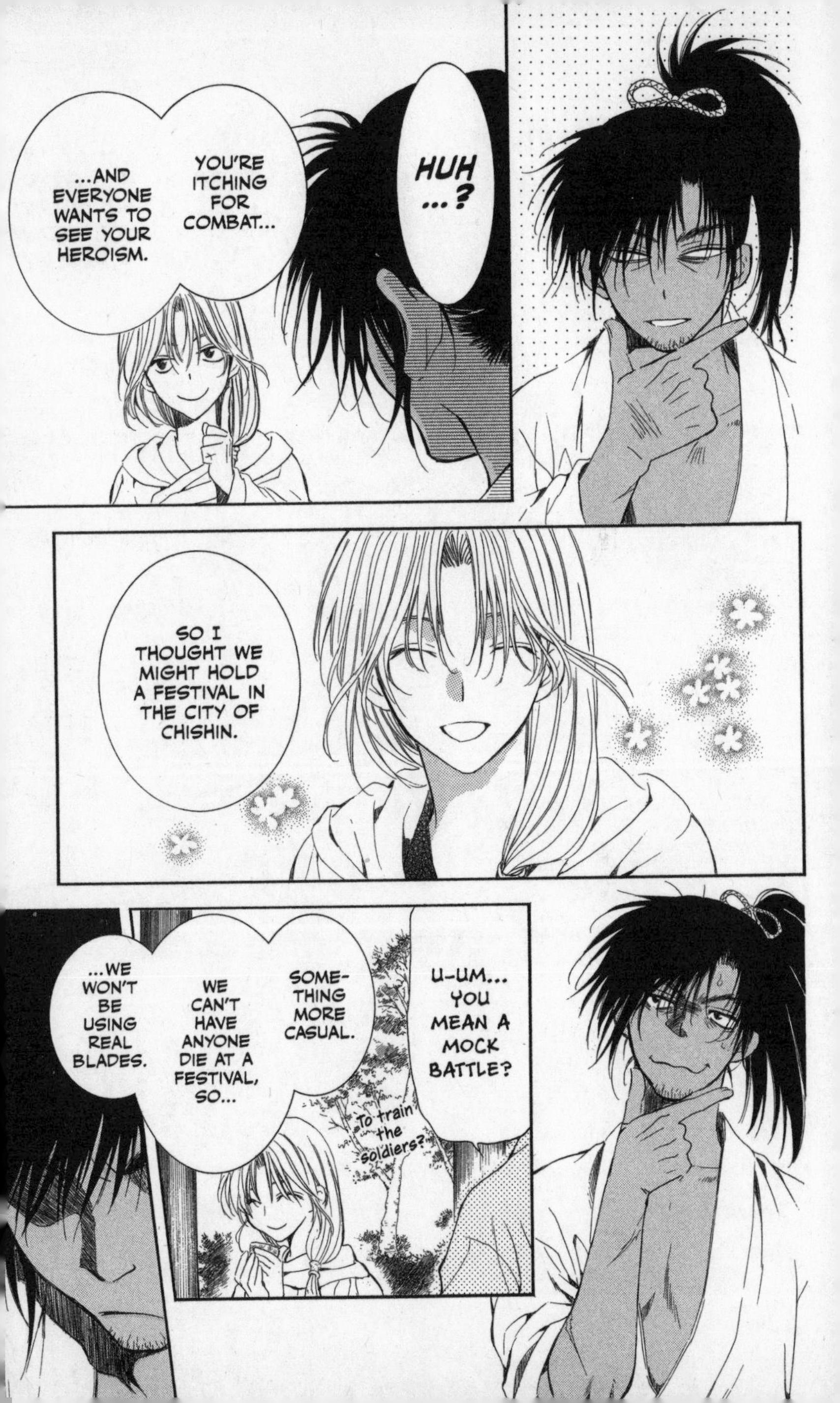
HUH ...?
YOU'RE ITCHING FOR COMBAT...
...AND EVERYONE WANTS TO SEE YOUR HEROISM.
SO I THOUGHT WE MIGHT HOLD A FESTIVAL IN THE CITY OF CHISHIN.
U-UM... YOU MEAN A MOCK BATTLE?
To train the soldiers?
SOME-THING MORE CASUAL.
WE CAN'T HAVE ANYONE DIE AT A FESTIVAL, SO...
...WE WON'T BE USING REAL BLADES.

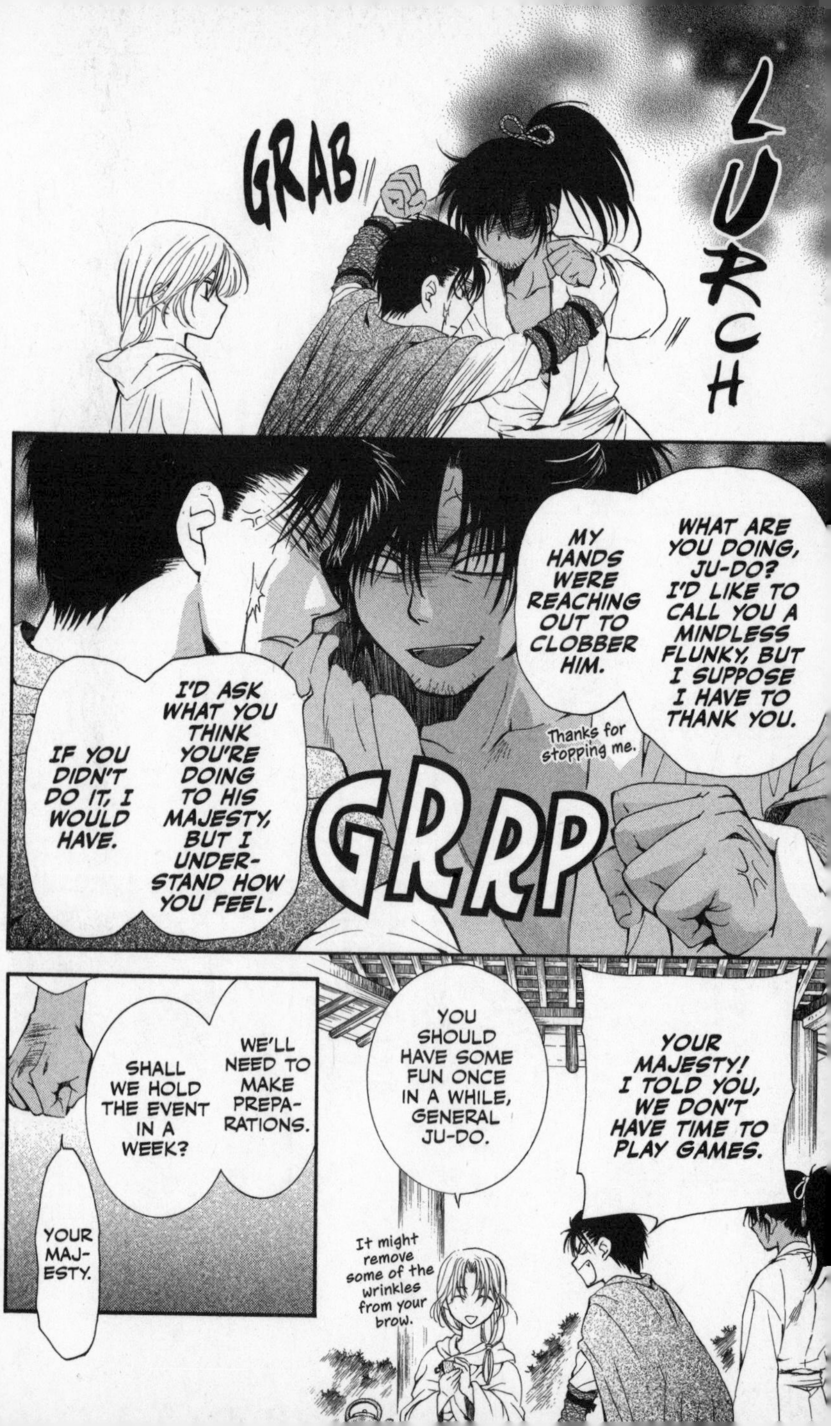
LURCH
GRAB
WHAT ARE YOU DOING, JU-DO? I'D LIKE TO CALL YOU A MINDLESS FLUNKY, BUT I SUPPOSE I HAVE TO THANK YOU.
MY HANDS WERE REACHING OUT TO CLOBBER HIM.
Thanks for stopping me.
GRRP
I'D ASK WHAT YOU THINK YOU'RE DOING TO HIS MAJESTY, BUT I UNDER-STAND HOW YOU FEEL.
IF YOU DIDN'T DO IT, I WOULD HAVE.
YOUR MAJESTY! I TOLD YOU, WE DON'T HAVE TIME TO PLAY GAMES.
YOU SHOULD HAVE SOME FUN ONCE IN A WHILE, GENERAL JU-DO.
It might remove some of the wrinkles from your brow.
WE'LL NEED TO MAKE PREPA-RATIONS.
SHALL WE HOLD THE EVENT IN A WEEK?
YOUR MAJ-ESTY.

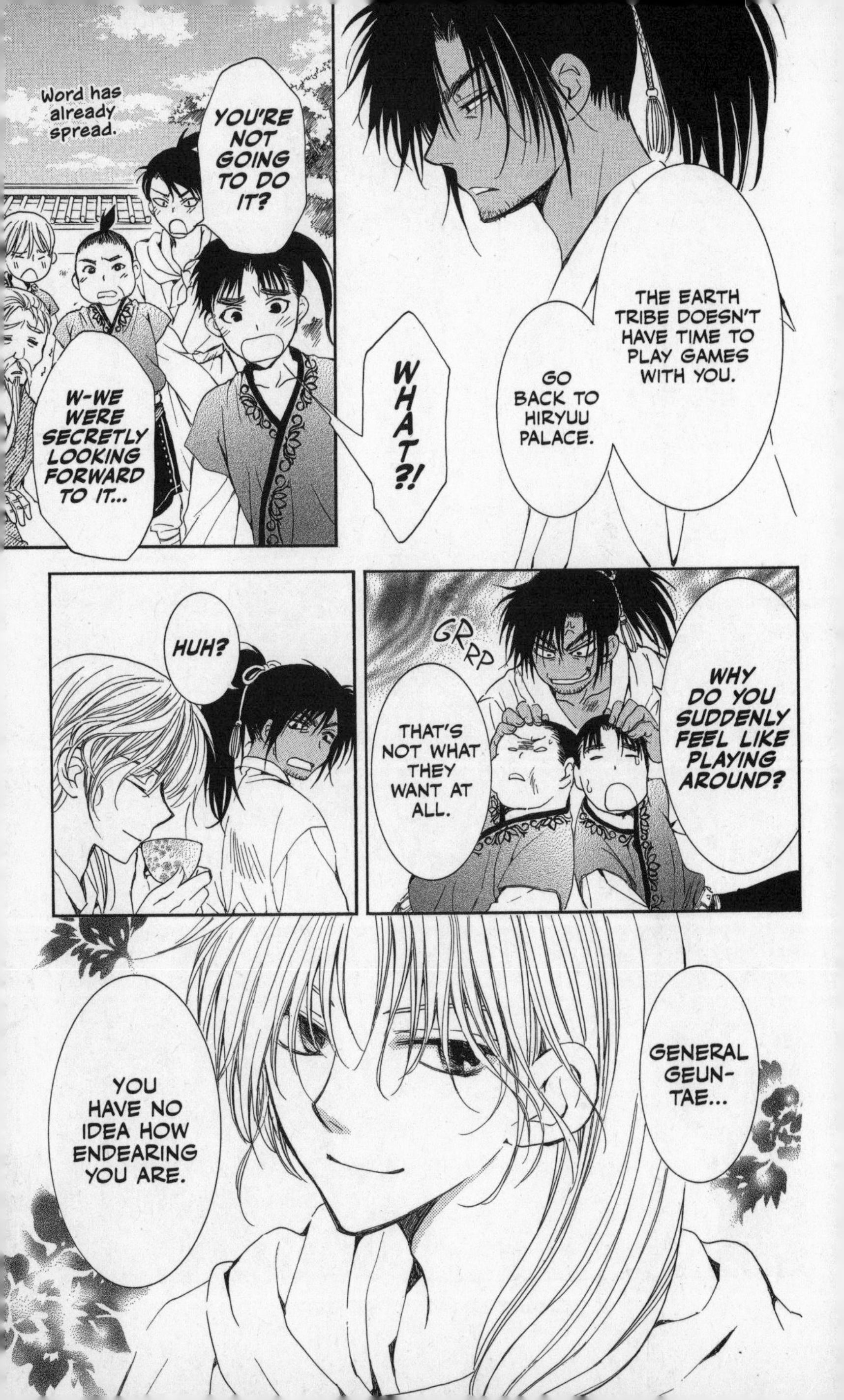
THE EARTH TRIBE DOESN'T HAVE TIME TO PLAY GAMES WITH YOU.
GO BACK TO HIRYUU PALACE.
WHAT?!
YOU'RE NOT GOING TO DO IT?
Word has already spread.
W-WE WERE SECRETLY LOOKING FORWARD TO IT...
WHY DO YOU SUDDENLY FEEL LIKE PLAYING AROUND?
GRRP
THAT'S NOT WHAT THEY WANT AT ALL.
HUH?
GENERAL GEUN-TAE...
YOU HAVE NO IDEA HOW ENDEARING YOU ARE.

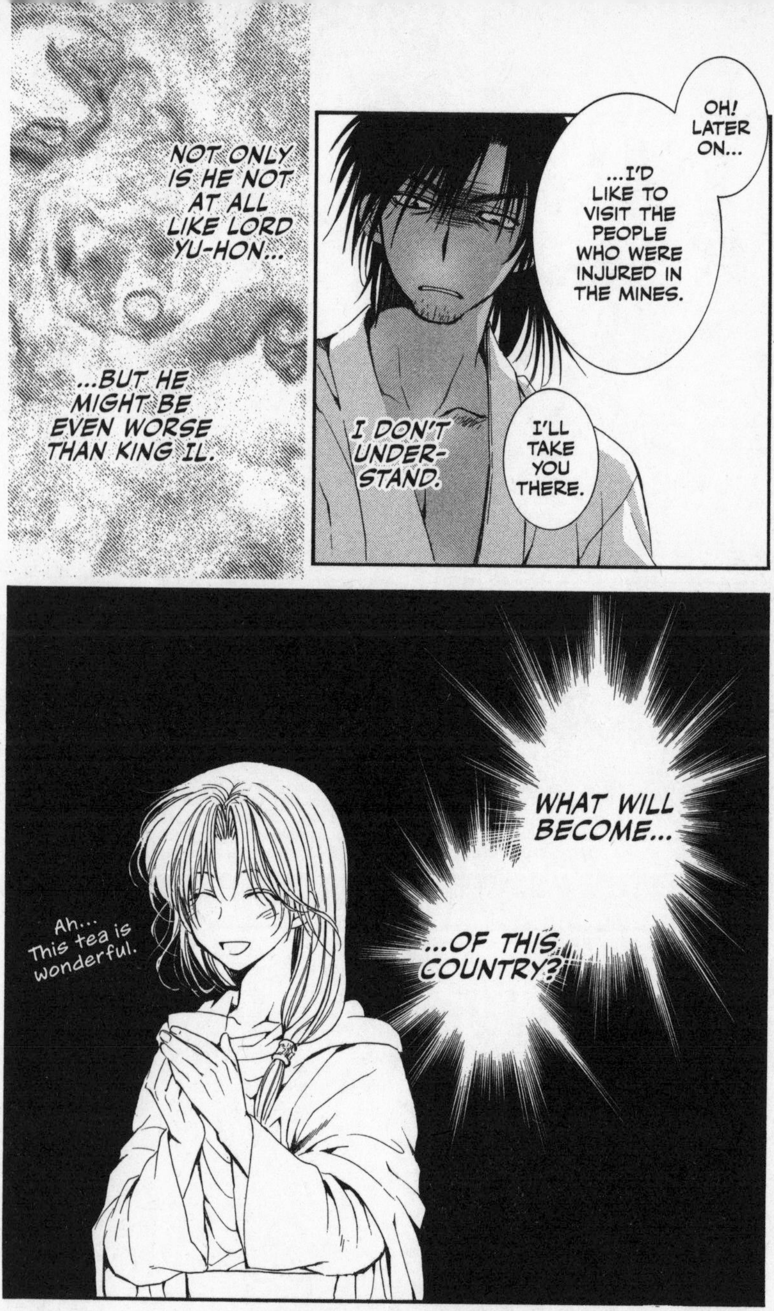
OH! LATER ON...
...I'D LIKE TO VISIT THE PEOPLE WHO WERE INJURED IN THE MINES.
I'LL TAKE YOU THERE.
I DON'T UNDER-STAND.
NOT ONLY IS HE NOT AT ALL LIKE LORD YU-HON...
...BUT HE MIGHT BE EVEN WORSE THAN KING IL.
WHAT WILL BECOME...
...OF THIS COUNTRY?
Ah... This tea is wonderful.

CHAPTER 44 / THE END

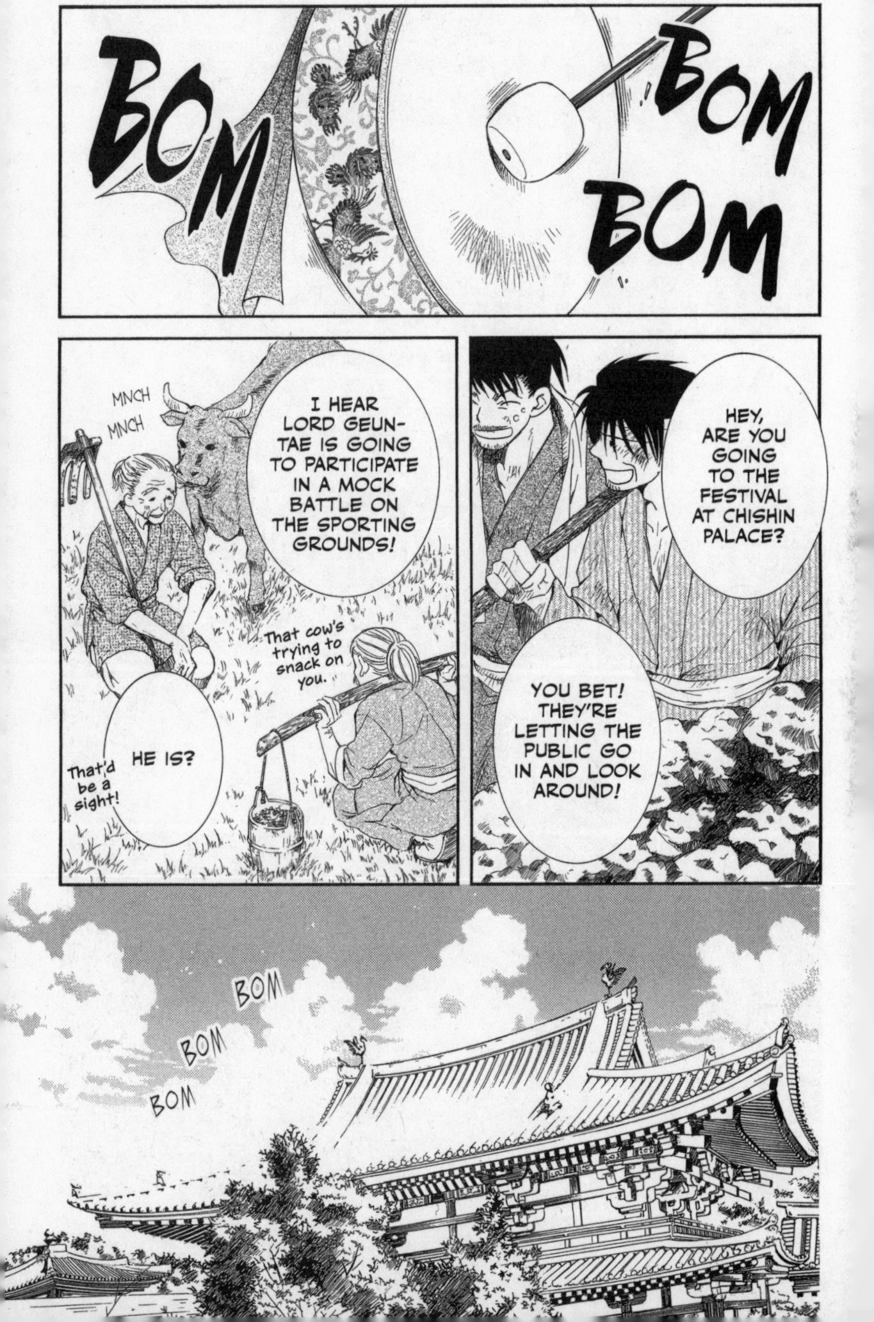
BOM
BOM
BOM
HEY, ARE YOU GOING TO THE FESTIVAL AT CHISHIN PALACE?
YOU BET! THEY'RE LETTING THE PUBLIC GO IN AND LOOK AROUND!
MNCH MNCH
I HEAR LORD GEUN-TAE IS GOING TO PARTICIPATE IN A MOCK BATTLE ON THE SPORTING GROUNDS!
That cow's trying to snack on you.
HE IS?
That'd be a sight!
BOM
BOM
BOM

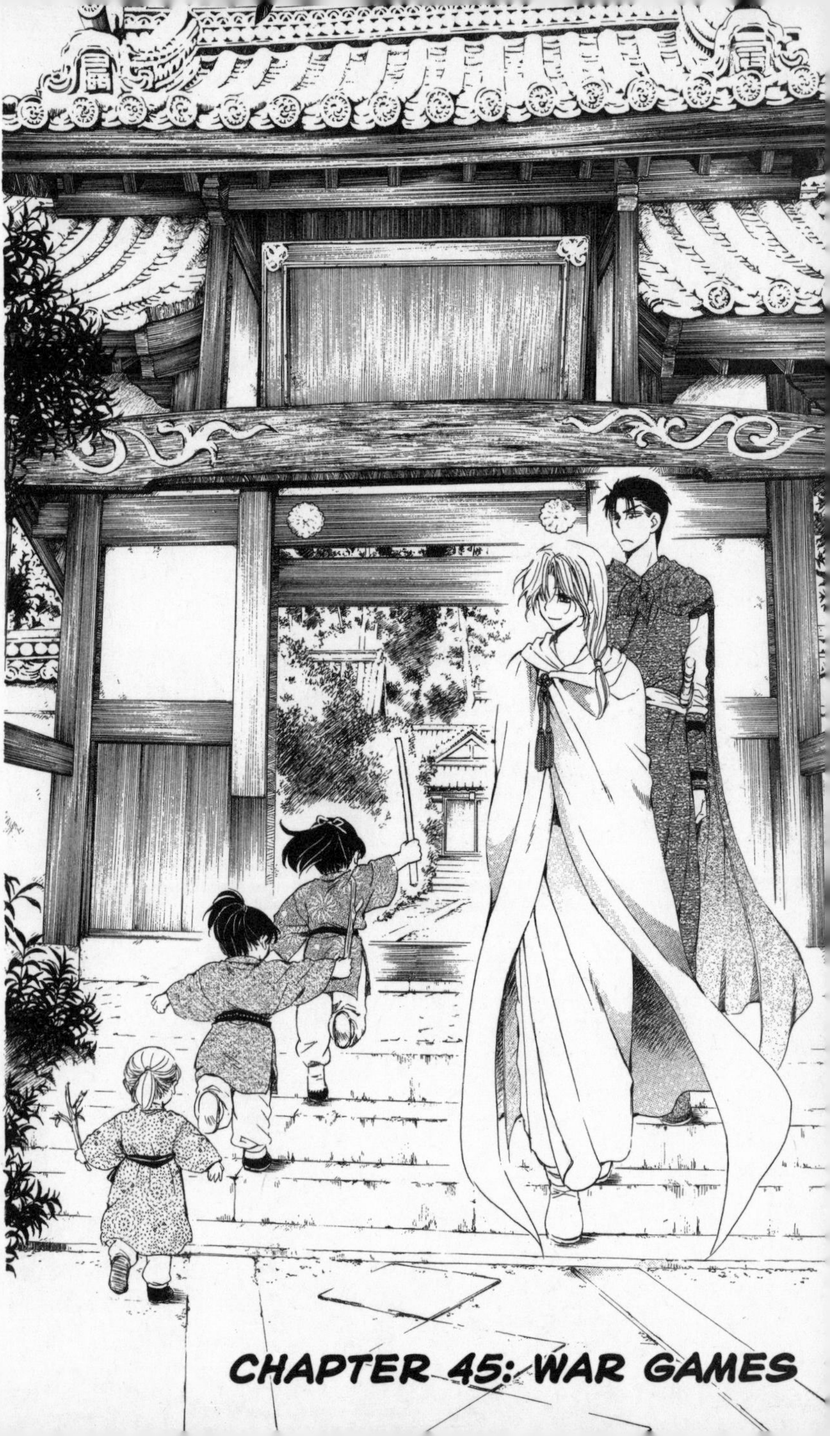
CHAPTER 45: WAR GAMES

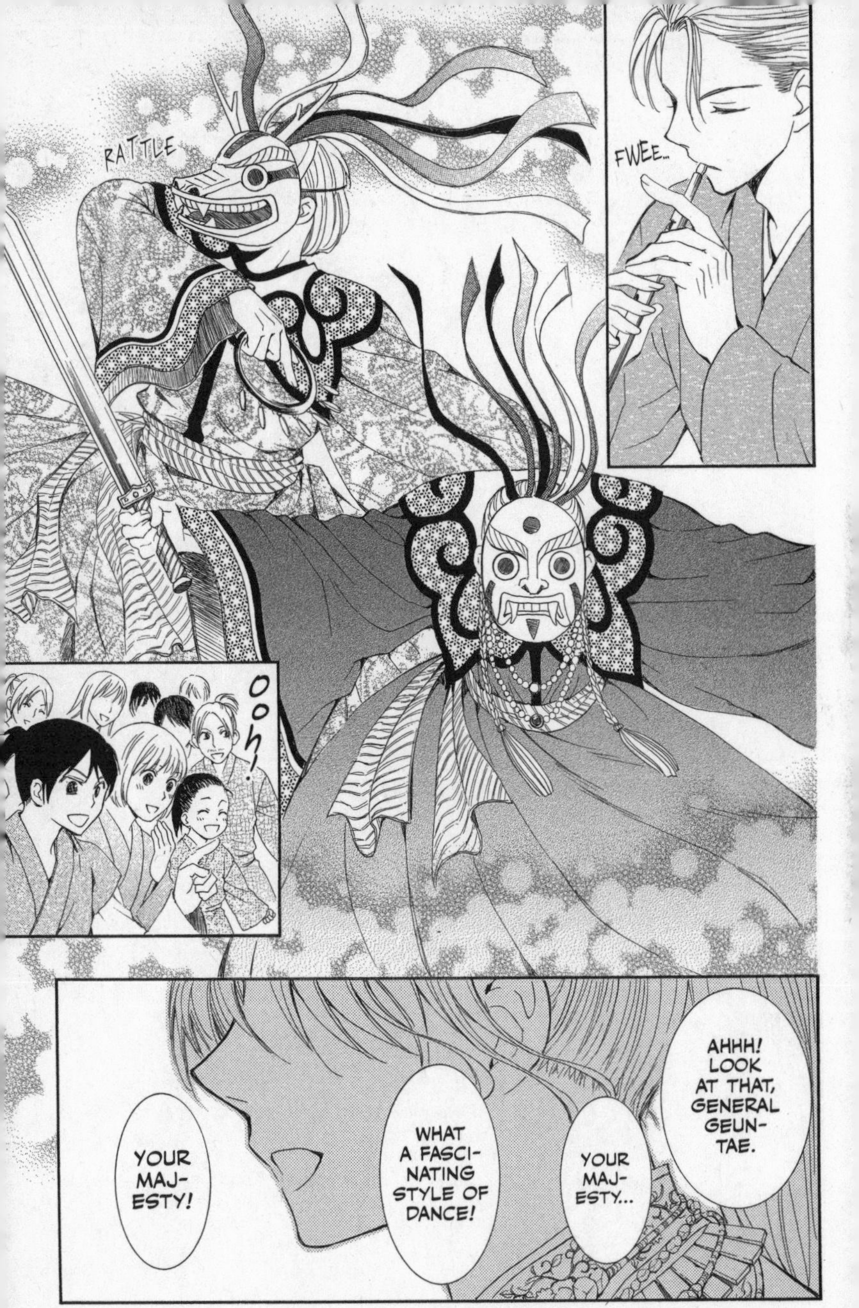
FWEE...
RATTLE
Ooh!
AHHH! LOOK AT THAT, GENERAL GEUN-TAE.
YOUR MAJ-ESTY...
WHAT A FASCI-NATING STYLE OF DANCE!
YOUR MAJ-ESTY!

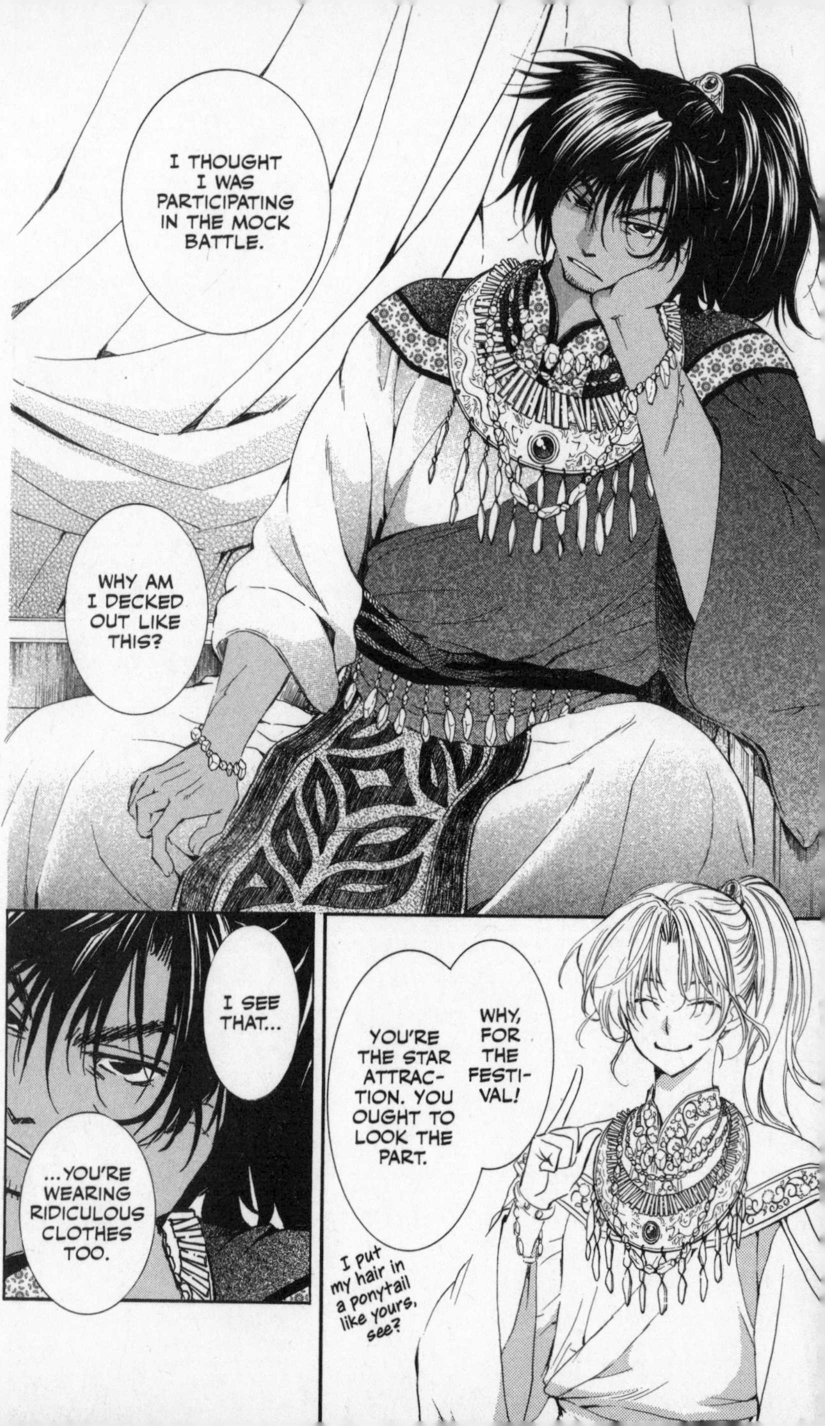
I THOUGHT I WAS PARTICIPATING IN THE MOCK BATTLE.
WHY AM I DECKED OUT LIKE THIS?
WHY, FOR THE FESTI-VAL!
YOU'RE THE STAR ATTRAC-TION. YOU OUGHT TO LOOK THE PART.
I put my hair in a ponytail like yours, see?
I SEE THAT...
...YOU'RE WEARING RIDICULOUS CLOTHES TOO.

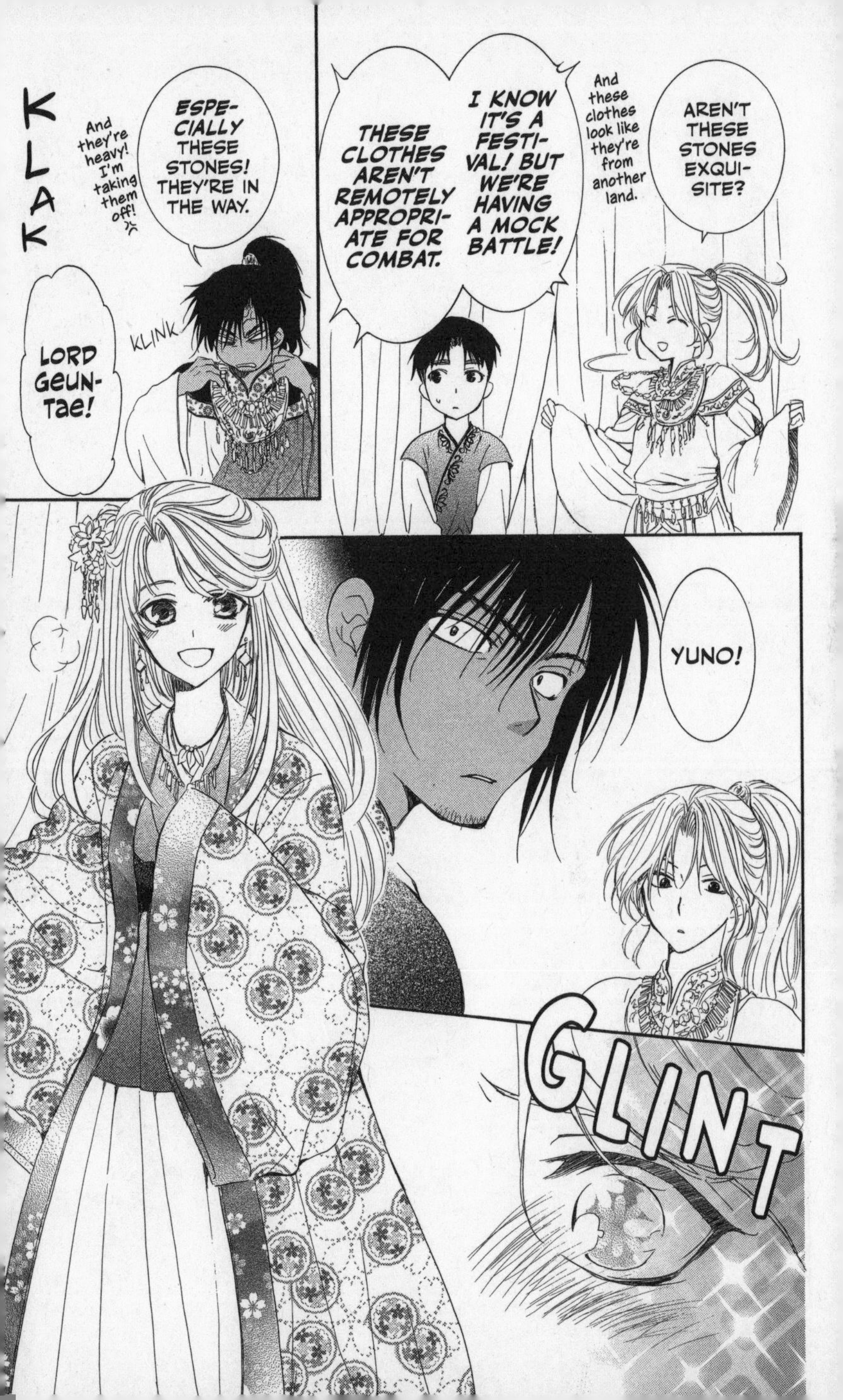
AREN'T THESE STONES EXQUI-SITE?
And these clothes look like they're from another land.
I KNOW IT'S A FESTI-VAL! BUT WE'RE HAVING A MOCK BATTLE!
THESE CLOTHES AREN'T REMOTELY APPROPRI-ATE FOR COMBAT.
ESPE-CIALLY THESE STONES! THEY'RE IN THE WAY.
And they're heavy! I'm taking them off!
KLINK
KLAK
LORD GEUN-TAE!
YUNO!
GLINT

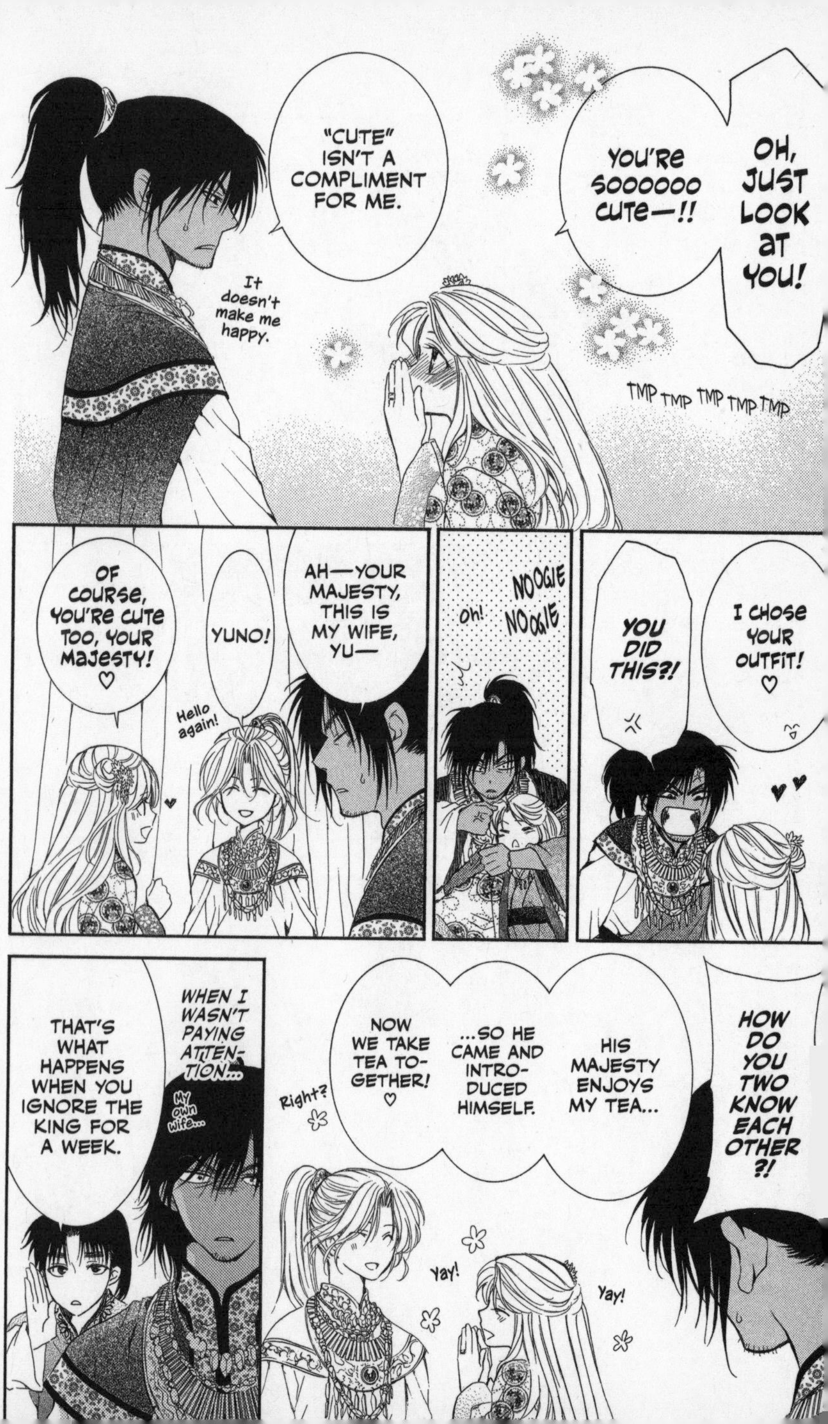
OH, JUST LOOK AT YOU!
YOU'RE SOOOOOO CUTE—!!
TMP TMP TMP TMP TMP
"CUTE" ISN'T A COMPLIMENT FOR ME.
It doesn't make me happy.
I CHOSE YOUR OUTFIT! ♡
YOU DID THIS?!
NOOGIE NOOGIE
Oh!
AH—YOUR MAJESTY, THIS IS MY WIFE, YU—
YUNO!
OF COURSE, YOU'RE CUTE TOO, YOUR MAJESTY! ♡
Hello again!
HOW DO YOU TWO KNOW EACH OTHER?!
HIS MAJESTY ENJOYS MY TEA...
...SO HE CAME AND INTRODUCED HIMSELF.
NOW WE TAKE TEA TOGETHER! ♡
Right?
Yay!
Yay!
WHEN I WASN'T PAYING ATTENTION...
My own wife...
THAT'S WHAT HAPPENS WHEN YOU IGNORE THE KING FOR A WEEK.

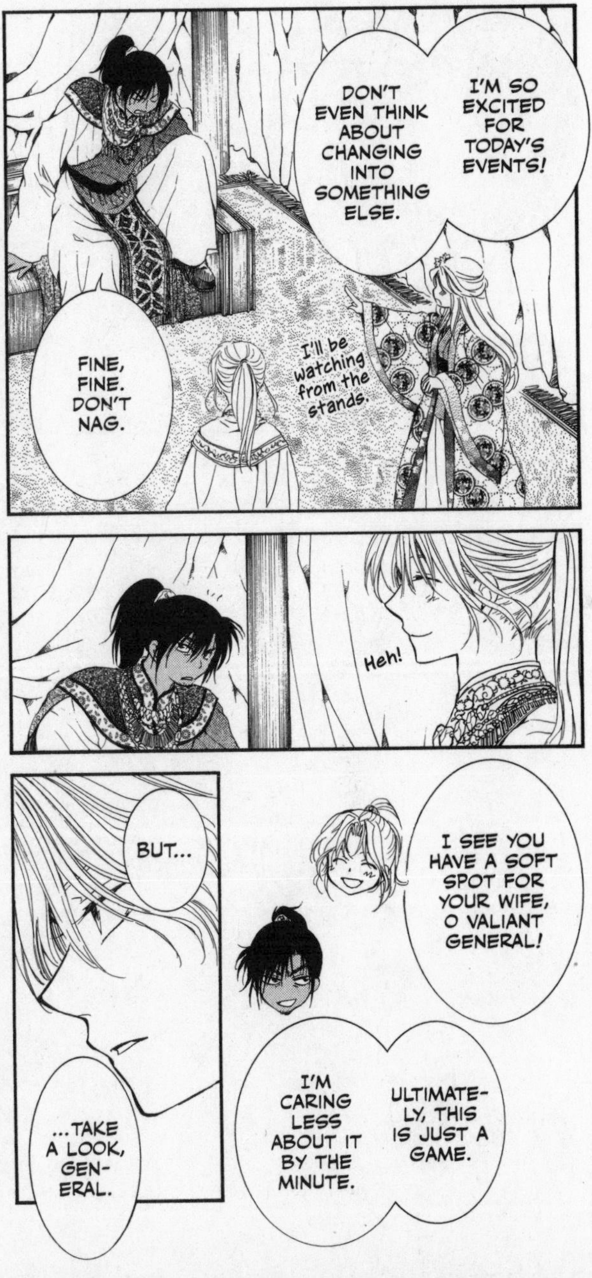
I'M SO EXCITED FOR TODAY'S EVENTS!
DON'T EVEN THINK ABOUT CHANGING INTO SOMETHING ELSE.
I'll be watching from the stands.
FINE, FINE. DON'T NAG.
Heh!
I SEE YOU HAVE A SOFT SPOT FOR YOUR WIFE, O VALIANT GENERAL!
ULTIMATE-LY, THIS IS JUST A GAME.
I'M CARING LESS ABOUT IT BY THE MINUTE.
BUT...
...TAKE A LOOK, GEN-ERAL.

I wrote this while considering that, if I were to enter Yona's world, I'd like to be Yuno. (*Laugh*) I'd have a wild husband everyone admired, and I'd be able to spend my days working on my hobbies. Sounds great! ^^

Just as a side note, Yuno picks out the clothing that Geun-tae wears when he visits the palace. Her taste is a bit quirky.

As we embarked on the Su-won arc, all of the characters were older men. This was a bit rough for some of my readers, so they asked me to introduce a girl. They were like wanderers in a desert begging for water. I felt bad, so I brought Yuno into the story. What do you think? (*Laugh*) She seems childlike, but she's actually 25 years old.

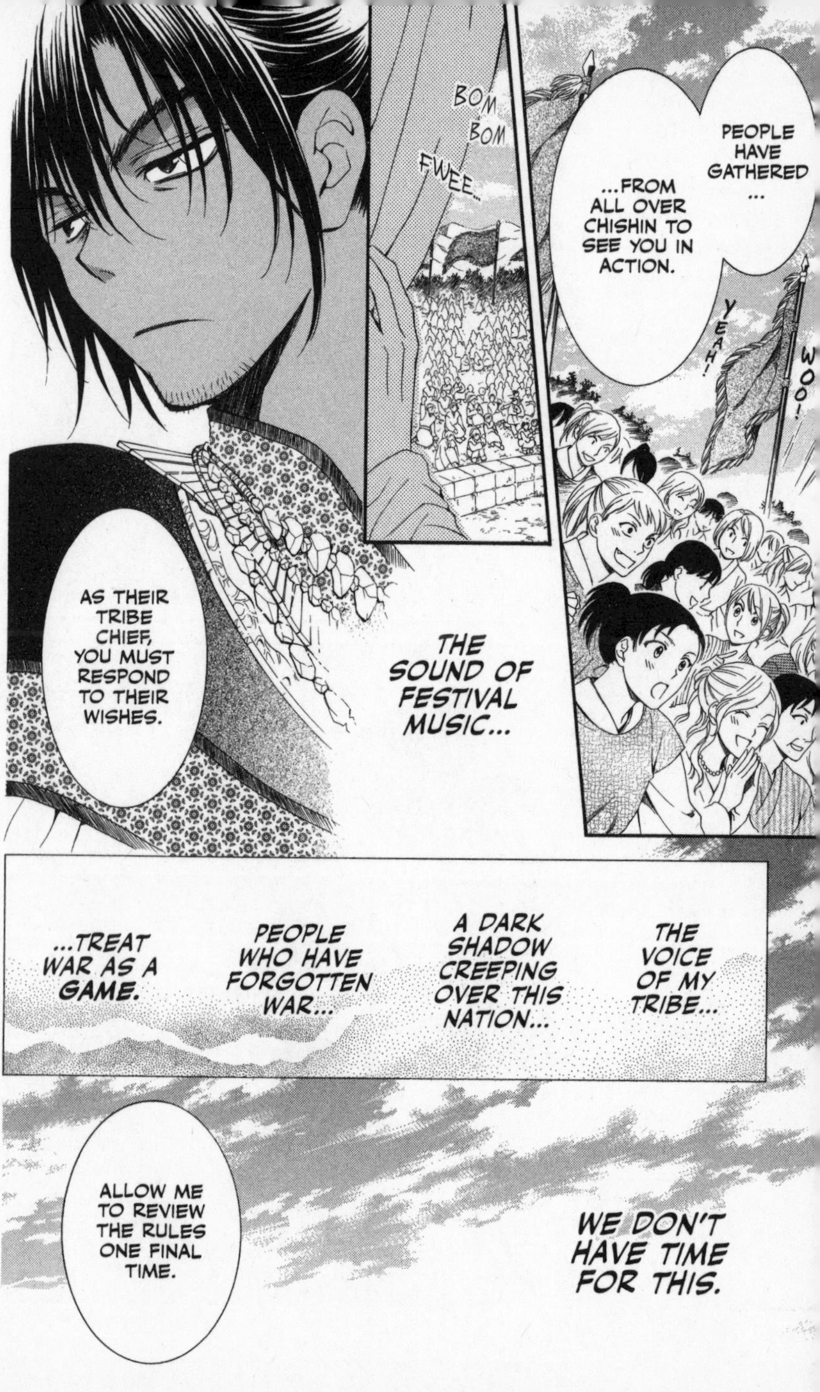
PEOPLE HAVE GATHERED...
...FROM ALL OVER CHISHIN TO SEE YOU IN ACTION.
YEAH!
WOO!
BOM
BOM
FWEE...
THE SOUND OF FESTIVAL MUSIC...
AS THEIR TRIBE CHIEF, YOU MUST RESPOND TO THEIR WISHES.
THE VOICE OF MY TRIBE...
A DARK SHADOW CREEPING OVER THIS NATION...
PEOPLE WHO HAVE FORGOTTEN WAR...
...TREAT WAR AS A GAME.
WE DON'T HAVE TIME FOR THIS.
ALLOW ME TO REVIEW THE RULES ONE FINAL TIME.

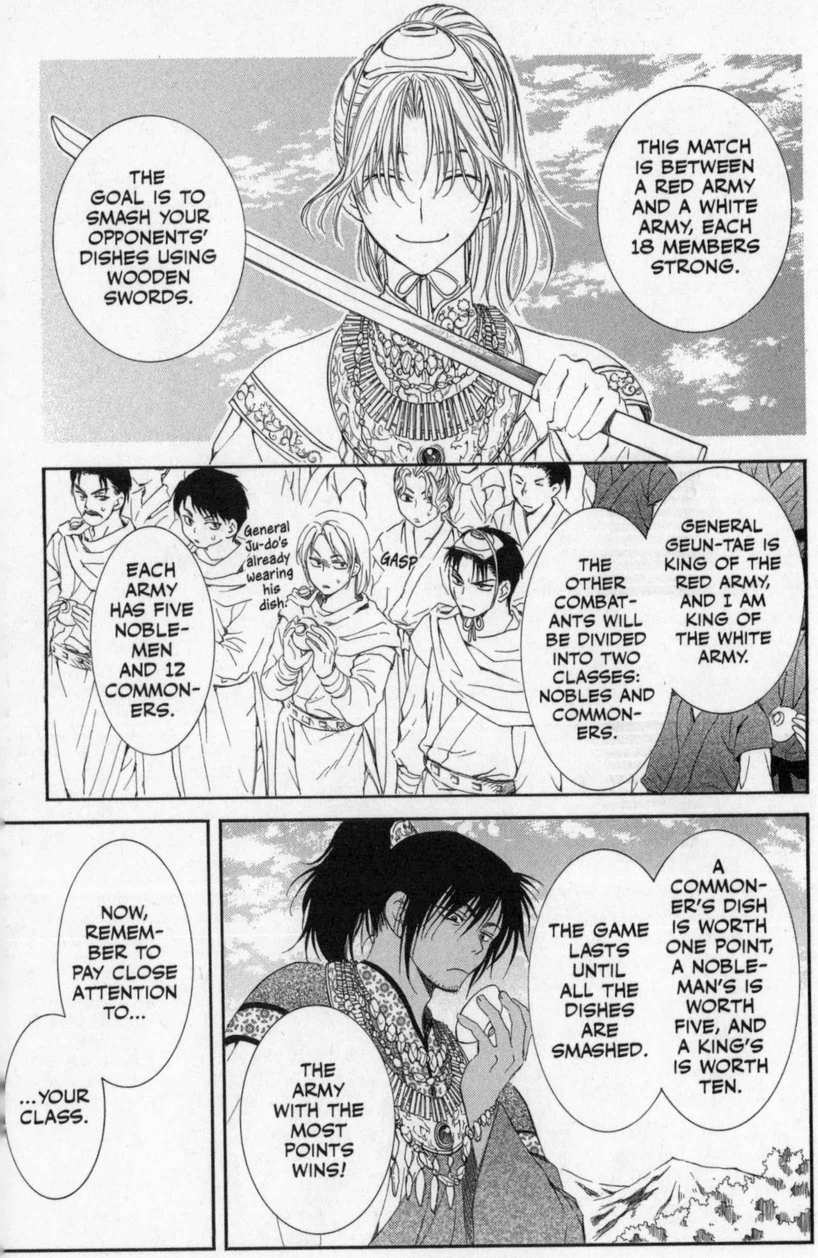
THIS MATCH IS BETWEEN A RED ARMY AND A WHITE ARMY, EACH 18 MEMBERS STRONG.
THE GOAL IS TO SMASH YOUR OPPONENTS' DISHES USING WOODEN SWORDS.
GENERAL GEUN-TAE IS KING OF THE RED ARMY, AND I AM KING OF THE WHITE ARMY.
THE OTHER COMBATANTS WILL BE DIVIDED INTO TWO CLASSES: NOBLES AND COMMONERS.
GASP
General Ju-do's already wearing his dish.
EACH ARMY HAS FIVE NOBLEMEN AND 12 COMMONERS.
A COMMONER'S DISH IS WORTH ONE POINT, A NOBLEMAN'S IS WORTH FIVE, AND A KING'S IS WORTH TEN.
THE GAME LASTS UNTIL ALL THE DISHES ARE SMASHED.
THE ARMY WITH THE MOST POINTS WINS!
NOW, REMEMBER TO PAY CLOSE ATTENTION TO...
...YOUR CLASS.

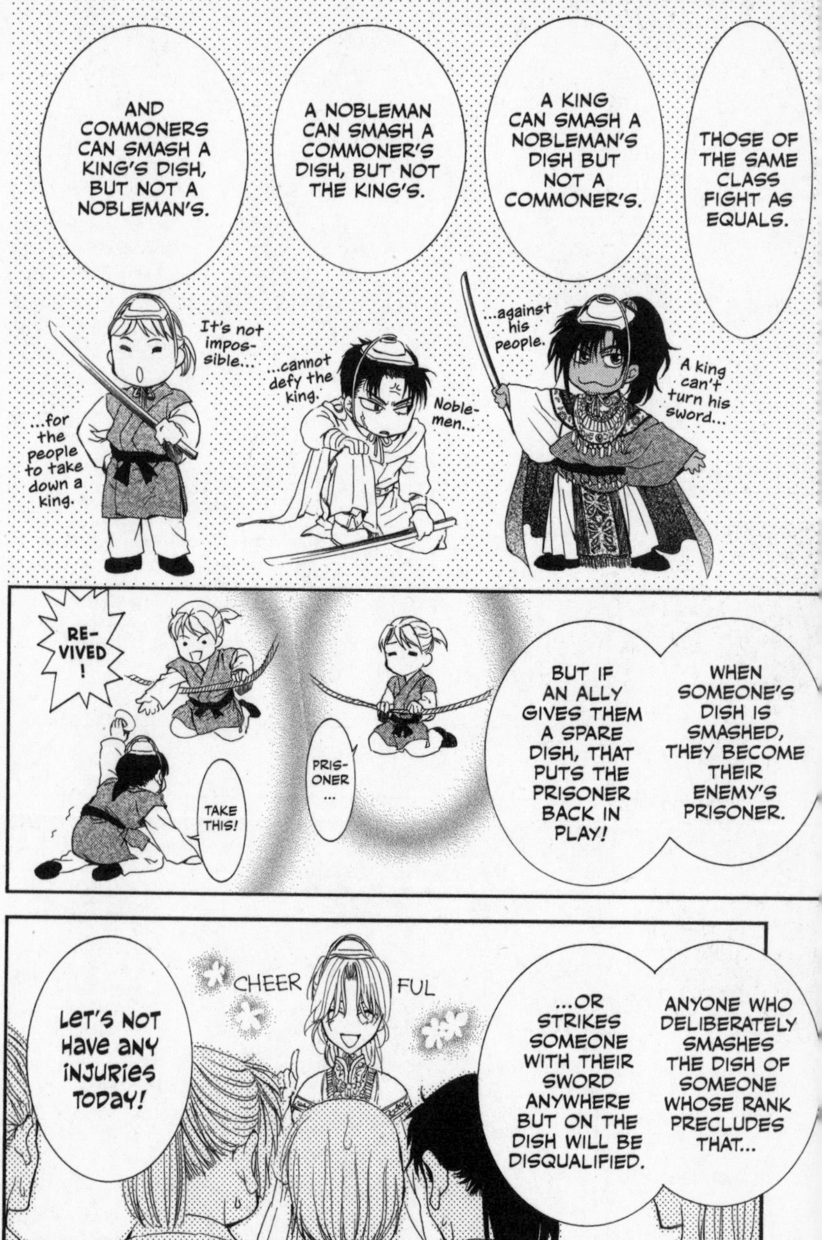
THOSE OF THE SAME CLASS FIGHT AS EQUALS.
A KING CAN SMASH A NOBLEMAN'S DISH BUT NOT A COMMONER'S.
A NOBLEMAN CAN SMASH A COMMONER'S DISH, BUT NOT THE KING'S.
AND COMMONERS CAN SMASH A KING'S DISH, BUT NOT A NOBLEMAN'S.
A king can't turn his sword...
...against his people.
Noble-men...
...cannot defy the king.
It's not impos-sible...
...for the people to take down a king.
WHEN SOMEONE'S DISH IS SMASHED, THEY BECOME THEIR ENEMY'S PRISONER.
BUT IF AN ALLY GIVES THEM A SPARE DISH, THAT PUTS THE PRISONER BACK IN PLAY!
PRIS-ONER...
TAKE THIS!
RE-VIVED!
ANYONE WHO DELIBERATELY SMASHES THE DISH OF SOMEONE WHOSE RANK PRECLUDES THAT...
...OR STRIKES SOMEONE WITH THEIR SWORD ANYWHERE BUT ON THE DISH WILL BE DISQUALIFIED.
CHEER FUL
LET'S NOT HAVE ANY INJURIES TODAY!

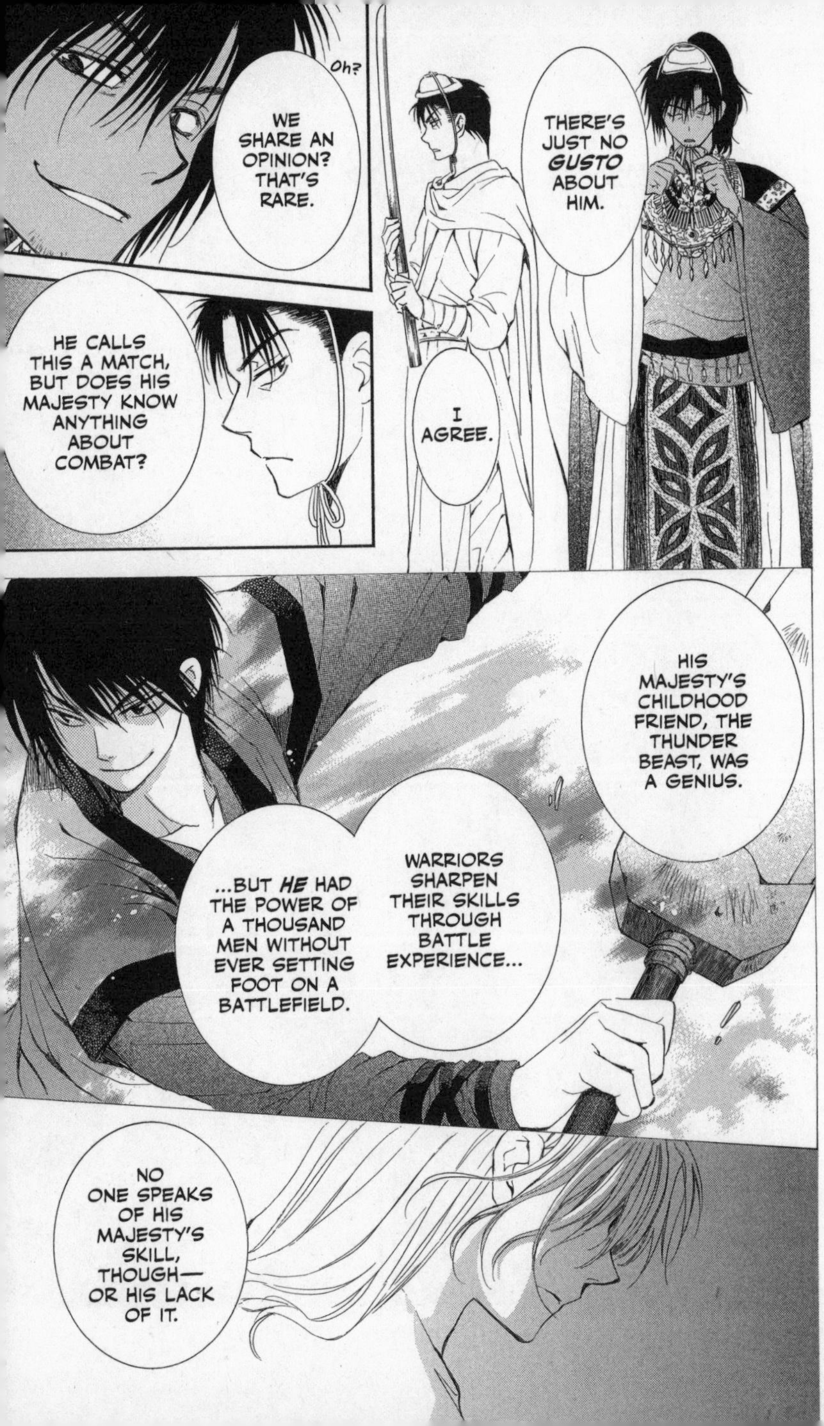

THERE'S JUST NO *GUSTO* ABOUT HIM.
I AGREE.
Oh?
WE SHARE AN OPINION? THAT'S RARE.
HE CALLS THIS A MATCH, BUT DOES HIS MAJESTY KNOW ANYTHING ABOUT COMBAT?
HIS MAJESTY'S CHILDHOOD FRIEND, THE THUNDER BEAST, WAS A GENIUS.
WARRIORS SHARPEN THEIR SKILLS THROUGH BATTLE EXPERIENCE...
...BUT *HE* HAD THE POWER OF A THOUSAND MEN WITHOUT EVER SETTING FOOT ON A BATTLEFIELD.
NO ONE SPEAKS OF HIS MAJESTY'S SKILL, THOUGH—OR HIS LACK OF IT.

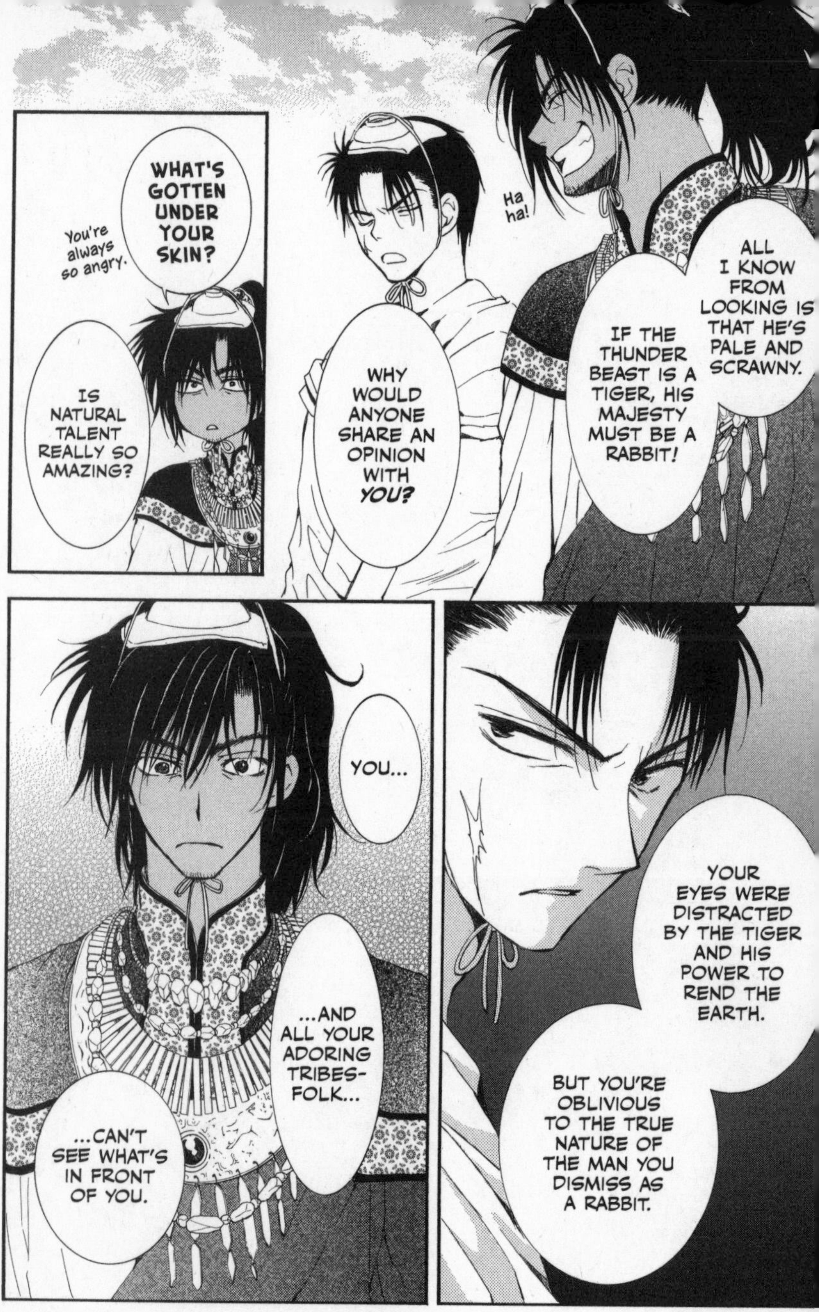
Ha ha!
ALL I KNOW FROM LOOKING IS THAT HE'S PALE AND SCRAWNY.
IF THE THUNDER BEAST IS A TIGER, HIS MAJESTY MUST BE A RABBIT!
WHY WOULD ANYONE SHARE AN OPINION WITH *YOU?*
WHAT'S GOTTEN UNDER YOUR SKIN?
You're always so angry.
IS NATURAL TALENT REALLY SO AMAZING?
YOUR EYES WERE DISTRACTED BY THE TIGER AND HIS POWER TO REND THE EARTH.
BUT YOU'RE OBLIVIOUS TO THE TRUE NATURE OF THE MAN YOU DISMISS AS A RABBIT.
YOU...
...AND ALL YOUR ADORING TRIBES-FOLK...
...CAN'T SEE WHAT'S IN FRONT OF YOU.

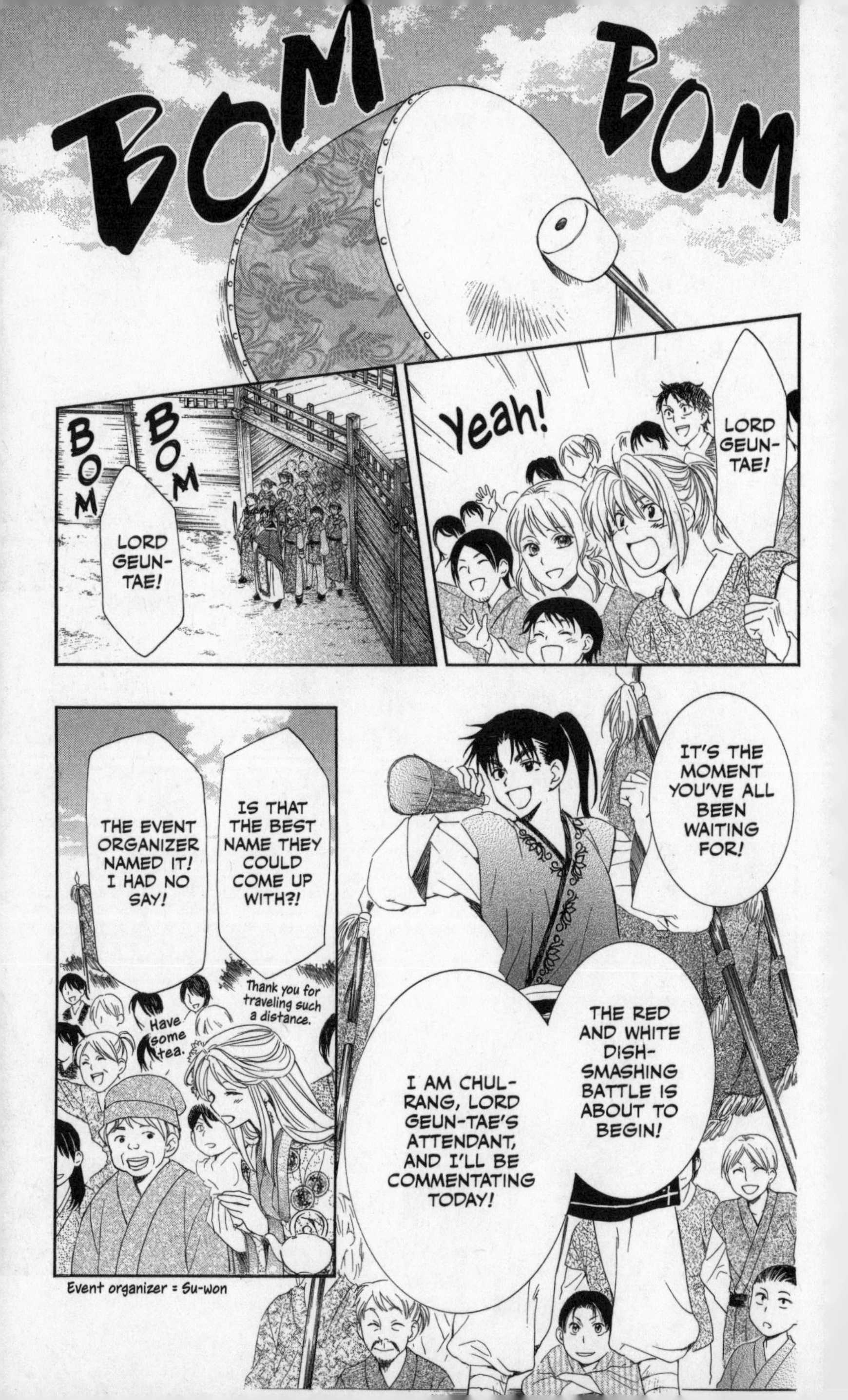
BOM BOM
Yeah!
LORD GEUN-TAE!
BOM BOM
LORD GEUN-TAE!
IT'S THE MOMENT YOU'VE ALL BEEN WAITING FOR!
THE RED AND WHITE DISH-SMASHING BATTLE IS ABOUT TO BEGIN!
I AM CHUL-RANG, LORD GEUN-TAE'S ATTENDANT, AND I'LL BE COMMENTATING TODAY!
IS THAT THE BEST NAME THEY COULD COME UP WITH?!
THE EVENT ORGANIZER NAMED IT! I HAD NO SAY!
Thank you for traveling such a distance.
Have some tea.
Event organizer = Su-won

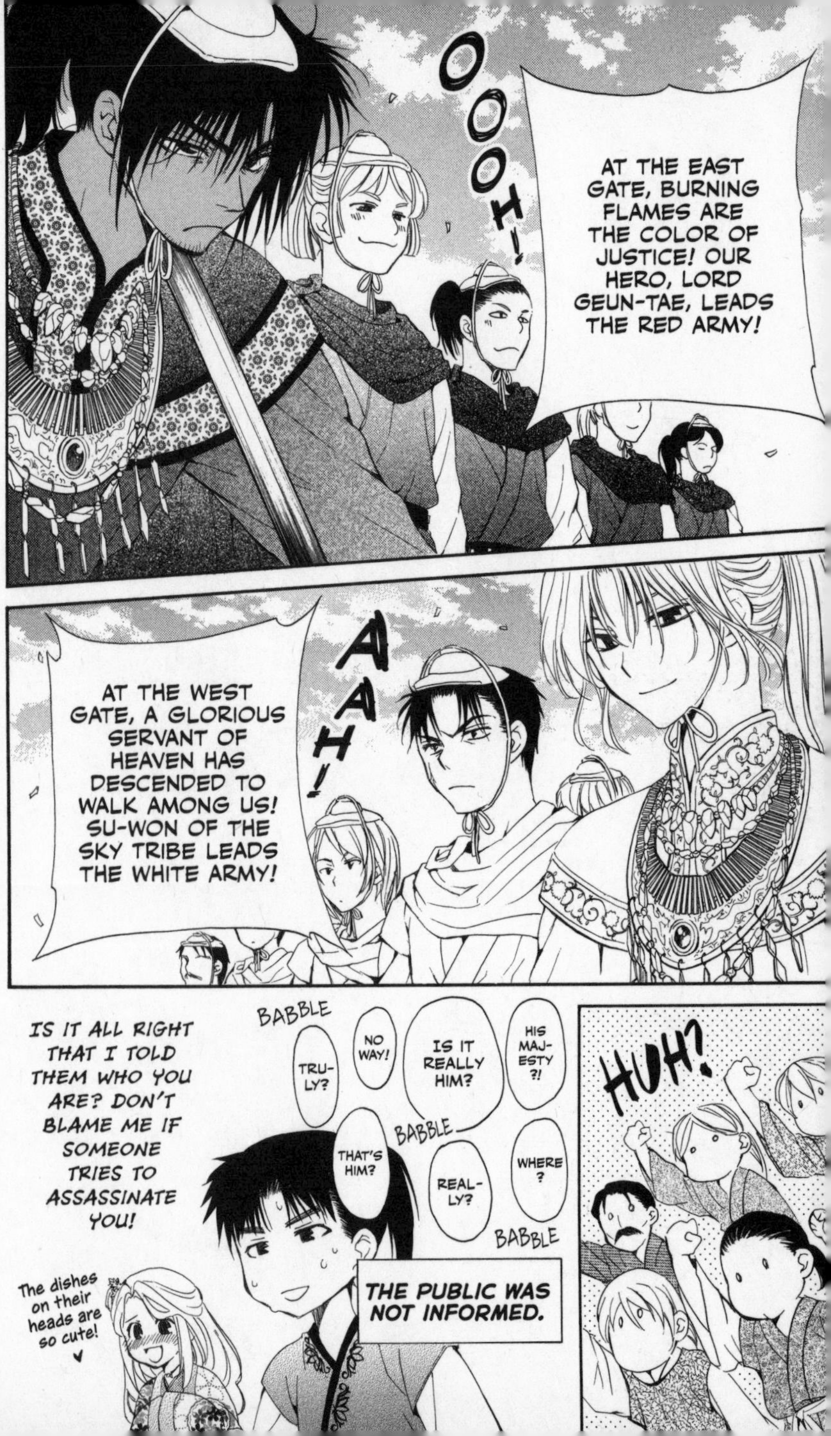
OOOOH!
AT THE EAST GATE, BURNING FLAMES ARE THE COLOR OF JUSTICE! OUR HERO, LORD GEUN-TAE, LEADS THE RED ARMY!
AAAH!
AT THE WEST GATE, A GLORIOUS SERVANT OF HEAVEN HAS DESCENDED TO WALK AMONG US! SU-WON OF THE SKY TRIBE LEADS THE WHITE ARMY!
HUH?
BABBLE
HIS MAJ-ESTY ?!
IS IT REALLY HIM?
NO WAY!
TRU-LY?
BABBLE
WHERE ?
REAL-LY?
THAT'S HIM?
BABBLE
IS IT ALL RIGHT THAT I TOLD THEM WHO YOU ARE? DON'T BLAME ME IF SOMEONE TRIES TO ASSASSINATE YOU!
THE PUBLIC WAS NOT INFORMED.
The dishes on their heads are so cute! ♥

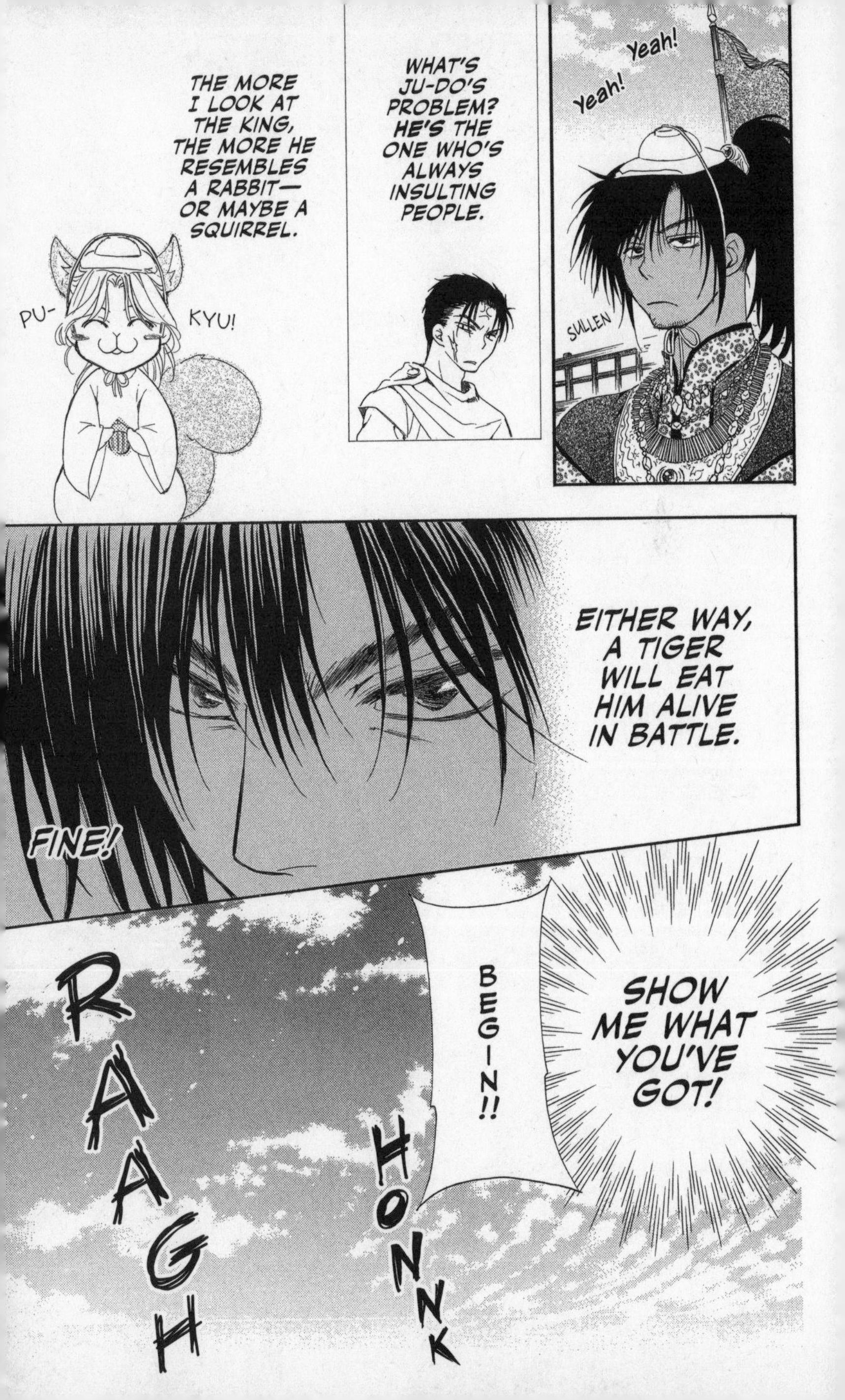
Yeah!
Yeah!
SULLEN
WHAT'S JU-DO'S PROBLEM? HE'S THE ONE WHO'S ALWAYS INSULTING PEOPLE.
THE MORE I LOOK AT THE KING, THE MORE HE RESEMBLES A RABBIT— OR MAYBE A SQUIRREL.
PU-
KYU!
EITHER WAY, A TIGER WILL EAT HIM ALIVE IN BATTLE.
FINE!
SHOW ME WHAT YOU'VE GOT!
BEGIN!!
HONNK
RAAGH

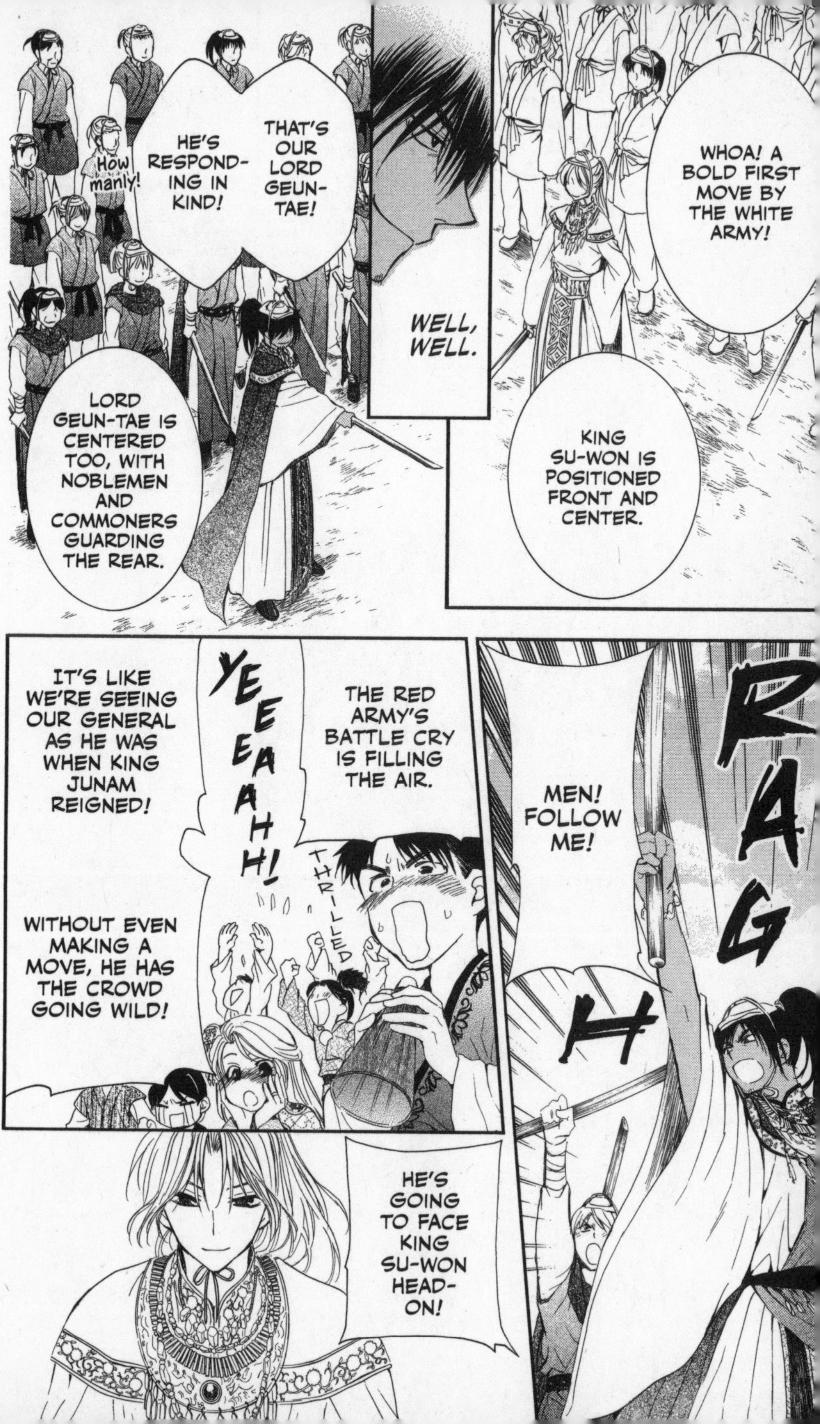
WHOA! A BOLD FIRST MOVE BY THE WHITE ARMY!
KING SU-WON IS POSITIONED FRONT AND CENTER.
WELL, WELL.
THAT'S OUR LORD GEUN-TAE!
HE'S RESPOND-ING IN KIND!
How manly!
LORD GEUN-TAE IS CENTERED TOO, WITH NOBLEMEN AND COMMONERS GUARDING THE REAR.
RAGH
MEN! FOLLOW ME!
THE RED ARMY'S BATTLE CRY IS FILLING THE AIR.
YEEEAAHH!
THRILLED
IT'S LIKE WE'RE SEEING OUR GENERAL AS HE WAS WHEN KING JUNAM REIGNED!
WITHOUT EVEN MAKING A MOVE, HE HAS THE CROWD GOING WILD!
HE'S GOING TO FACE KING SU-WON HEAD-ON!

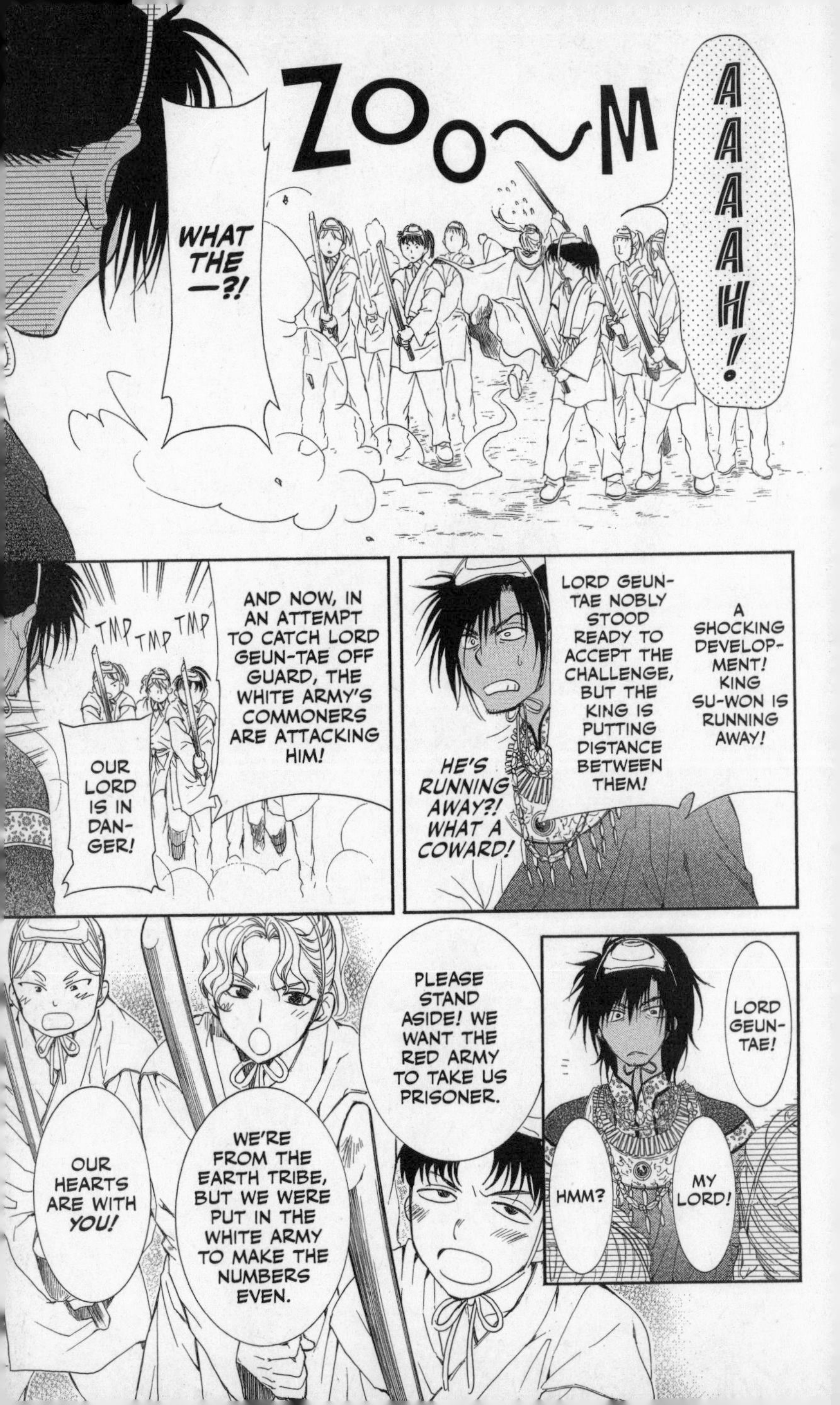
AAAAAH!
ZOO~M
WHAT THE—?!
A SHOCKING DEVELOPMENT! KING SU-WON IS RUNNING AWAY!
LORD GEUN-TAE NOBLY STOOD READY TO ACCEPT THE CHALLENGE, BUT THE KING IS PUTTING DISTANCE BETWEEN THEM!
HE'S RUNNING AWAY?! WHAT A COWARD!
AND NOW, IN AN ATTEMPT TO CATCH LORD GEUN-TAE OFF GUARD, THE WHITE ARMY'S COMMONERS ARE ATTACKING HIM!
TMP TMP TMP
OUR LORD IS IN DANGER!
LORD GEUN-TAE!
MY LORD!
HMM?
PLEASE STAND ASIDE! WE WANT THE RED ARMY TO TAKE US PRISONER.
WE'RE FROM THE EARTH TRIBE, BUT WE WERE PUT IN THE WHITE ARMY TO MAKE THE NUMBERS EVEN.
OUR HEARTS ARE WITH YOU!

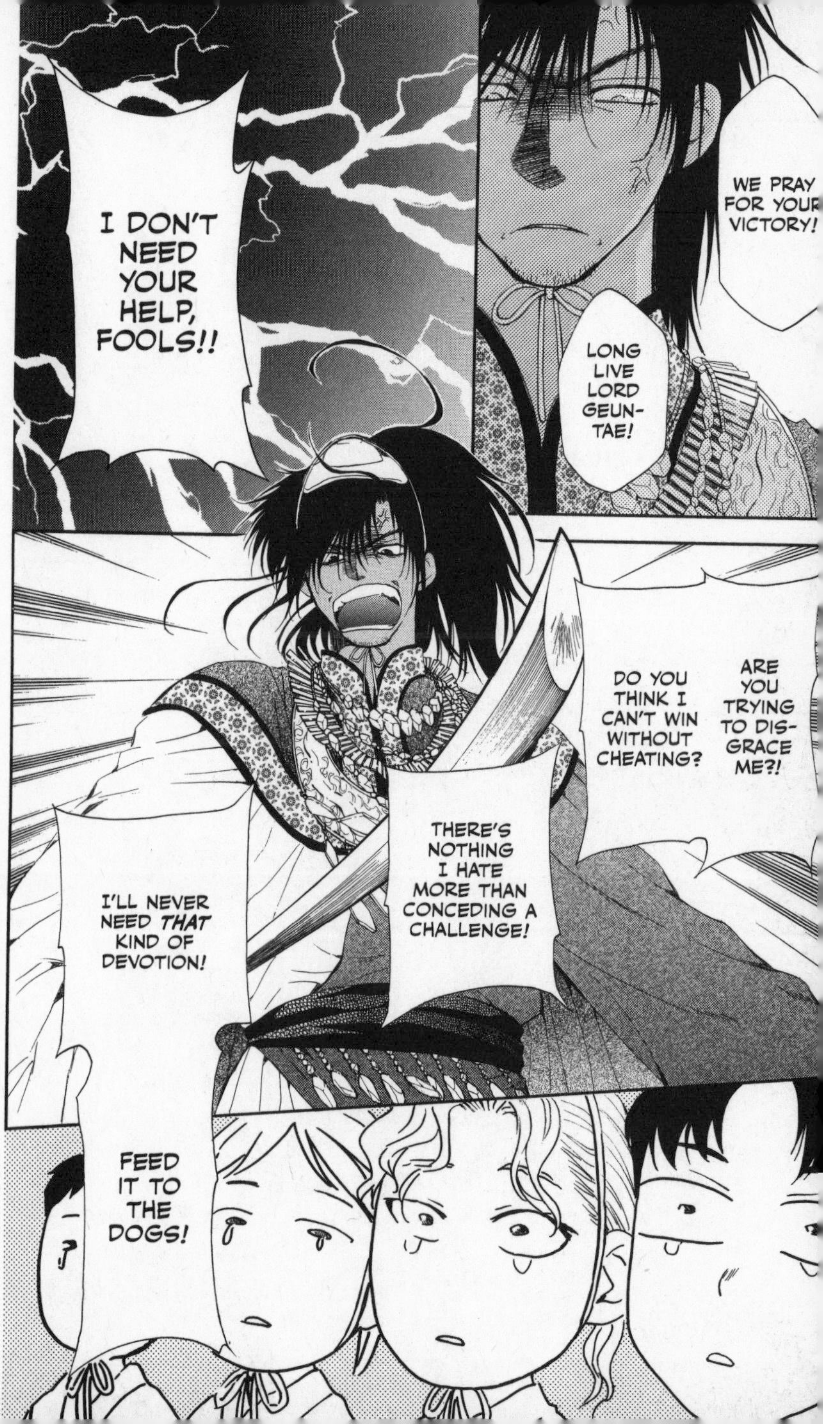
WE PRAY FOR YOUR VICTORY!
LONG LIVE LORD GEUN-TAE!
I DON'T NEED YOUR HELP, FOOLS!!
ARE YOU TRYING TO DIS-GRACE ME?!
DO YOU THINK I CAN'T WIN WITHOUT CHEATING?
THERE'S NOTHING I HATE MORE THAN CONCEDING A CHALLENGE!
I'LL NEVER NEED *THAT* KIND OF DEVOTION!
FEED IT TO THE DOGS!

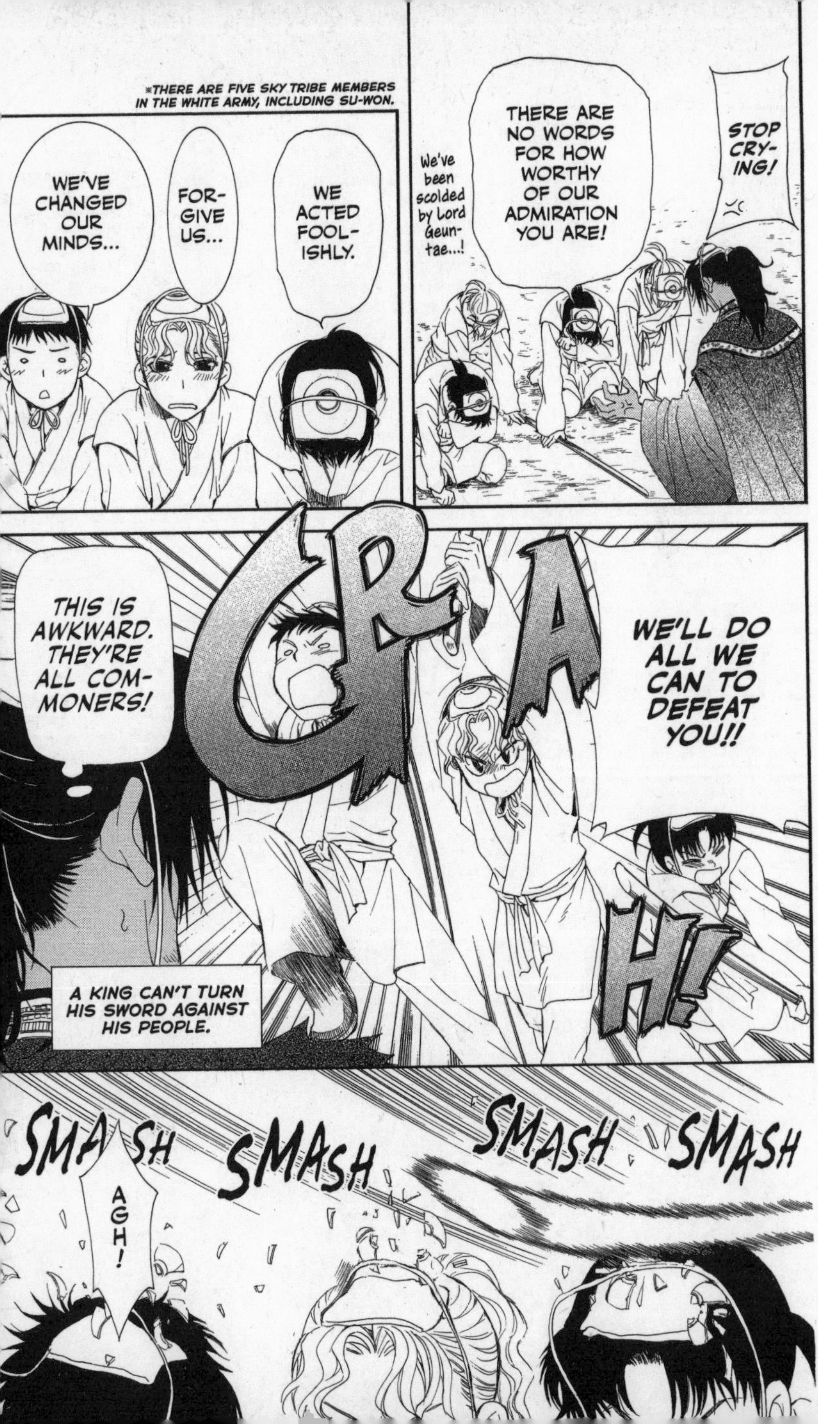
STOP CRY-ING!
THERE ARE NO WORDS FOR HOW WORTHY OF OUR ADMIRATION YOU ARE!
We've been scolded by Lord Geun-tae...!
WE ACTED FOOL-ISHLY.
FOR-GIVE US...
WE'VE CHANGED OUR MINDS...
*THERE ARE FIVE SKY TRIBE MEMBERS IN THE WHITE ARMY, INCLUDING SU-WON.
WE'LL DO ALL WE CAN TO DEFEAT YOU!!
CRASH!
THIS IS AWKWARD. THEY'RE ALL COM-MONERS!
A KING CAN'T TURN HIS SWORD AGAINST HIS PEOPLE.
SMASH SMASH SMASH SMASH
AGH!

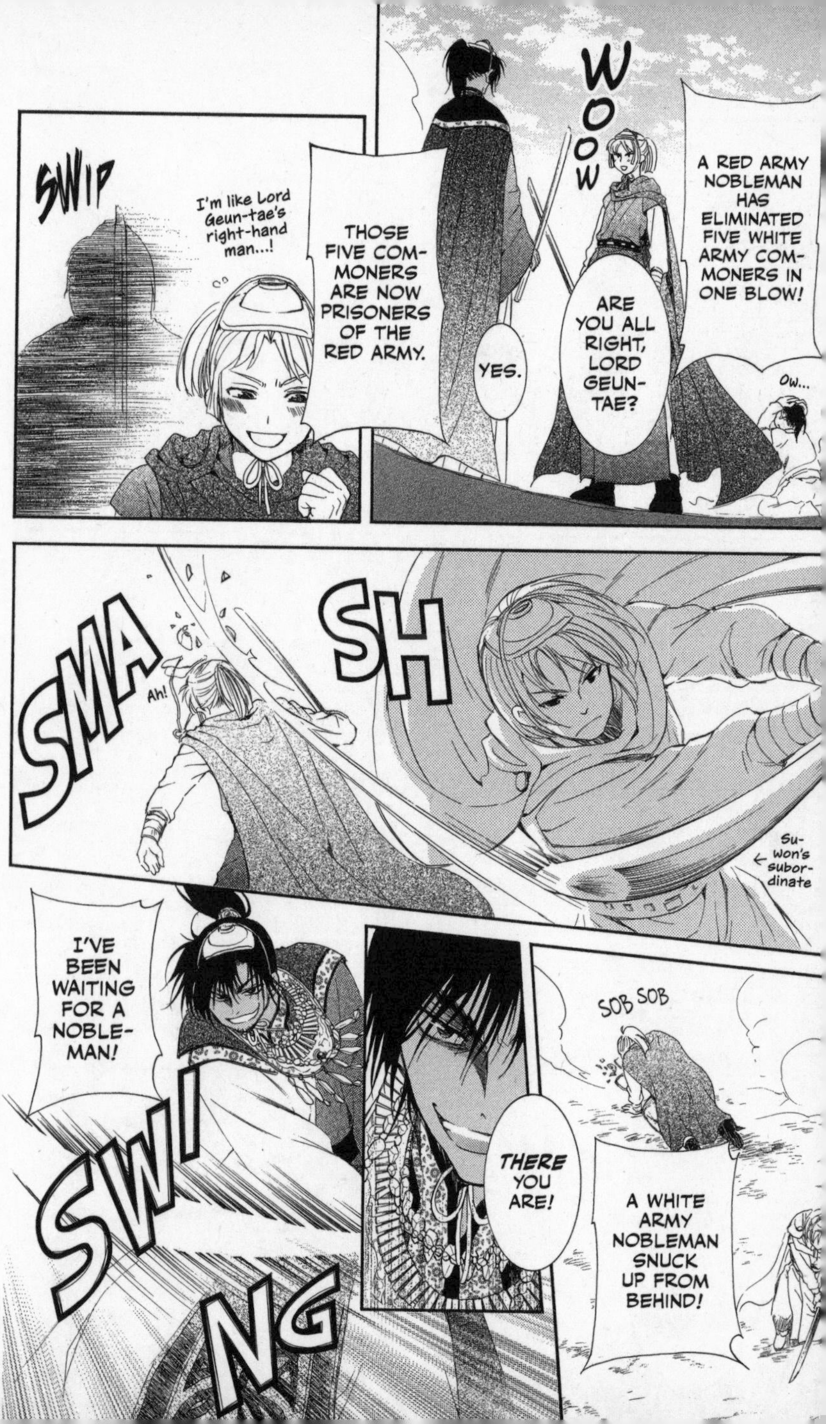
WOOW
A RED ARMY NOBLEMAN HAS ELIMINATED FIVE WHITE ARMY COMMONERS IN ONE BLOW!
ARE YOU ALL RIGHT, LORD GEUN-TAE?
YES.
Ow...
THOSE FIVE COMMONERS ARE NOW PRISONERS OF THE RED ARMY.
SWIP
I'm like Lord Geun-tae's right-hand man...!
SH
SMA
Ah!
← Su-won's subordinate
SOB SOB
A WHITE ARMY NOBLEMAN SNUCK UP FROM BEHIND!
THERE YOU ARE!
I'VE BEEN WAITING FOR A NOBLEMAN!
SWI
NG

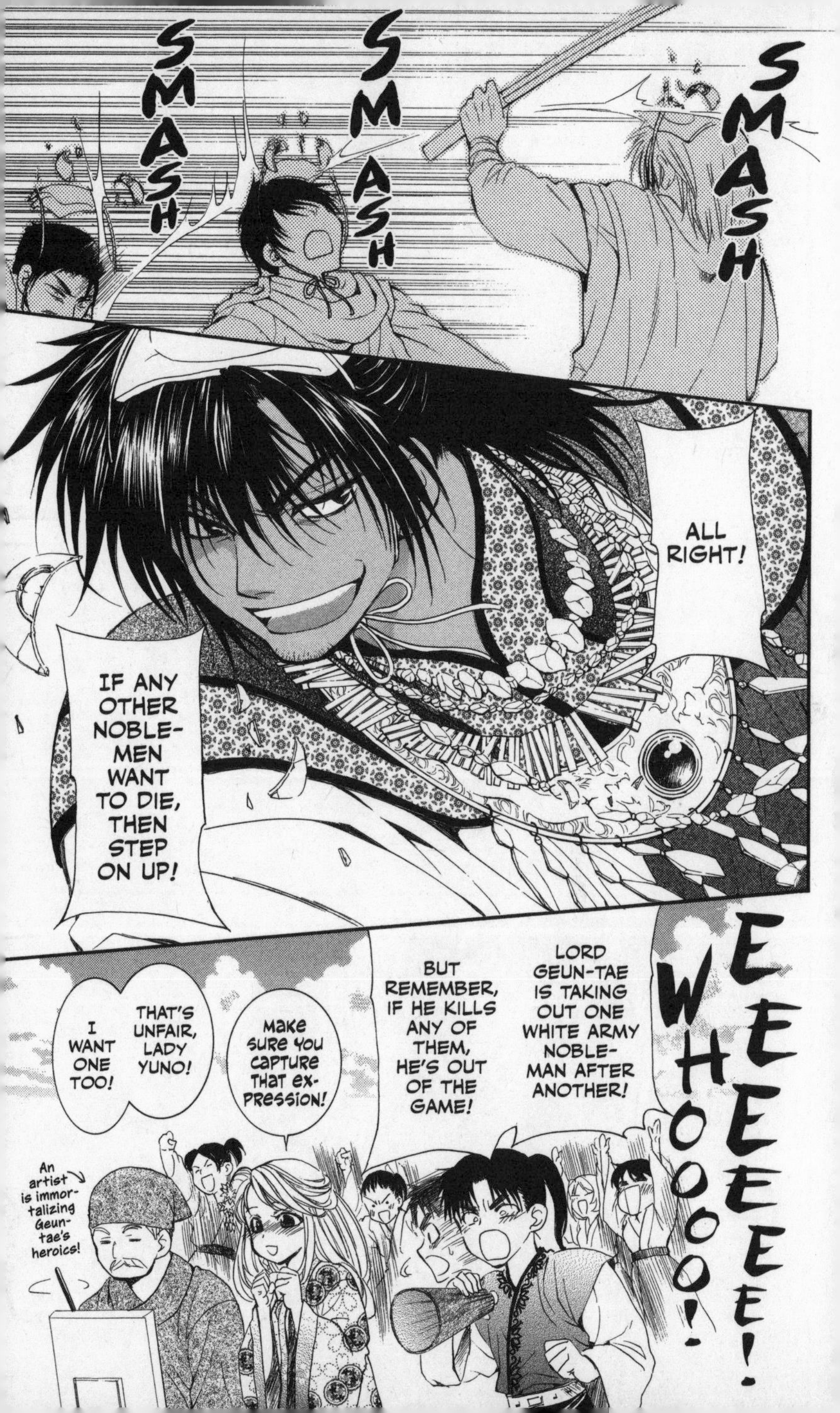
SMASH
SMASH
SMASH
ALL RIGHT!
IF ANY OTHER NOBLEMEN WANT TO DIE, THEN STEP ON UP!
EEEEEEEE!
WHOOOOO!
LORD GEUN-TAE IS TAKING OUT ONE WHITE ARMY NOBLEMAN AFTER ANOTHER!
BUT REMEMBER, IF HE KILLS ANY OF THEM, HE'S OUT OF THE GAME!
Make sure you capture that expression!
THAT'S UNFAIR, LADY YUNO!
I WANT ONE TOO!
An artist is immortalizing Geun-tae's heroics!

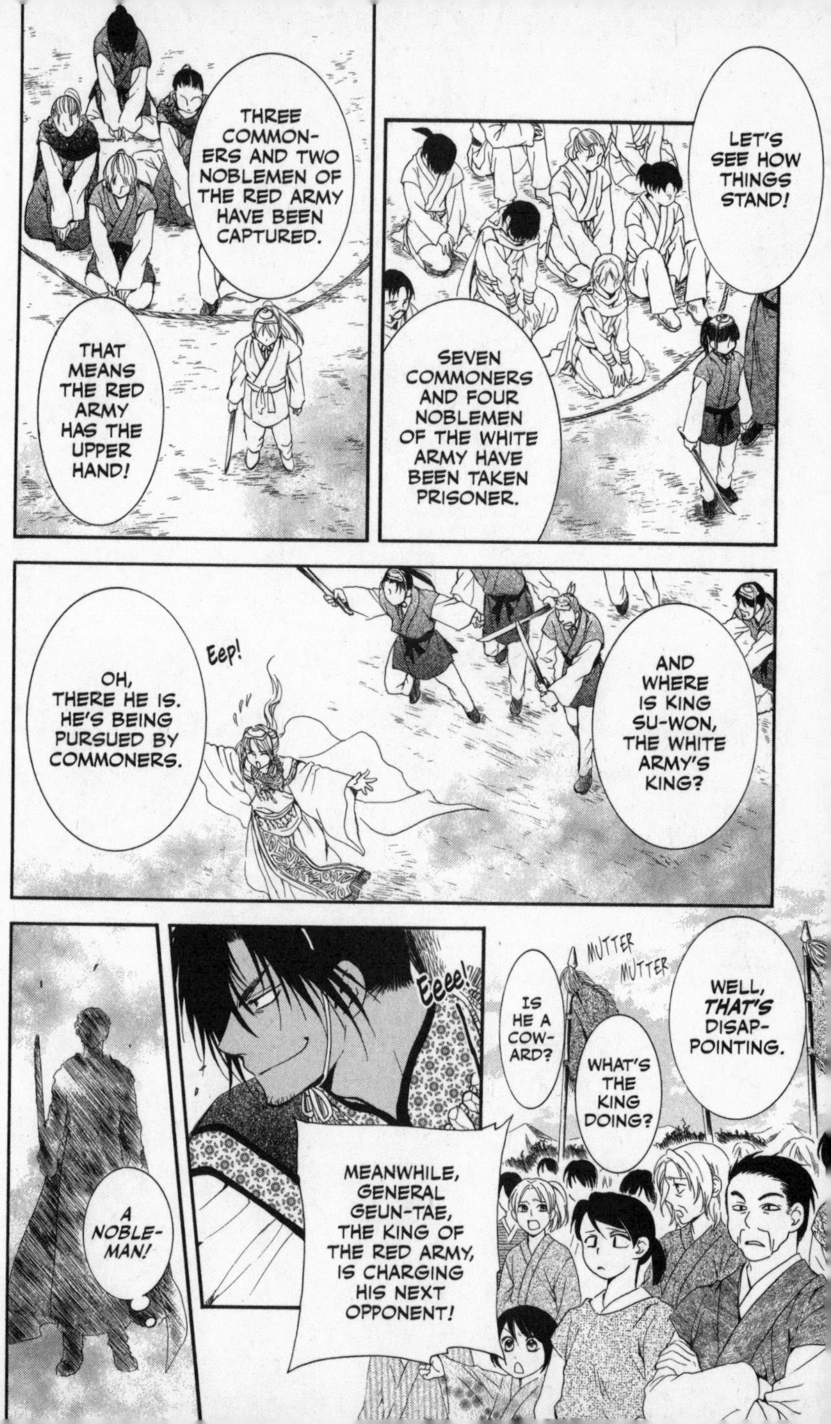
LET'S SEE HOW THINGS STAND!
SEVEN COMMONERS AND FOUR NOBLEMEN OF THE WHITE ARMY HAVE BEEN TAKEN PRISONER.
THREE COMMONERS AND TWO NOBLEMEN OF THE RED ARMY HAVE BEEN CAPTURED.
THAT MEANS THE RED ARMY HAS THE UPPER HAND!
AND WHERE IS KING SU-WON, THE WHITE ARMY'S KING?
Eep!
OH, THERE HE IS. HE'S BEING PURSUED BY COMMONERS.
MUTTER MUTTER
WELL, *THAT'S* DISAPPOINTING.
IS HE A COWARD?
WHAT'S THE KING DOING?
Eeee!
MEANWHILE, GENERAL GEUN-TAE, THE KING OF THE RED ARMY, IS CHARGING HIS NEXT OPPONENT!
A NOBLEMAN!

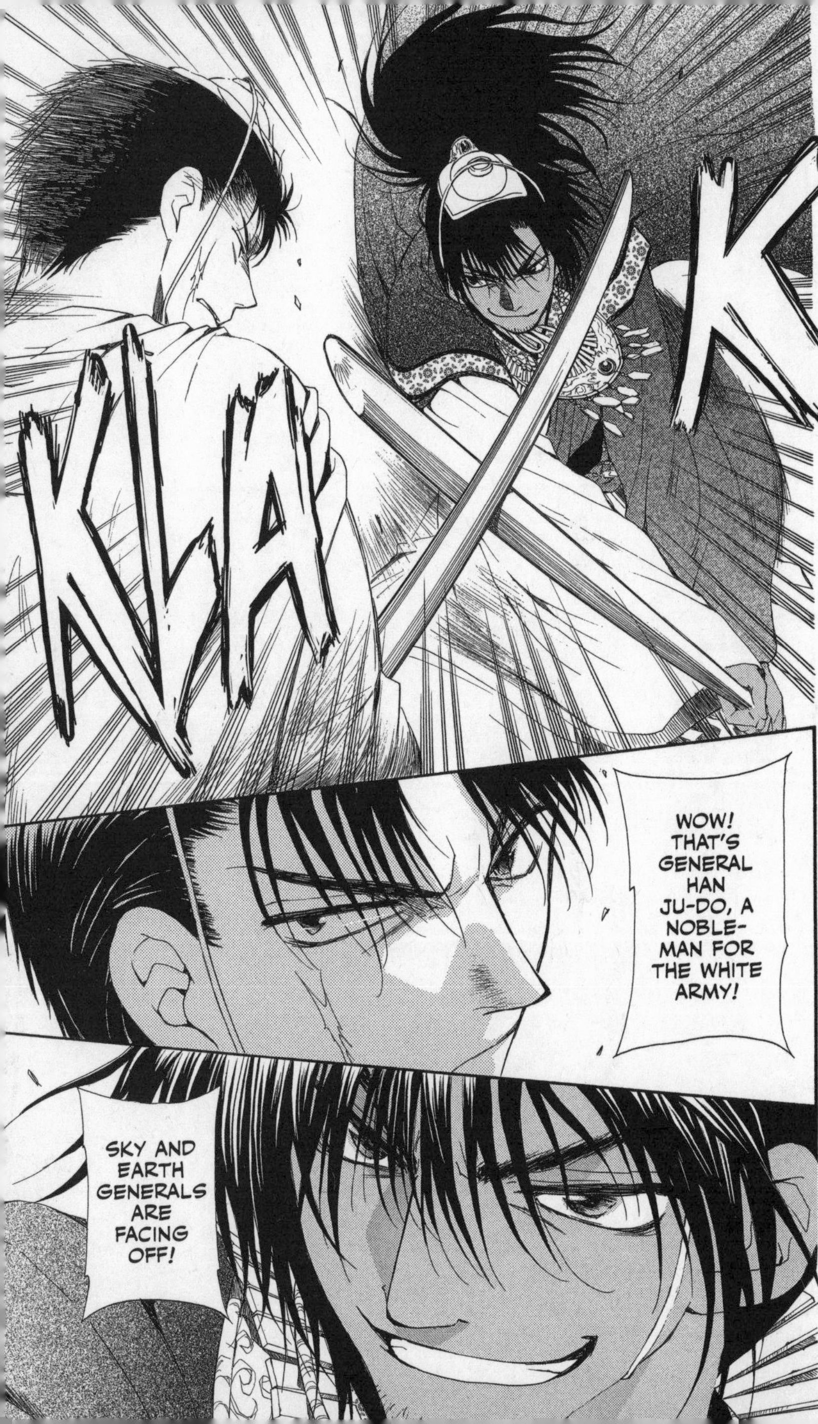
KLAK
WOW! THAT'S GENERAL HAN JU-DO, A NOBLE-MAN FOR THE WHITE ARMY!
SKY AND EARTH GENERALS ARE FACING OFF!

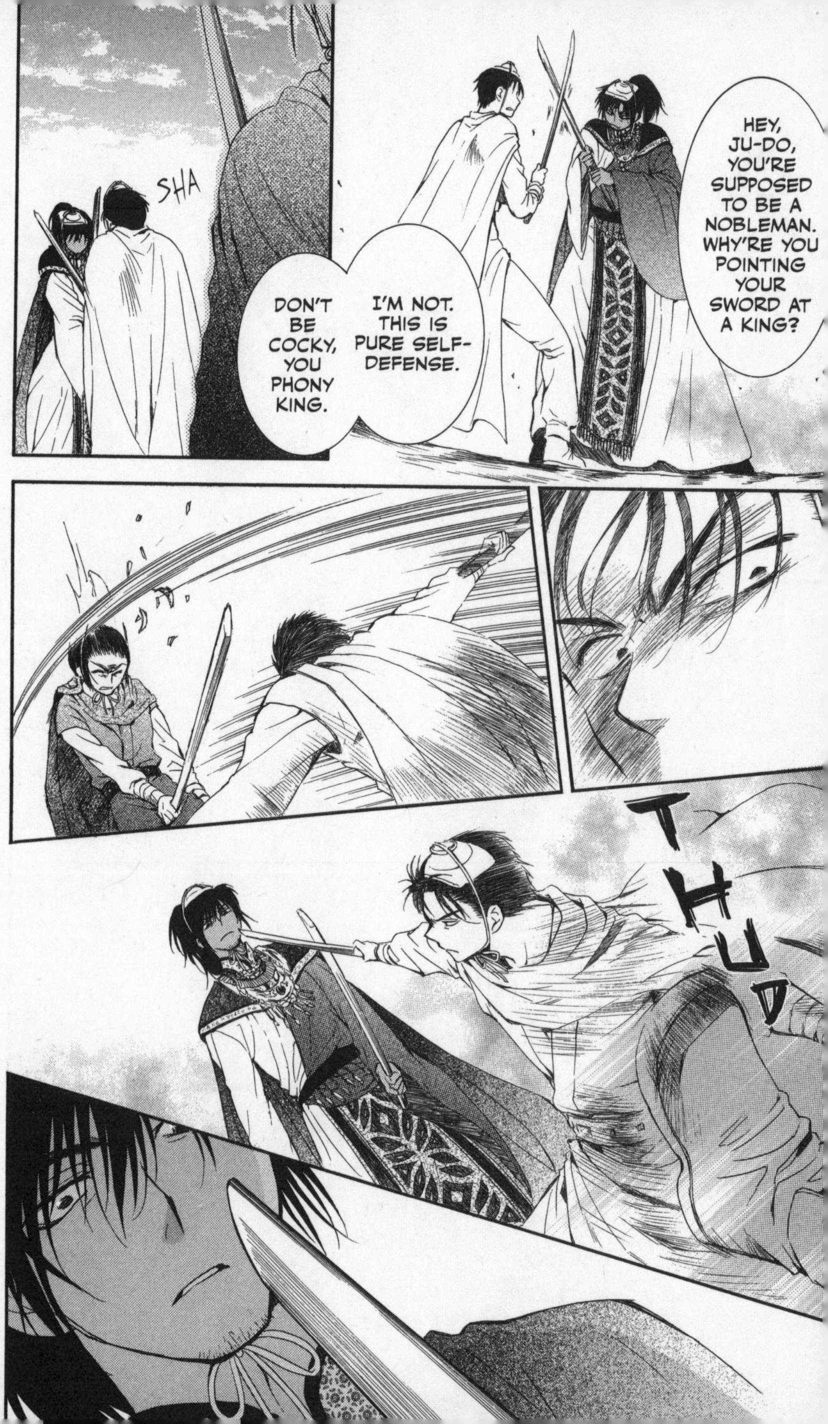

HEY, JU-DO, YOU'RE SUPPOSED TO BE A NOBLEMAN. WHY'RE YOU POINTING YOUR SWORD AT A KING?
I'M NOT. THIS IS PURE SELF-DEFENSE.
DON'T BE COCKY, YOU PHONY KING.
SHA
THUD

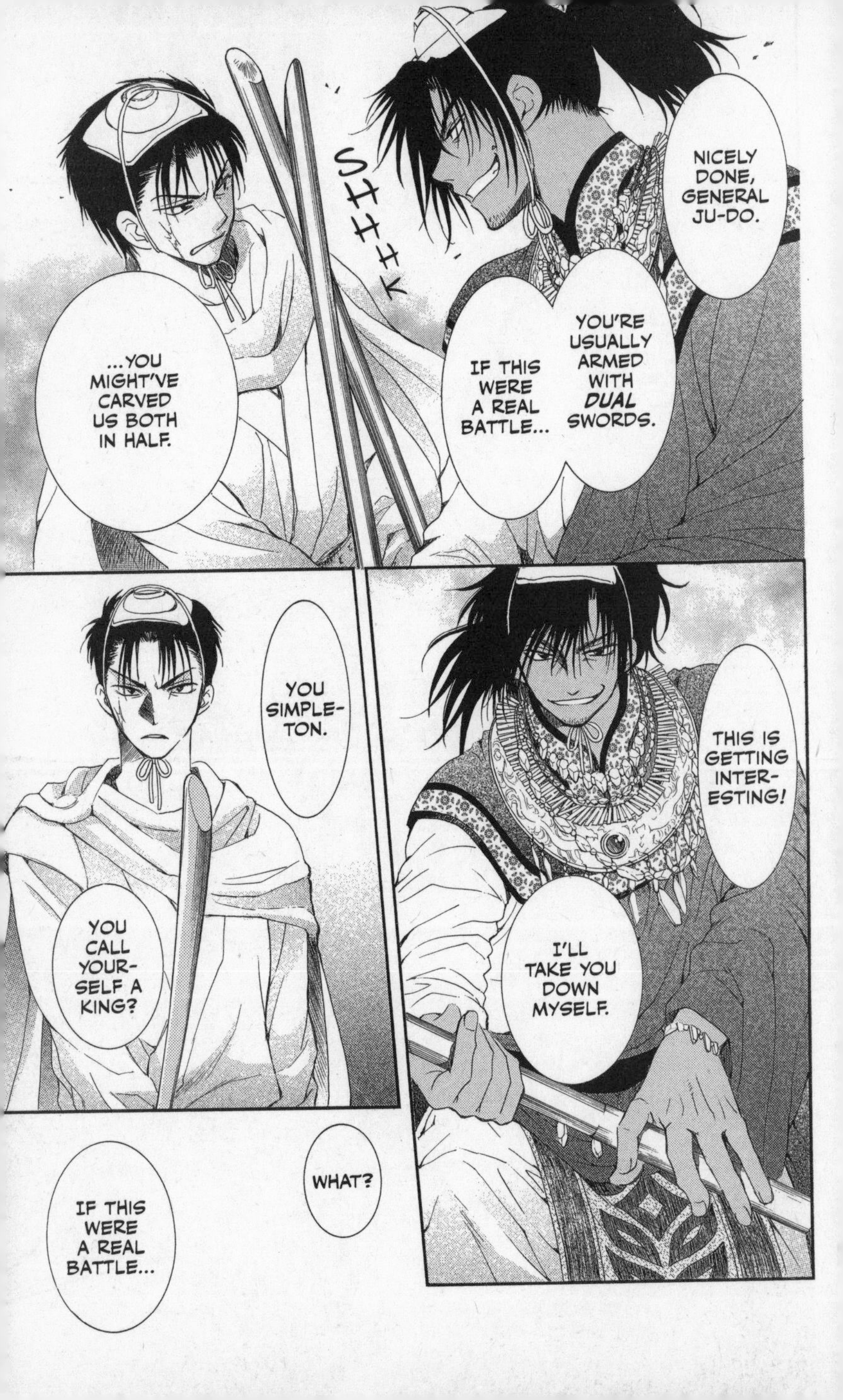
NICELY DONE, GENERAL JU-DO.
YOU'RE USUALLY ARMED WITH *DUAL* SWORDS.
IF THIS WERE A REAL BATTLE...
SHHHK
...YOU MIGHT'VE CARVED US BOTH IN HALF.
THIS IS GETTING INTER-ESTING!
I'LL TAKE YOU DOWN MYSELF.
YOU SIMPLE-TON.
YOU CALL YOUR-SELF A KING?
WHAT?
IF THIS WERE A REAL BATTLE...

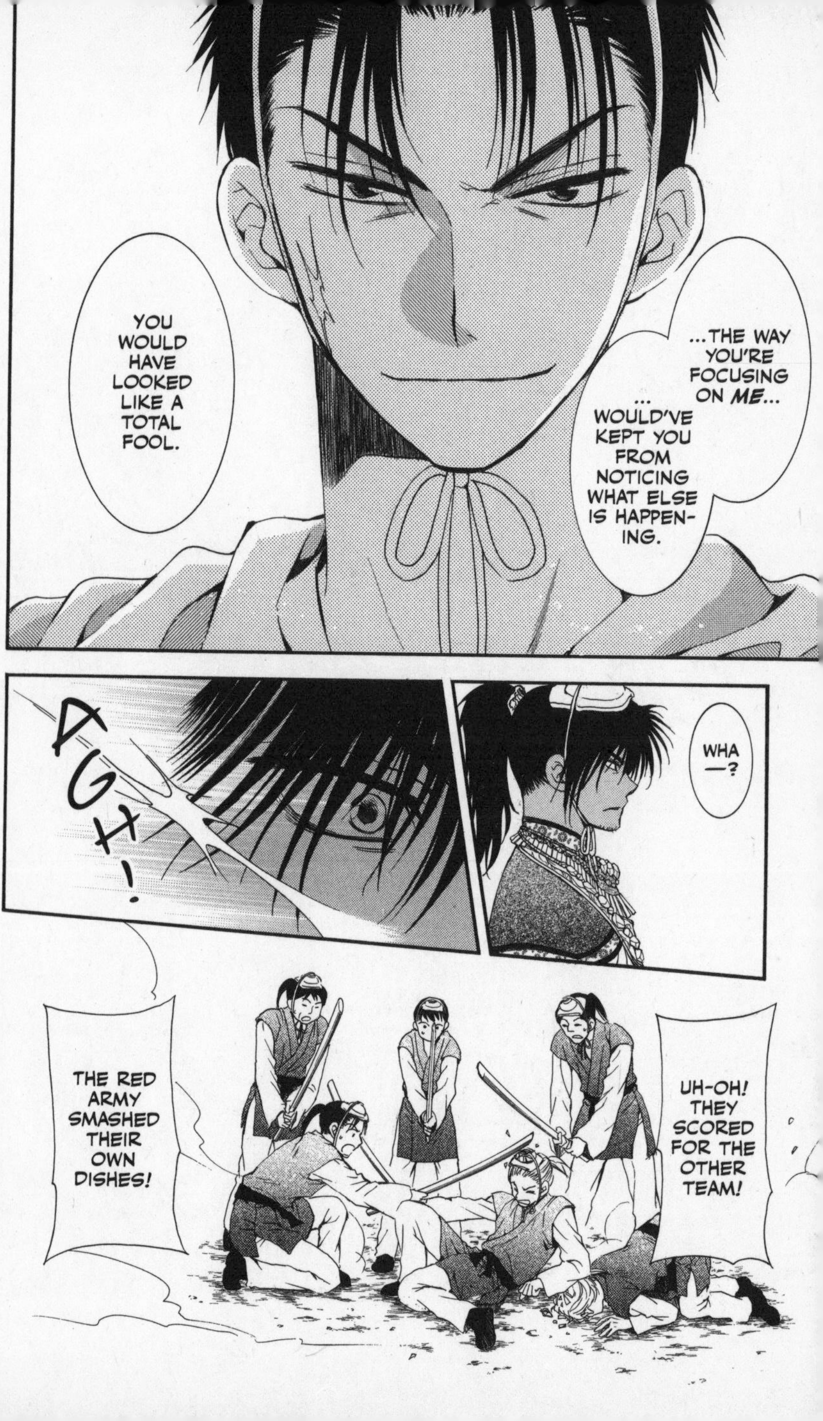
...THE WAY YOU'RE FOCUSING ON *ME*...
... WOULD'VE KEPT YOU FROM NOTICING WHAT ELSE IS HAPPEN-ING.
YOU WOULD HAVE LOOKED LIKE A TOTAL FOOL.
WHA—?
AGH!
UH-OH! THEY SCORED FOR THE OTHER TEAM!
THE RED ARMY SMASHED THEIR OWN DISHES!

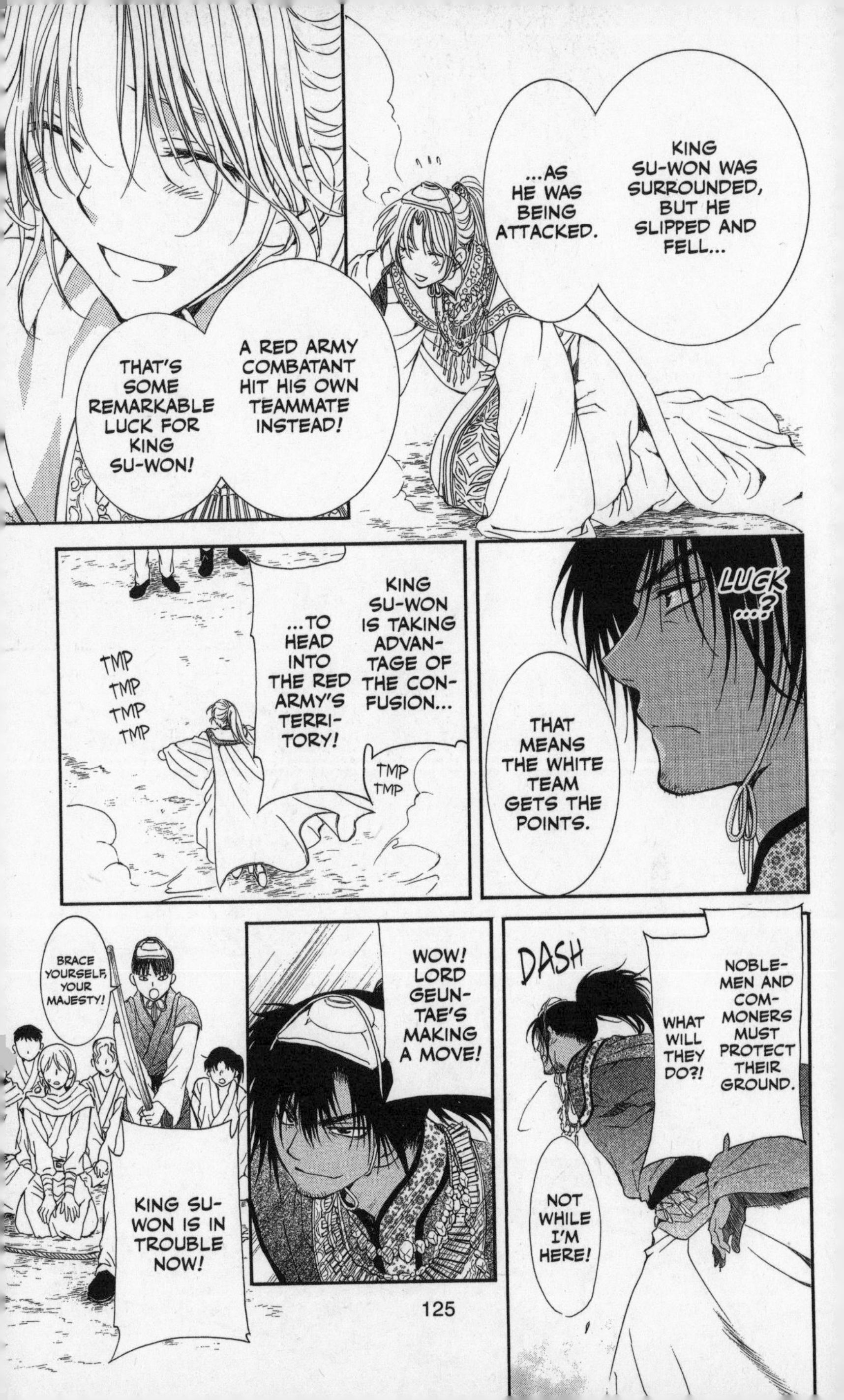

KING SU-WON WAS SURROUNDED, BUT HE SLIPPED AND FELL...
...AS HE WAS BEING ATTACKED.
A RED ARMY COMBATANT HIT HIS OWN TEAMMATE INSTEAD!
THAT'S SOME REMARKABLE LUCK FOR KING SU-WON!
LUCK ...?
THAT MEANS THE WHITE TEAM GETS THE POINTS.
KING SU-WON IS TAKING ADVANTAGE OF THE CONFUSION...
...TO HEAD INTO THE RED ARMY'S TERRITORY!
TMP TMP TMP TMP
TMP TMP
DASH
NOBLEMEN AND COMMONERS MUST PROTECT THEIR GROUND.
WHAT WILL THEY DO?!
NOT WHILE I'M HERE!
WOW! LORD GEUN-TAE'S MAKING A MOVE!
BRACE YOURSELF, YOUR MAJESTY!
KING SU-WON IS IN TROUBLE NOW!

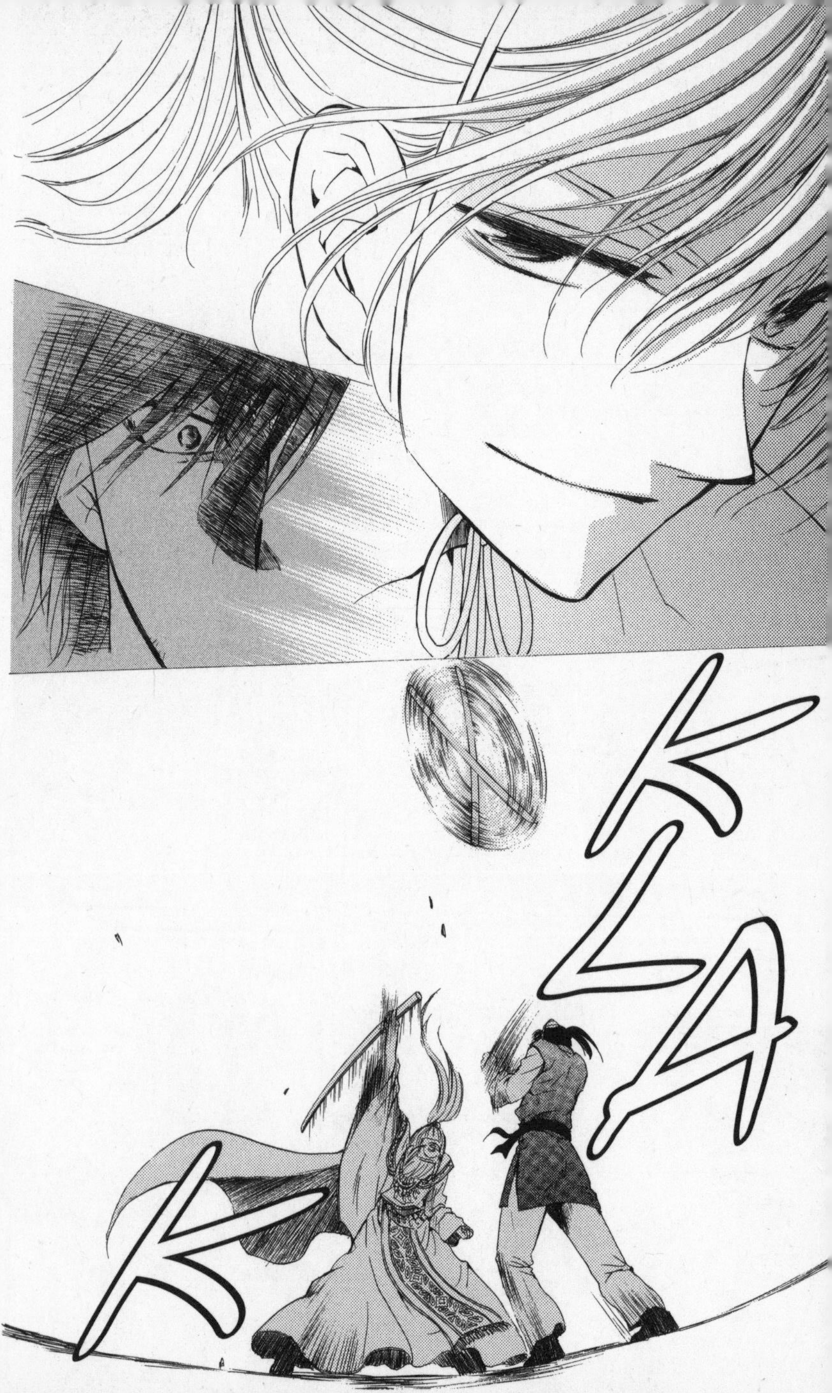
KLAK

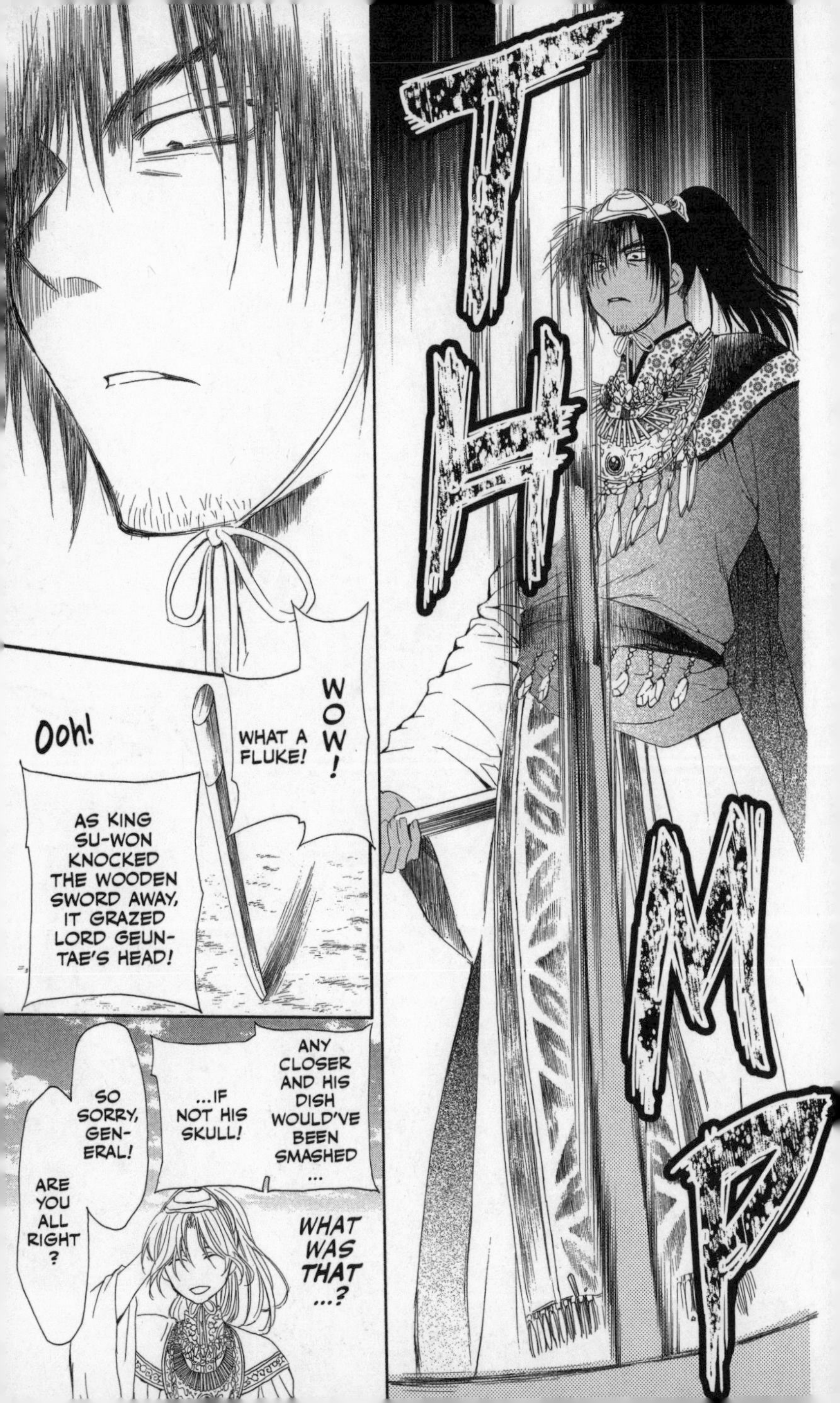
THMP
WOW!
WHAT A FLUKE!
Ooh!
AS KING SU-WON KNOCKED THE WOODEN SWORD AWAY, IT GRAZED LORD GEUN-TAE'S HEAD!
ANY CLOSER AND HIS DISH WOULD'VE BEEN SMASHED...
...IF NOT HIS SKULL!
SO SORRY, GEN-ERAL!
ARE YOU ALL RIGHT?
WHAT WAS THAT...?

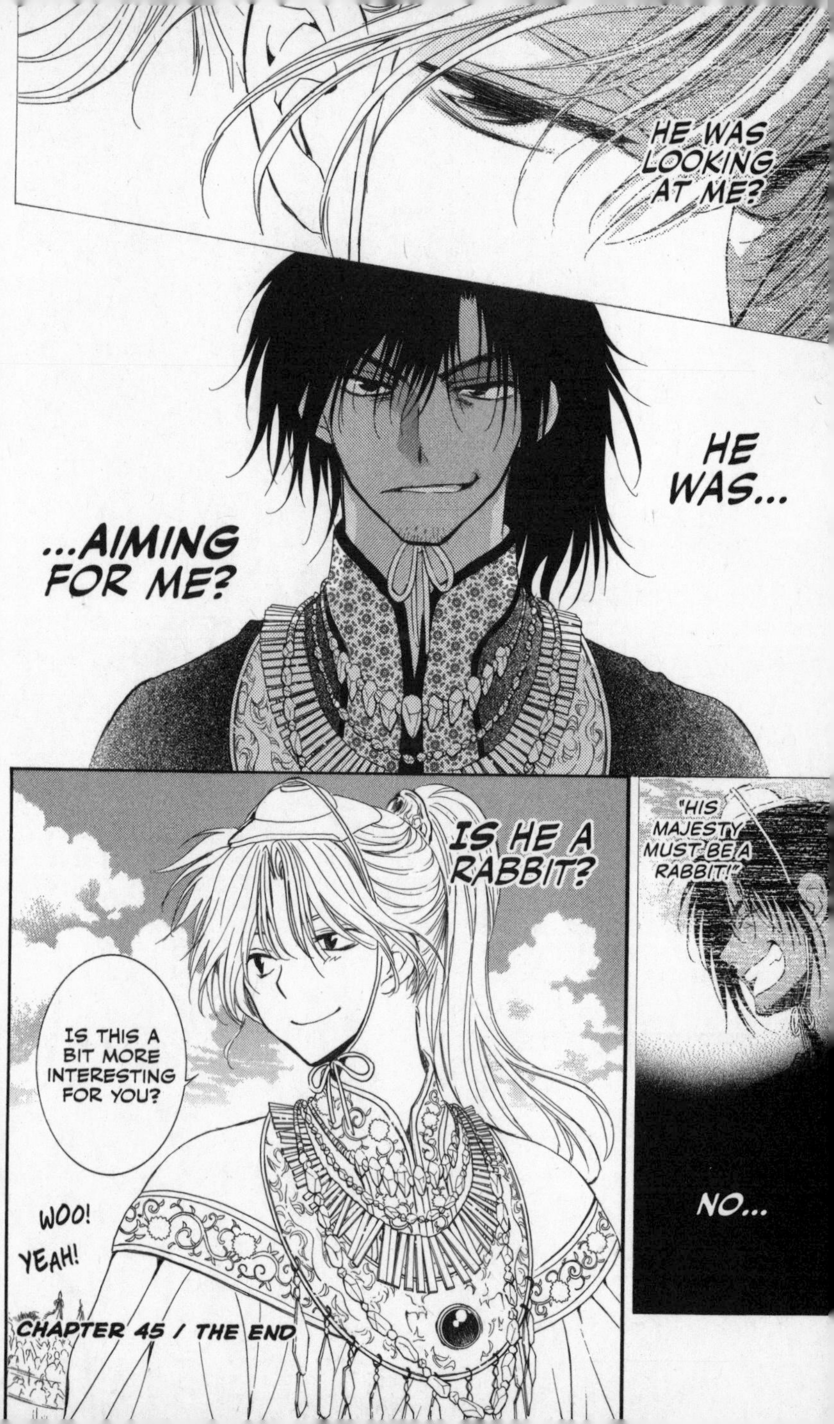
HE WAS LOOKING AT ME?
HE WAS...
...AIMING FOR ME?
"HIS MAJESTY MUST BE A RABBIT!"
NO...
IS HE A RABBIT?
IS THIS A BIT MORE INTERESTING FOR YOU?
WOO!
YEAH!
CHAPTER 45 / THE END

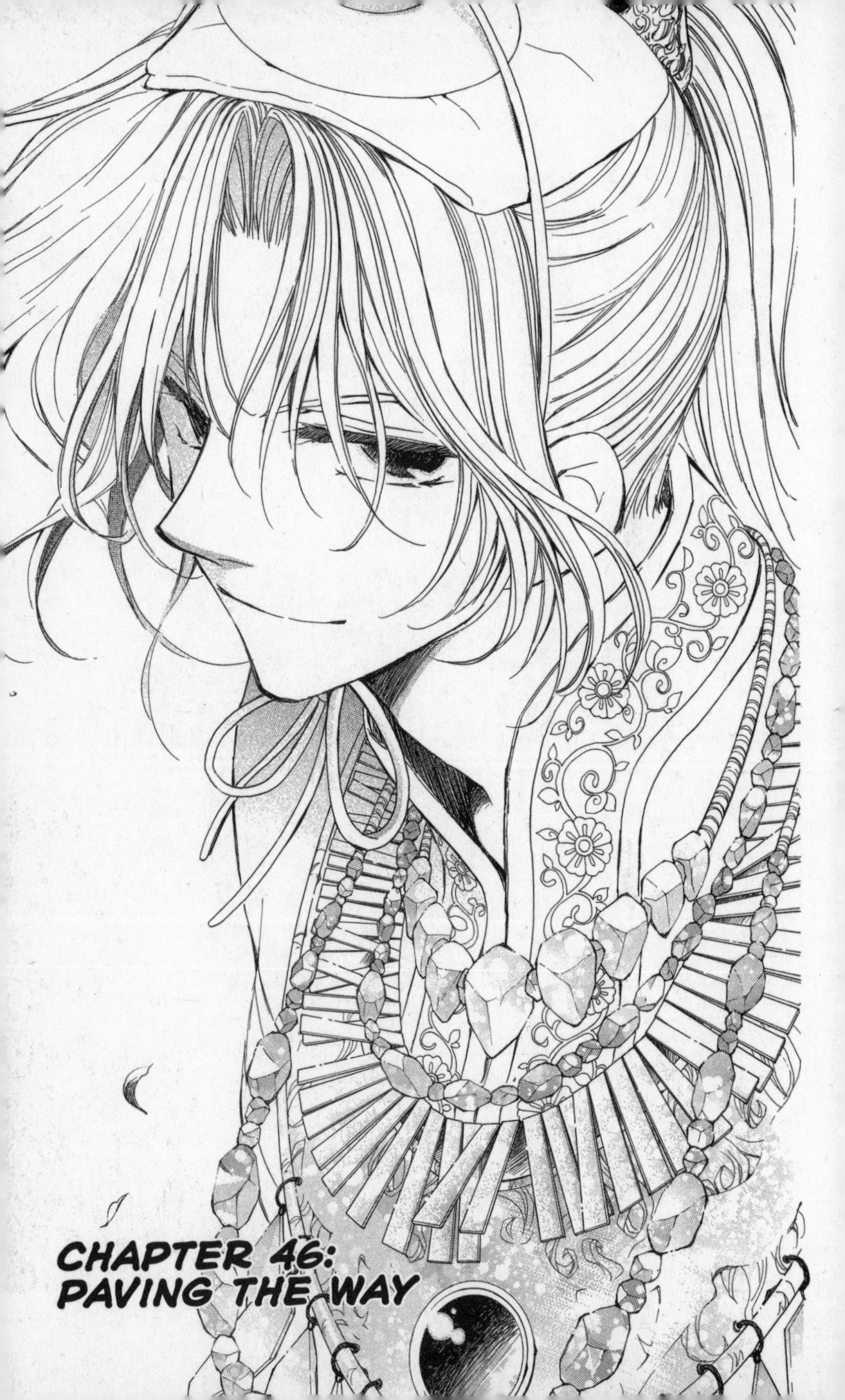
CHAPTER 46:
PAVING THE WAY

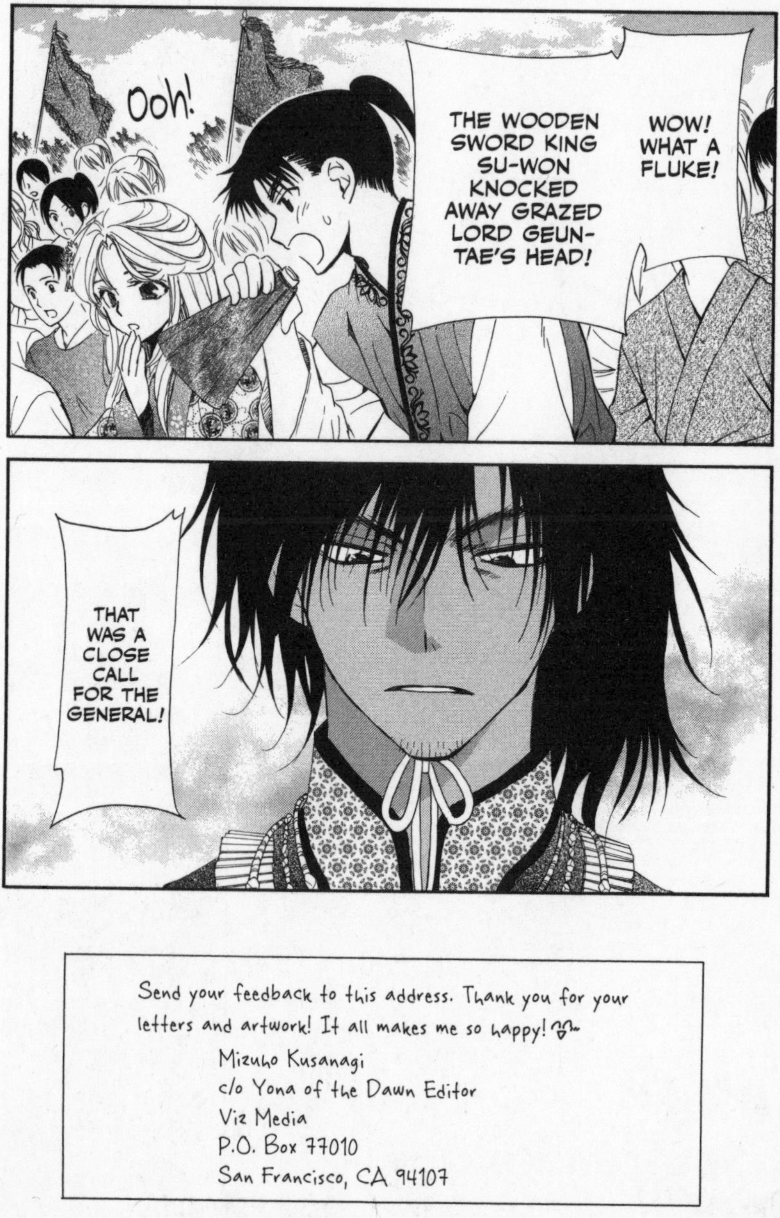
WOW! WHAT A FLUKE!
THE WOODEN SWORD KING SU-WON KNOCKED AWAY GRAZED LORD GEUN-TAE'S HEAD!
Ooh!
THAT WAS A CLOSE CALL FOR THE GENERAL!

Send your feedback to this address. Thank you for your letters and artwork! It all makes me so happy!

Mizuho Kusanagi
c/o Yona of the Dawn Editor
Viz Media
P.O. Box 77010
San Francisco, CA 94107

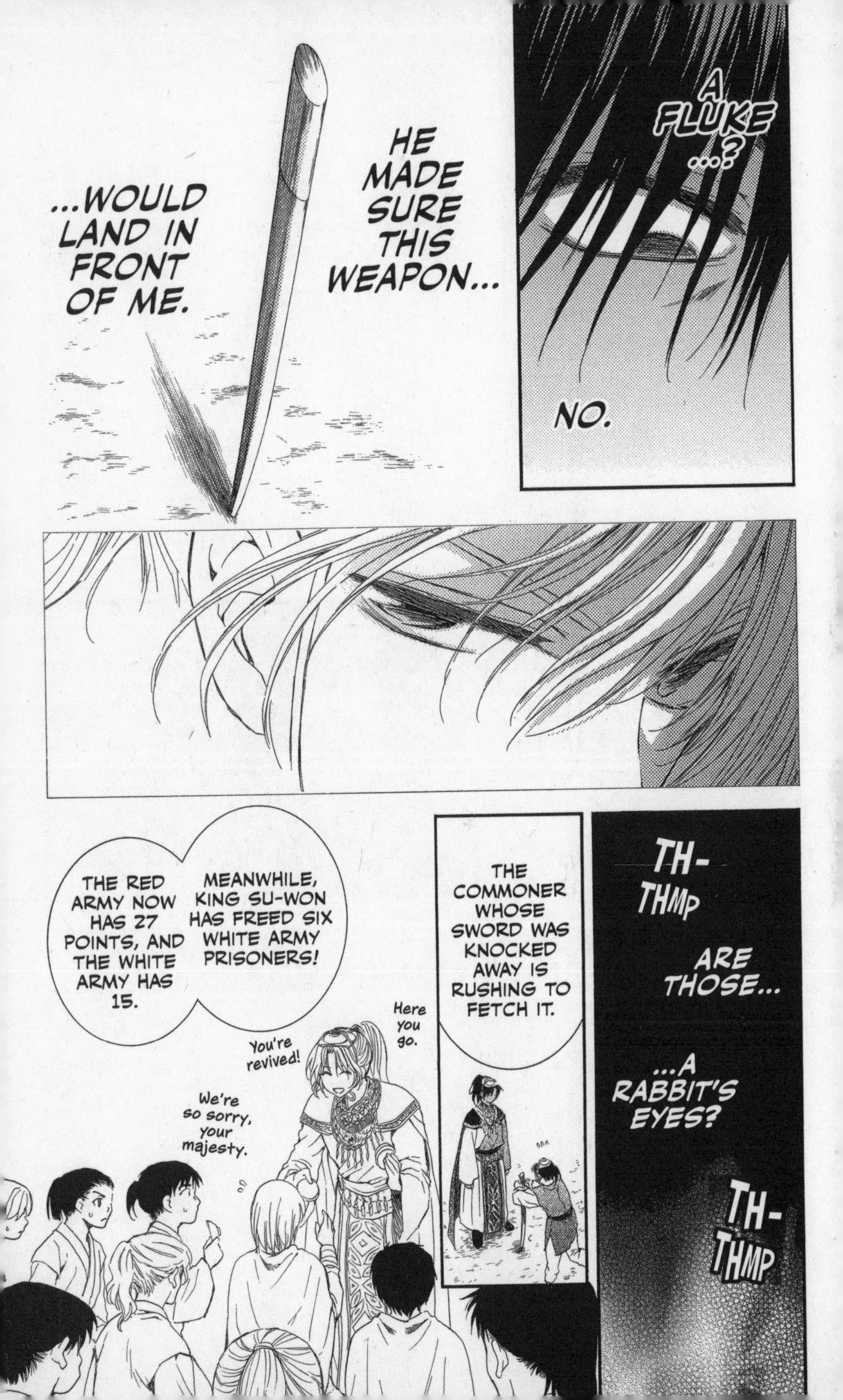
A FLUKE...?
NO.
HE MADE SURE THIS WEAPON...
...WOULD LAND IN FRONT OF ME.
TH-THMP
ARE THOSE...
...A RABBIT'S EYES?
TH-THMP
THE COMMONER WHOSE SWORD WAS KNOCKED AWAY IS RUSHING TO FETCH IT.
MEANWHILE, KING SU-WON HAS FREED SIX WHITE ARMY PRISONERS!
THE RED ARMY NOW HAS 27 POINTS, AND THE WHITE ARMY HAS 15.
Here you go.
You're revived!
We're so sorry, your majesty.

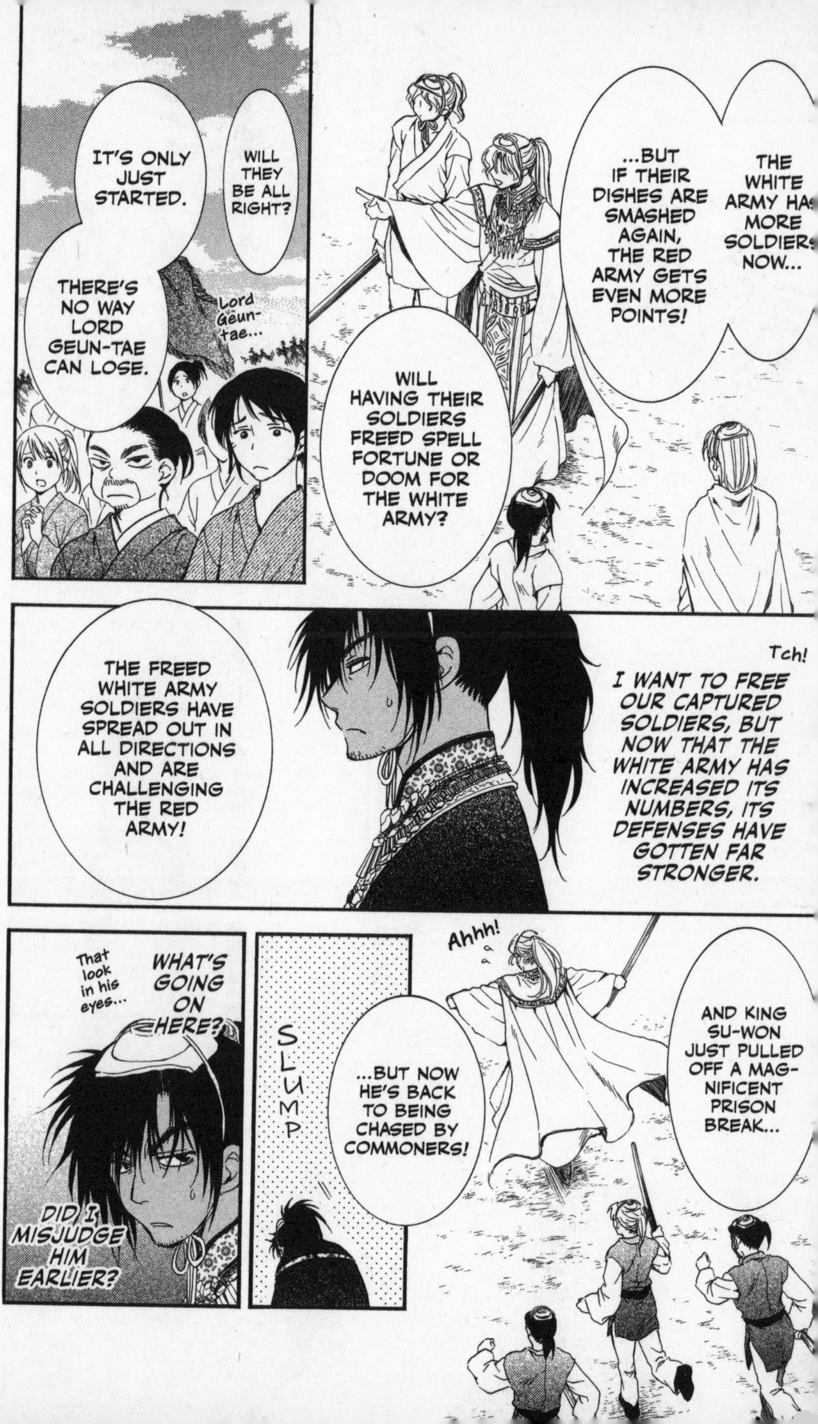
THE WHITE ARMY HAS MORE SOLDIERS NOW...
...BUT IF THEIR DISHES ARE SMASHED AGAIN, THE RED ARMY GETS EVEN MORE POINTS!
WILL HAVING THEIR SOLDIERS FREED SPELL FORTUNE OR DOOM FOR THE WHITE ARMY?
WILL THEY BE ALL RIGHT?
IT'S ONLY JUST STARTED.
Lord Geun-tae...
THERE'S NO WAY LORD GEUN-TAE CAN LOSE.
Tch!
I WANT TO FREE OUR CAPTURED SOLDIERS, BUT NOW THAT THE WHITE ARMY HAS INCREASED ITS NUMBERS, ITS DEFENSES HAVE GOTTEN FAR STRONGER.
THE FREED WHITE ARMY SOLDIERS HAVE SPREAD OUT IN ALL DIRECTIONS AND ARE CHALLENGING THE RED ARMY!
Ahhh!
AND KING SU-WON JUST PULLED OFF A MAGNIFICENT PRISON BREAK...
...BUT NOW HE'S BACK TO BEING CHASED BY COMMONERS!
SLUMP
WHAT'S GOING ON HERE?
That look in his eyes...
DID I MISJUDGE HIM EARLIER?

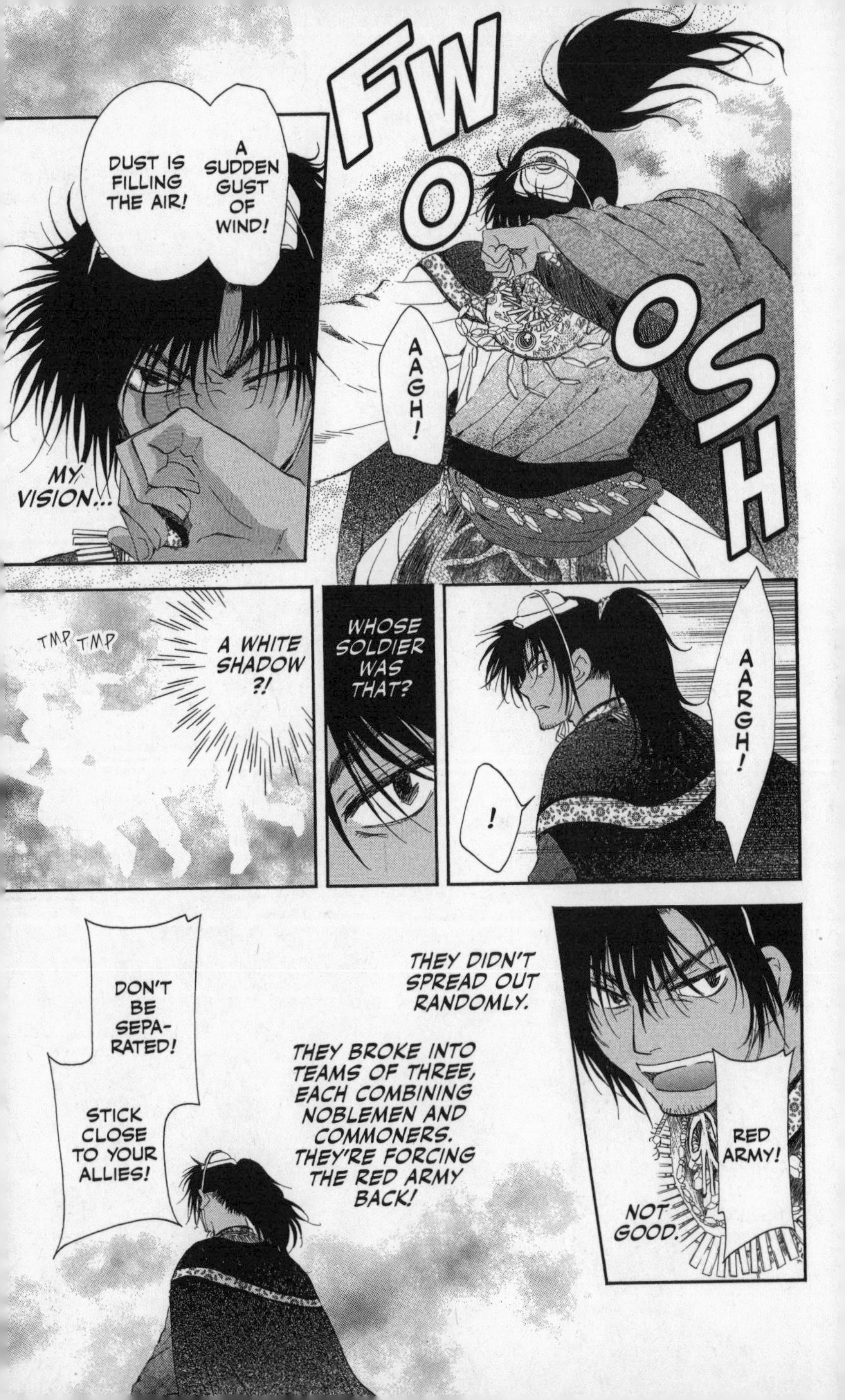
FWOOSH
AAGH!
A SUDDEN GUST OF WIND!
DUST IS FILLING THE AIR!
MY VISION...
AARGH!
!
WHOSE SOLDIER WAS THAT?
A WHITE SHADOW?!
TMP TMP
RED ARMY!
NOT GOOD.
THEY DIDN'T SPREAD OUT RANDOMLY.
THEY BROKE INTO TEAMS OF THREE, EACH COMBINING NOBLEMEN AND COMMONERS. THEY'RE FORCING THE RED ARMY BACK!
DON'T BE SEPARATED!
STICK CLOSE TO YOUR ALLIES!

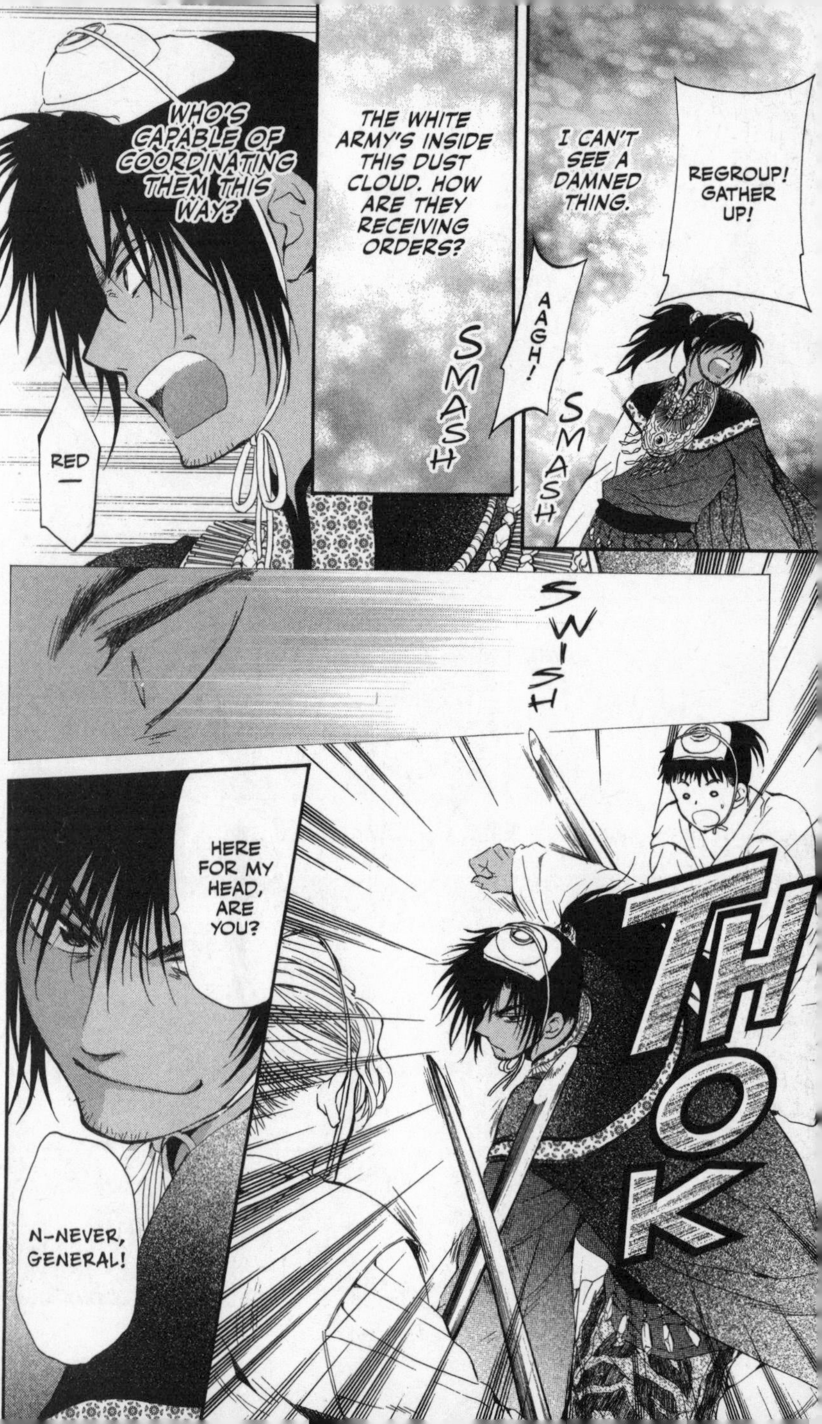
REGROUP! GATHER UP!
I CAN'T SEE A DAMNED THING.
AAGH!
SMASH
THE WHITE ARMY'S INSIDE THIS DUST CLOUD. HOW ARE THEY RECEIVING ORDERS?
SMASH
WHO'S CAPABLE OF COORDINATING THEM THIS WAY?
RED—
SWISH
THOK
HERE FOR MY HEAD, ARE YOU?
N-NEVER, GENERAL!

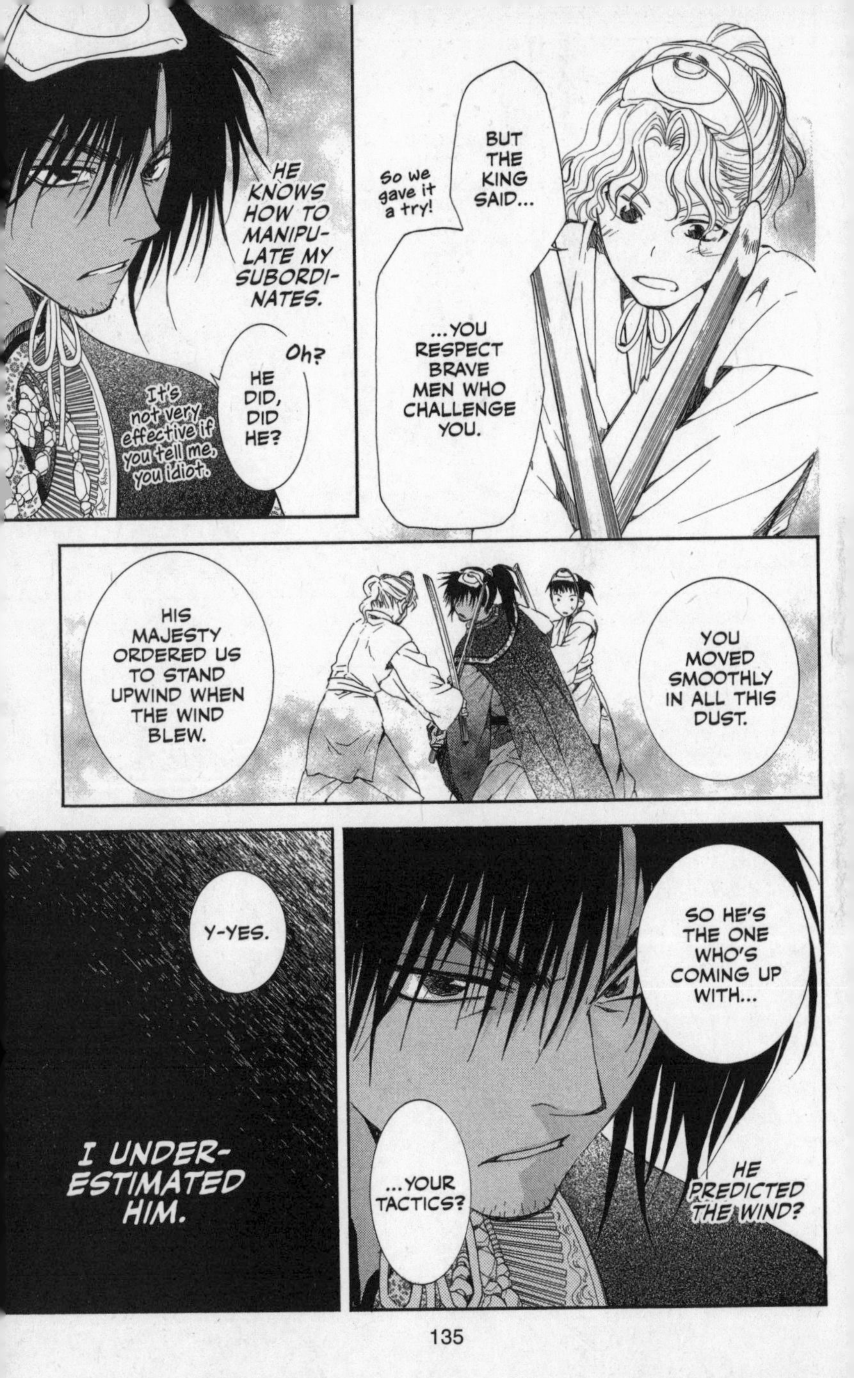

BUT THE KING SAID...
So we gave it a try!
...YOU RESPECT BRAVE MEN WHO CHALLENGE YOU.
HE KNOWS HOW TO MANIPULATE MY SUBORDINATES.
Oh?
HE DID, DID HE?
It's not very effective if you tell me, you idiot.
YOU MOVED SMOOTHLY IN ALL THIS DUST.
HIS MAJESTY ORDERED US TO STAND UPWIND WHEN THE WIND BLEW.
SO HE'S THE ONE WHO'S COMING UP WITH...
HE PREDICTED THE WIND?
...YOUR TACTICS?
Y-YES.
I UNDERESTIMATED HIM.

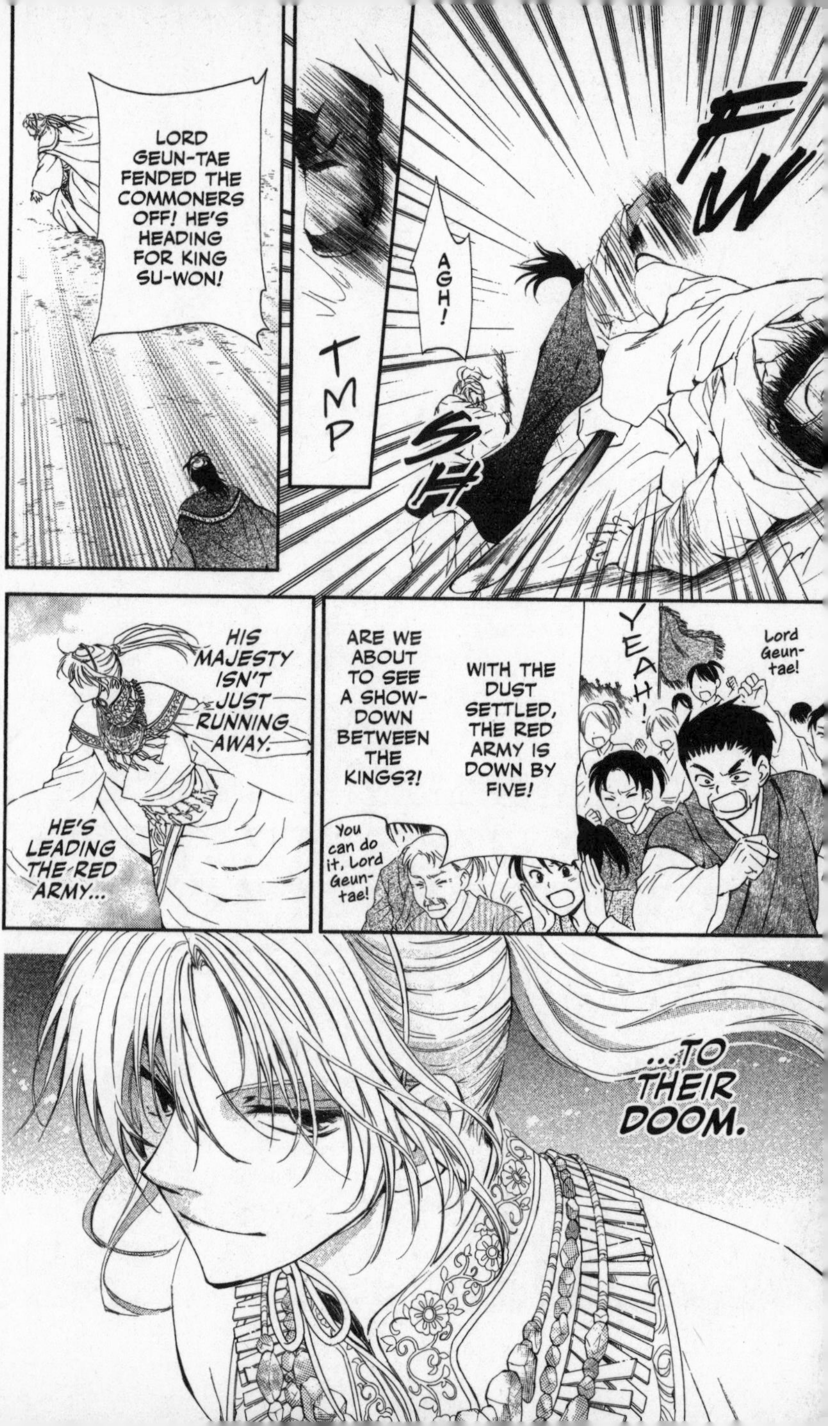
FW
AGH!
TMP
SH
LORD GEUN-TAE FENDED THE COMMONERS OFF! HE'S HEADING FOR KING SU-WON!
YEAH!
Lord Geun-tae!
WITH THE DUST SETTLED, THE RED ARMY IS DOWN BY FIVE!
ARE WE ABOUT TO SEE A SHOW-DOWN BETWEEN THE KINGS?!
You can do it, Lord Geun-tae!
HIS MAJESTY ISN'T JUST RUNNING AWAY.
HE'S LEADING THE RED ARMY...
...TO THEIR DOOM.

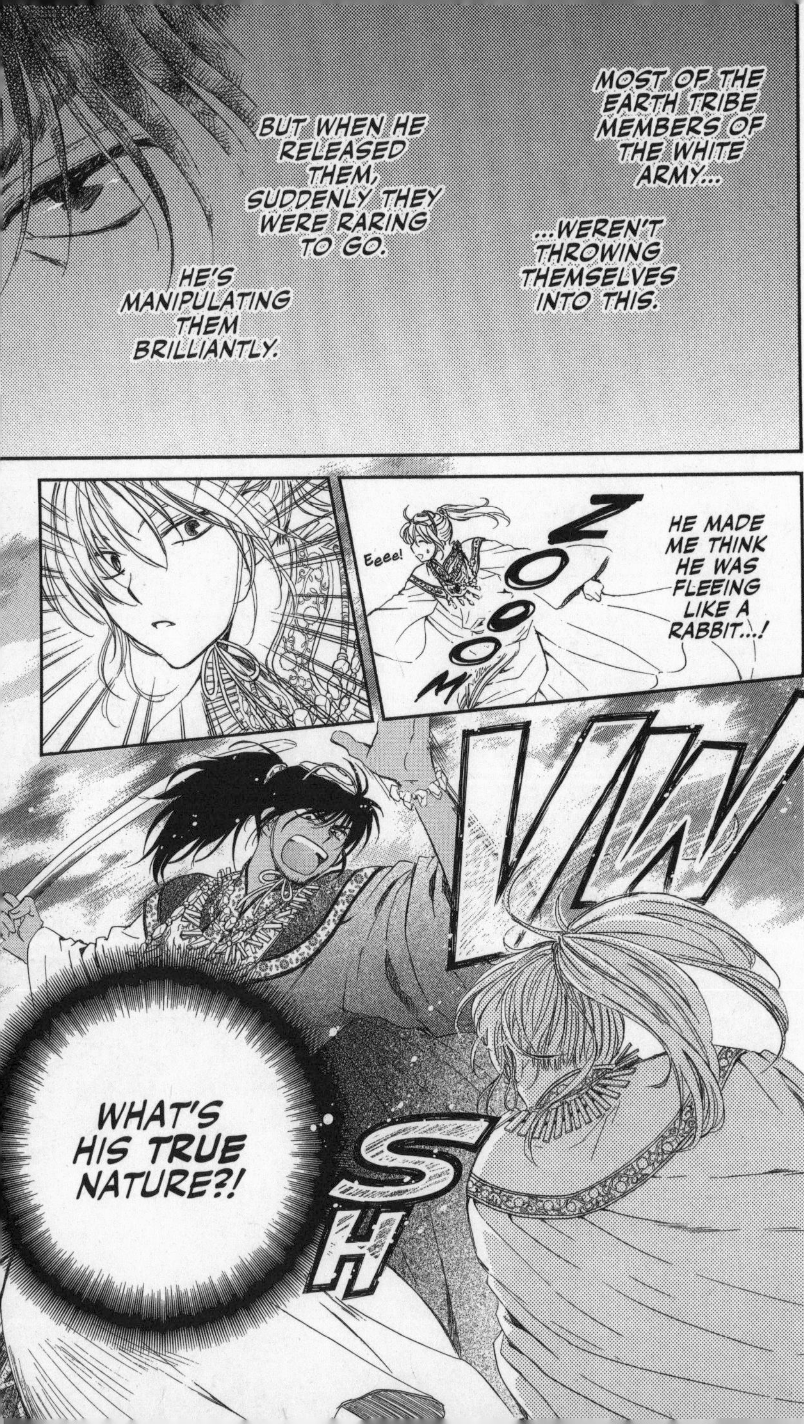
MOST OF THE EARTH TRIBE MEMBERS OF THE WHITE ARMY...
...WEREN'T THROWING THEMSELVES INTO THIS.
BUT WHEN HE RELEASED THEM, SUDDENLY THEY WERE RARING TO GO.
HE'S MANIPULATING THEM BRILLIANTLY.
HE MADE ME THINK HE WAS FLEEING LIKE A RABBIT...!
ZOOOOM
Eeee!
VW
WHAT'S HIS TRUE NATURE?!
SH

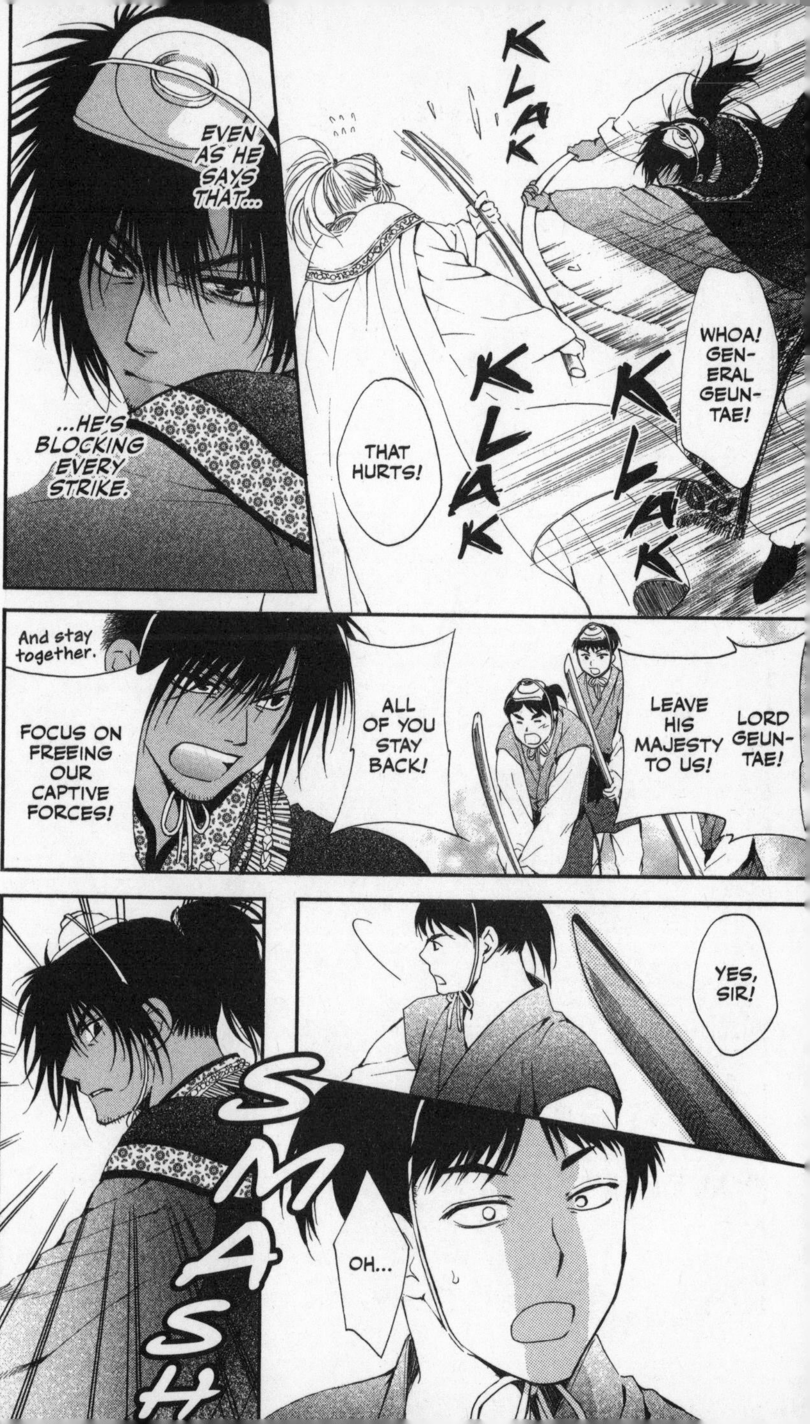
KLAK
WHOA! GEN-ERAL GEUN-TAE!
KLAK
THAT HURTS!
KLAK
EVEN AS HE SAYS THAT...
...HE'S BLOCKING EVERY STRIKE.
LORD GEUN-TAE!
LEAVE HIS MAJESTY TO US!
ALL OF YOU STAY BACK!
FOCUS ON FREEING OUR CAPTIVE FORCES!
And stay together.
YES, SIR!
OH...
SMASH

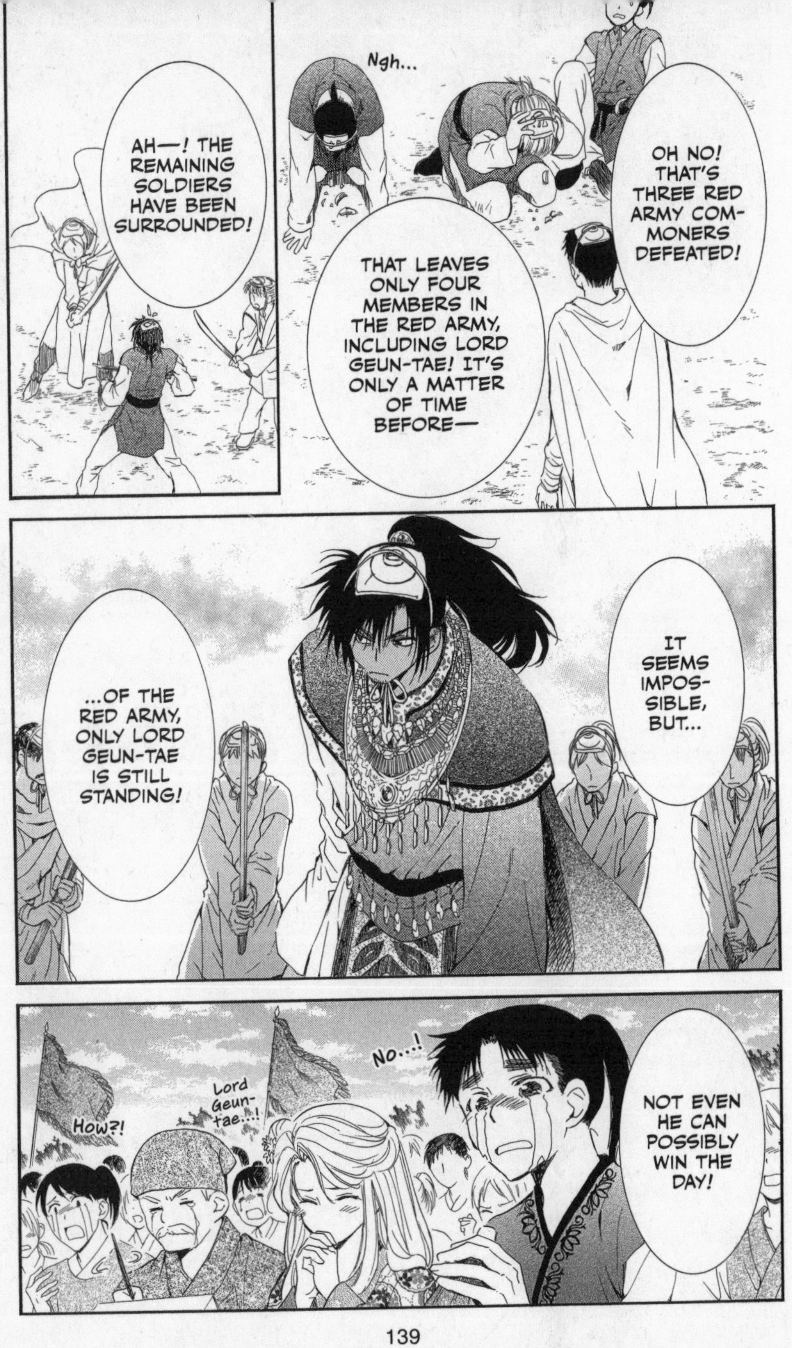
Ngh...
OH NO! THAT'S THREE RED ARMY COMMONERS DEFEATED!
THAT LEAVES ONLY FOUR MEMBERS IN THE RED ARMY, INCLUDING LORD GEUN-TAE! IT'S ONLY A MATTER OF TIME BEFORE—
AH—! THE REMAINING SOLDIERS HAVE BEEN SURROUNDED!
IT SEEMS IMPOSSIBLE, BUT...
...OF THE RED ARMY, ONLY LORD GEUN-TAE IS STILL STANDING!
NOT EVEN HE CAN POSSIBLY WIN THE DAY!
No...!
Lord Geun-tae...!
How?!

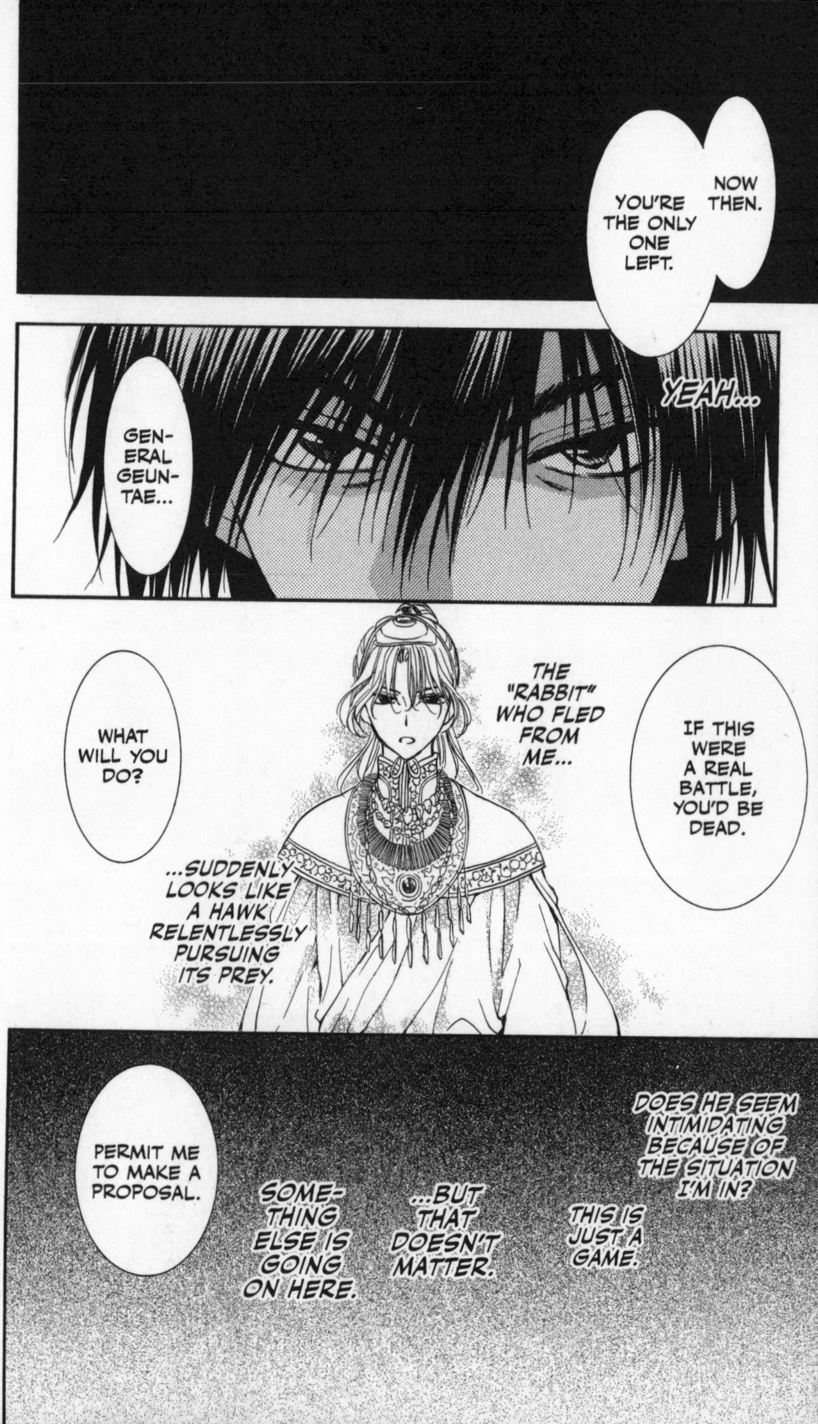
NOW THEN.
YOU'RE THE ONLY ONE LEFT.
YEAH...
GEN-ERAL GEUN-TAE...
IF THIS WERE A REAL BATTLE, YOU'D BE DEAD.
THE "RABBIT" WHO FLED FROM ME...
...SUDDENLY LOOKS LIKE A HAWK RELENTLESSLY PURSUING ITS PREY.
WHAT WILL YOU DO?
DOES HE SEEM INTIMIDATING BECAUSE OF THE SITUATION I'M IN?
THIS IS JUST A GAME.
...BUT THAT DOESN'T MATTER.
SOME-THING ELSE IS GOING ON HERE.
PERMIT ME TO MAKE A PROPOSAL.

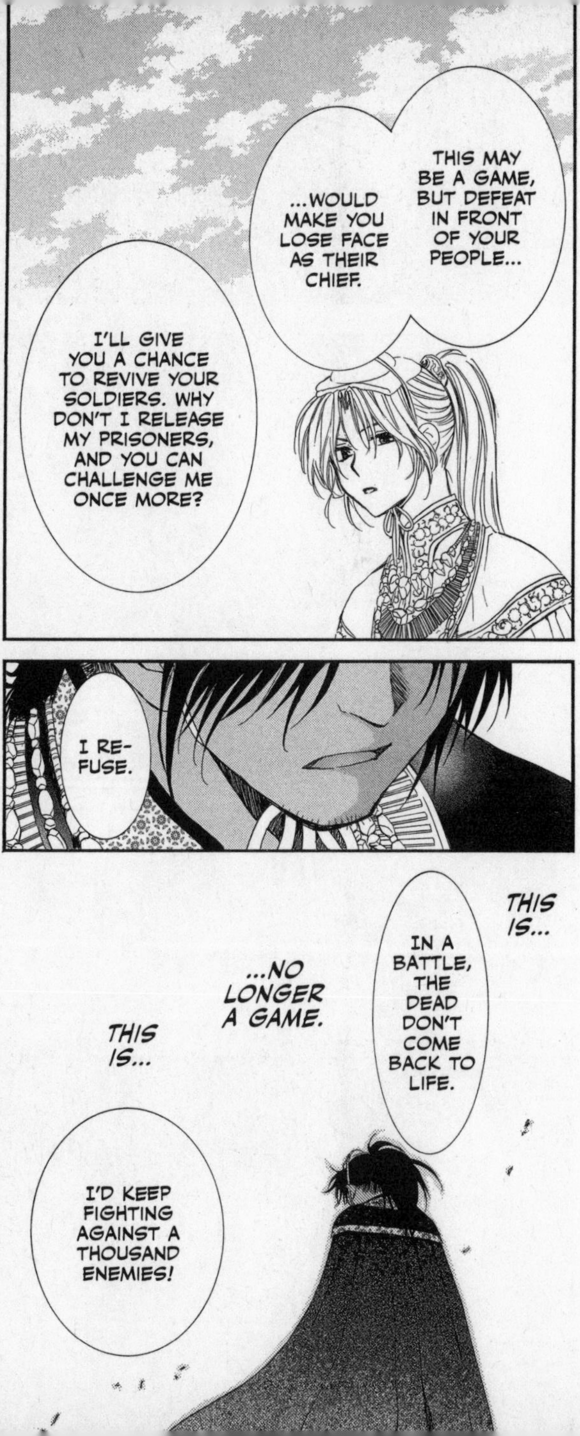
THIS MAY BE A GAME, BUT DEFEAT IN FRONT OF YOUR PEOPLE...
...WOULD MAKE YOU LOSE FACE AS THEIR CHIEF.
I'LL GIVE YOU A CHANCE TO REVIVE YOUR SOLDIERS. WHY DON'T I RELEASE MY PRISONERS, AND YOU CAN CHALLENGE ME ONCE MORE?
I RE-FUSE.
THIS IS...
IN A BATTLE, THE DEAD DON'T COME BACK TO LIFE.
...NO LONGER A GAME.
THIS IS...
I'D KEEP FIGHTING AGAINST A THOUSAND ENEMIES!

Yona and her friends aren't around, but I'm quite excited to be drawing old men like Geun-tae and Ju-do. (They're in their thirties.) ^^ It's great to draw people who are very expressive! But even Su-won or Ju-do look silly with dishes on their heads.

I have to tell you that I regret a choice I made. I'm sorry that the names of the characters in Yona are tricky to keep straight, especially the ones like Gija, Jaeha, Ju-do, Junam, Su-jin, Tae-jun, etc.... Many of the names with the letter "j" in them are rather confusing, aren't they? Apparently I like the sound of names that include "s" or "j."

I'm trying to be careful, but...I'll try harder.

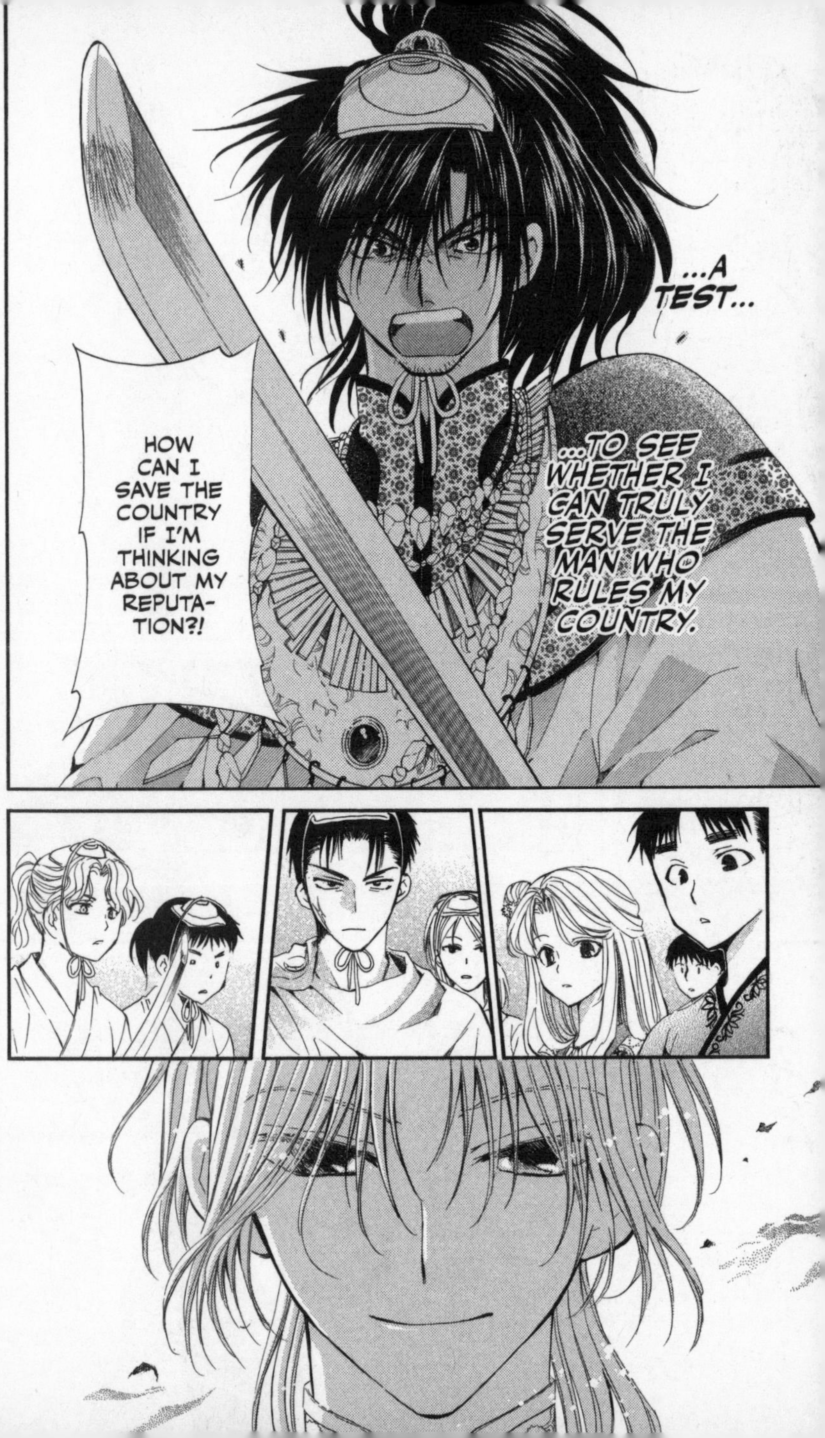
...A TEST...
...TO SEE WHETHER I CAN TRULY SERVE THE MAN WHO RULES MY COUNTRY.
HOW CAN I SAVE THE COUNTRY IF I'M THINKING ABOUT MY REPUTA-TION?!

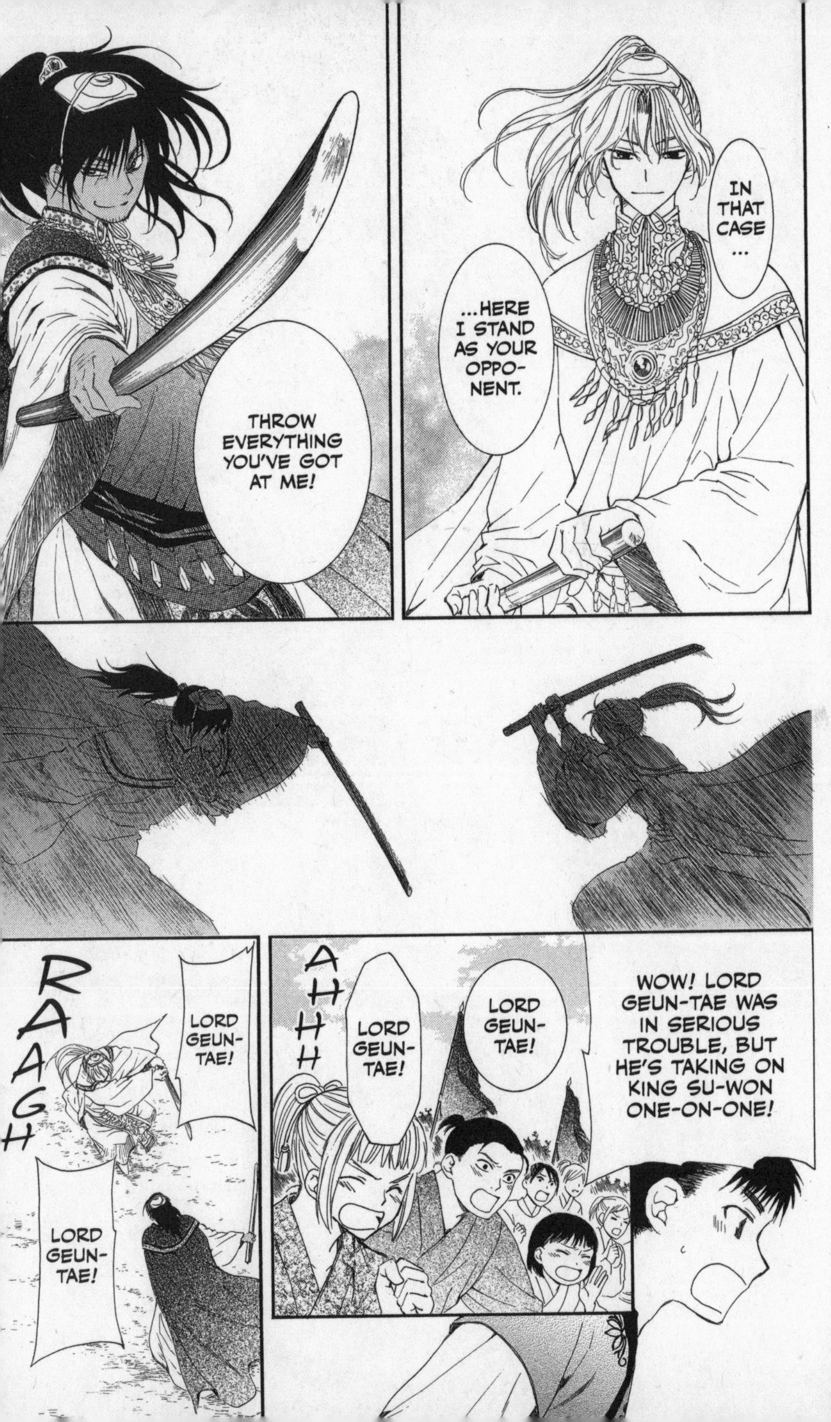
IN THAT CASE ...
...HERE I STAND AS YOUR OPPONENT.
THROW EVERYTHING YOU'VE GOT AT ME!
WOW! LORD GEUN-TAE WAS IN SERIOUS TROUBLE, BUT HE'S TAKING ON KING SU-WON ONE-ON-ONE!
LORD GEUN-TAE!
LORD GEUN-TAE!
AHHH
RAAGH
LORD GEUN-TAE!
LORD GEUN-TAE!

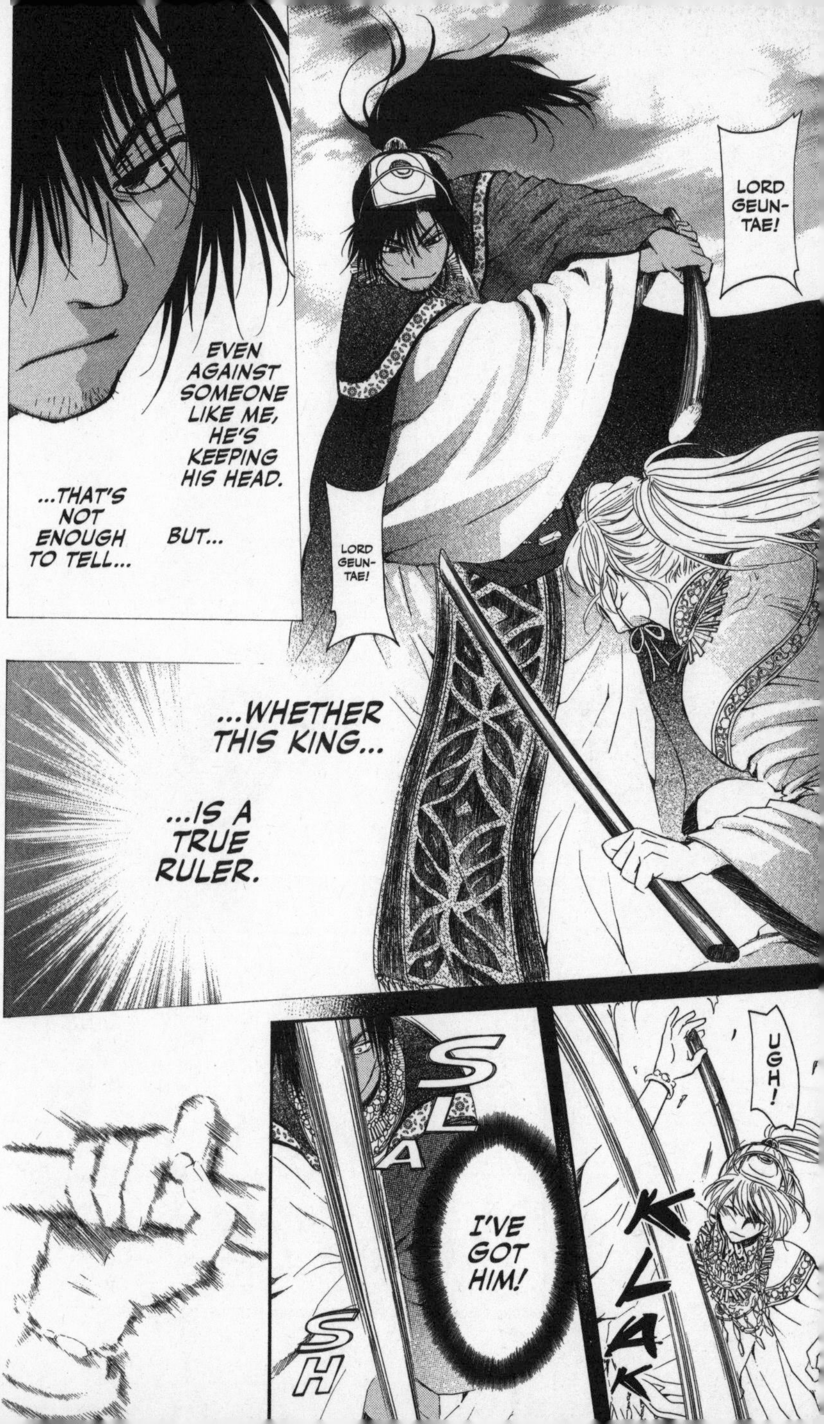
LORD GEUN-TAE!
LORD GEUN-TAE!
EVEN AGAINST SOMEONE LIKE ME, HE'S KEEPING HIS HEAD.
BUT...
...THAT'S NOT ENOUGH TO TELL...
...WHETHER THIS KING...
...IS A TRUE RULER.
UGH!
KLAK
SLASH
I'VE GOT HIM!

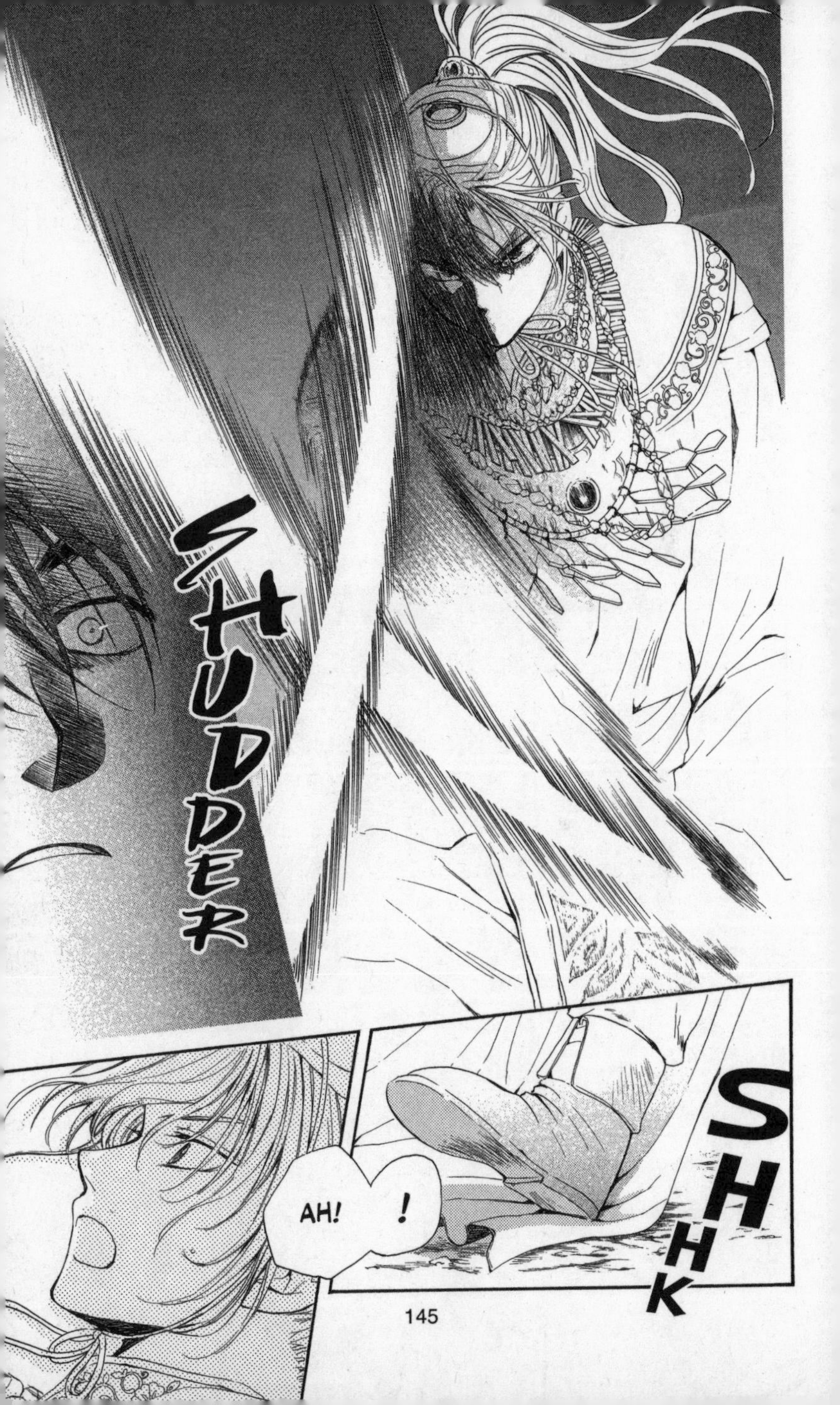
SHUDDER
SHHK
!
AH!

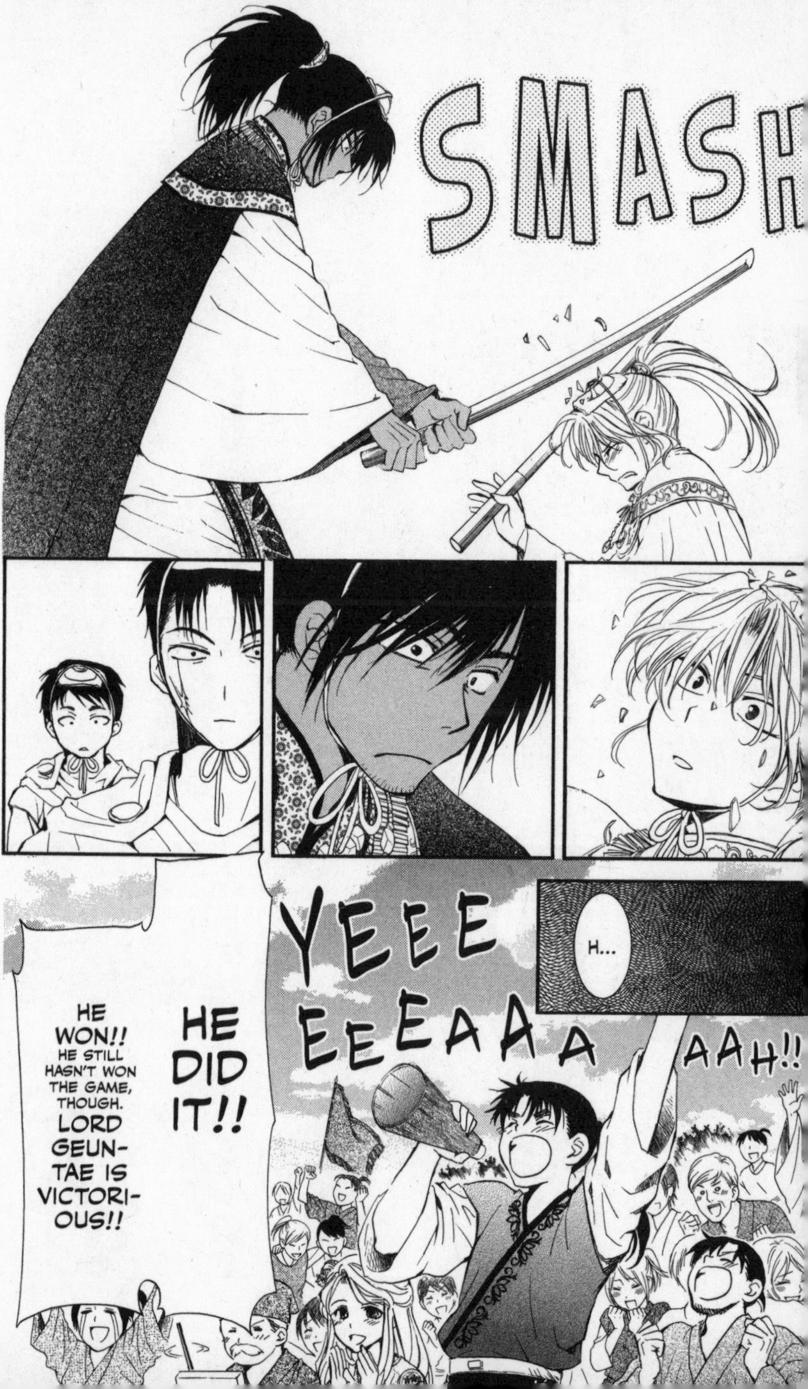
SMASH
H...
YEEEEEEAAAAAAH!!
HE DID IT!!
HE WON!!
HE STILL HASN'T WON THE GAME, THOUGH.
LORD GEUN-TAE IS VICTORIOUS!!

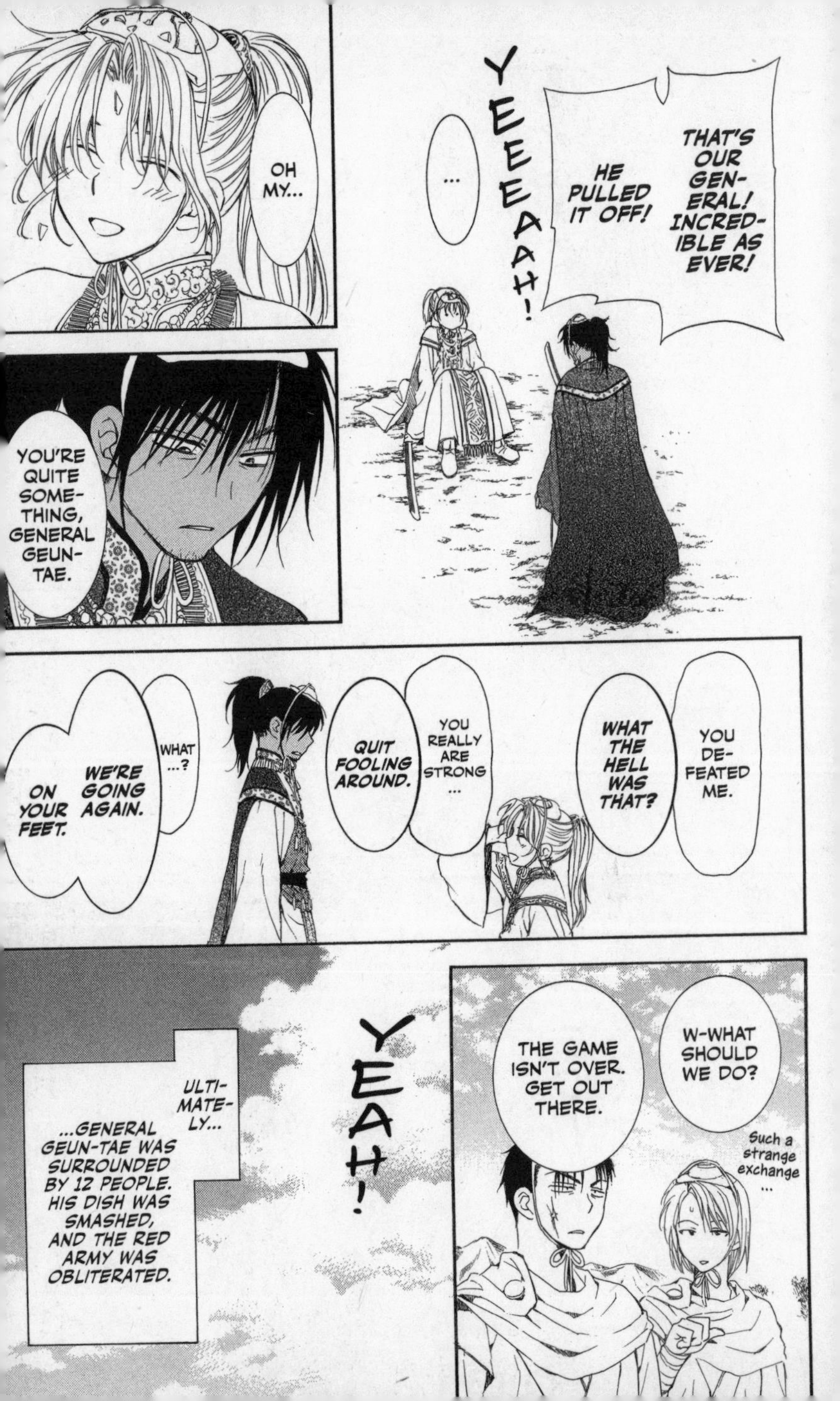
THAT'S OUR GEN-ERAL! INCRED-IBLE AS EVER!
HE PULLED IT OFF!
YEEEAAH!
...
OH MY...
YOU'RE QUITE SOME-THING, GENERAL GEUN-TAE.
YOU DE-FEATED ME.
WHAT THE HELL WAS THAT?
YOU REALLY ARE STRONG...
QUIT FOOLING AROUND.
WHAT...?
WE'RE GOING AGAIN.
ON YOUR FEET.
W-WHAT SHOULD WE DO?
THE GAME ISN'T OVER. GET OUT THERE.
Such a strange exchange...
YEAH!
ULTI-MATE-LY...
...GENERAL GEUN-TAE WAS SURROUNDED BY 12 PEOPLE. HIS DISH WAS SMASHED, AND THE RED ARMY WAS OBLITERATED.

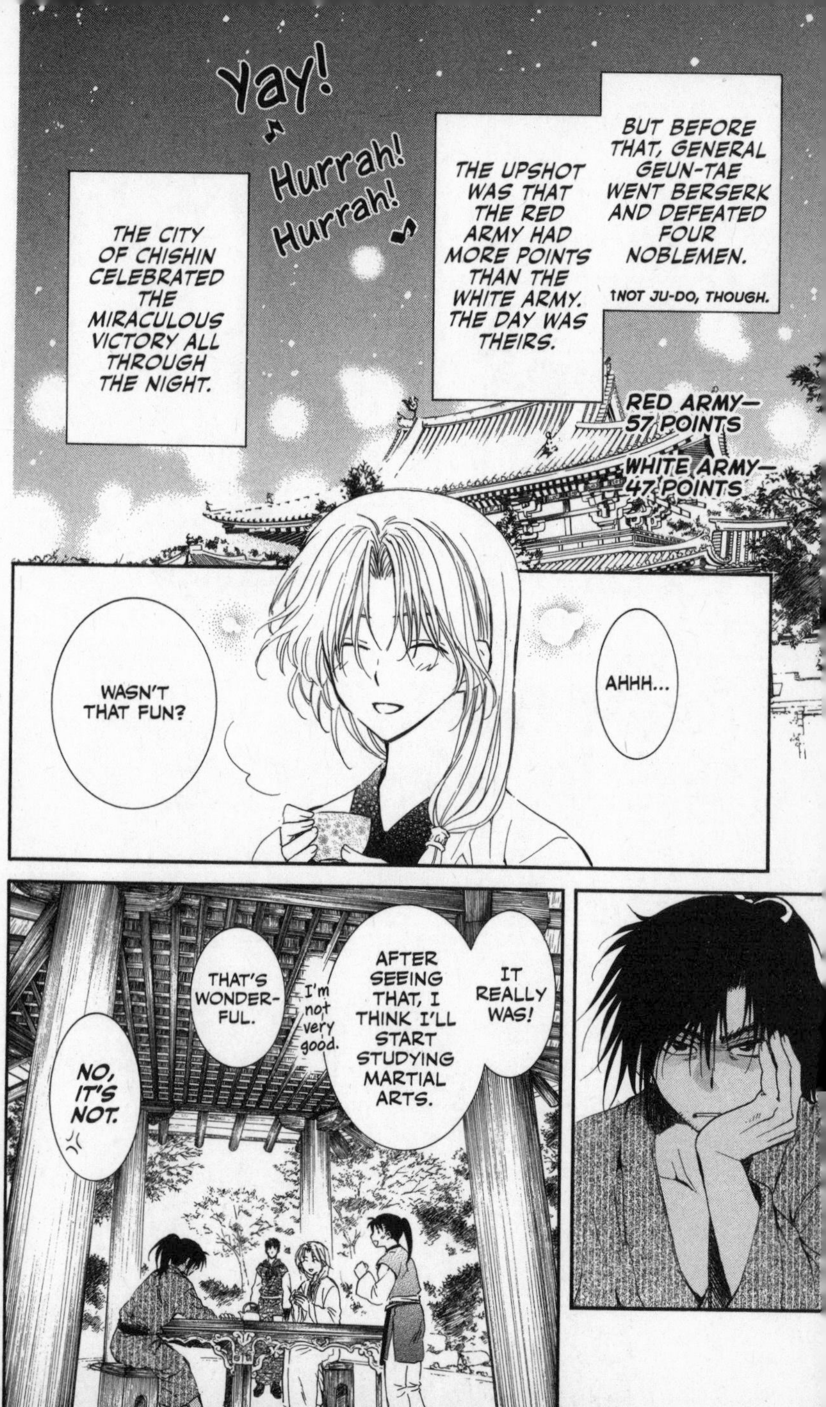
BUT BEFORE THAT, GENERAL GEUN-TAE WENT BERSERK AND DEFEATED FOUR NOBLEMEN.
†NOT JU-DO, THOUGH.
THE UPSHOT WAS THAT THE RED ARMY HAD MORE POINTS THAN THE WHITE ARMY. THE DAY WAS THEIRS.
Yay!
Hurrah! Hurrah!
THE CITY OF CHISHIN CELEBRATED THE MIRACULOUS VICTORY ALL THROUGH THE NIGHT.
RED ARMY—57 POINTS
WHITE ARMY—47 POINTS
AHHH...
WASN'T THAT FUN?
IT REALLY WAS!
AFTER SEEING THAT, I THINK I'LL START STUDYING MARTIAL ARTS.
I'm not very good.
THAT'S WONDERFUL.
NO, IT'S NOT.

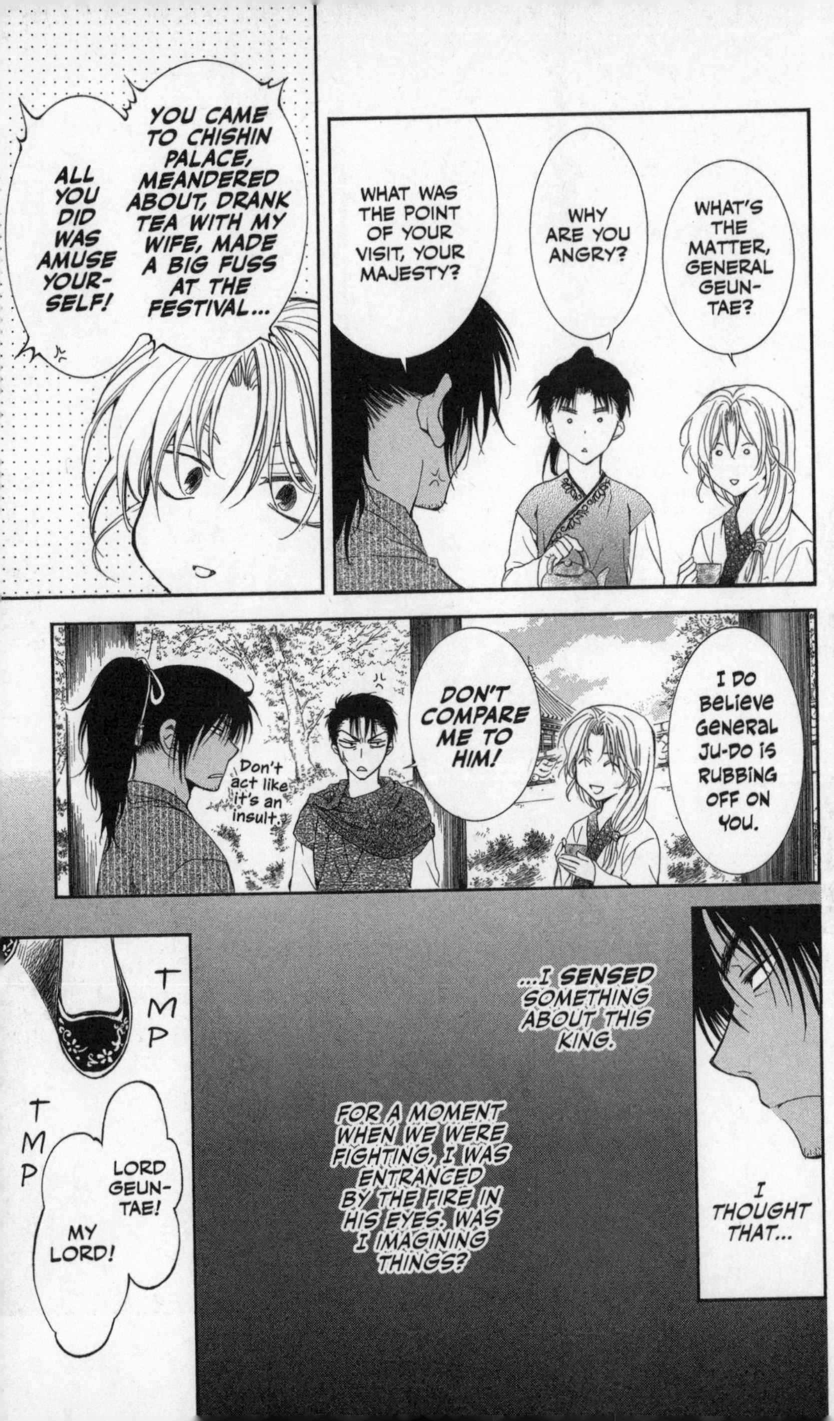
WHAT'S THE MATTER, GENERAL GEUN-TAE?
WHY ARE YOU ANGRY?
WHAT WAS THE POINT OF YOUR VISIT, YOUR MAJESTY?
YOU CAME TO CHISHIN PALACE, MEANDERED ABOUT, DRANK TEA WITH MY WIFE, MADE A BIG FUSS AT THE FESTIVAL...
ALL YOU DID WAS AMUSE YOURSELF!
I DO BELIEVE GENERAL JU-DO IS RUBBING OFF ON YOU.
DON'T COMPARE ME TO HIM!
Don't act like it's an insult.
I THOUGHT THAT...
...I SENSED SOMETHING ABOUT THIS KING.
FOR A MOMENT WHEN WE WERE FIGHTING, I WAS ENTRANCED BY THE FIRE IN HIS EYES. WAS I IMAGINING THINGS?
TMP
TMP
LORD GEUN-TAE!
MY LORD!
TMP

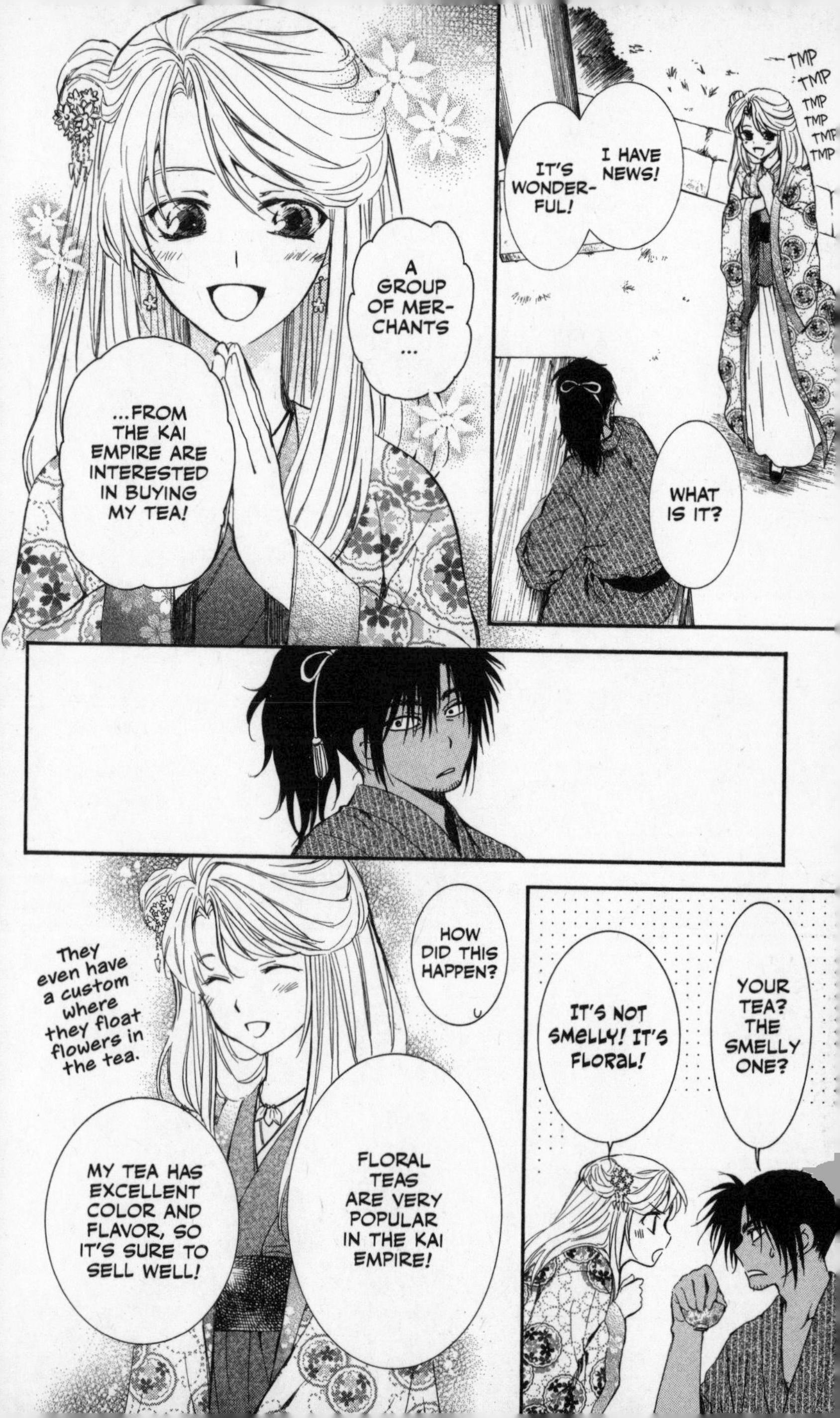
TMP TMP TMP TMP TMP TMP
I HAVE NEWS!
IT'S WONDER-FUL!
WHAT IS IT?
A GROUP OF MER-CHANTS ...
...FROM THE KAI EMPIRE ARE INTERESTED IN BUYING MY TEA!
YOUR TEA? THE SMELLY ONE?
IT'S NOT SMELLY! IT'S FLORAL!
HOW DID THIS HAPPEN?
FLORAL TEAS ARE VERY POPULAR IN THE KAI EMPIRE!
MY TEA HAS EXCELLENT COLOR AND FLAVOR, SO IT'S SURE TO SELL WELL!
They even have a custom where they float flowers in the tea.

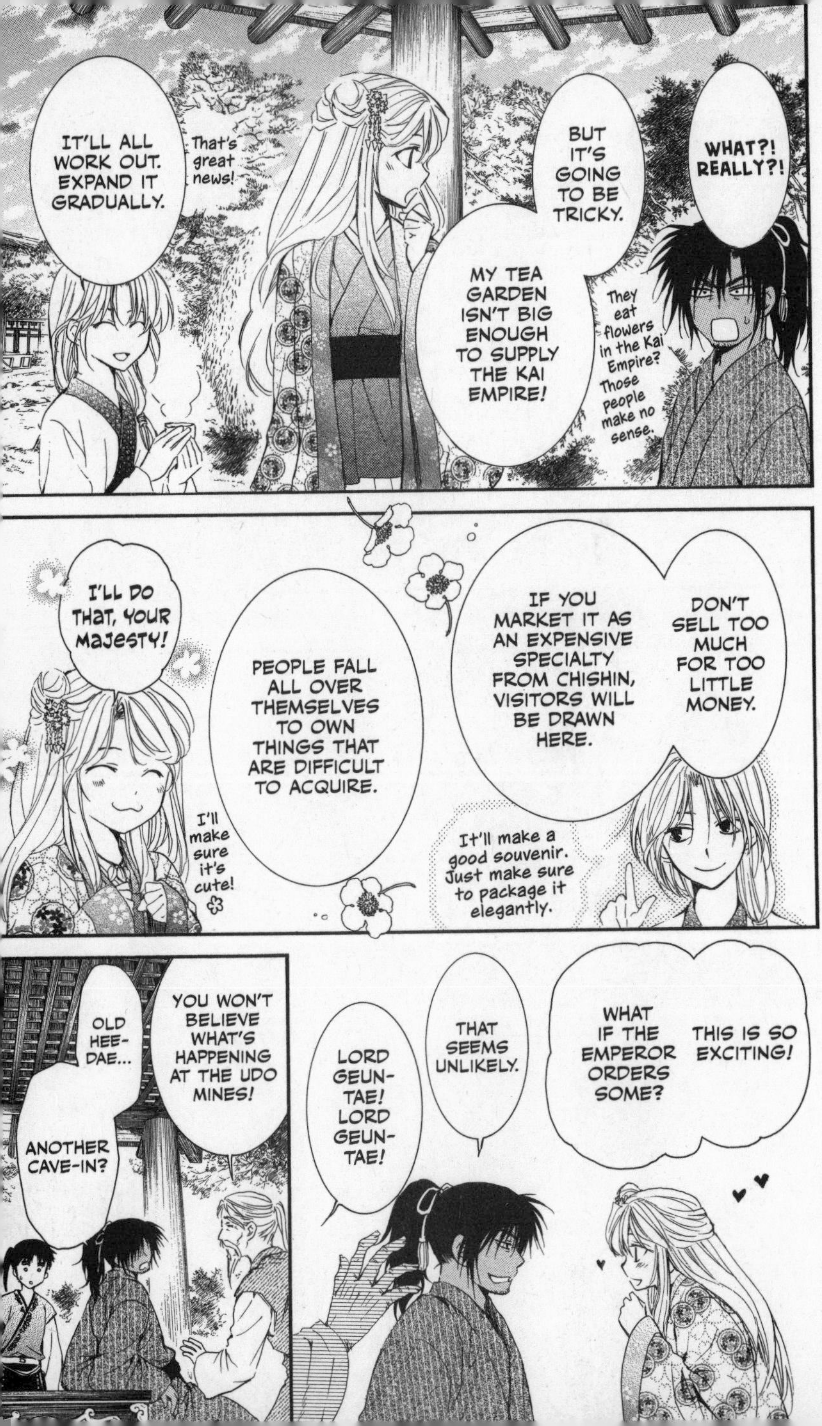
WHAT?! REALLY?!
They eat flowers in the Kai Empire? Those people make no sense.
BUT IT'S GOING TO BE TRICKY.
MY TEA GARDEN ISN'T BIG ENOUGH TO SUPPLY THE KAI EMPIRE!
That's great news!
IT'LL ALL WORK OUT. EXPAND IT GRADUALLY.
DON'T SELL TOO MUCH FOR TOO LITTLE MONEY.
IF YOU MARKET IT AS AN EXPENSIVE SPECIALTY FROM CHISHIN, VISITORS WILL BE DRAWN HERE.
It'll make a good souvenir. Just make sure to package it elegantly.
PEOPLE FALL ALL OVER THEMSELVES TO OWN THINGS THAT ARE DIFFICULT TO ACQUIRE.
I'LL DO THAT, YOUR MAJESTY!
I'll make sure it's cute!
THIS IS SO EXCITING!
WHAT IF THE EMPEROR ORDERS SOME?
THAT SEEMS UNLIKELY.
LORD GEUN-TAE! LORD GEUN-TAE!
YOU WON'T BELIEVE WHAT'S HAPPENING AT THE UDO MINES!
OLD HEE-DAE...
ANOTHER CAVE-IN?

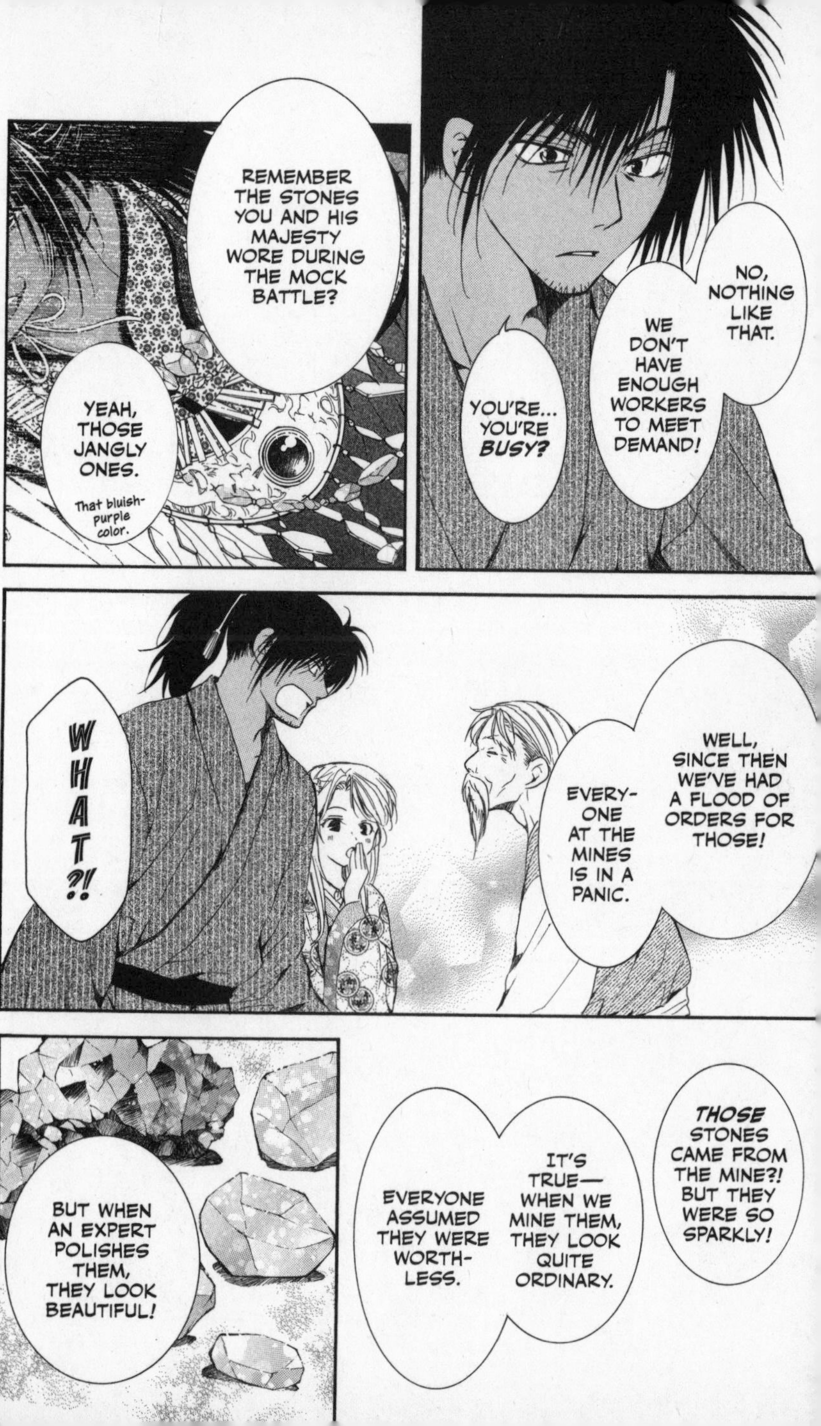
NO, NOTHING LIKE THAT.
WE DON'T HAVE ENOUGH WORKERS TO MEET DEMAND!
YOU'RE... YOU'RE *BUSY?*
REMEMBER THE STONES YOU AND HIS MAJESTY WORE DURING THE MOCK BATTLE?
YEAH, THOSE JANGLY ONES.
That bluish-purple color.
WELL, SINCE THEN WE'VE HAD A FLOOD OF ORDERS FOR THOSE!
EVERY-ONE AT THE MINES IS IN A PANIC.
WHAT?!
THOSE STONES CAME FROM THE MINE?! BUT THEY WERE SO SPARKLY!
IT'S TRUE— WHEN WE MINE THEM, THEY LOOK QUITE ORDINARY.
EVERYONE ASSUMED THEY WERE WORTH-LESS.
BUT WHEN AN EXPERT POLISHES THEM, THEY LOOK BEAUTIFUL!

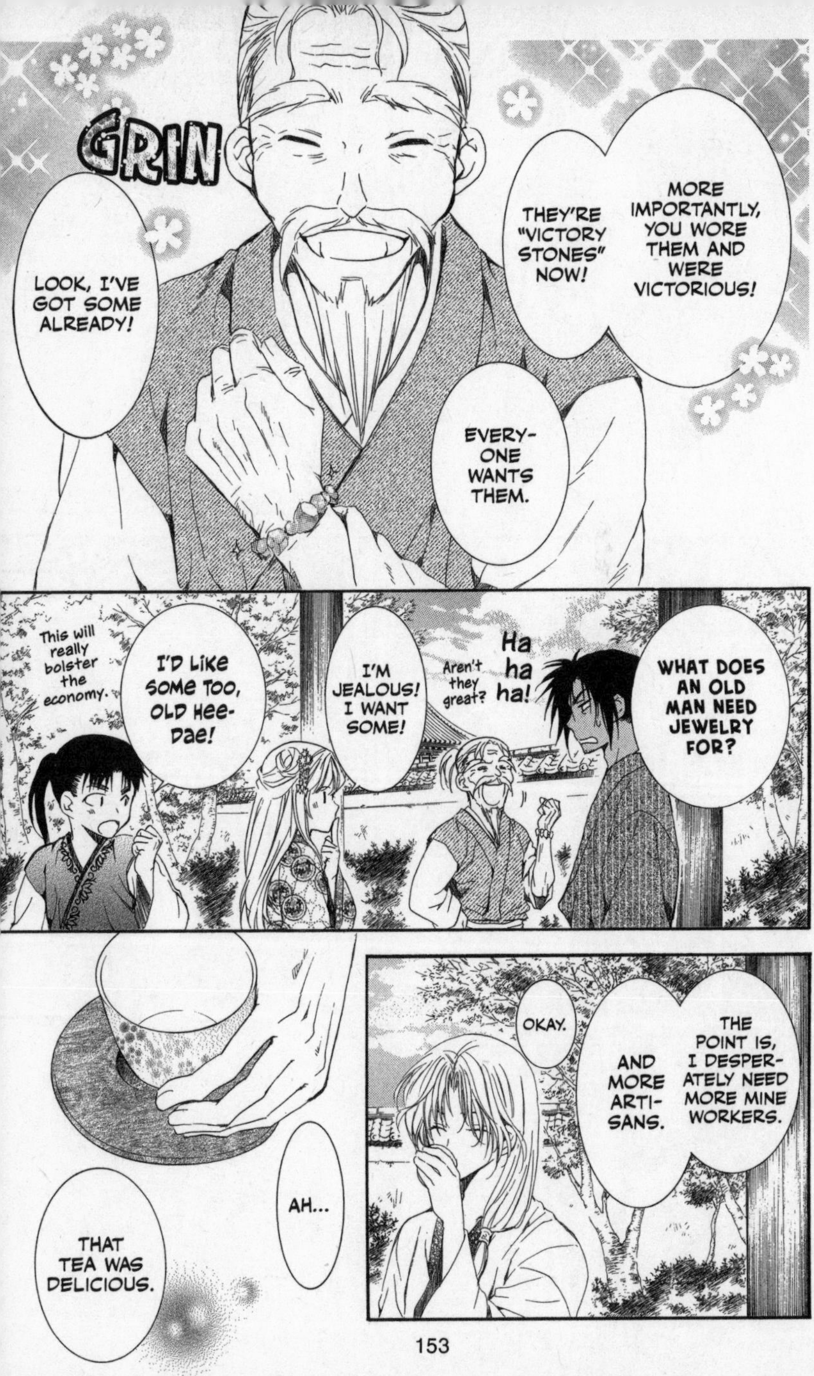
MORE IMPORTANTLY, YOU WORE THEM AND WERE VICTORIOUS!
THEY'RE "VICTORY STONES" NOW!
GRIN
LOOK, I'VE GOT SOME ALREADY!
EVERY-ONE WANTS THEM.
WHAT DOES AN OLD MAN NEED JEWELRY FOR?
Ha ha ha!
Aren't they great?
I'M JEALOUS! I WANT SOME!
I'D LIKE SOME TOO, OLD HEE-DAE!
This will really bolster the economy.
THE POINT IS, I DESPERATELY NEED MORE MINE WORKERS.
AND MORE ARTI-SANS.
OKAY.
AH...
THAT TEA WAS DELICIOUS.

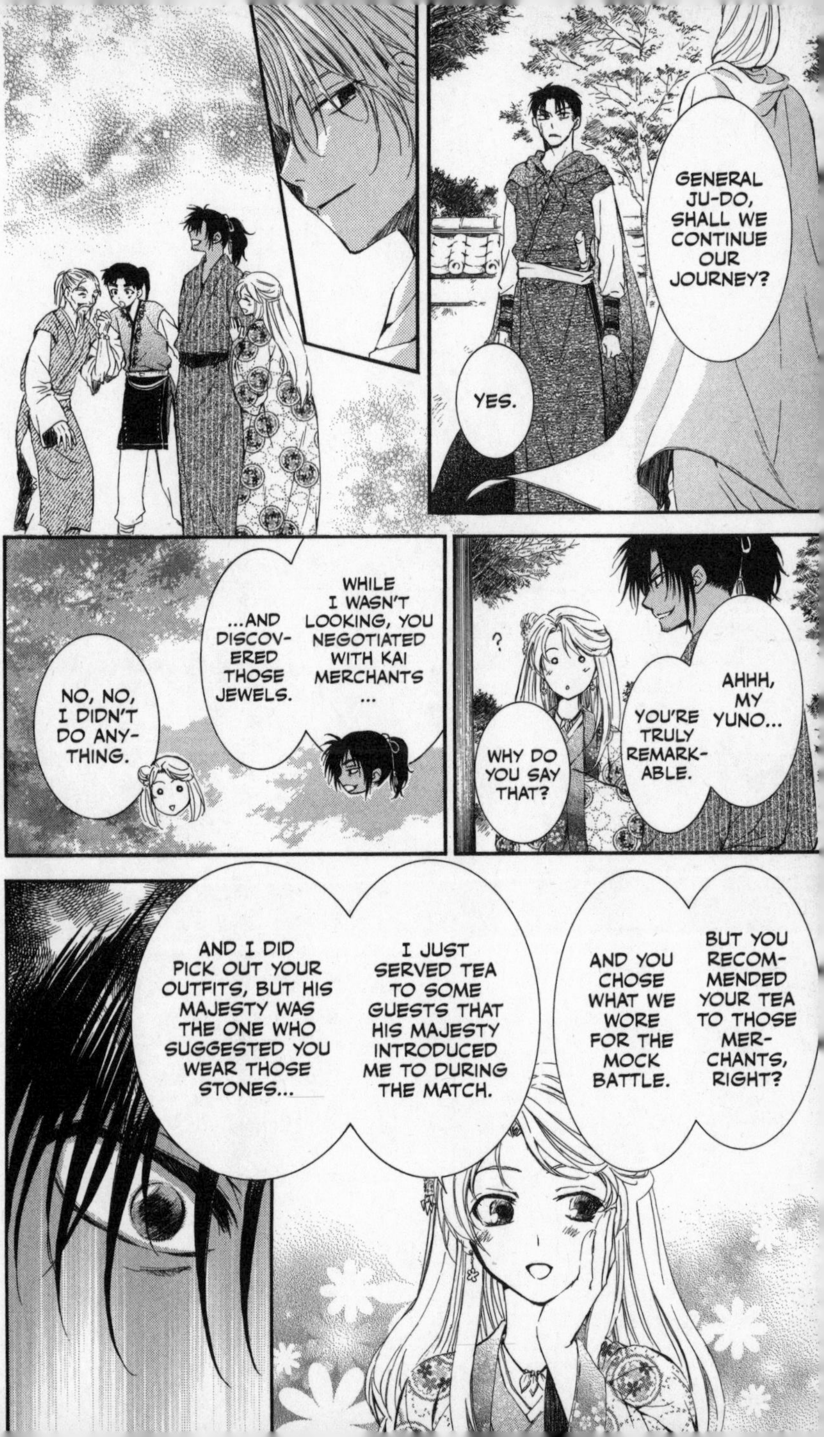
GENERAL JU-DO, SHALL WE CONTINUE OUR JOURNEY?
YES.
AHHH, MY YUNO...
YOU'RE TRULY REMARKABLE.
?
WHY DO YOU SAY THAT?
WHILE I WASN'T LOOKING, YOU NEGOTIATED WITH KAI MERCHANTS ...
...AND DISCOVERED THOSE JEWELS.
NO, NO, I DIDN'T DO ANYTHING.
BUT YOU RECOMMENDED YOUR TEA TO THOSE MERCHANTS, RIGHT?
AND YOU CHOSE WHAT WE WORE FOR THE MOCK BATTLE.
I JUST SERVED TEA TO SOME GUESTS THAT HIS MAJESTY INTRODUCED ME TO DURING THE MATCH.
AND I DID PICK OUT YOUR OUTFITS, BUT HIS MAJESTY WAS THE ONE WHO SUGGESTED YOU WEAR THOSE STONES...

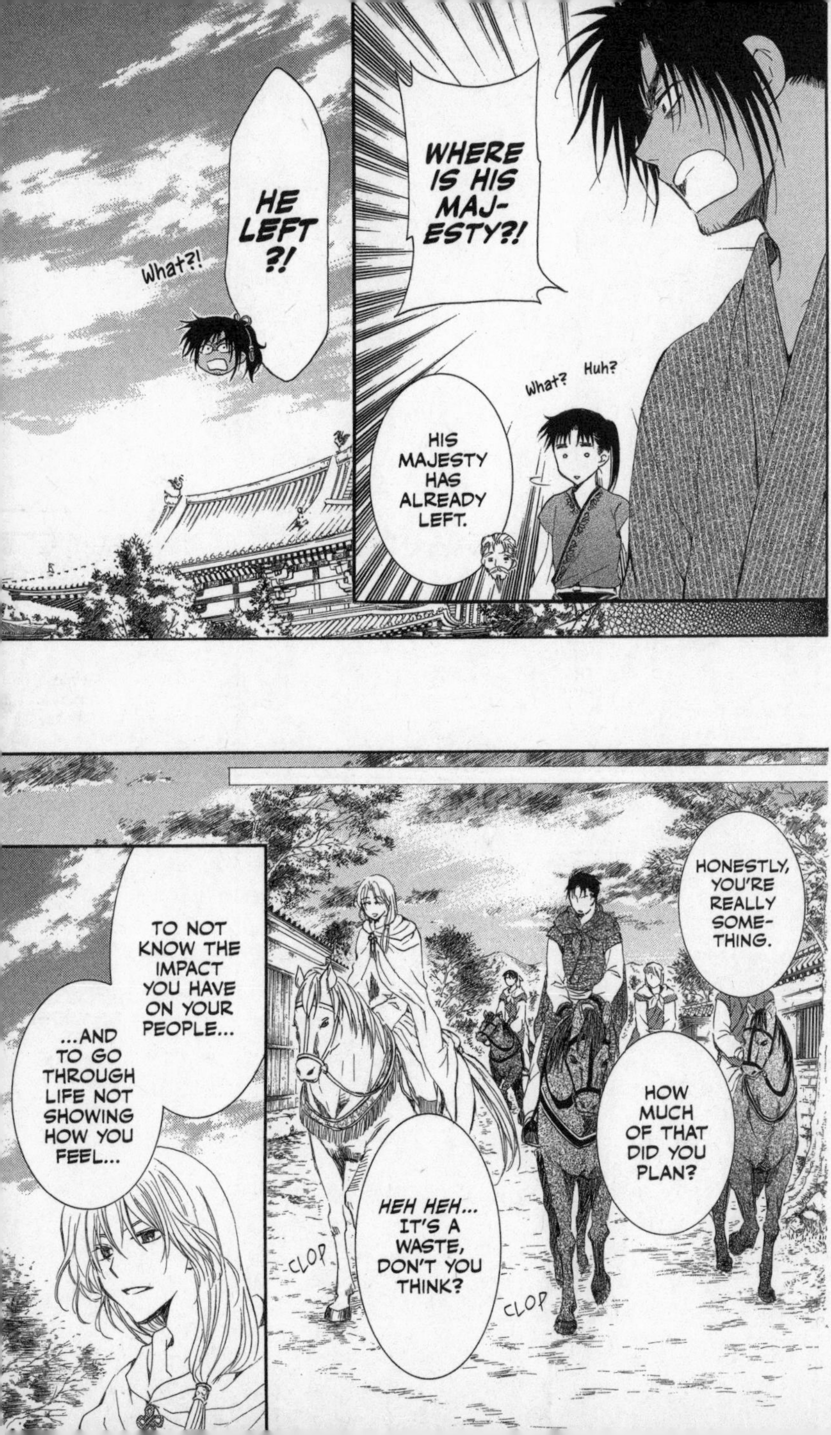
WHERE IS HIS MAJESTY?!
Huh?
What?
HIS MAJESTY HAS ALREADY LEFT.
HE LEFT ?!
What?!
HONESTLY, YOU'RE REALLY SOMETHING.
HOW MUCH OF THAT DID YOU PLAN?
HEH HEH... IT'S A WASTE, DON'T YOU THINK?
CLOP
CLOP
TO NOT KNOW THE IMPACT YOU HAVE ON YOUR PEOPLE...
...AND TO GO THROUGH LIFE NOT SHOWING HOW YOU FEEL...

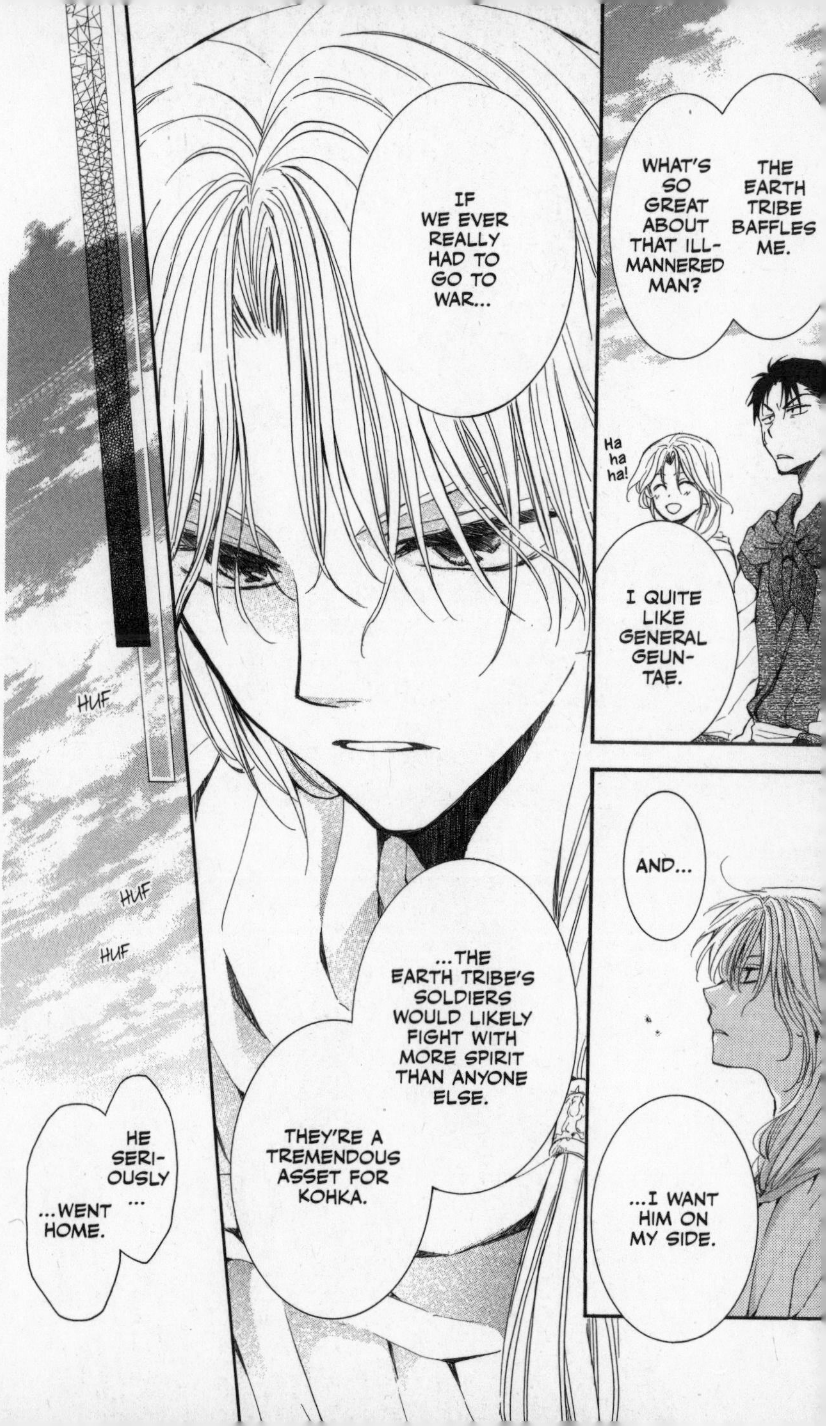
THE EARTH TRIBE BAFFLES ME.
WHAT'S SO GREAT ABOUT THAT ILL-MANNERED MAN?
Ha ha ha!
I QUITE LIKE GENERAL GEUN-TAE.
AND...
...I WANT HIM ON MY SIDE.
IF WE EVER REALLY HAD TO GO TO WAR...
...THE EARTH TRIBE'S SOLDIERS WOULD LIKELY FIGHT WITH MORE SPIRIT THAN ANYONE ELSE.
THEY'RE A TREMENDOUS ASSET FOR KOHKA.
HUF
HUF
HUF
HE SERIOUSLY...
...WENT HOME.

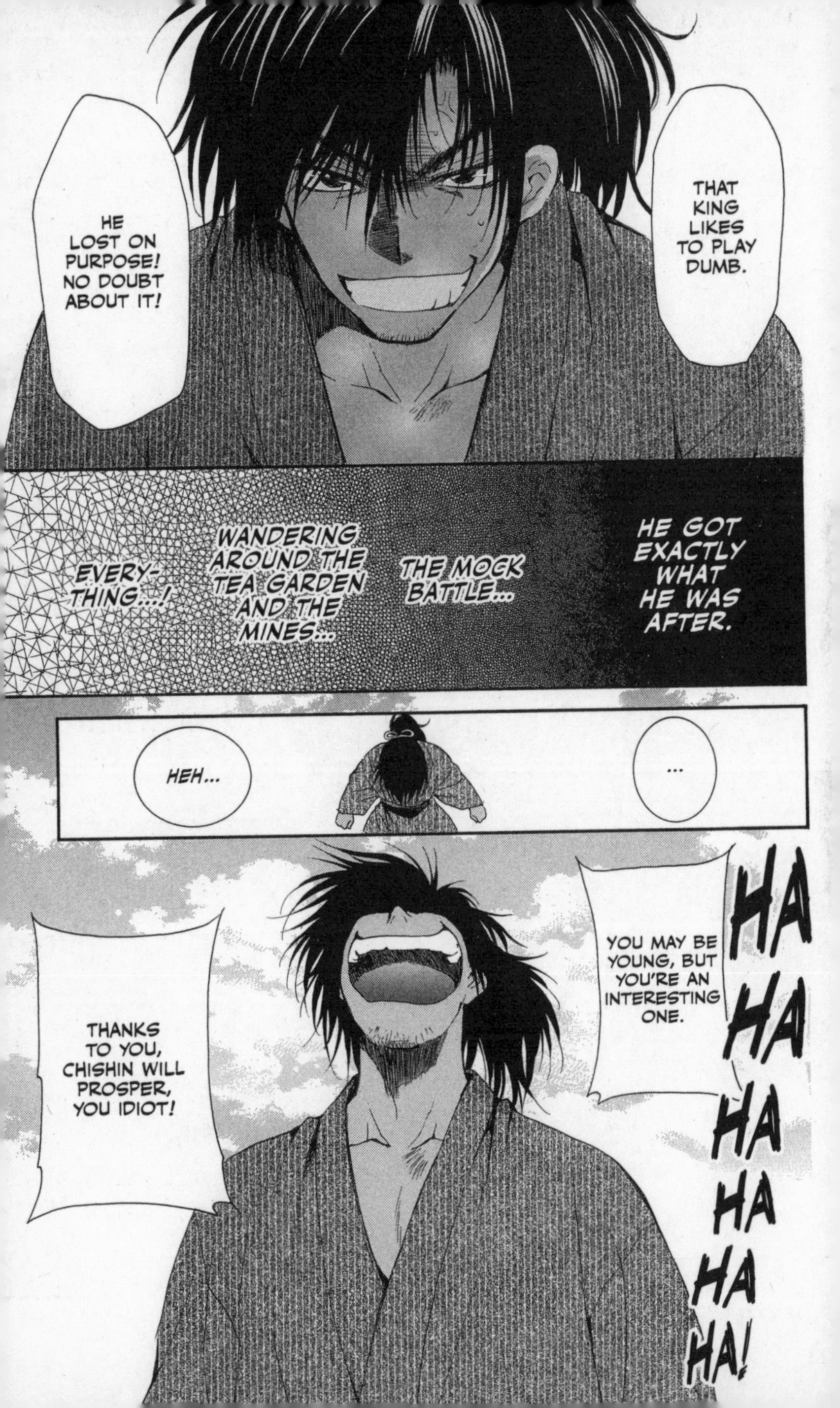
THAT KING LIKES TO PLAY DUMB.
HE LOST ON PURPOSE! NO DOUBT ABOUT IT!
HE GOT EXACTLY WHAT HE WAS AFTER.
THE MOCK BATTLE...
WANDERING AROUND THE TEA GARDEN AND THE MINES...
EVERY-THING...!
...
HEH...
HA HA HA HA HA HA HA HA!
YOU MAY BE YOUNG, BUT YOU'RE AN INTERESTING ONE.
THANKS TO YOU, CHISHIN WILL PROSPER, YOU IDIOT!

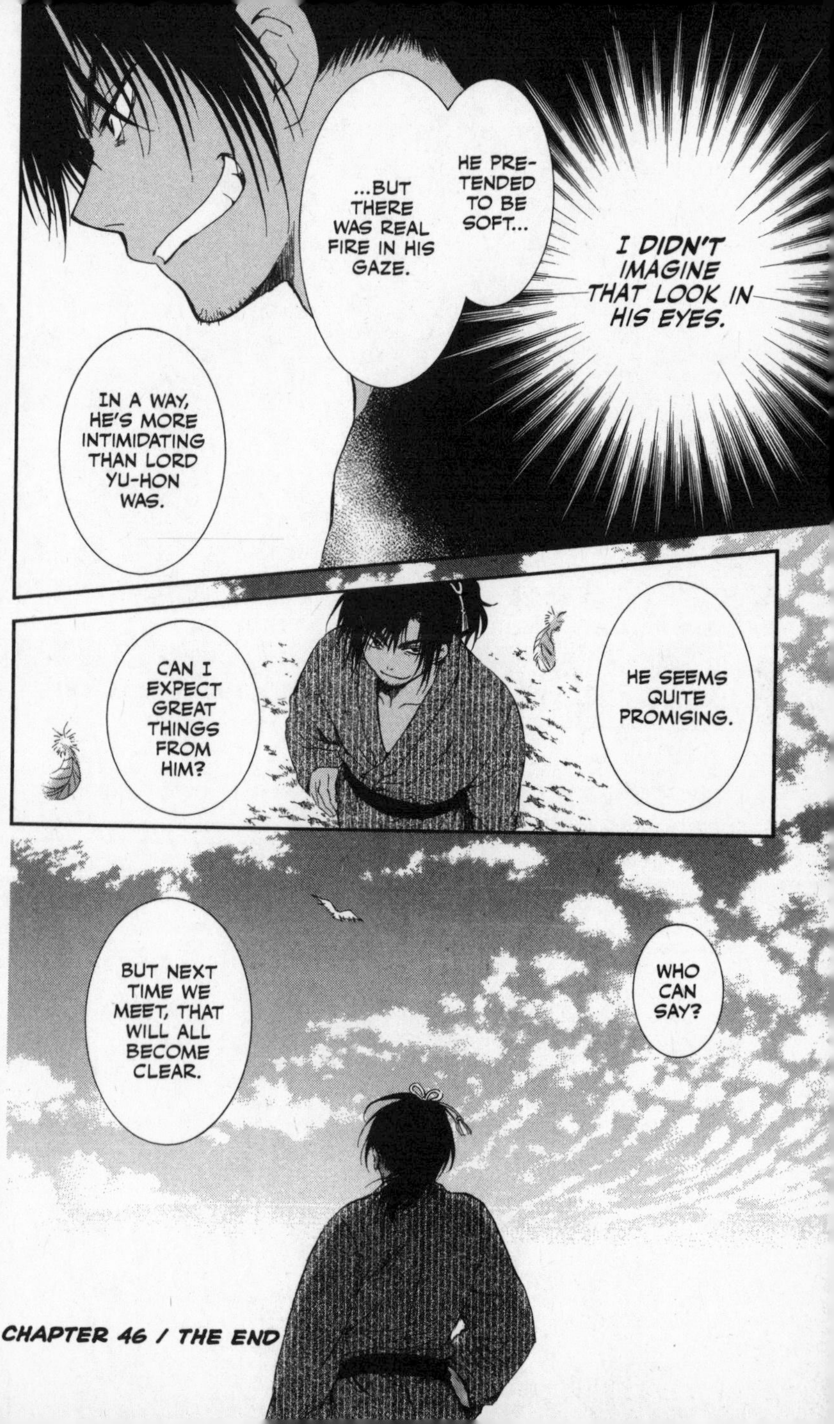
I DIDN'T IMAGINE THAT LOOK IN HIS EYES.
HE PRE-TENDED TO BE SOFT...
...BUT THERE WAS REAL FIRE IN HIS GAZE.
IN A WAY, HE'S MORE INTIMIDATING THAN LORD YU-HON WAS.
HE SEEMS QUITE PROMISING.
CAN I EXPECT GREAT THINGS FROM HIM?
WHO CAN SAY?
BUT NEXT TIME WE MEET, THAT WILL ALL BECOME CLEAR.
CHAPTER 46 / THE END

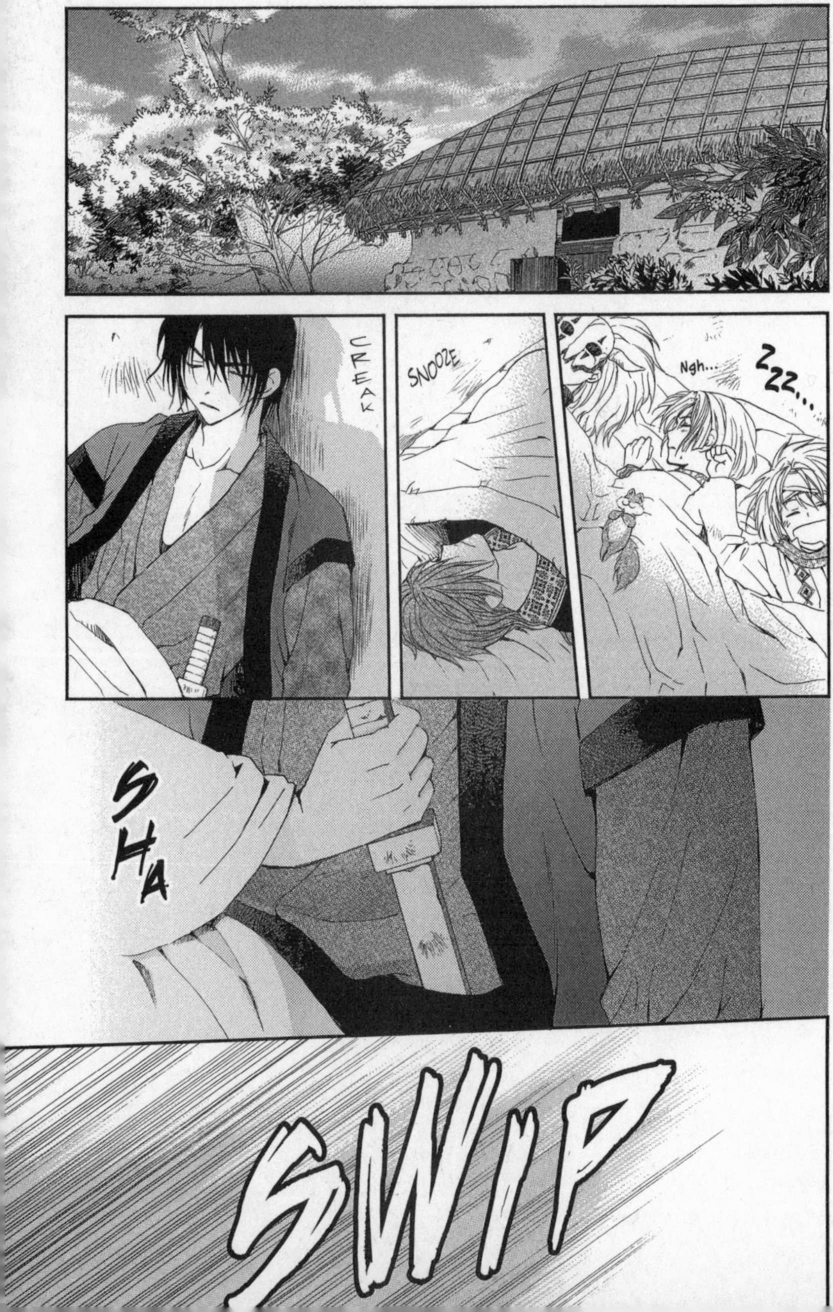
Ngh...
ZZZ...
SNOOZE
CREAK
SHA
SWIP

CHAPTER 47: A WELCOME RAIN

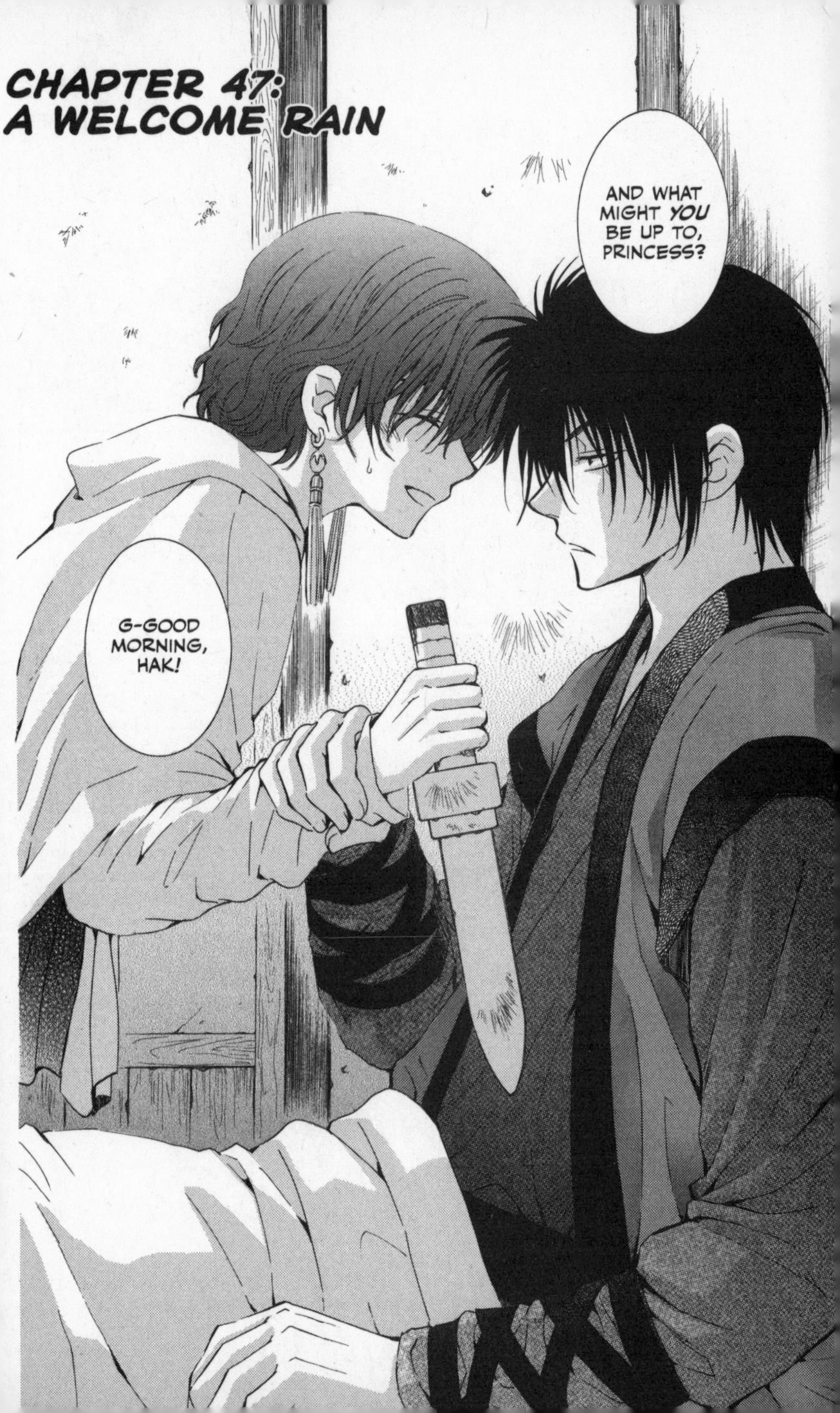
AND WHAT MIGHT *YOU* BE UP TO, PRINCESS?
G-GOOD MORNING, HAK!

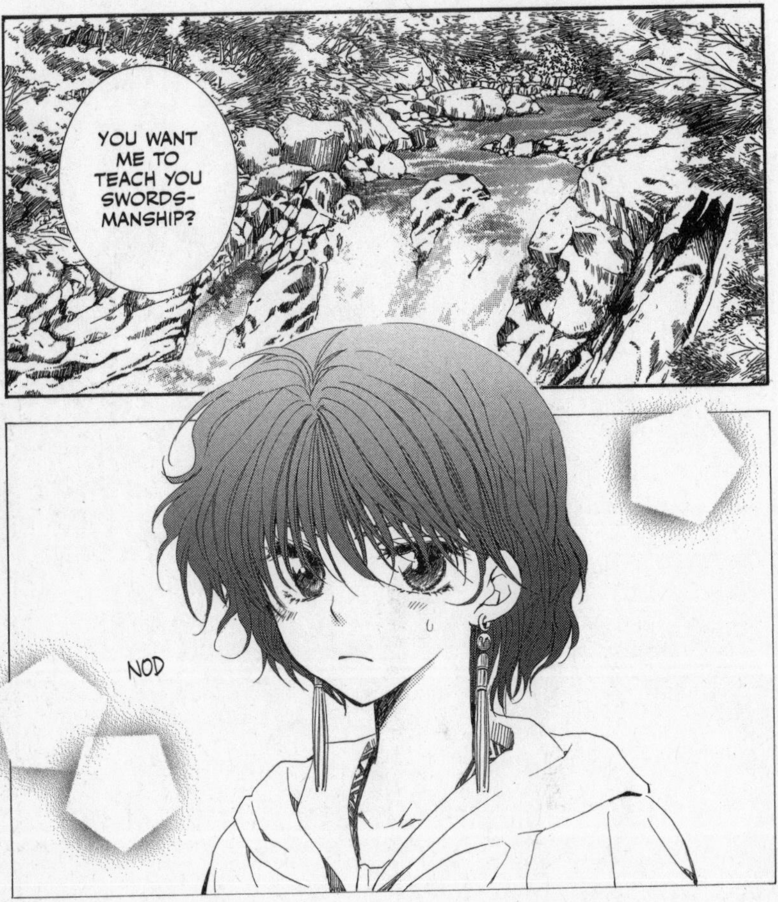
YOU WANT ME TO TEACH YOU SWORDS-MANSHIP?
NOD

Special thanks to all the people who've helped me.
My assistants → Mikorun, Kyoko, Oka, C.F., Ryo and my little sister...
My editor Yamashita, the *Hana to Yume* editorial office...
Everyone who's helped me create and sell this manga...
Family, friends and readers who've supported me...! ♥
I'm truly grateful that you've all supported Yona!
I'll keep trying my best.

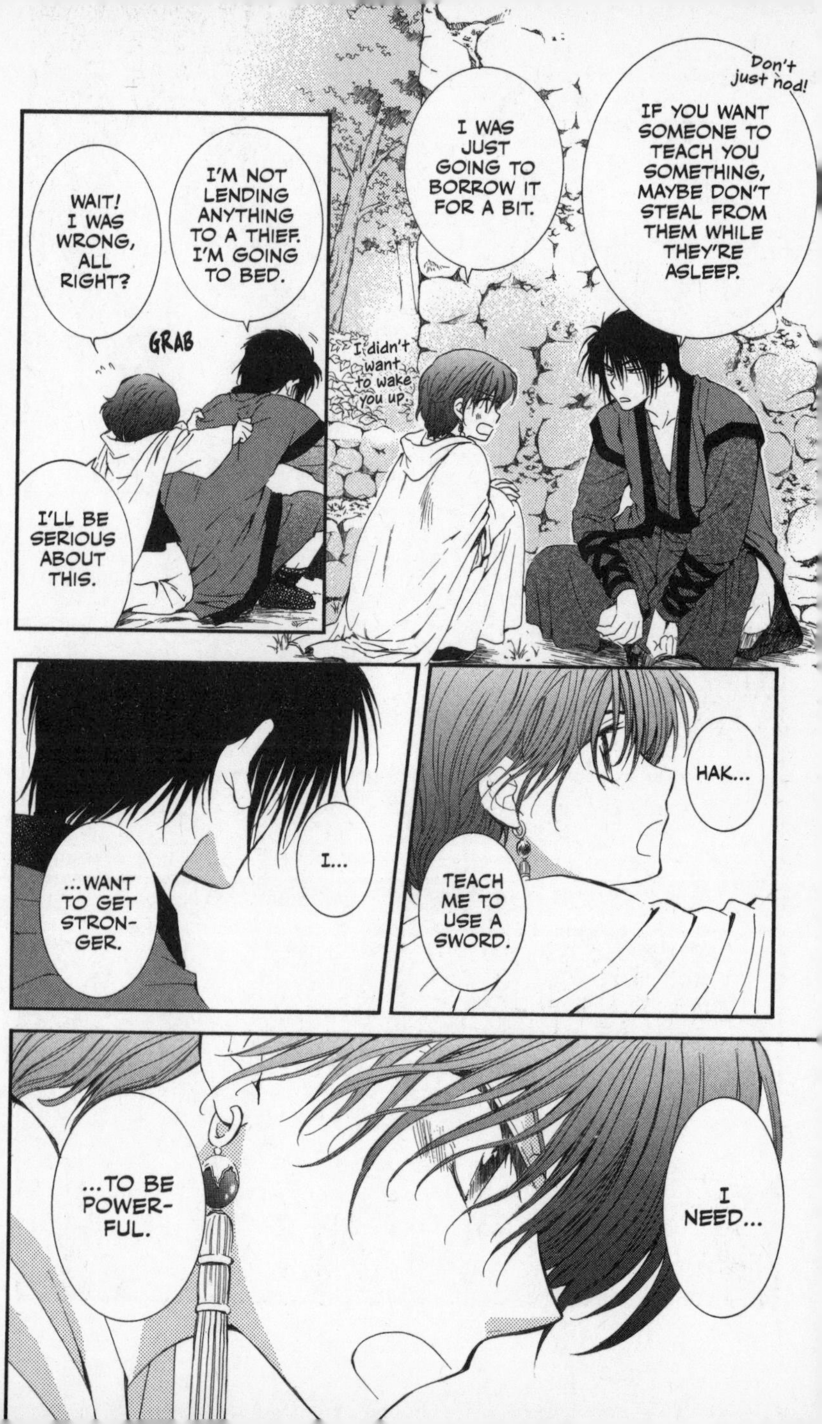
Don't just nod!
IF YOU WANT SOMEONE TO TEACH YOU SOMETHING, MAYBE DON'T STEAL FROM THEM WHILE THEY'RE ASLEEP.
I WAS JUST GOING TO BORROW IT FOR A BIT.
I didn't want to wake you up.
I'M NOT LENDING ANYTHING TO A THIEF. I'M GOING TO BED.
WAIT! I WAS WRONG, ALL RIGHT?
GRAB
I'LL BE SERIOUS ABOUT THIS.
HAK...
TEACH ME TO USE A SWORD.
I...
...WANT TO GET STRONGER.
I NEED...
...TO BE POWERFUL.

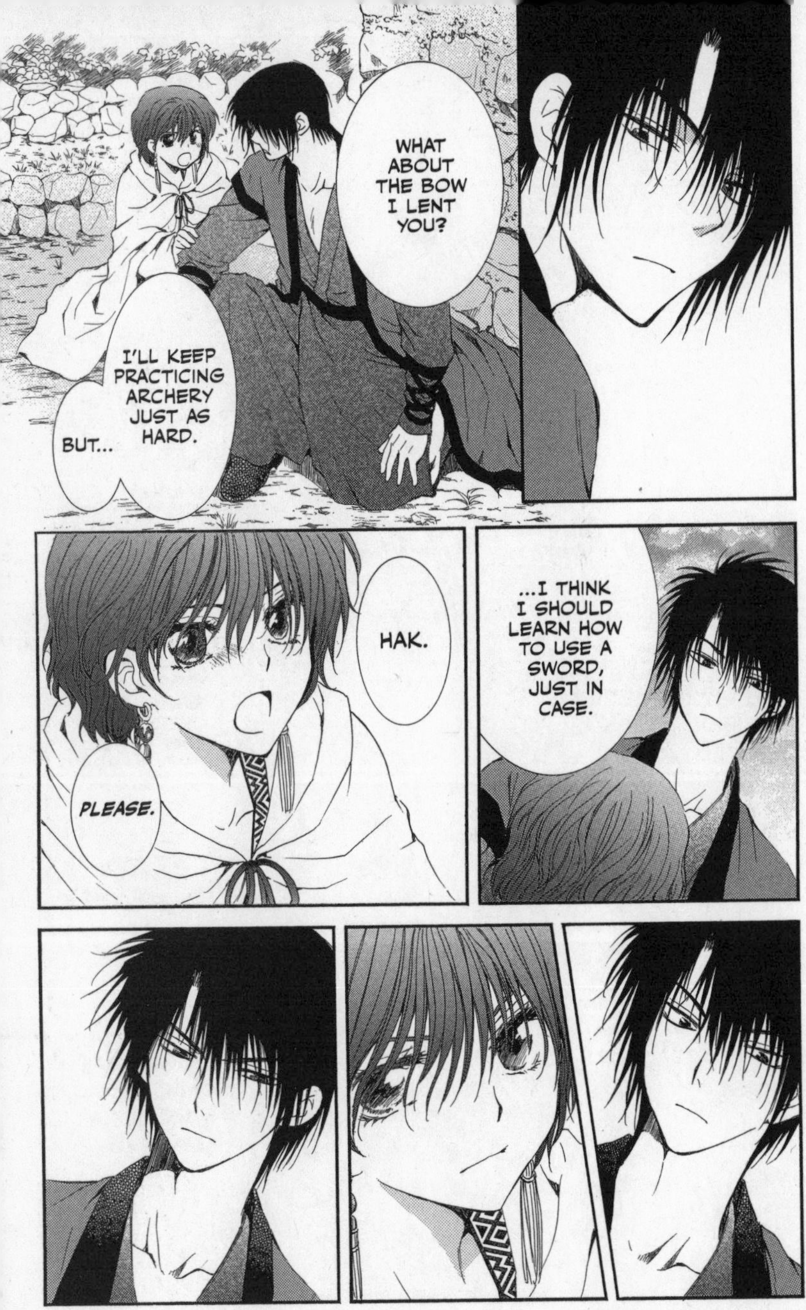
WHAT ABOUT THE BOW I LENT YOU?
I'LL KEEP PRACTICING ARCHERY JUST AS HARD.
BUT...
...I THINK I SHOULD LEARN HOW TO USE A SWORD, JUST IN CASE.
HAK.
PLEASE.

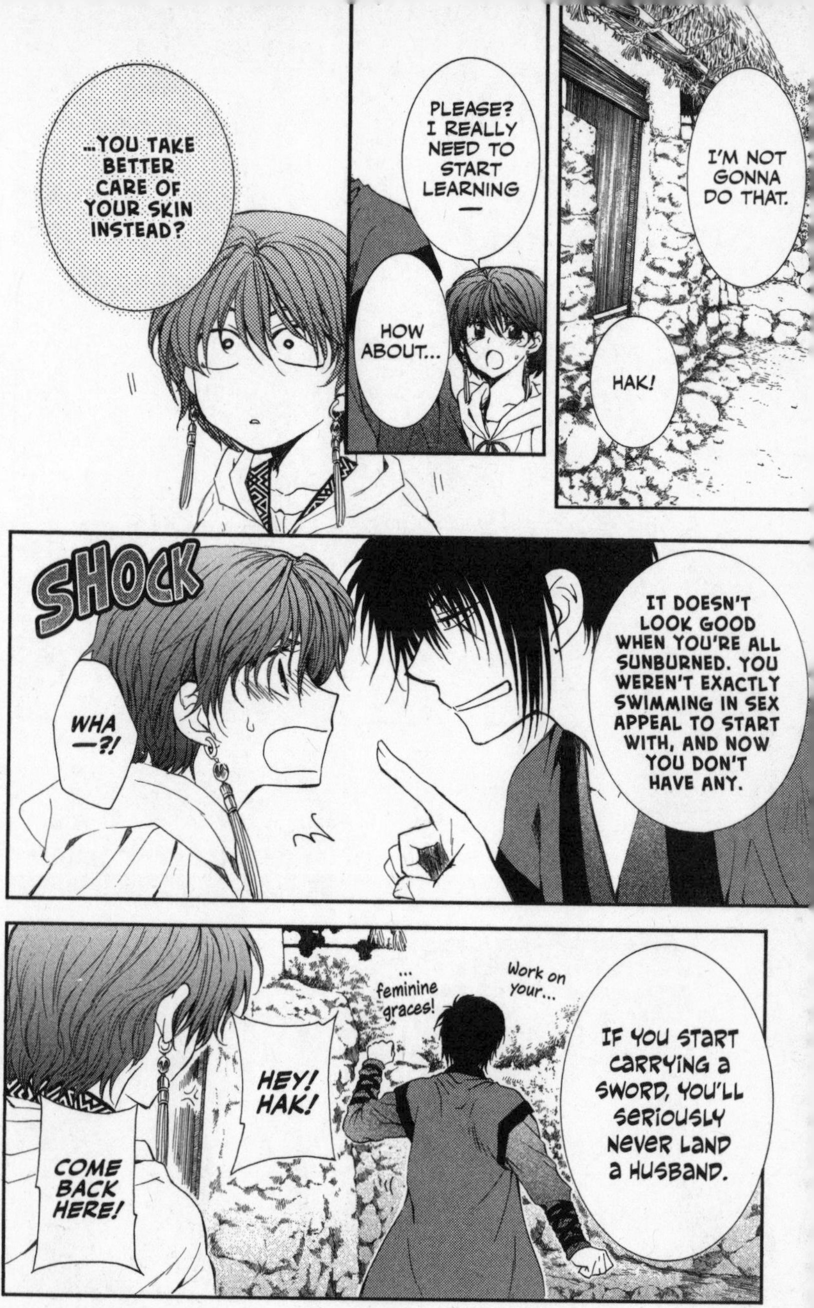
I'M NOT GONNA DO THAT.
HAK!
PLEASE? I REALLY NEED TO START LEARNING—
HOW ABOUT...
...YOU TAKE BETTER CARE OF YOUR SKIN INSTEAD?
IT DOESN'T LOOK GOOD WHEN YOU'RE ALL SUNBURNED. YOU WEREN'T EXACTLY SWIMMING IN SEX APPEAL TO START WITH, AND NOW YOU DON'T HAVE ANY.
SHOCK
WHA—?!
IF YOU START CARRYING A SWORD, YOU'LL SERIOUSLY NEVER LAND A HUSBAND.
Work on your...
... feminine graces!
HEY! HAK!
COME BACK HERE!

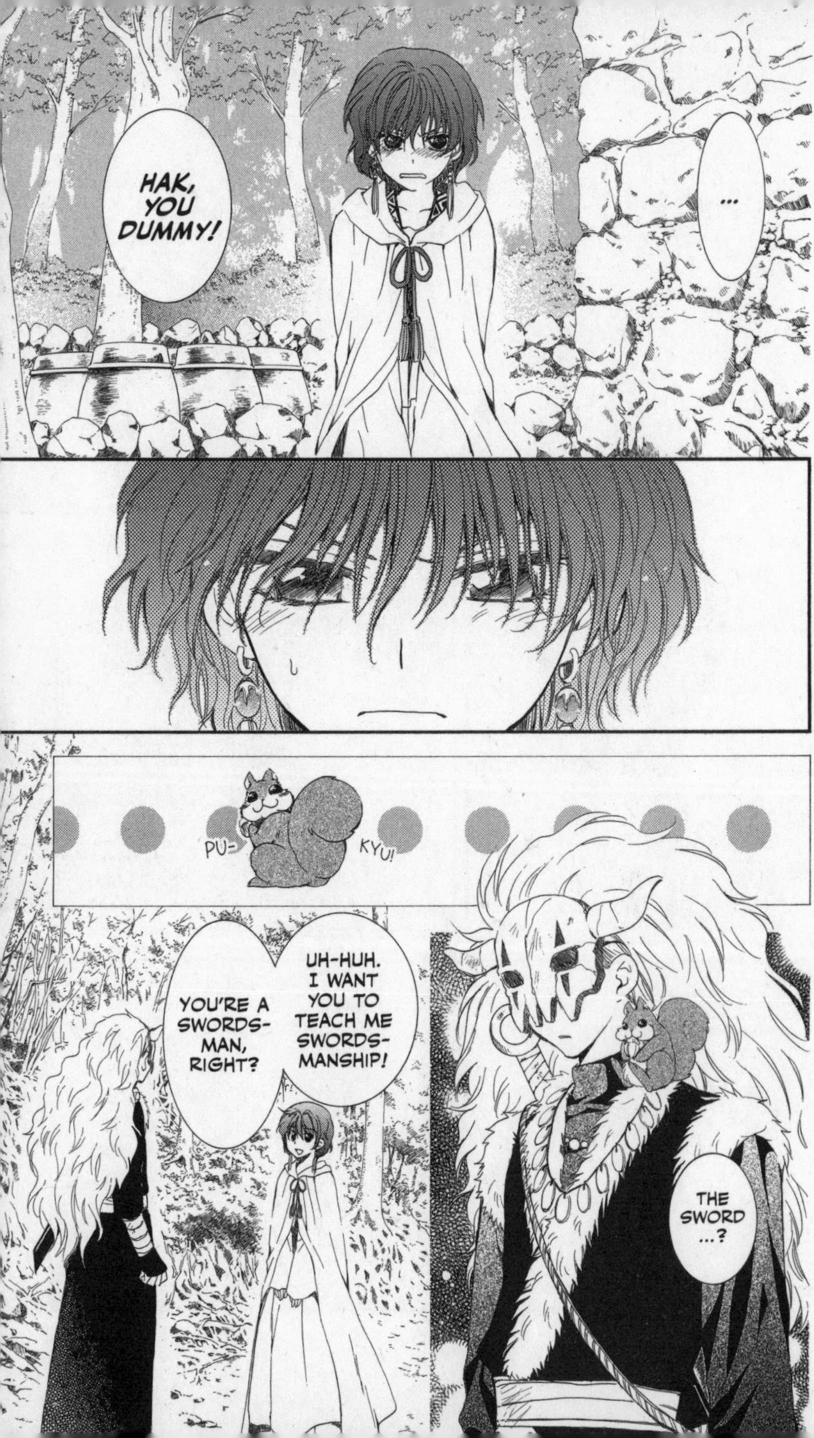
...
HAK, YOU DUMMY!
PU-KYU!
THE SWORD ...?
UH-HUH. I WANT YOU TO TEACH ME SWORDS-MANSHIP!
YOU'RE A SWORDS-MAN, RIGHT?

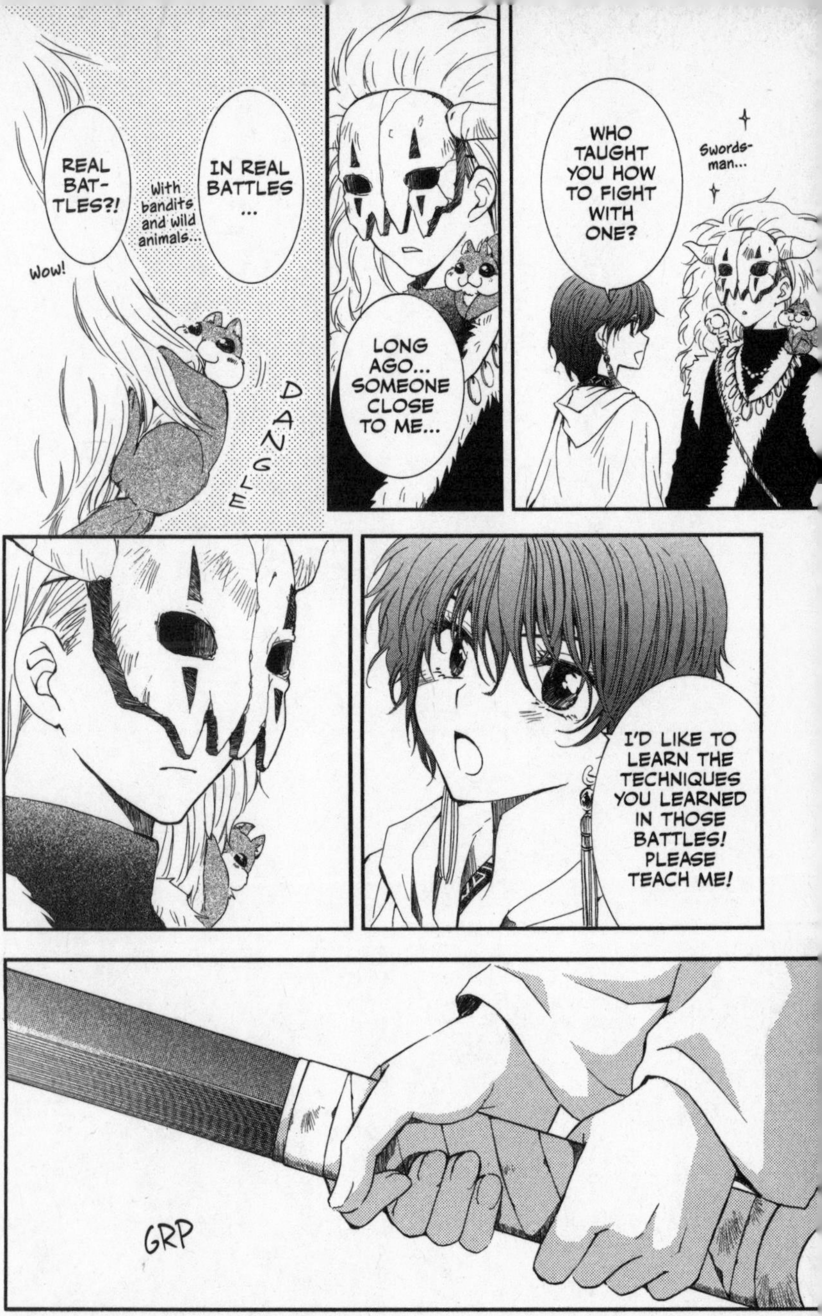
Swords-man...
WHO TAUGHT YOU HOW TO FIGHT WITH ONE?
LONG AGO... SOMEONE CLOSE TO ME...
IN REAL BATTLES ...
With bandits and wild animals...
REAL BAT-TLES?!
Wow!
DANGLE
I'D LIKE TO LEARN THE TECHNIQUES YOU LEARNED IN THOSE BATTLES! PLEASE TEACH ME!
GRP

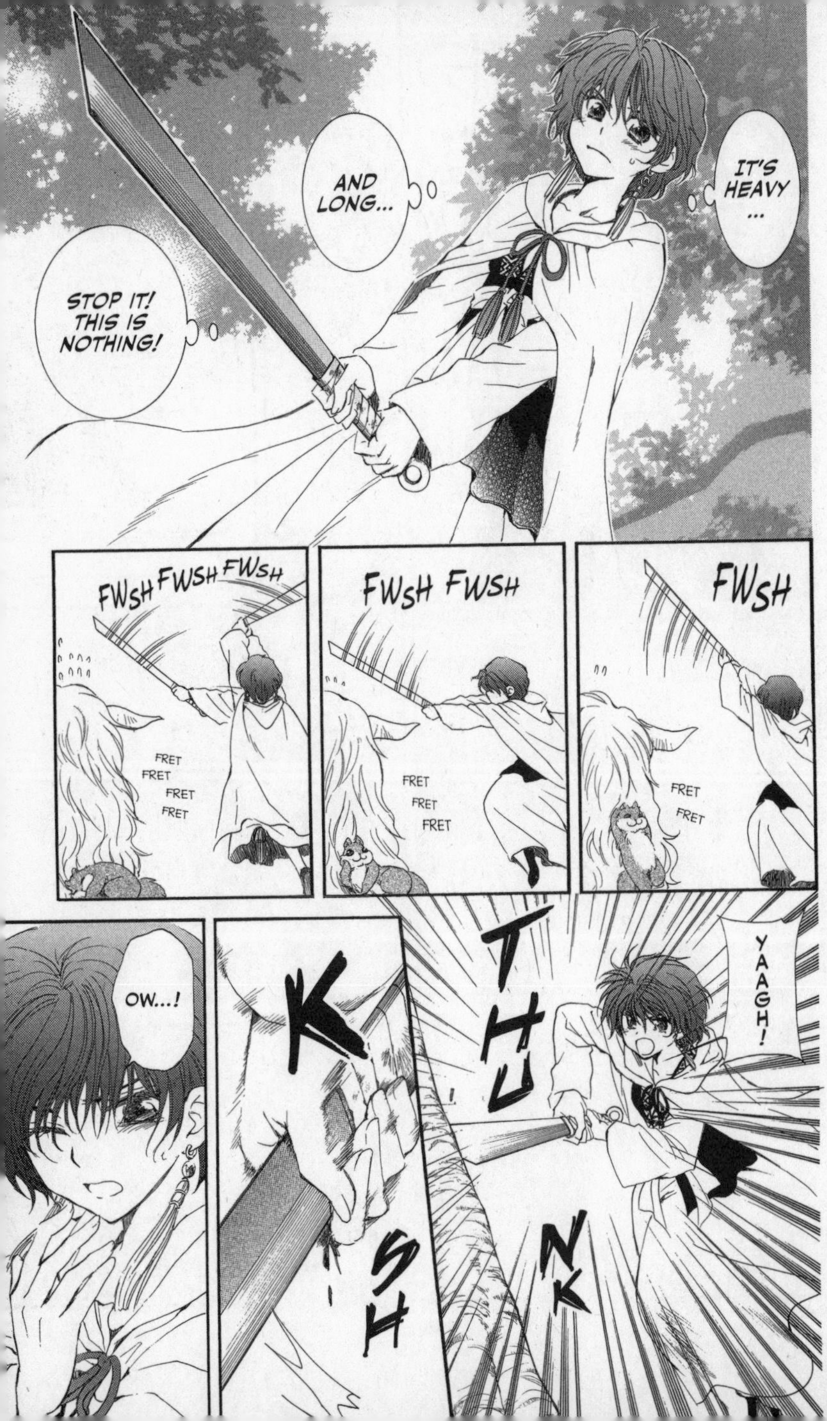
IT'S HEAVY ...
AND LONG...
STOP IT! THIS IS NOTHING!
FWSH
FRET
FRET
FWSH FWSH
FRET
FRET
FRET
FWSH FWSH FWSH
FRET
FRET
FRET
FRET
YAAGH!
THU
NK
K
SH
OW...!

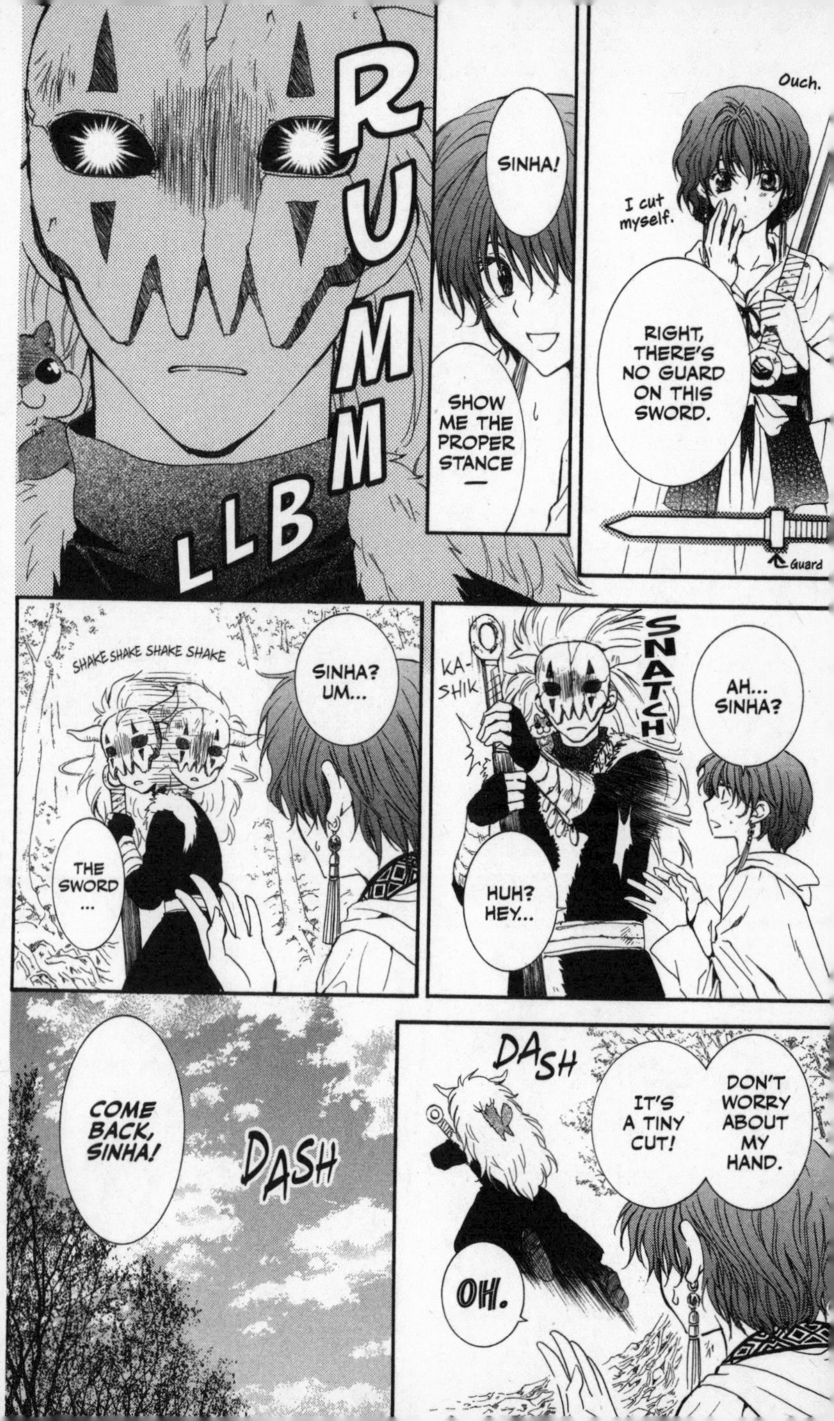

Ouch.
I cut myself.
RIGHT, THERE'S NO GUARD ON THIS SWORD.
Guard
SINHA!
SHOW ME THE PROPER STANCE —
RUMMBLL
AH... SINHA?
SNATCH
KA-SHIK
HUH? HEY...
SINHA? UM...
SHAKE SHAKE SHAKE SHAKE
THE SWORD ...
DON'T WORRY ABOUT MY HAND.
IT'S A TINY CUT!
DASH
OH.
DASH
COME BACK, SINHA!

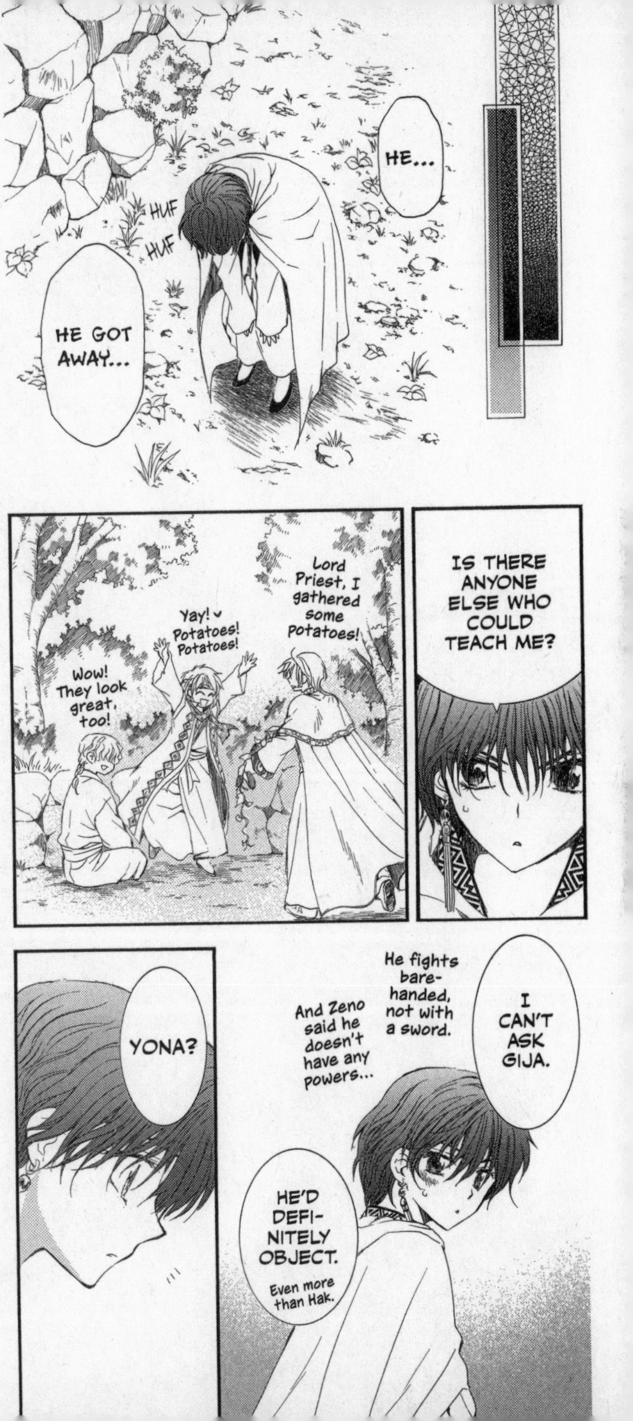

HE...
HUF
HUF
HE GOT AWAY...
IS THERE ANYONE ELSE WHO COULD TEACH ME?
Lord Priest, I gathered some potatoes!
Yay! ♡ Potatoes! Potatoes!
Wow! They look great, too!
I CAN'T ASK GIJA.
He fights bare-handed, not with a sword.
And Zeno said he doesn't have any powers...
YONA?
HE'D DEFINITELY OBJECT.
Even more than Hak.

Now that I think about it, after I finished my last series, *NG Life*, that series' editor told me to make my male characters sexier. What about Keidai? (The hero of my last series.)

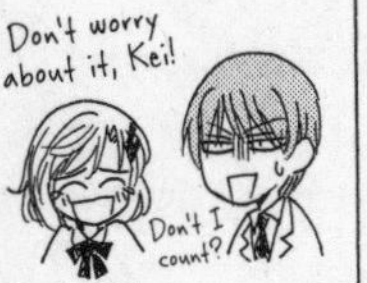

Don't worry about it, Kei!
Don't I count?

So what do you think about my new series, Editor H? Do you like Hak? *NG Life* is a bit more (?) fast-paced than *Yona*. I'm a little embarrassed by how amateurish it is, but I'm also quite fond of it. It gave me the experience I needed to create *Yona*. So what do you think of Hak? (laughs) See you in volume 9!

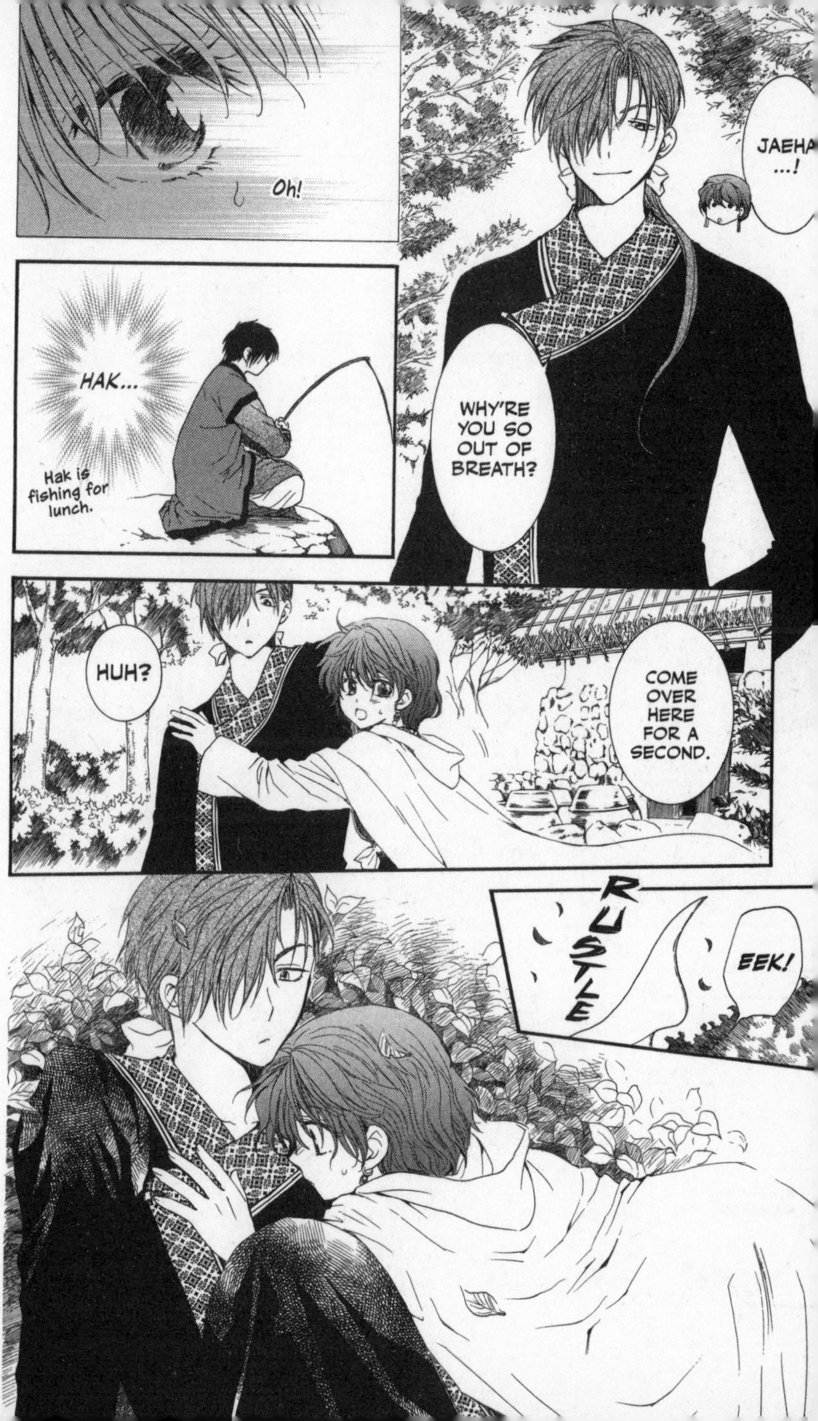
JAEHA ...!
WHY'RE YOU SO OUT OF BREATH?
Oh!
HAK...
Hak is fishing for lunch.
COME OVER HERE FOR A SECOND.
HUH?
RUSTLE
EEK!

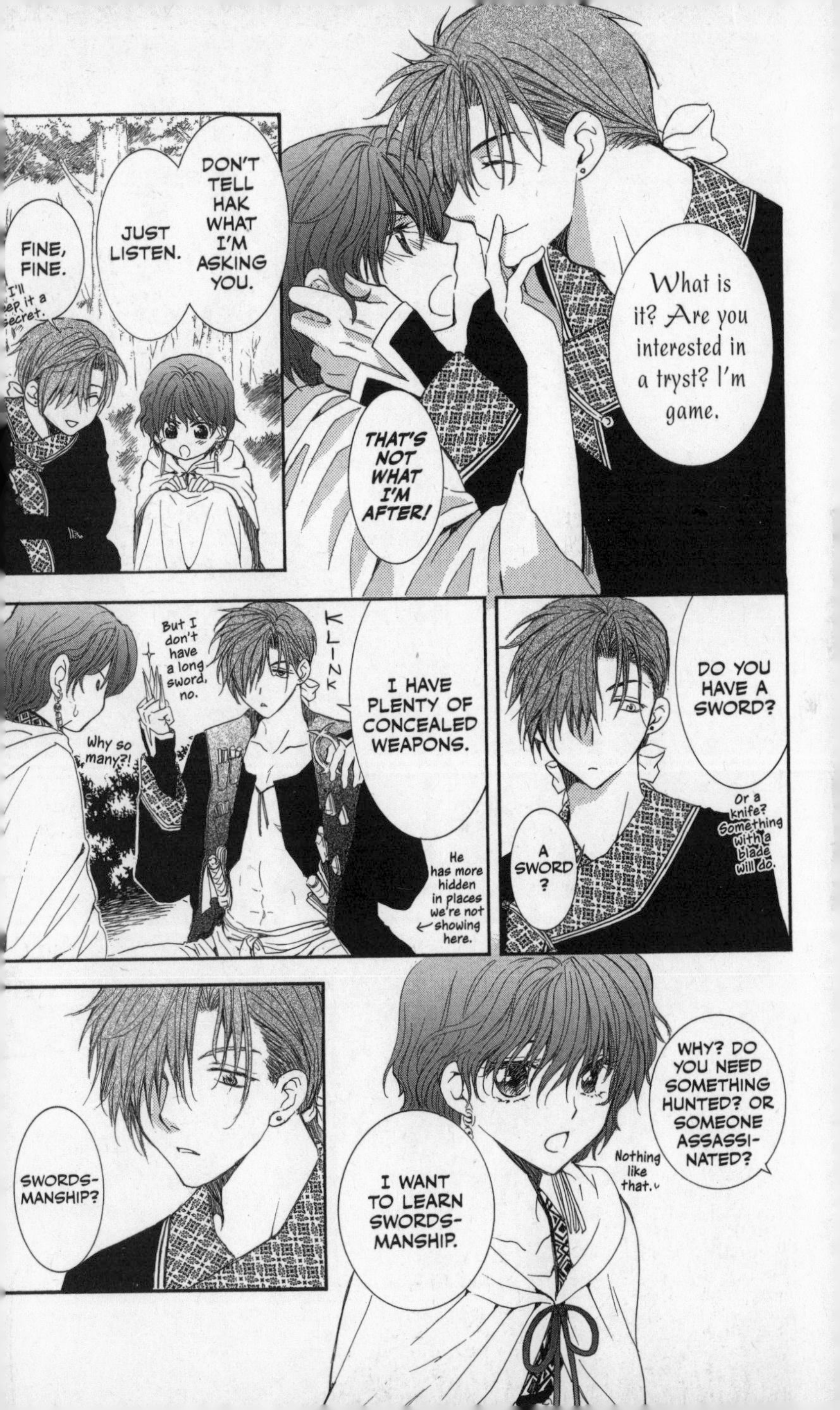
What is it? Are you interested in a tryst? I'm game.
THAT'S NOT WHAT I'M AFTER!
DON'T TELL HAK WHAT I'M ASKING YOU.
JUST LISTEN.
FINE, FINE.
I'll ep it a secret.
DO YOU HAVE A SWORD?
Or a knife? Something with a blade will do.
A SWORD?
KLINK
I HAVE PLENTY OF CONCEALED WEAPONS.
But I don't have a long sword, no.
Why so many?!
He has more hidden in places we're not showing here.
WHY? DO YOU NEED SOMETHING HUNTED? OR SOMEONE ASSASSI-NATED?
Nothing like that.
I WANT TO LEARN SWORDS-MANSHIP.
SWORDS-MANSHIP?

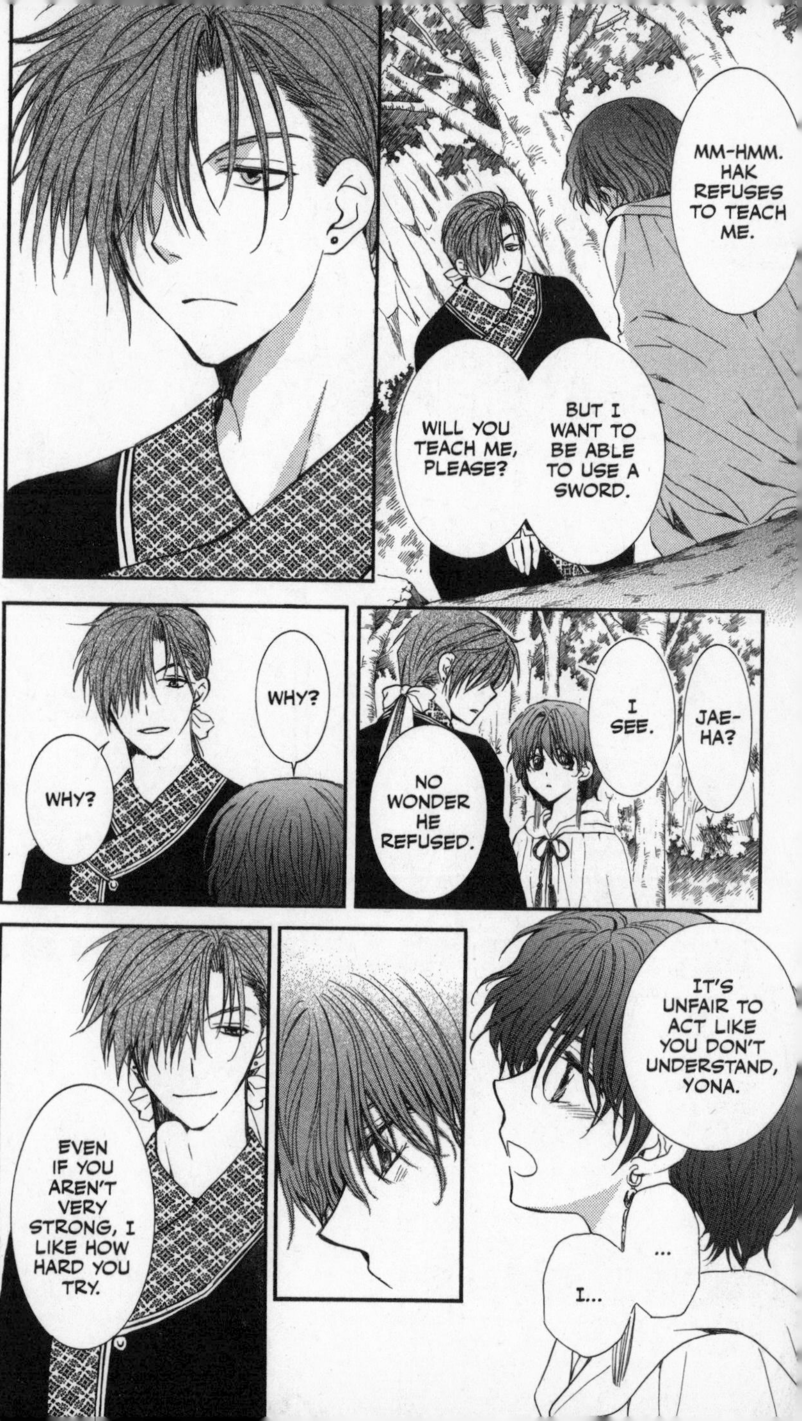
MM-HMM. HAK REFUSES TO TEACH ME.
BUT I WANT TO BE ABLE TO USE A SWORD.
WILL YOU TEACH ME, PLEASE?
JAE-HA?
I SEE.
NO WONDER HE REFUSED.
WHY?
WHY?
IT'S UNFAIR TO ACT LIKE YOU DON'T UNDERSTAND, YONA.
...
I...
EVEN IF YOU AREN'T VERY STRONG, I LIKE HOW HARD YOU TRY.

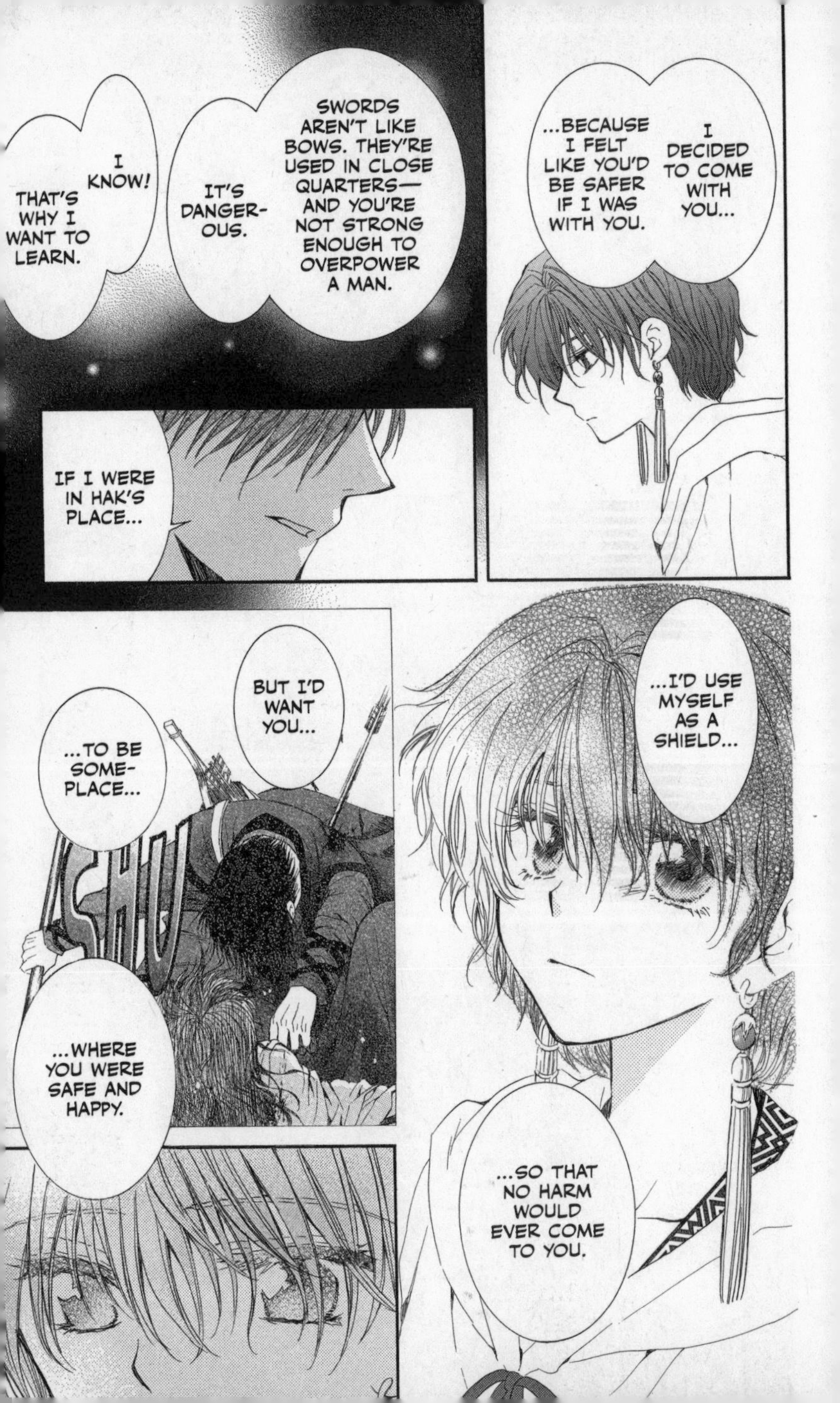
I DECIDED TO COME WITH YOU...
...BECAUSE I FELT LIKE YOU'D BE SAFER IF I WAS WITH YOU.
SWORDS AREN'T LIKE BOWS. THEY'RE USED IN CLOSE QUARTERS—AND YOU'RE NOT STRONG ENOUGH TO OVERPOWER A MAN.
IT'S DANGER-OUS.
I KNOW!
THAT'S WHY I WANT TO LEARN.
IF I WERE IN HAK'S PLACE...
...I'D USE MYSELF AS A SHIELD...
...SO THAT NO HARM WOULD EVER COME TO YOU.
BUT I'D WANT YOU...
...TO BE SOME-PLACE...
SHU
...WHERE YOU WERE SAFE AND HAPPY.

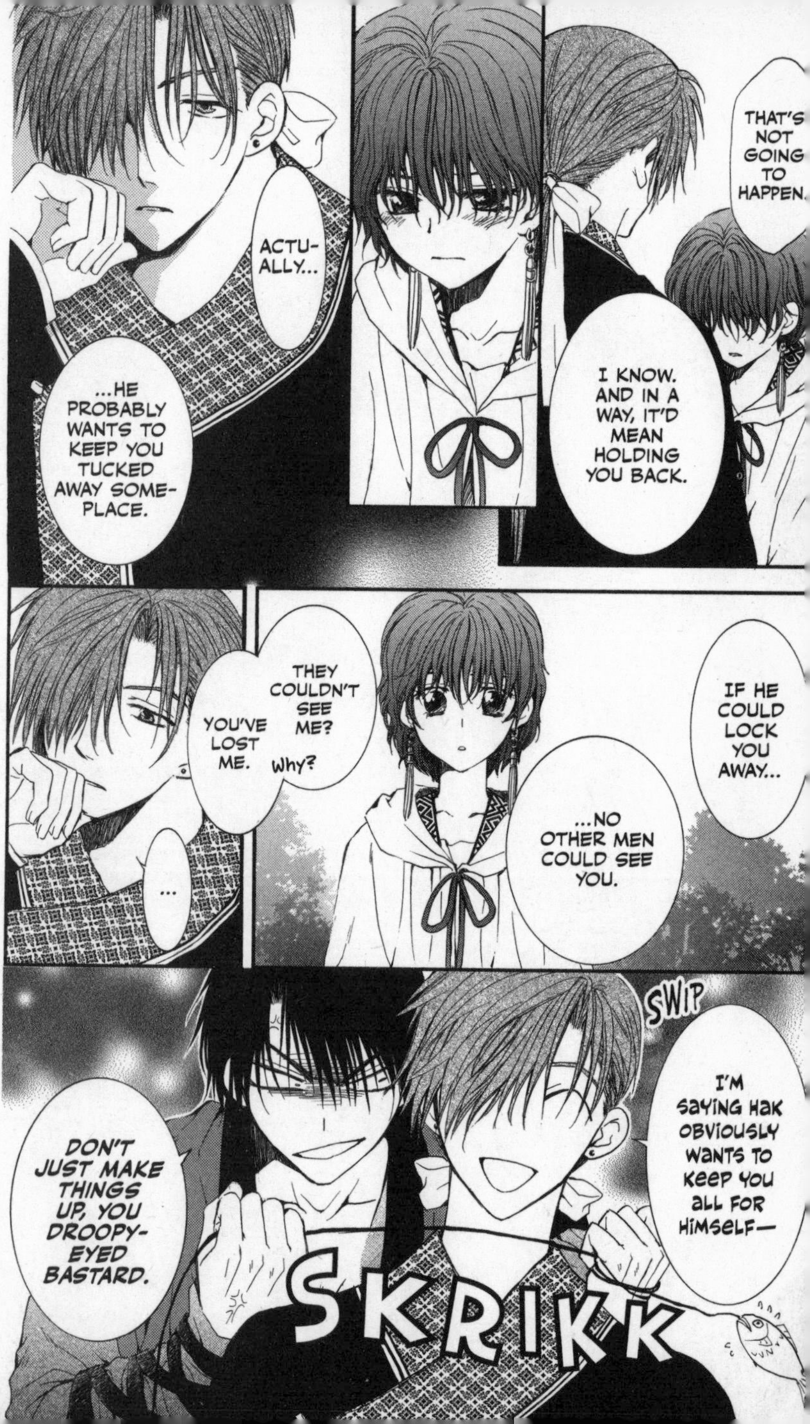
THAT'S NOT GOING TO HAPPEN.
I KNOW. AND IN A WAY, IT'D MEAN HOLDING YOU BACK.
ACTU-ALLY...
...HE PROBABLY WANTS TO KEEP YOU TUCKED AWAY SOME-PLACE.
IF HE COULD LOCK YOU AWAY...
...NO OTHER MEN COULD SEE YOU.
THEY COULDN'T SEE ME?
Why?
YOU'VE LOST ME.
...
SWIP
I'M SAYING HAK OBVIOUSLY WANTS TO KEEP YOU ALL FOR HIMSELF—
SKRIKK
DON'T JUST MAKE THINGS UP, YOU DROOPY-EYED BASTARD.

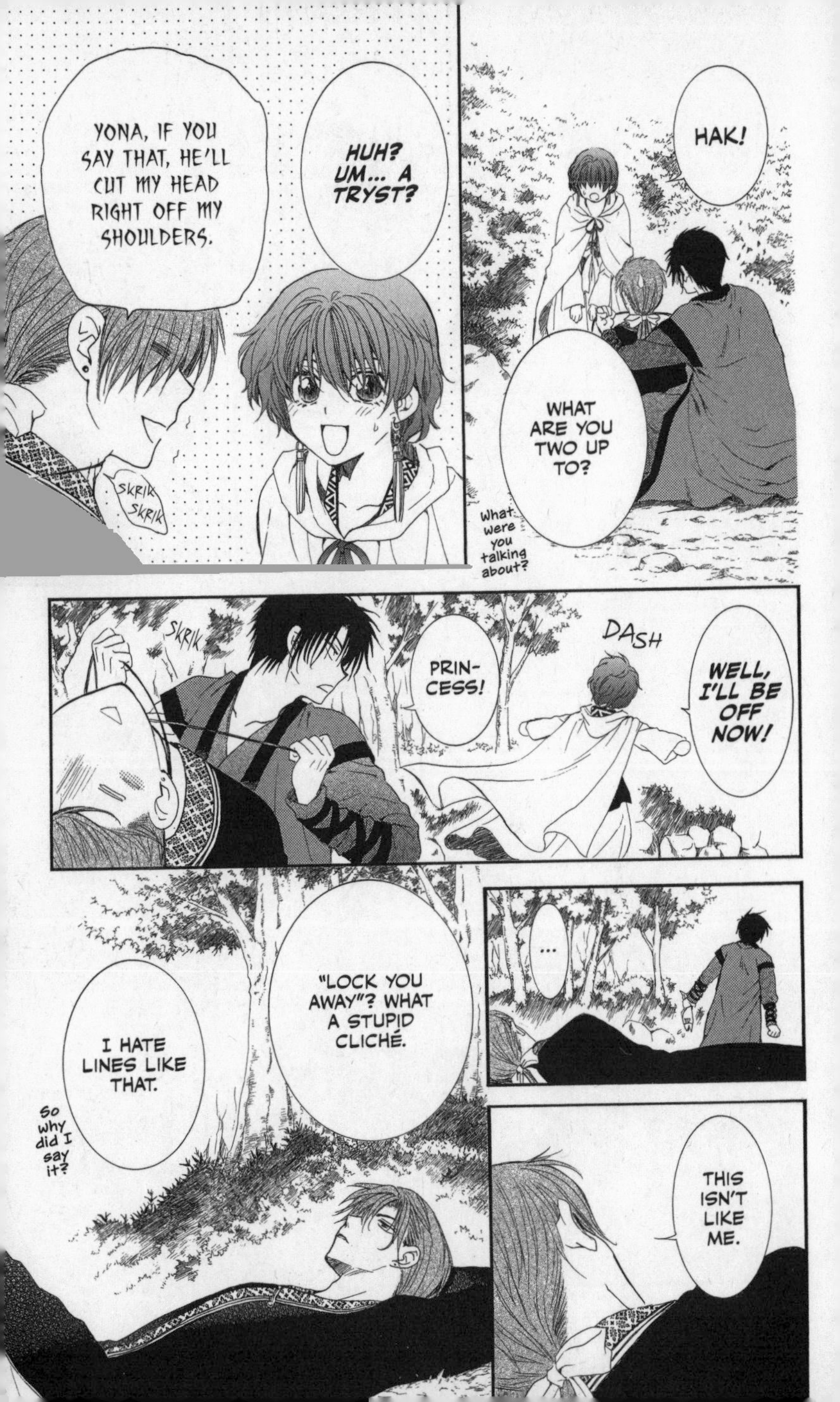
HAK!
WHAT ARE YOU TWO UP TO?
What were you talking about?
HUH? UM... A TRYST?
YONA, IF YOU SAY THAT, HE'LL CUT MY HEAD RIGHT OFF MY SHOULDERS.
SKRIK SKRIK
WELL, I'LL BE OFF NOW!
DASH
PRIN-CESS!
SKRIK
...
THIS ISN'T LIKE ME.
"LOCK YOU AWAY"? WHAT A STUPID CLICHÉ.
I HATE LINES LIKE THAT.
So why did I say it?

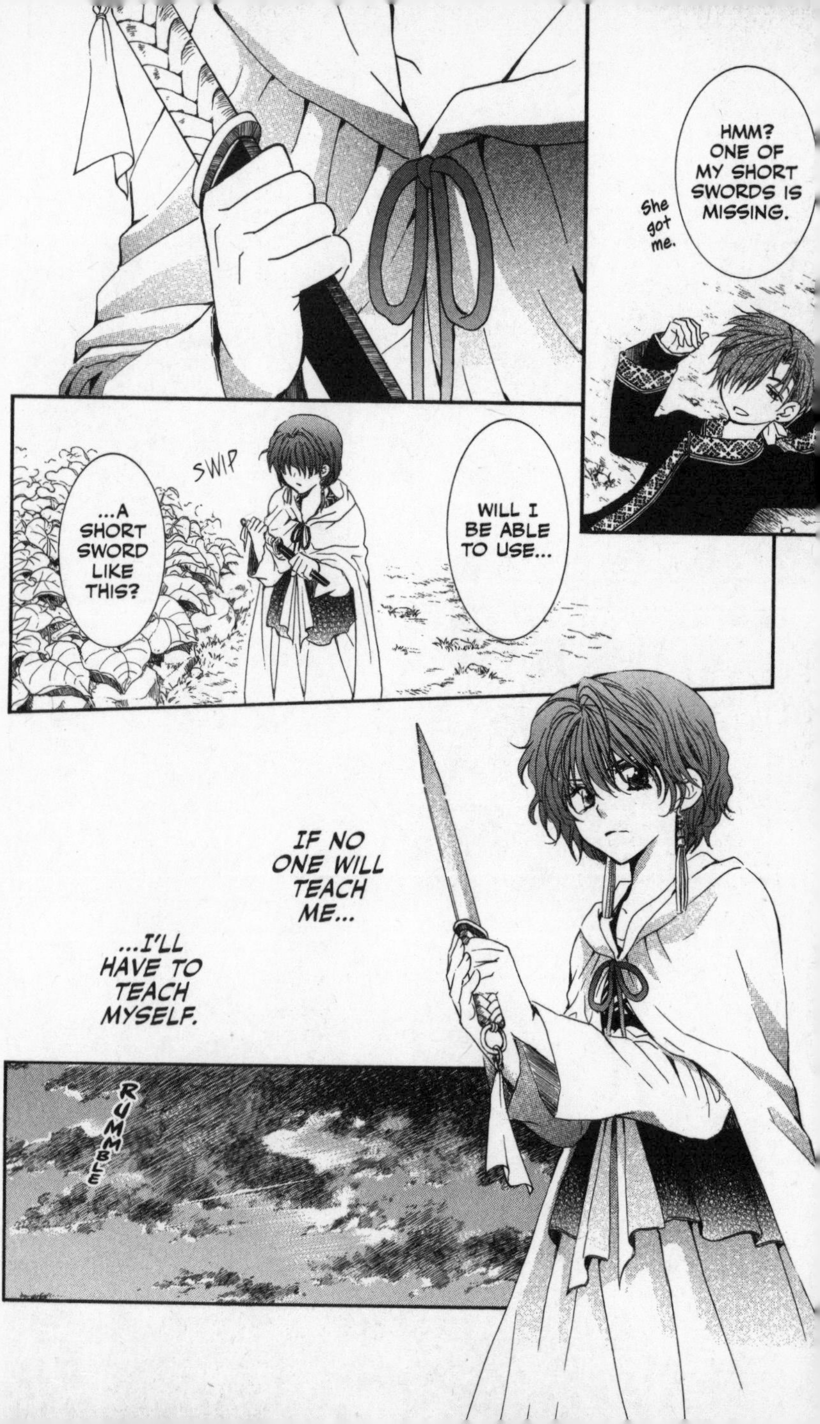
HMM? ONE OF MY SHORT SWORDS IS MISSING.
She got me.
WILL I BE ABLE TO USE...
SWIP
...A SHORT SWORD LIKE THIS?
IF NO ONE WILL TEACH ME...
...I'LL HAVE TO TEACH MYSELF.
RUMMBLE

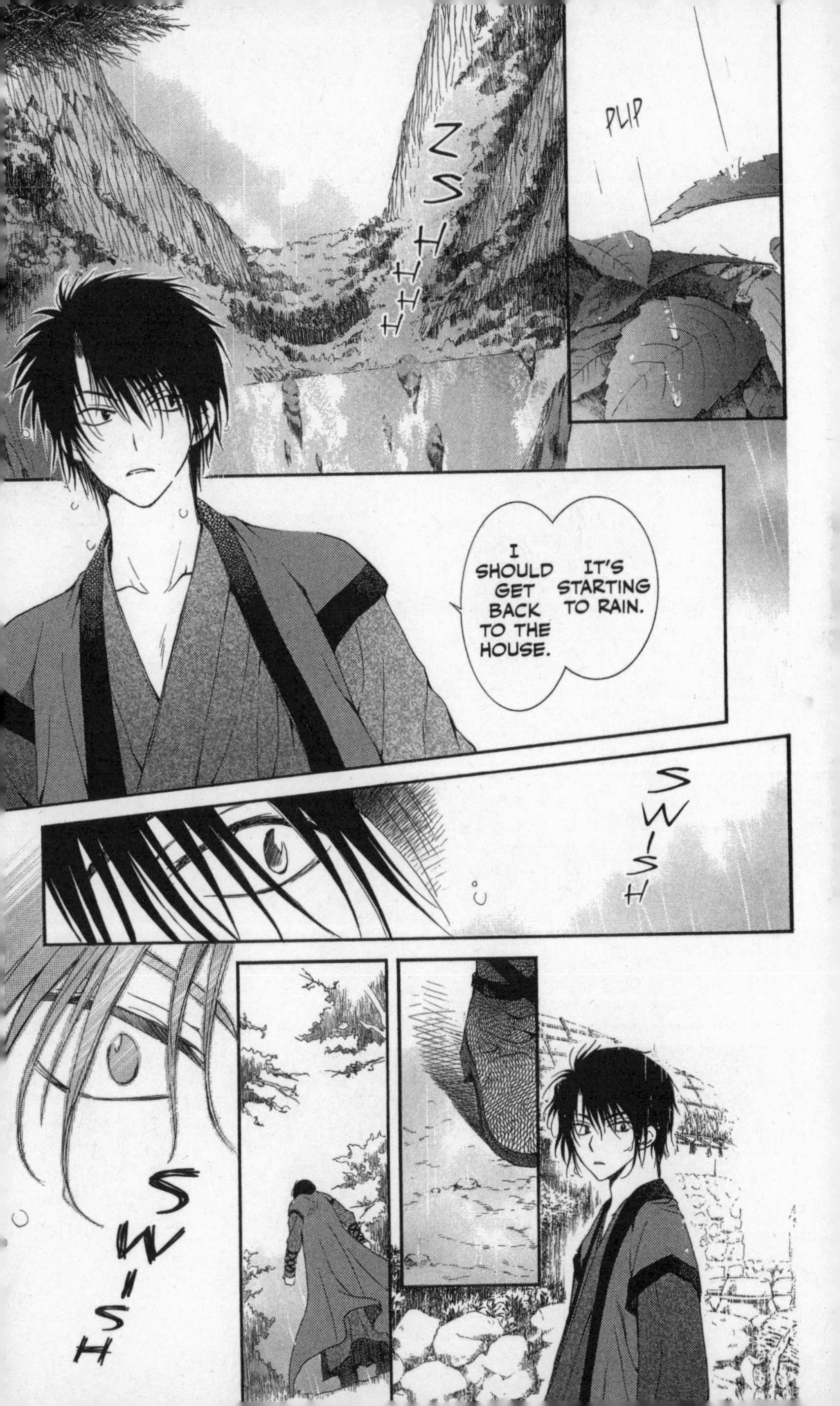
PLIP
ZSHHHH
IT'S STARTING TO RAIN.
I SHOULD GET BACK TO THE HOUSE.
SWISH
SWISH

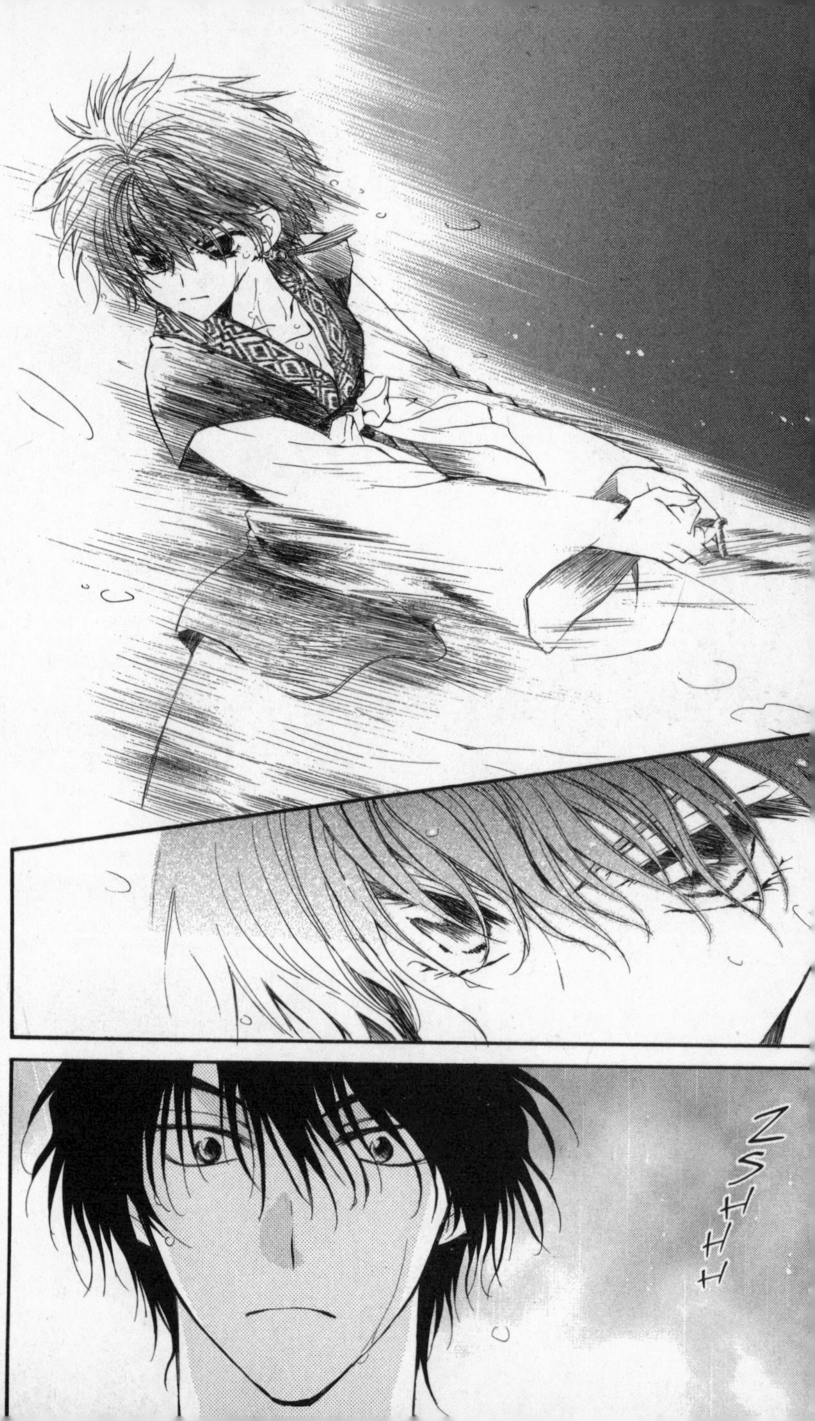
ZSHHH

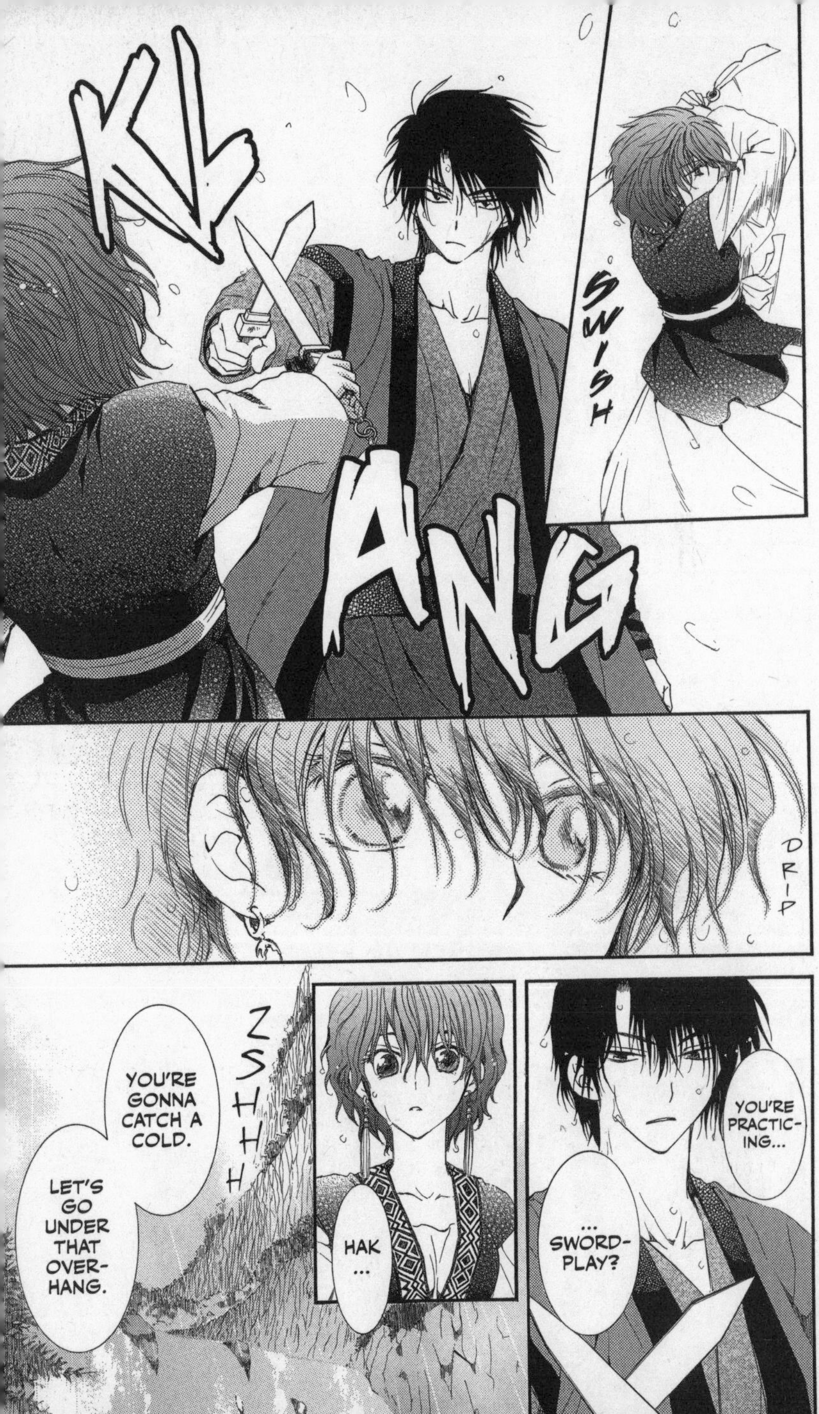
SWISH
KLANG
DRIP
YOU'RE PRACTIC-ING...
...SWORD-PLAY?
HAK...
ZSHHH
YOU'RE GONNA CATCH A COLD.
LET'S GO UNDER THAT OVER-HANG.

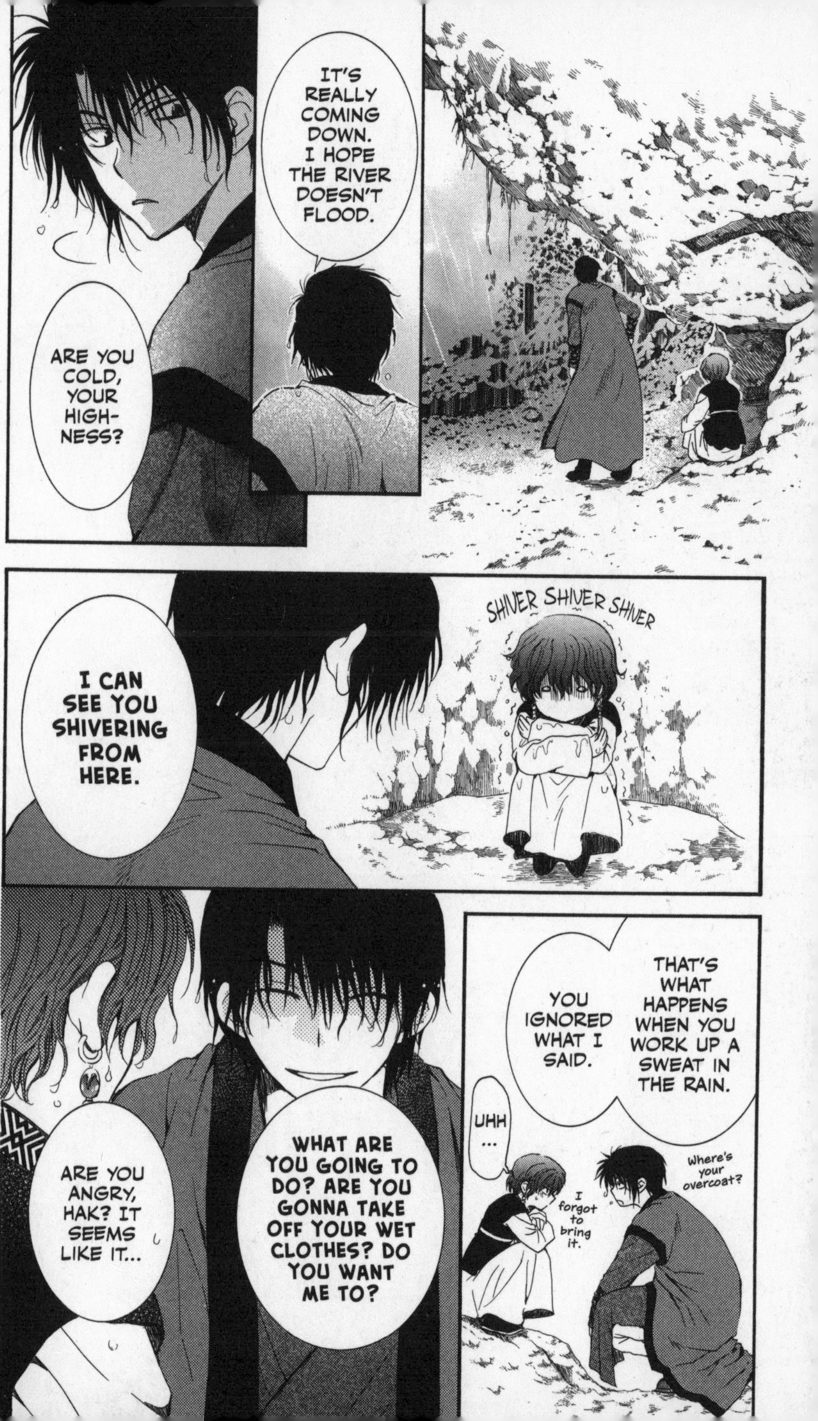
IT'S REALLY COMING DOWN. I HOPE THE RIVER DOESN'T FLOOD.
ARE YOU COLD, YOUR HIGHNESS?
SHIVER SHIVER SHIVER
I CAN SEE YOU SHIVERING FROM HERE.
THAT'S WHAT HAPPENS WHEN YOU WORK UP A SWEAT IN THE RAIN.
YOU IGNORED WHAT I SAID.
Where's your overcoat?
I forgot to bring it.
UHH ...
WHAT ARE YOU GOING TO DO? ARE YOU GONNA TAKE OFF YOUR WET CLOTHES? DO YOU WANT ME TO?
ARE YOU ANGRY, HAK? IT SEEMS LIKE IT...

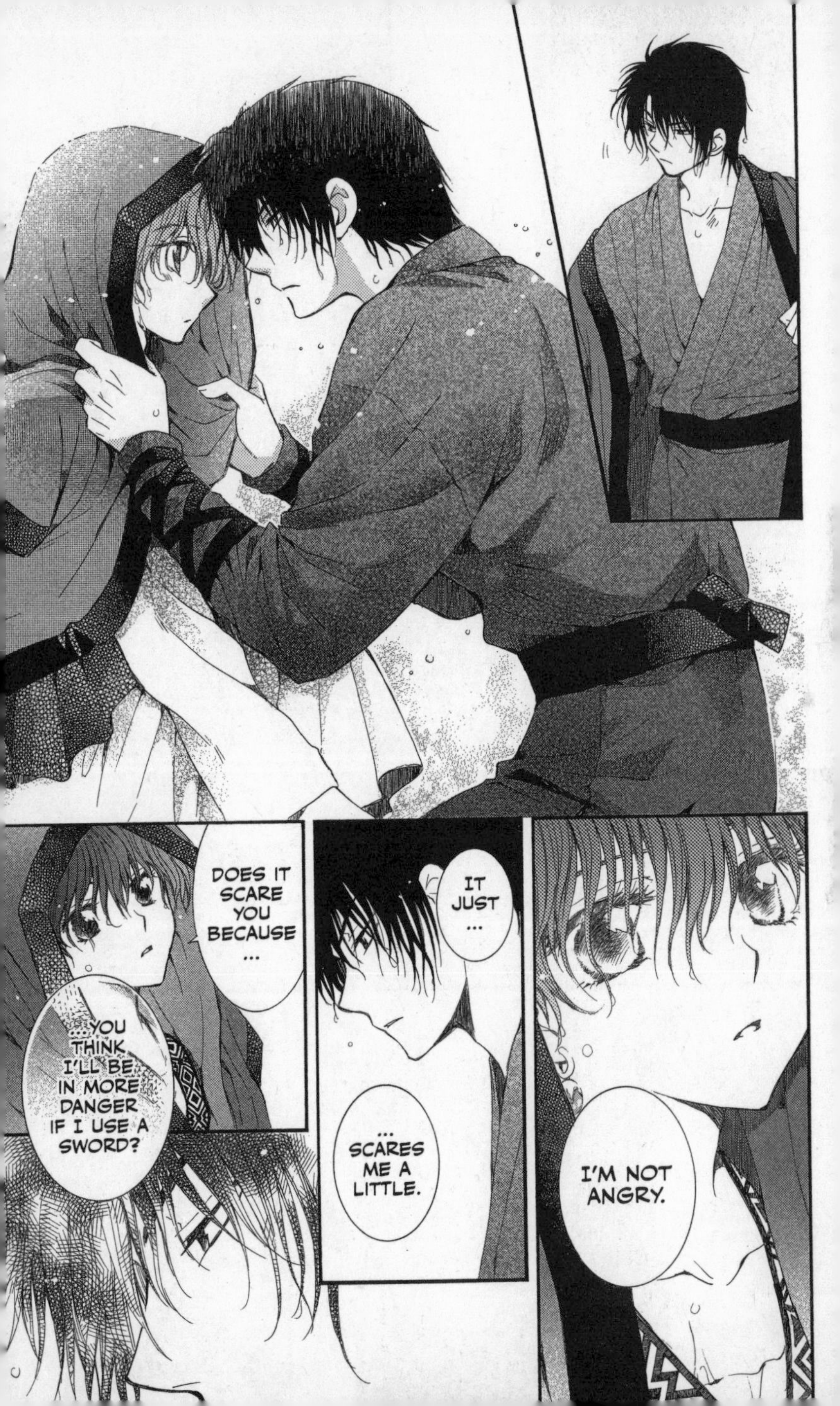
I'M NOT ANGRY.
IT JUST ...
... SCARES ME A LITTLE.
DOES IT SCARE YOU BECAUSE ...
... YOU THINK I'LL BE IN MORE DANGER IF I USE A SWORD?

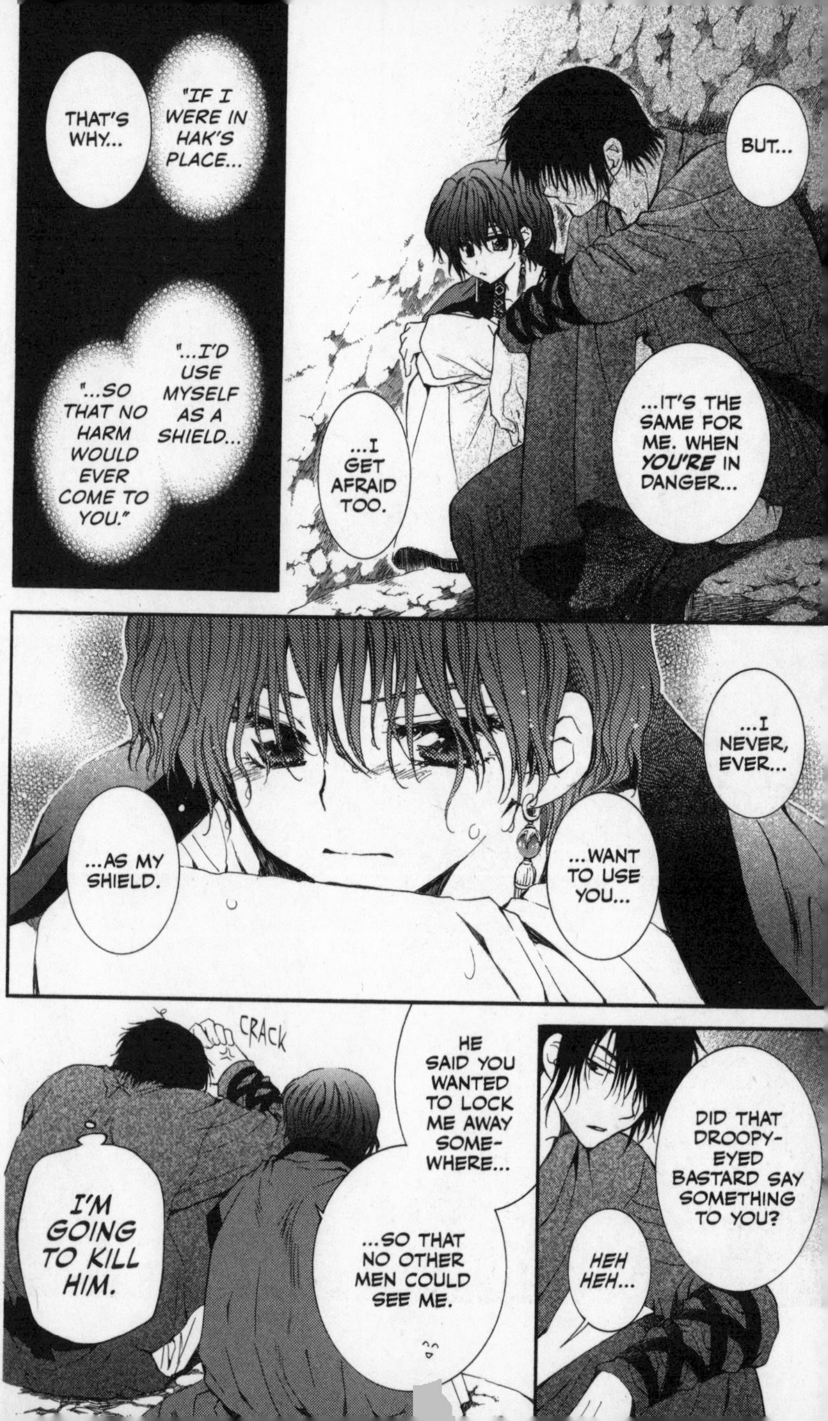
BUT...
...IT'S THE SAME FOR ME. WHEN YOU'RE IN DANGER...
...I GET AFRAID TOO.
"IF I WERE IN HAK'S PLACE...
THAT'S WHY...
"...I'D USE MYSELF AS A SHIELD...
"...SO THAT NO HARM WOULD EVER COME TO YOU."
...I NEVER, EVER...
...WANT TO USE YOU...
...AS MY SHIELD.
DID THAT DROOPY-EYED BASTARD SAY SOMETHING TO YOU?
HEH HEH...
HE SAID YOU WANTED TO LOCK ME AWAY SOME-WHERE...
...SO THAT NO OTHER MEN COULD SEE ME.
CRACK
I'M GOING TO KILL HIM.

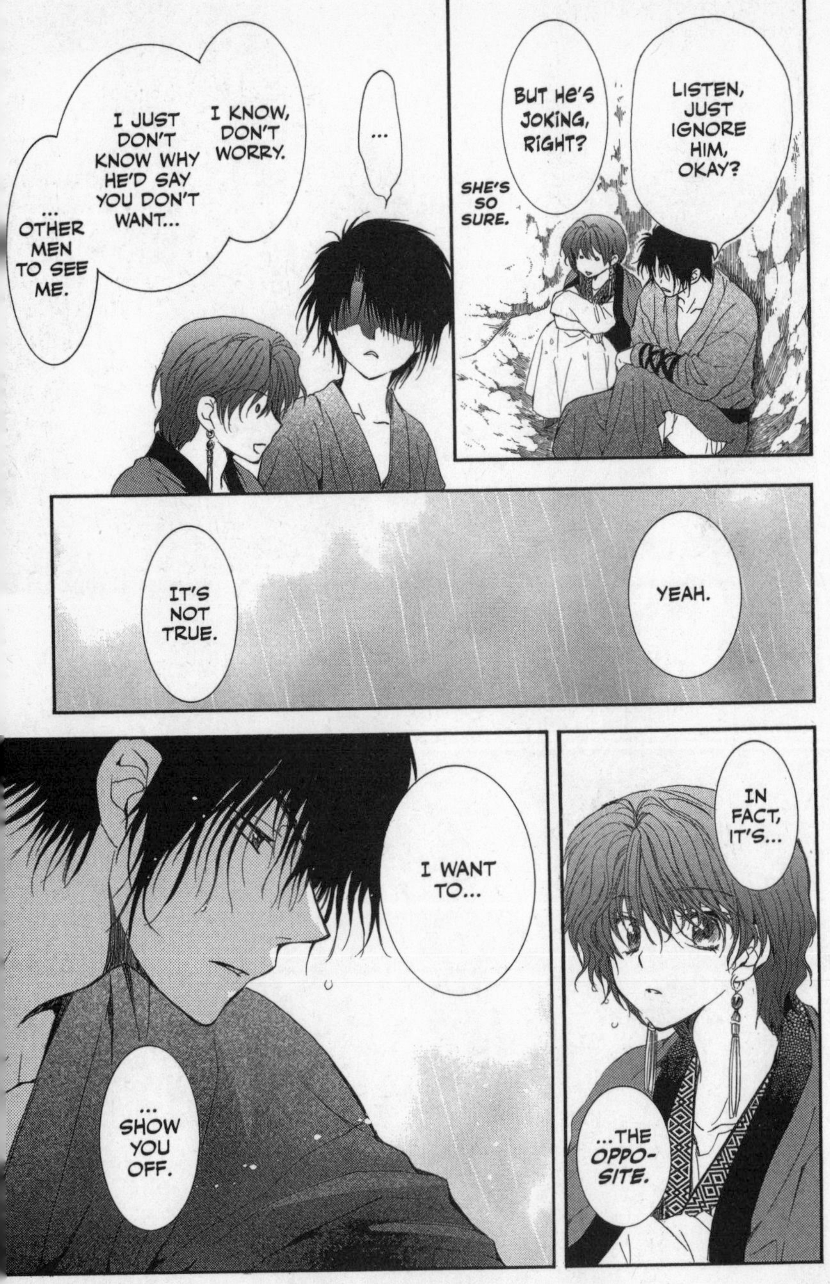
LISTEN, JUST IGNORE HIM, OKAY?
BUT HE'S JOKING, RIGHT?
SHE'S SO SURE.
...
I KNOW, DON'T WORRY.
I JUST DON'T KNOW WHY HE'D SAY YOU DON'T WANT...
...OTHER MEN TO SEE ME.
YEAH.
IT'S NOT TRUE.
IN FACT, IT'S...
...THE OPPOSITE.
I WANT TO...
...SHOW YOU OFF.

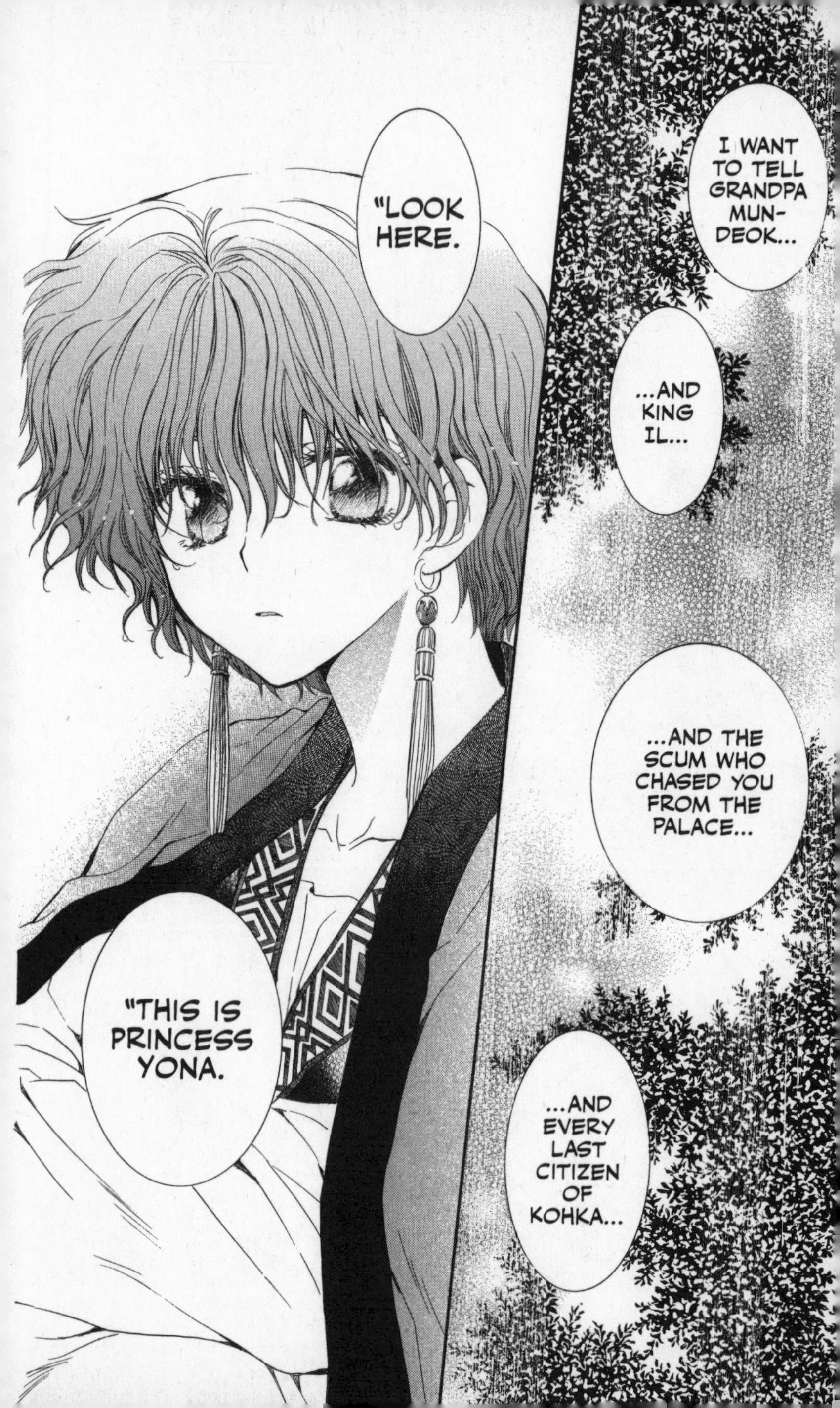
I WANT TO TELL GRANDPA MUN-DEOK...
...AND KING IL...
...AND THE SCUM WHO CHASED YOU FROM THE PALACE...
...AND EVERY LAST CITIZEN OF KOHKA...
"LOOK HERE.
"THIS IS PRINCESS YONA.

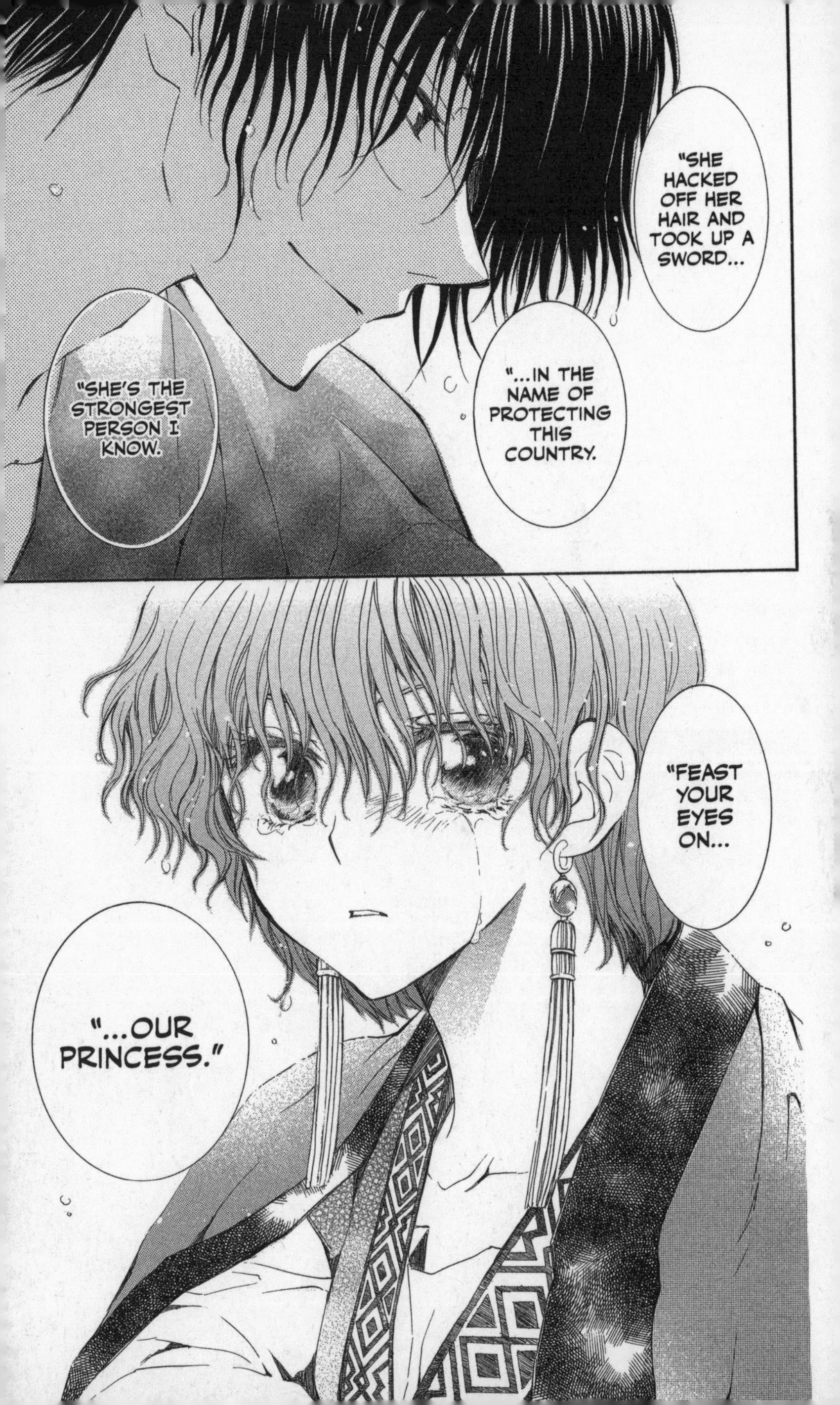
"SHE HACKED OFF HER HAIR AND TOOK UP A SWORD...
"...IN THE NAME OF PROTECTING THIS COUNTRY.
"SHE'S THE STRONGEST PERSON I KNOW.
"FEAST YOUR EYES ON...
"...OUR PRINCESS."

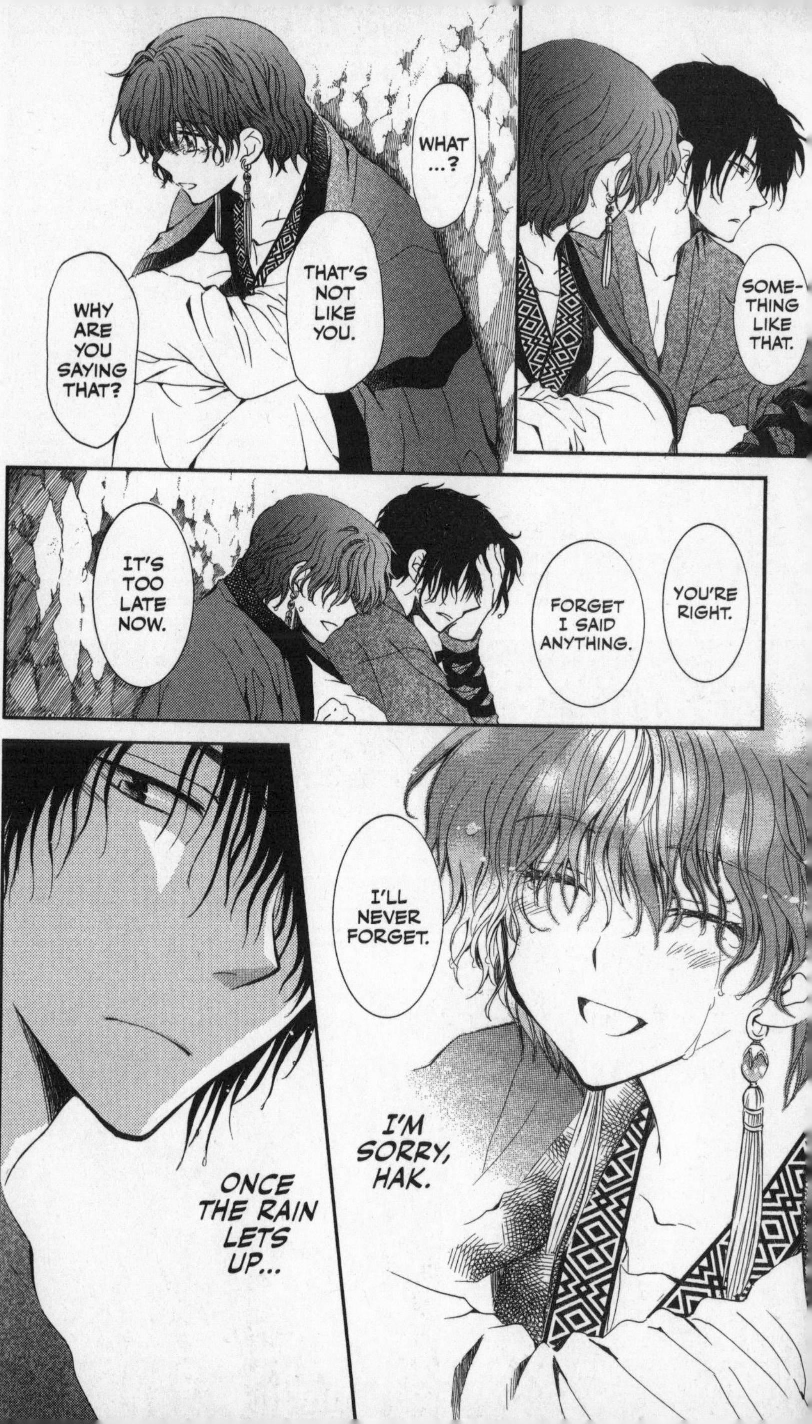
SOME-THING LIKE THAT.
WHAT ...?
THAT'S NOT LIKE YOU.
WHY ARE YOU SAYING THAT?
YOU'RE RIGHT.
FORGET I SAID ANYTHING.
IT'S TOO LATE NOW.
I'LL NEVER FORGET.
I'M SORRY, HAK.
ONCE THE RAIN LETS UP...

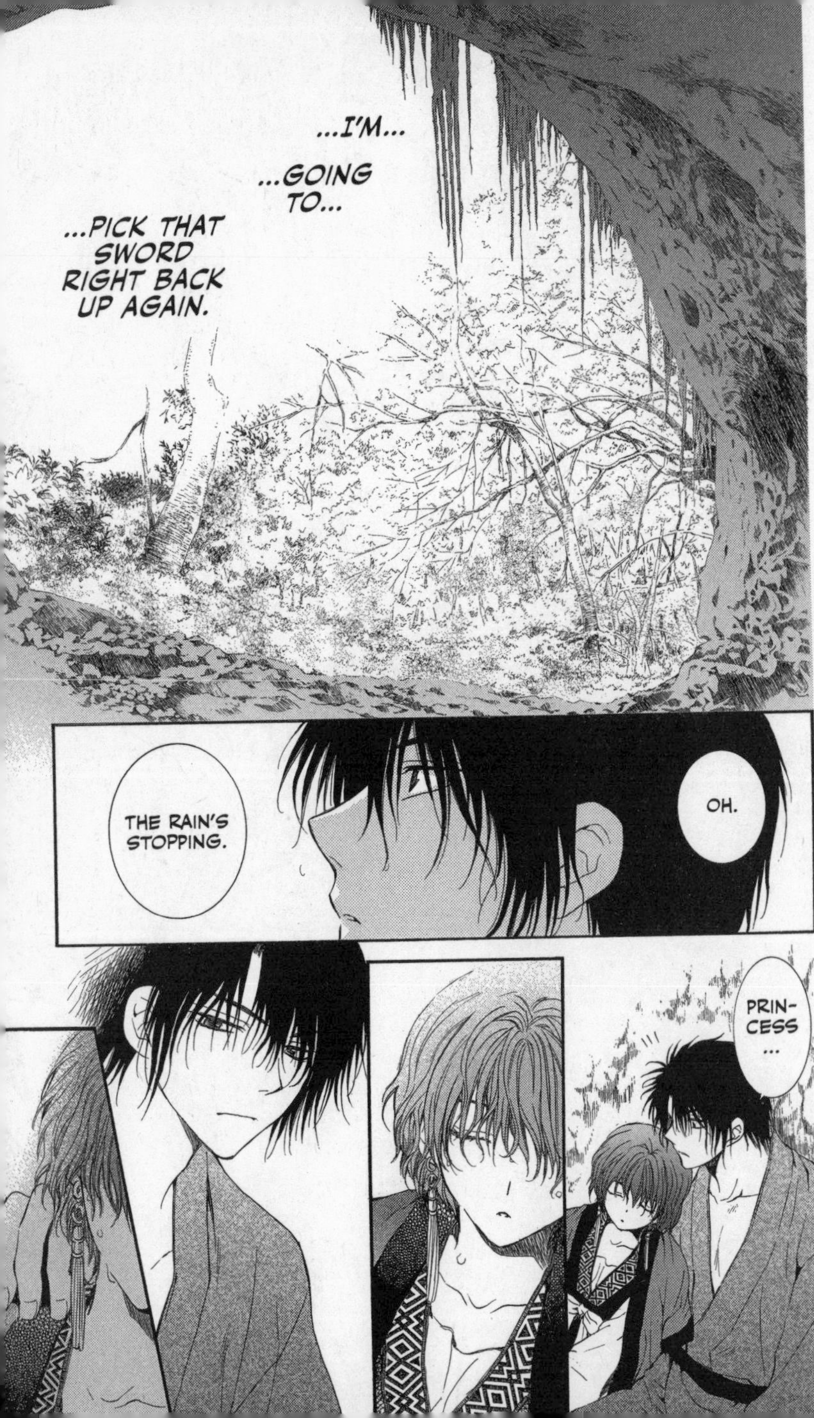
...I'M...
...GOING TO...
...PICK THAT SWORD RIGHT BACK UP AGAIN.
OH.
THE RAIN'S STOPPING.
PRIN-CESS ...

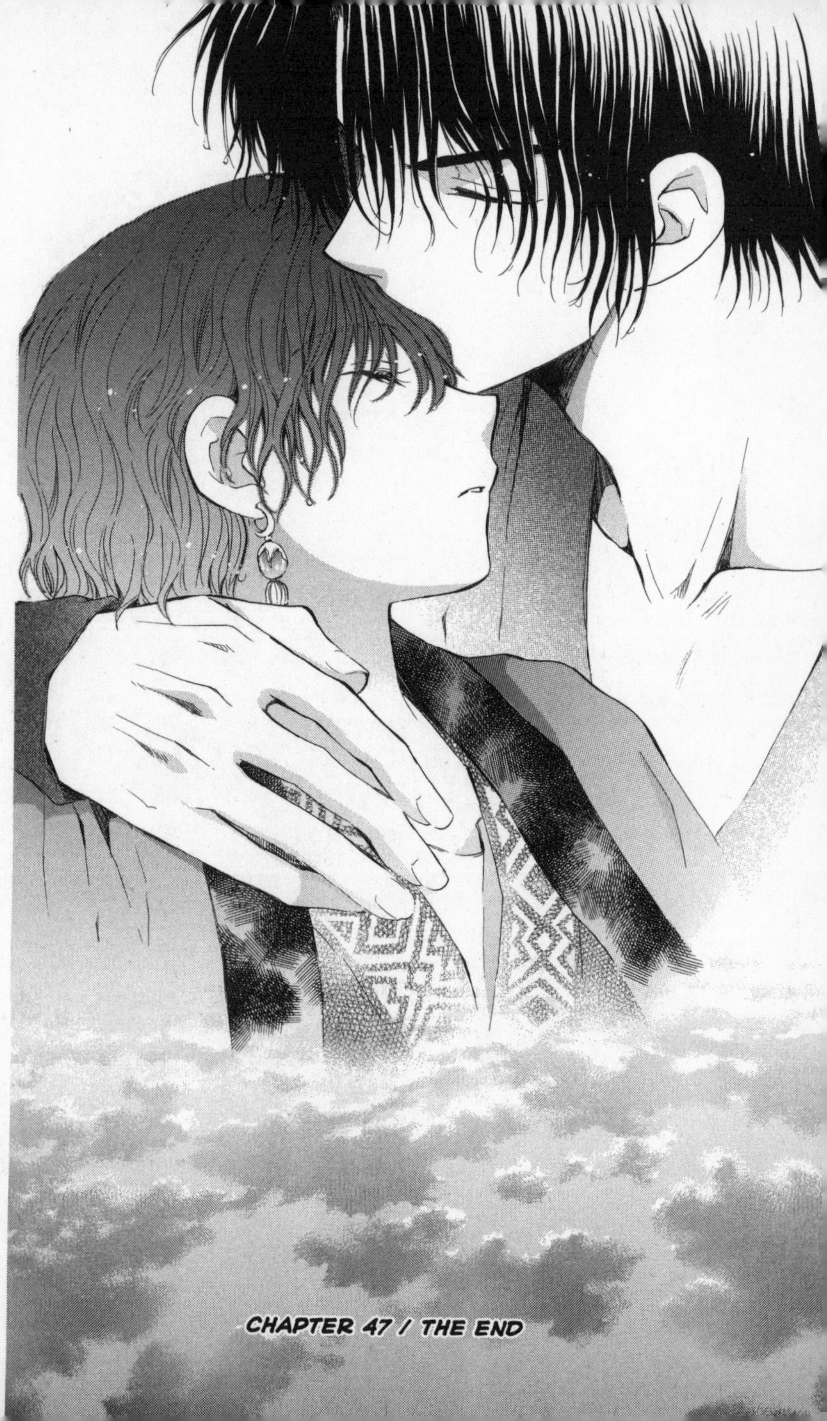
CHAPTER 47 / THE END

BONUS COMIC

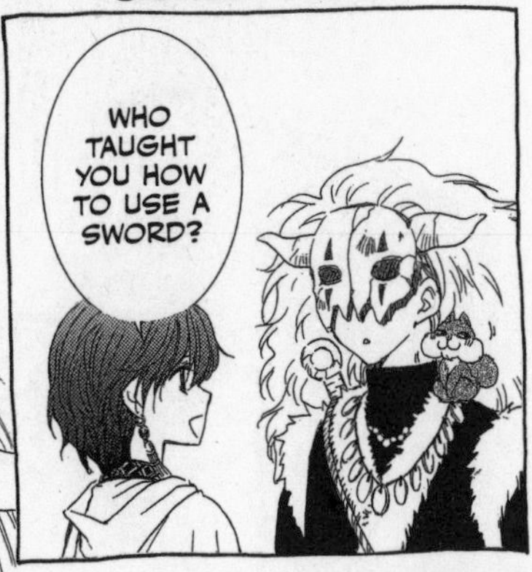
WHO TAUGHT YOU HOW TO USE A SWORD?

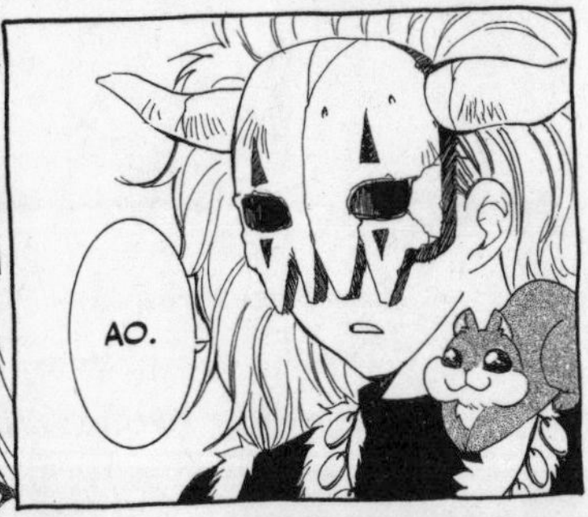
AO.

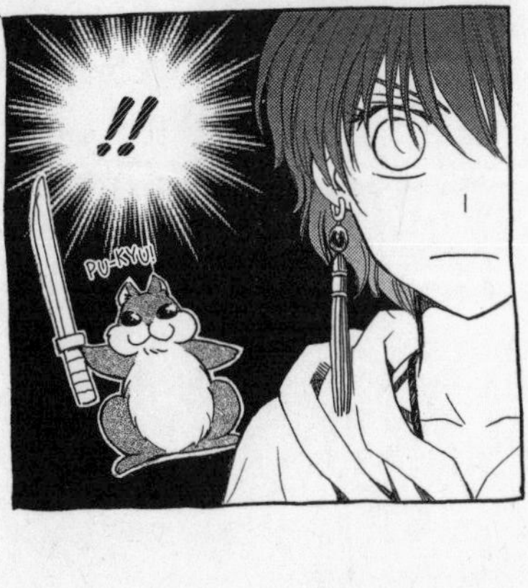
!!
PU-KYU!

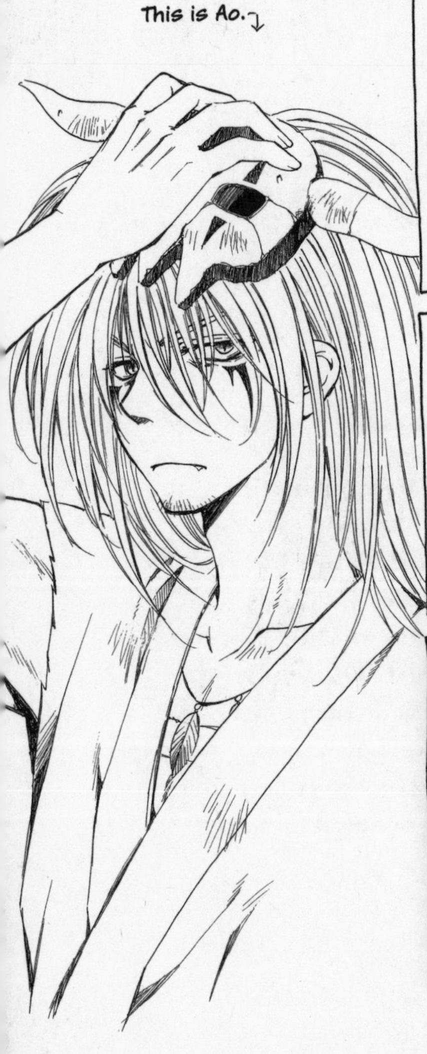
This is Ao.

Born on February 3 in Kumamoto
Prefecture in Japan, Mizuho Kusanagi
began her professional manga
career with *Yoiko no Kokoroe* (The
Rules of a Good Child) in 2003. Her
other works include *NG Life*, which
was serialized in *Hana to Yume* and
The Hana to Yume magazines and
published by Hakusensha in Japan.
Yona of the Dawn was adapted into an
anime in 2014.

YONA OF THE DAWN
VOL.8
Shojo Beat Edition

STORY AND ART BY
MIZUHO KUSANAGI

English Adaptation/Ysabet Reinhardt MacFarlane
Translation/JN Productions
Touch-Up Art & Lettering/Lys Blakeslee
Design/Yukiko Whitley
Editor/Amy Yu

Akatsuki no Yona by Mizuho Kusanagi
© Mizuho Kusanagi 2012
All rights reserved.
First published in Japan in 2012 by HAKUSENSHA, Inc., Tokyo.
English language translation rights arranged with
HAKUSENSHA, Inc., Tokyo.

Printed in the U.S.A.

Published by VIZ Media, LLC
P.O. Box 77010
San Francisco, CA 94107

10 9 8 7 6 5 4 3 2 1
First printing, October 2017

www.viz.com   www.shojobeat.com

This is the last page.

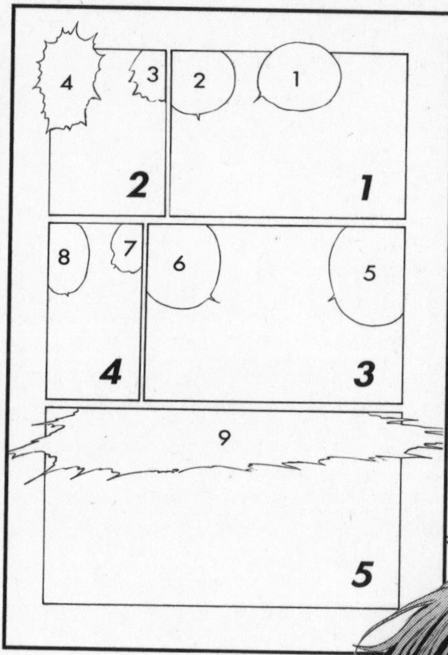

1
2
1
3
4
2
5
6
3
7
8
4
9
5

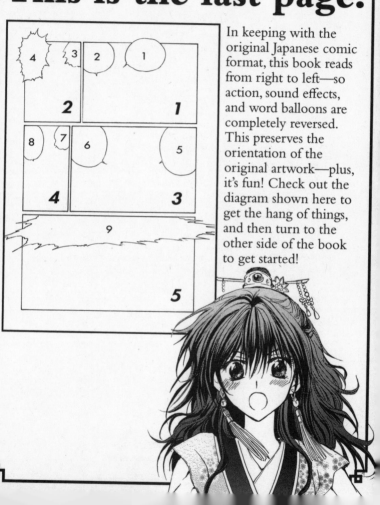

In keeping with the original Japanese comic format, this book reads from right to left—so action, sound effects, and word balloons are completely reversed. This preserves the orientation of the original artwork—plus, it's fun! Check out the diagram shown here to get the hang of things, and then turn to the other side of the book to get started!

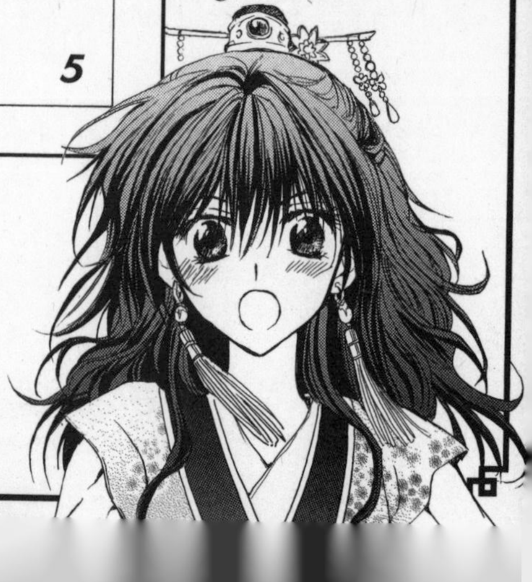